MW01365882

DB2® Express

IBM Press Series—Information Management

On Demand Computing Books

On Demand Computing
Fellenstein

Autonomic Computing
Murch

Grid Computing
Joseph and Fellenstein

Business Intelligence for the Enterprise
Biere

DB2 Books

DB2 Express: Application Development and Deployment
Yip, Cheung, Gartner, Liu, and O'Connell

DB2 Universal Database v8.1 Certification Exam 703 Study Guide
Sanders

The Official Introduction to DB2 for z/OS
Sloan

High Availability Guide to DB2
Eaton and Cialini

DB2 Universal Database v8.1 Certification Exams 701 and 706 Study Guide
Sanders

Integrated Solutions with DB2
Cutlip and Medicke

DB2 Universal Database v8.1 Certification Exam 700 Study Guide
Sanders

DB2 for Solaris: The Official Guide
Bauch and Wilding

DB2 Universal Database v8 Handbook for Windows, UNIX, and Linux
Gunning

Advanced DBA Certification Guide and Reference for DB2 Universal Database v8 for Linux, UNIX, and Windows
Snow and Phan

DB2 Universal Database v8 Application Development Certification Guide, Second Edition
Martineau, Sanyal, Gashyna, and Kyprianou

DB2 Universal Database v8 for Linux, UNIX, and Windows Database Administration Certification Guide, Fifth Edition
Baklarz and Wong

DB2 SQL Procedural Language for Linux, UNIX, and Windows
Yip, Bradstock, Curtis, Gao, Janmohamed, Liu, and McArthur

DB2 Universal Database for OS/390 Version 7.1 Certification Guide
Lawson and Yevich

DB2 Version 8: The Official Guide
Zikopoulos, Baklarz, deRoos, and Melnyk

DB2 UDB for OS/390: An Introduction to DB2 OS/390
Sloan and Hernandez

More Books from IBM Press

The Inventor's Guide to Trademarks and Patents
Fellenstein

WebSphere and Lotus: Implementing Collaboration Solutions
Lamb and Laskey

IBM WebSphere: Deployment and Advanced Configuration
Barcia, Hines, Alcott, and Botzum

IBM WebSphere System Administration
Williamson, Chan, Cundiff, Lauzon, and Mitchell

Developing Quality Technical Information, Second Edition
Hargis, Carey, Hernandez, Hughes, Longo, Rouiller, and Wilde

Enterprise Messaging Using JMS and IBM WebSphere
Yusuf

Enterprise Java Programming with IBM WebSphere, Second Edition
Brown, Craig, Hester, Pitt, Stinehour, Weitzel, Amsden, Jakab, and Berg

DB2® Express

Easy Development and Administration

Paul Yip

Kit Man Cheung

Jason Gartner

Clara Liu

Stephen O'Connell

Prentice Hall Professional Technical Reference
Upper Saddle River, New Jersey 07458
www.phptr.com

Cover design: *IBM Corporation*
IBM Consulting Editor: *Susan Visser*

Published by Pearson Education, Inc.
Publishing as IBM Press
Upper Saddle River, NJ 07458

IBM Press offers excellent discounts on this book when ordered in quantity for bulk purchases or special sales. For more information, please contact: U.S. Corporate and Government Sales, 1-800-382-3419, corpsales@pearsontechgroup.com. For sales outside of the U.S., please contact: International Sales, international@pearsoned.com.

Library of Congress Cataloging-in-Publication Data

DB2 Express : easy development and administration / Paul Yip ... [et al.].
p. cm.
Includes bibliographical references and indexes.
ISBN 0-13-146397-7 (hardback : alk. paper)
1. IBM Database 2. 2. Relational databases. I. Yip, Paul.
QA76.9.D3D15645 2004
005.75'65—dc22 2004017218

Printed in the United States of America
First Printing
ISBN 0-13-146397-7

Pearson Education LTD.
Pearson Education Australia PTY, Limited
Pearson Education Singapore, Pte. Ltd.
Pearson Education North Asia Ltd.
Pearson Education Canada, Ltd.
Pearson Educación de Mexico, S.A. de C.V.
Pearson Education — Japan
Pearson Education Malaysia, Pte. Ltd.

Contents

Dedication and Acknowledgments

I would like to dedicate this book to Justine for her continuous support, especially in the final stages of this work, where she helped edit and proofread almost the entire book. And to my parents, thank you. None of this would have been possible without your love, guidance, and care. –Paul

I would like to thank my family for their love and support over the years. I would also like to thank Darcy for her incredible patience and support. And finallly, to all my friends from work and elsewhere: Thank you for all the little things! –Kit Man

I would like to dedicate this book to my wife Tammy and daughter Rebecca. Tammy for the late nights of editing and proofing and my daughter for her unending energy as inspiration to all of us. I would also like to thank the entire KD3 team (you know who you are) for 3 of my most rewarding years in IBM, a great team with great zest for life. –Jason

I would like to thank Heison for being patient with all the long nights and weekends I spent on this book. The support from my family and friends is invaluable. I think this book team is a perfect match with such a great leader, Paul. Without your dedication, it would not have been as successful as it is. –Clara

I'd like to dedicate this book to my family and friends who kindly put up with me boring them about databases and to my old friend and tutor Danny Heaney. –Stephen

We would like to recognize several key individuals who made this book possible.

- Phil Gunning and James Huddleston, our technical reviewers.
- Susan Visser, who helps take care of everything else in between.
- Jeffrey Pepper, Elizabeth Ryan, and all the folks involved behind the scenes in producing this book.

We would like to thank the following people for their time and support in the production of this book:

Gustavo Arocena
Abdul Al Azzawe
George Baklarz
John Botsford
Jessica Escott
Louisa Ford
Kelvin Ho
Peter Kohlmann
Guy Lau
Leo Lau
Amelia Lou
Marie Ma
Abby Mac
Rob Mauhar
Nancy Miller
Melinda Pfeiffer
David Ready
Bridget Reid
Belal Tassi
Craig Tobias
Carmen Wong
Theresa Xu
Justine Yau
Paul Zikopoulos

Foreword

From its inception more than twenty years ago, relational database technology has been making the storage, retrieval, and interpretation of data easier. IBM Research delivered the first commercially available database in the early 1980s. This technology created the unique ability to represent data in a simple tabular form, access it through the powerful Structured Query Language (SQL), and make it readily available to the business community. Today, tens of thousands of businesses all over the world rely on DB2 databases to store their data and run their businesses, both traditionally and over the Web.

After more than twenty years of innovation and exponential growth in data volume, the promise of DB2 UDB is still to safely store, retrieve, and interpret data. But today it's not just about more function. It's about making function accessible to people who don't want to be database experts. It's about high performance without a dedicated database administrator. It's about automatic database maintenance. It's about automatic query optimization. And, it's about fitting seamlessly into the development environment of your choice and getting results as quickly as possible.

This book will take you through the full process of creating a point of sale business application using either Java or Microsoft Visual Basic, from design to deployment and management.

If you are new to DB2 UDB, Express is an excellent way to discover how easy it can be to make DB2 UDB work for you. It will also open a depth of function, capability, performance, and scalability surprising in something that works so well right out of the box.

—Peter Kohlmann
DB2 UDB Express Product Development Manager
IBM

DB2 EXPRESS BOOK WEB SITE

Hosted by:

developerWorks®

IBM's resource for developers

http://ibm.com/developerworks/offers/db2expressbook.html

- Downloadable code samples
- Solutions to exercises
- Useful tips
- Updates and errata

For additional DB2 technical resources, visit the developerWorks main site:

http://ibm.com/developerWorks/db2

CHAPTER 1 Introduction

Among the dozens of major enhancements delivered in DB2 version 8.2 are features created specifically for deployment in small and medium-sized businesses (or in departments within large businesses) where highly skilled database administrators are not available. This book shows you how to leverage these features to dramatically reduce time to market and total cost of ownership for solutions built on DB2.

1.1 About This Book

This book is a concise guide for developing and deploying a DB2 application from the ground up. You will be guided through every step of the way, including

- Installing DB2 for Windows
- Creating databases and objects
- Developing an application
- Performance tuning
- Deploying to production and configuring automatic maintainence
- Troubleshooting techniques

To aid your understanding, a sample point-of-sale database application will be developed from start to finish to get you up and running quickly with DB2. We will teach you how to use DB2 tools effectively so that you can focus on what you do best—building applications. When the database application is complete, we'll show you how to deploy the database into production.

Each chapter's discussion and examples build on one another, with concrete examples and source code that you can reuse in your own applications. Most chapters have additional exercises to reinforce what you've learned. As you progress through this book you will master core skills to develop and deploy DB2 applications.

Code and solutions for each chapter are available from the book's Web site.

1.2 Who Should Read This Book

This book was written for anyone whose day-to-day activities include database application development but whose job description does not include database administration. This book does not discuss advanced database administration; instead it focuses on how to leverage what IBM calls DB2's autonomic (self-managing) capabilities when deployed into production environments where a full-time database administrator may not be available (such as in small and medium-sized businesses).

It's been our experience that database application developers just want to get up and running as soon as possible without needing to learn every detail of a product. The DB2 product manuals are very detailed and comprehensive. Although these manuals are good resources for seasoned DB2 application developers, they may not be the ideal starting point for novice DB2 application developers.

Therefore, this book is for you if you

- Are new to DB2 Universal Database
- Don't want another reference book exhaustively covering every option and feature
- Don't have the time to learn and memorize command-line commands
- Just want to *cut to the chase:* create a database and some objects, load it with data, build an application, and deploy it to production

This book

- Does not assume prior knowledge of DB2 Universal Database (UDB)
- Is written for anyone who wants to create database applications with minimal grief
- Shows you how to do the most frequent database application development tasks, using the most common options, while highlighting advanced capabilities
- Demonstrates how to perform all tasks through graphical tools
- Shows you how to take an application from design and development to deployment

Prerequisites

The only skill assumed is a very basic understanding of Structured Query Language (SQL). Some previous database exposure would be beneficial but is not necessary.

We will refer to examples that include actual source code. Therefore, you're assumed to have some background in either Visual Basic .NET or Java. Experience with database programming interfaces such as Java Database Connectivity (JDBC) or ADO.NET, however, is not required.

1.3 What Is DB2 Express?

DB2 Express is a member of the DB2 Universal Database family of products. Other members of the family are as follows:

- DB2 UDB for Linux, UNIX, and Windows
  - Personal Edition
  - Express Edition
  - Workgroup Server Edition and Workgroup Server Unlimited Edition
  - Enterprise Server Edition, with the optional database partitioning facility (DPF)
- DB2 for z/OS (mainframe)
- DB2 for iSeries (formerly known as AS400)

The Express branding is used to identify IBM software products that have been specifically tailored to meet the needs of small and medium-sized businesses (SMB). "Express" implies simplified installation, enhanced ease of use provided through graphical user interfaces, and autonomic capabilities. DB2 Express has all these qualities while offering professional-grade relational database management features and industry-leading performance. The use of open standards in DB2 simplifies the integration of the product with other software.

1.4 What's Cool about DB2 Express v8.2

You may have heard about IBM's new major initiative called "on demand." A significant part of this strategy is autonomic computing: software and hardware that is self-managing, self-tuning, and self-healing to reduce the cost and complexity of technology.

DB2 v8.2 has industry-leading autonomic technologies that make developing and maintaining DB2 database applications easier. The entire list of new features in DB2 v8.2 is too substantial to list here. Instead, we highlight some key technologies that are relevant to the target audience of this book:

- Application development features: features that enhance developer productivity
- Autonomic features: features that are part of DB2's self-monitoring, self-healing, and self-tuning capabilities

Application Development Features

Application development tooling has been significantly enhanced with DB2 v8.2.

For Microsoft Visual Studio .NET Developers

- An enhanced .NET Data Provider that supports Microsoft's .NET Framework 1.1 and Visual Studio .NET 2003
- Support for Microsoft .NET CLR (Common Language Runtime) stored procedures and user-defined functions
- An enhanced DB2 development add-in for Visual Studio .NET 2003 that allows you to develop for DB2 seamlessly without leaving the Visual Studio .NET development environment

For Java Developers

- Improved DB2 Universal JDBC Driver that supports both JDBC type 2 (client-based) and type 4 (clientless) connections

- Support for Java Software Development Kit (SDK) 1.4.1

Autonomic Capabilities

DB2 provides many features to reduce the strain of database administration. These features work together to automatically manage the health of your database:

- Automatic database backup
- Automatic statistics collection
- Automatic statistics profiling
- Automatic reorganization
- Self-tuning backup and restore
- Autonomic log management
- Database Design Advisor
- Database Configuration Advisor
- Adaptive throttling utilities
- Health Monitor

1.5 Learning Objectives

After you have completed this book you will be able to

- Create DB2 Express databases and associated objects
- Develop applications for DB2 Express databases
- Apply data manipulation techniques to generate randomized data for testing
- Tune the performance of your database
- Work with advanced database objects
- Package and deploy database applications
- Set out a strategy for maintaining the database in production

1.6 Book Conventions

Supplemental

We have included a supplemental section in some chapters. These sections contain information that you don't need to move on to the next chapter but may be useful as you become more familiar with using DB2 Express.

Inquiring Minds

Inquiring Minds: Learn More

Sometimes, you want to know a little more about why something is happening. We have incorporated sections to expand on concepts raised in the text called *Inquiring Minds*. There is no requirement for you to read these sections but they will further expand your knowledge of DB2.

Notes

Note: Handy pointers to help you along.

Code Examples

We will show you sample code to illustrate concepts. Code examples can be identified by their distinctive font.

```
public class ClassName {
    public ClassName() {
        // This is sample code (SourceCode style)
    }
}
```

SQL statements and results are represented using a box with a gray background.

```
FNAME    INITIAL LNAME      HPHONE     CID
-------- ------- ---------- ---------- ---
Stephen          O'Connell  1115551234 111
Clara            Liu        2226543455 222
Paul             Yip        8886534534 777
Kitman           Cheung     9992112212 888
Jason            Gartner    1234256734 394
```

1.7 Book Web Site

The book Web site at http://ibm.com/developerworks/offers/db2expressbook.html contains the following:

- Link to where you may download a trial version of DB2 Express v8.2.
- Code examples of the sample application built throughout the book

CHAPTER 2

Getting Started

In this chapter, you will learn:

- How to install DB2 Express server and client
- How to create the DB2 SAMPLE database
- How to work with databases using the DB2 Control Center and Command Editor
- How to create your own database to be used for developing this book's sample application
- How to find information using the DB2 Information Center

2.1 Introduction

This chapter guides you through the process of installing DB2 and gives you a brief introduction to the graphical tools that accompany the product. In the process, you will learn how to create two databases. The first database, called SAMPLE, is shipped with DB2 and has a few simple tables and sample data. The second database, L8NITE, will be used for developing the application described in this book. The L8NITE database will be refined and tuned to demonstrate DB2 application development, deployment, and maintenance best practices.

To interact with the database, two important graphical tools will be introduced: the DB2 Control Center and the Command Editor.

The DB2 Control Center is DB2's primary graphical tool for database administration. The Command Editor is a graphical interface for executing DB2 commands or SQL. Other tools are provided with DB2, and they will be introduced as needed in later chapters.

2.2 Installing DB2 Express

A time limited trial edition of DB2 Express v8.2 can be downloaded from the IBM Web site at http://www.ibm.com/software/data/db2/udb/db2express/. A unlimited evaluation version of DB2 Express (and license) is available by registering at the IBM Virtual Innovation Center:

http://www.developer.ibm.com/welcome/vic.html

You can apply a license to a trial product at any time without having to reinstall DB2. Once you have the license file, use the DB2 License Center (which can be launched from the Tools menu of the Control Center) to register it.

Inquiring Minds: Virtual Innovation Center

The Virtual Innovation Center provides complimentary resources that enable mid-market Business Partners to build technical, sales, and product skills with IBM software products early in the product life cycle. By registering your company, you can get complimentary IBM software for development, get technical assistance via e-mail or chat, access online IBM education courses, and access sales and marketing materials.

A unlimited evaluation version of DB2 Personal Developer's Edition can also be downloaded from the IBM DB2 DeveloperWorks Web site at

http://www.ibm.com/developerworks/db2

Before you install, verify that your system meets the minimum requirements for DB2 Express v8.2 outlined in Table 2.1.

Table 2.1 Minimum System Requirements for DB2 Express

Hardware	For DB2 products running on Intel systems, a Pentium or later CPU; for AMD systems, an AMD Athlon CPU
Operating System	Windows 2003, Windows 2000, Windows NT, Windows XP, Linux Linux Distributions: For the latest information on supported distributions and kernel levels, see http://www-306.ibm.com/software/data/db2/linux/validate/

Note: DB2 servers are not supported on Windows XP Home Edition because of differences in how user authentication is handled. DB2 clients and DB2 Personal Edition, however, are supported on Home Edition.

Before starting the installation, log in to your system using a local administrator account or as the root user (on Linux). Then follow these steps:

1. Setup Launchpad. Installing DB2 Express is straightforward. Execute setup.exe and the IBM DB2 Setup Launchpad will automatically appear, as illustrated in Figure 2.1. From the launchpad, select the Install Product option to launch the Setup wizard.

Figure 2.1 Starting the installation

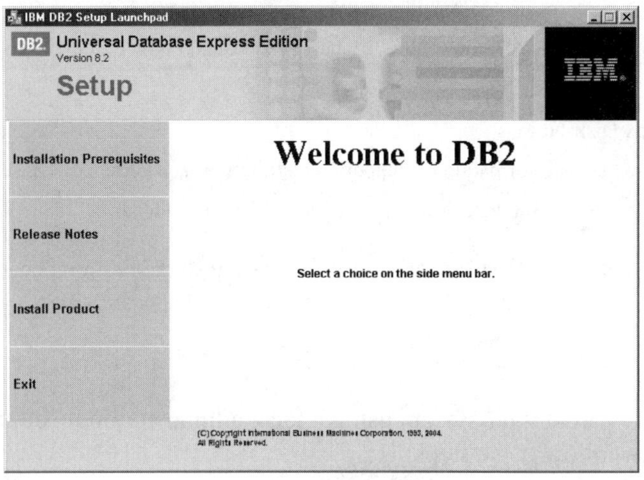

2. Setup wizard. The Setup wizard (Figure 2.2) will check your system for existing DB2 installations and minimum system requirements (this may take a few minutes). When the search is complete, the first of the installation screens will be displayed. To continue with the installation, click Next.

Figure 2.2 Setup wizard

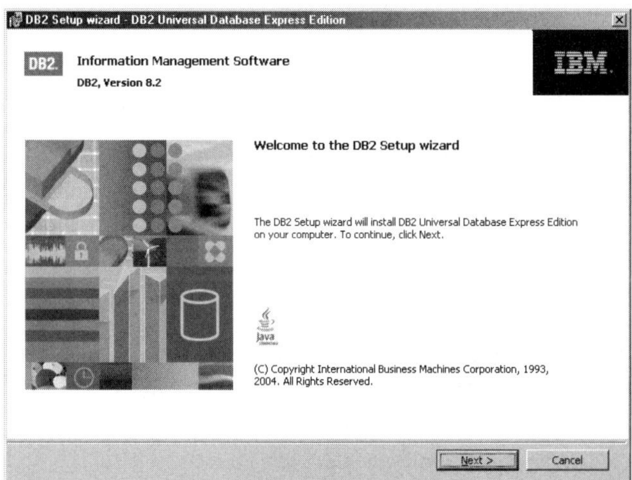

3. License Agreement. On this screen, you will be asked to accept the product licensing agreement (see Figure 2.3). To continue with the installation you will need to accept the terms and click Next.

Figure 2.3 License agreement screen

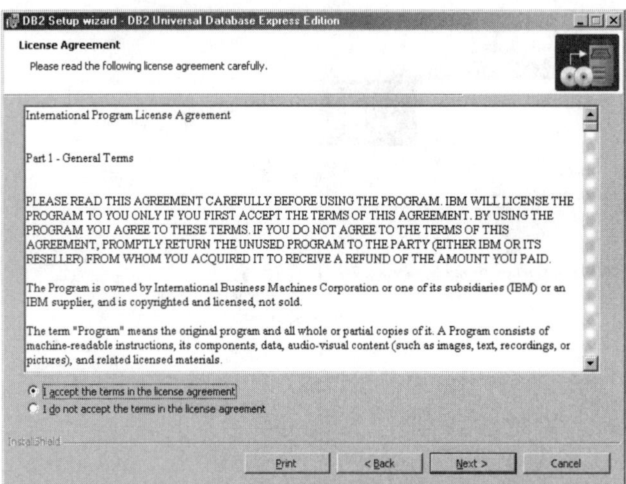

4. Installation Type. Using this screen you can choose from three installation options (see Figure 2.4).

- Typical: Install the most commonly used DB2 options.
- Compact: Perform only a basic installation.
- Custom: Select the specific features you want to install.

For the purposes of this book, select the Typical installation option.

Figure 2.4 Installation type

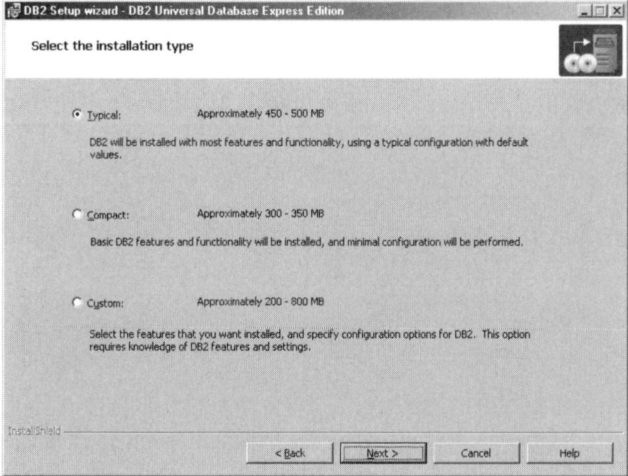

5. Select installation folder. Use this screen to specify the DB2 installation directory (see Figure 2.5). Ensure that you have enough free disk space as prescribed by the Typical installation. Click Next to move to the next screen.

If possible, we recommend using the default installation location:

C:\Program Files\IBM\SQLLIB

Figure 2.5 Installation folder

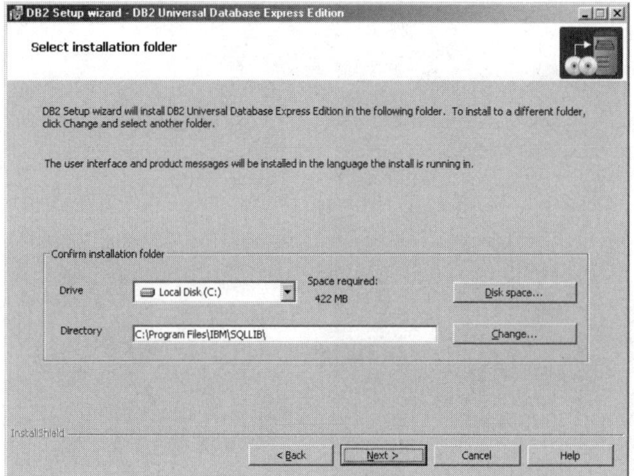

6. Set user information. When DB2 is installed, a set of DB2 processes is run as system services. These system services need to log in to the operating system before they can run.

On Windows, the default user ID db2admin is suggested (see Figure 2.6). On Linux, the default user ID db2inst1 is suggested. As for passwords, we use ibmdb2 for this book, but you can use whatever you like.

If the specified user does not already exist, it will be created automatically and granted local administrator privileges (therefore, be sure to protect this user ID). If you want to provide an existing user ID and password, the user must have local administrator authority.

Chapter 11, Implementing Security, shows you how to change user authentication information for DB2 services.

Figure 2.6 User information

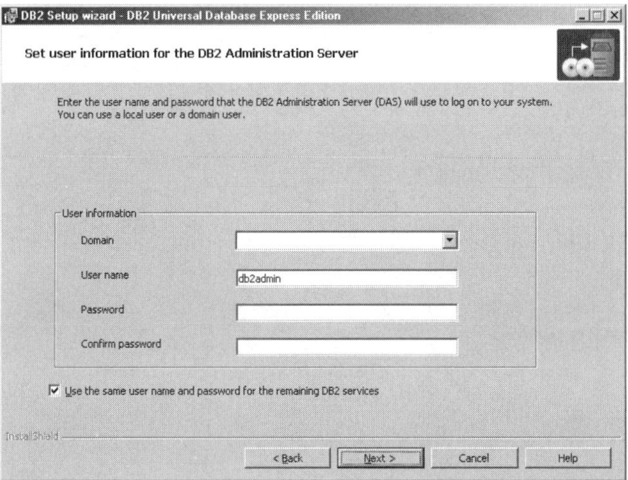

7. Configure DB2 instance. A DB2 *instance* is best thought of as a container for databases. An instance must exist before you create a database. During installation, a default instance called DB2 will be created so that you can create a database immediately after installation completes (see Figure 2.7).

Note: Often, there is confusion caused by the fact that both the product and the default instance name (on Windows) are called DB2. To be clear, the instance name and the product name are two separate entities and do not have any strict association. On Linux and UNIX environments, for example, the default instance is called db2inst1 rather than DB2.

By default, the DB2 server is configured to use Transmission Control Protocol/Internet Protocol (TCP/IP) as the communications method on port 50000 to listen for incoming remote connections. You can click the Protocols button to change this setting. However, unless you know that port 50000 is already being used by some other service (generally a rare event), there is no need to change this setting.

Figure 2.7 Configure DB2 instances

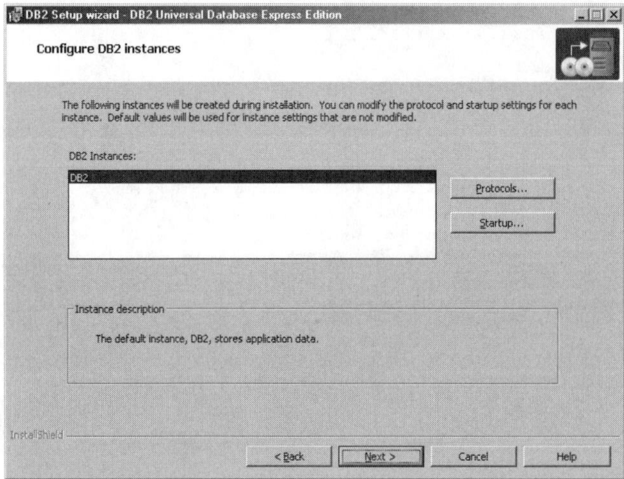

8. Start copying files. This screen will display a summary of the installation options (Figure 2.8). Review the selections before clicking the Install button to start the installation process.

Figure 2.8 Start installation

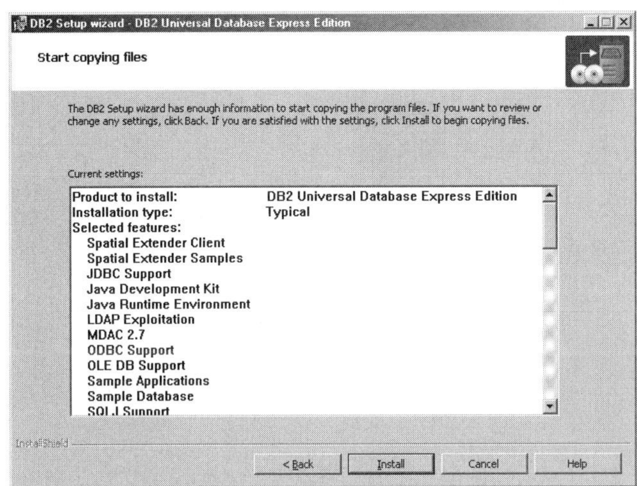

Note: The installation process for Linux is largely the same as for Windows. One difference is that, for security reasons, you will be prompted to provide a separate user ID for the instance owner and the fenced user. The fenced user ID will be used to run external (e.g., C or Java) stored procedures and user-defined functions.

Tip: Chapter 11 provides more information about how to simplify security on Windows by using the Local System account.

2.3 First Steps

After the installation is complete, a launchpad called First Steps is displayed (Figure 2.9). The First Steps launchpad offers you quick access to information to help get you started.

Figure 2.9 DB2 First Steps Launchpad

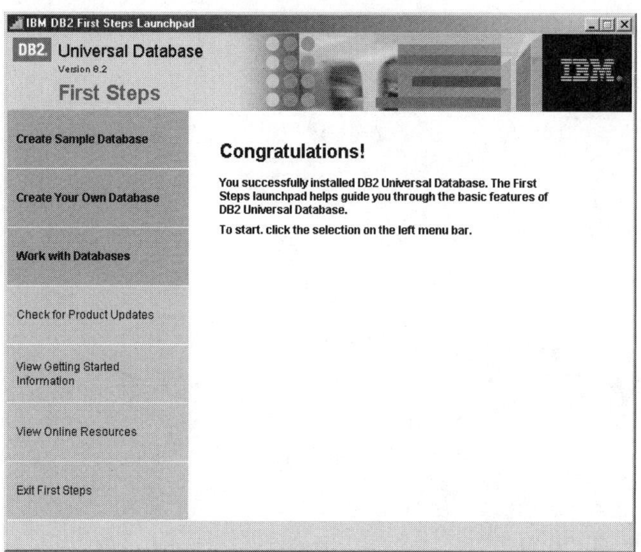

The First Steps page can help you create a sample database, called SAMPLE, that is shipped with DB2. Click the Create Sample Database task at the top of the page. While the database is being created a progress indicator will be shown. You will use this database later in this chapter.

2.4 DB2 Graphical Tools

DB2 Express includes an easy-to-use suite of tools to help you manage your database without having to learn the DB2 command-line environment. Over the course of this book you will see more of the capabilities of these graphical tools. This section gives you an initial look at two of these tools—the DB2 Control Center and the Command Editor—and explains what you can do with them.

The DB2 Control Center is used to administer DB2. Using the Control Center you can create, modify, and manage databases and their associated objects (tables, indexes, etc.) as well as launch many other tools to guide you through a vast array of tasks and activities.

The Control Center can be launched in a number of ways:

- From the Windows Start menu entry, as illustrated in Figure 2.10
- From the DB2 icon in the Windows system tray, shown in Figure 2.11
- By executing db2cc on a command prompt
- By clicking on the Control Center icon in the toolbar of any of the other DB2 tools

Figure 2.10 Launching the Control Center in Windows

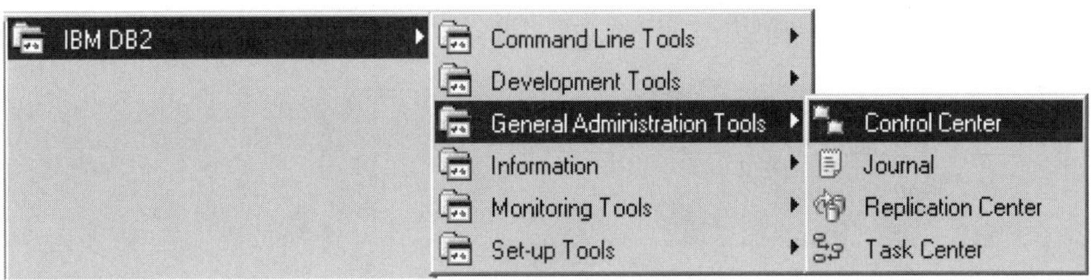

Figure 2.11 Launching the Control Center from the system tray

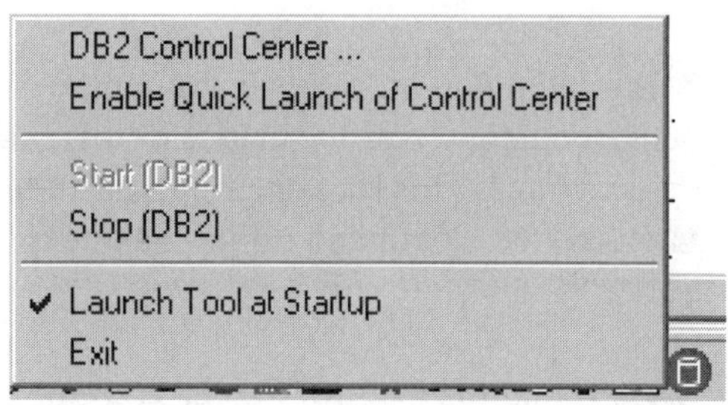

The first time the Control Center loads, you will see the Customize dialog (Figure 2.12) asking you which Control Center view you would like to use. The Control Center is a single point of access to a vast array of functionality. Exposing all the options and advanced features to new users, however, can be a bit overwhelming. Therefore, unless you have prior experience with DB2, we recommend that you select the Basic view, which will display only the essential database objects and features (as opposed to the default Advanced view setting).

Figure 2.12 Control Center View dialog

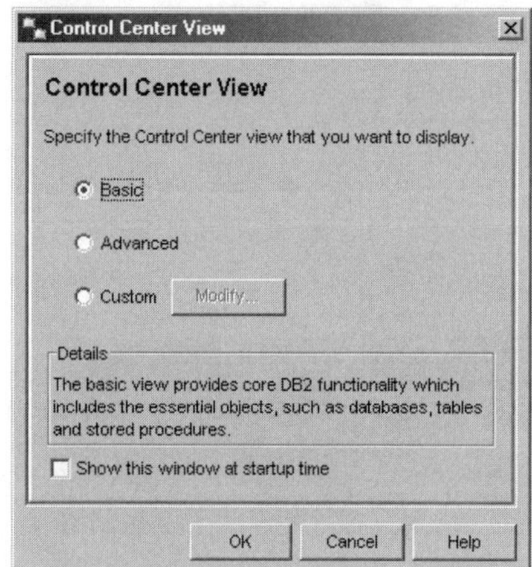

Note: We have also deselected the check box in the lower-left corner so that this dialog is not automatically displayed the next time the Control Center is launched.

After a view has been selected, the Control Center will continue to use that setting until you reinvoke the dialog and change it. When you have more experience with the Control Center, you can further customize it to show only those items and features you need.

If you choose the Advanced view, all available folders, objects, features, and functions will be displayed. The Custom view allows you to configure a customized view of the Control Center that shows only what you want to see. By clicking the Modify button, you can hide or show folders, objects, and their associated context menu items.

Figure 2.13 Relaunching the Customize dialog

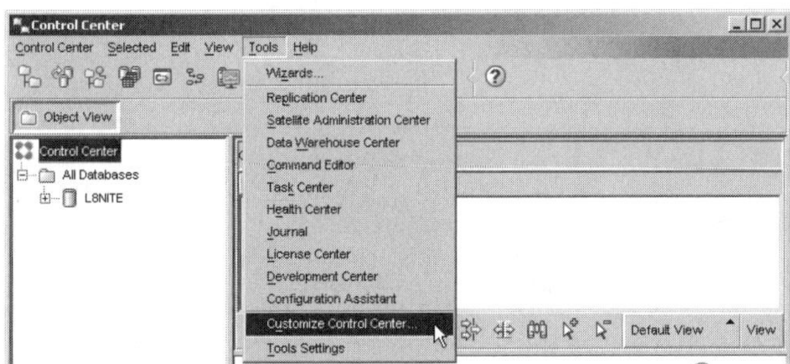

If you want to reinvoke the Control Center View dialog, select the Customize Control Center option (Figure 2.13) from the Tools menu. Or you can click on the Customize Control Center link in the object details panel when the root of the object tree (labeled "Control Center") is selected.

No matter which Control Center view is selected, the main interface will be laid out in three main sections (Figure 2.14):

- Left frame, object tree
- Upper-right frame, object listing
- Lower-right frame, object details

Figure 2.14 Control Center layout

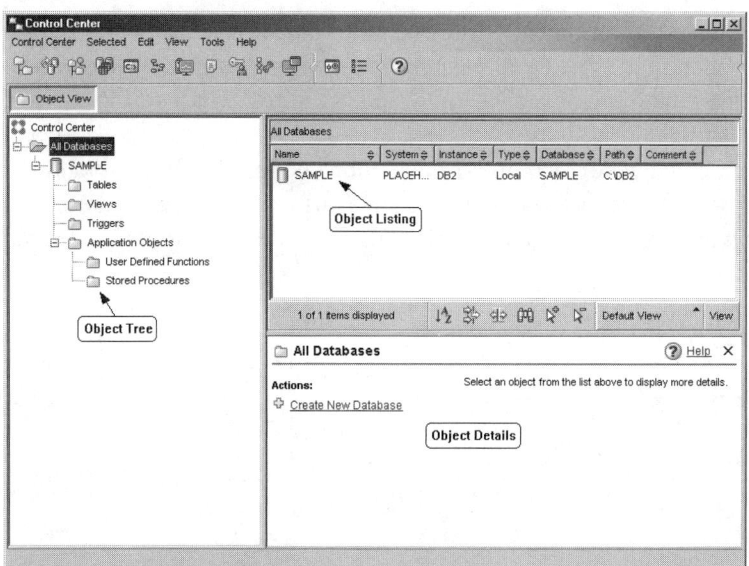

Selecting a folder from the object tree will display the contents of the folder in the object listings frame. The object details frame will show more detailed information for the selected object and will provide links to perform common tasks associated with the selected object.

The object tree is not expanded when the Control Center first loads. When expanded, it shows a list of all the databases registered on the client. By expanding the All Databases folder, you will see the SAMPLE database created in the previous section.

Inquiring Minds: Adding an Existing or Remote Database

If you have an existing database (possibly on another machine) and want to connect to it, it must first be registered with the DB2 client. To do this, right-click on the All Databases folder and select Add from the pop-up menu. The Add Database dialog

(Figure 2.15) can be used to search the local machine or network to catalog databases on the client.

Figure 2.15 Add Database dialog

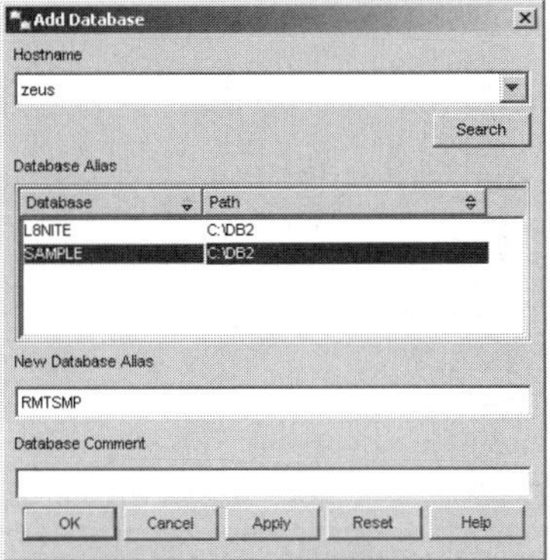

Note that database names are currently limited to eight characters and must be unique on each client. If the name of a database on a remote machine matches one that exists on your local machine, you need to alias it. In Figure 2.15, the SAMPLE database on a remote host called ZEUS is being aliased as RMTSMP.

2.5 Creating a Database

In subsequent chapters, you will build an application against a database called L8NITE.

From the Control Center, right-click the All Databases folder and select Create > With Automatic Maintenance (Figure 2.16).

Figure 2.16 Launching the Create Database wizard

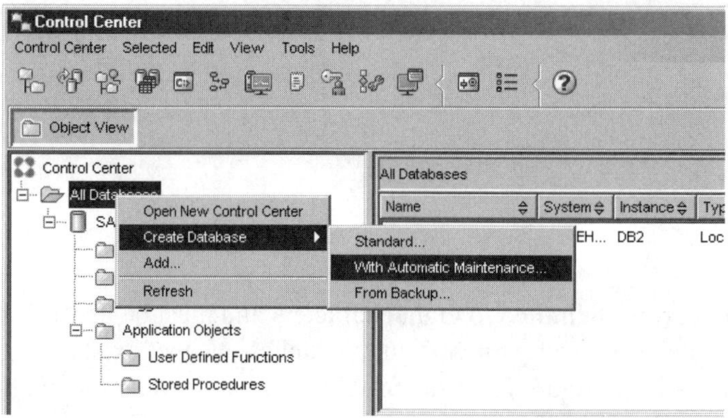

This will launch a wizard that creates and preconfigures a database to get you started. Follow these steps:

Step 1: Specify the database name and location.

Complete the following fields:

- **Database name:** L8NITE
- **Default drive:** C: (select a drive that has sufficient disk space)
- **Alias:** This will default to L8NITE if left blank.
- **Comment:** This is optional and can be left blank.

Click Next to continue.

Step 2: Configure the Maintenance Window.

The second step asks whether you can specify a period of time when DB2 can do some offline maintenance activities. Assuming that your database will not be used 24/7 we recommend you select Yes and click Next. If you don't want to specify a maintenance window, DB2 will still be able to do some online maintenance activities.

Step 3: Specify automatic offline maintenance timing.

The third step of the wizard (Timing) is available if you answered Yes to step 2. Set aside two or more hours a week when DB2 can perform automated tasks to ensure the health of your database.

Click Next to continue.

Step 4: Configure notification.

DB2 can automatically send you an e-mail (or send a message to a pager) if a problem or unhealthy condition is detected. If you wish to configure this, click the Add Contact button. Setting up notification can be skipped if you do not want to receive messages from DB2.

Step 5: Configure memory.

DB2 automatically detects how much physical memory is available on your system (Figure 2.17). All you are required to provide is the percentage of memory DB2 can use for tuning itself.

Figure 2.17 Configure memory usage

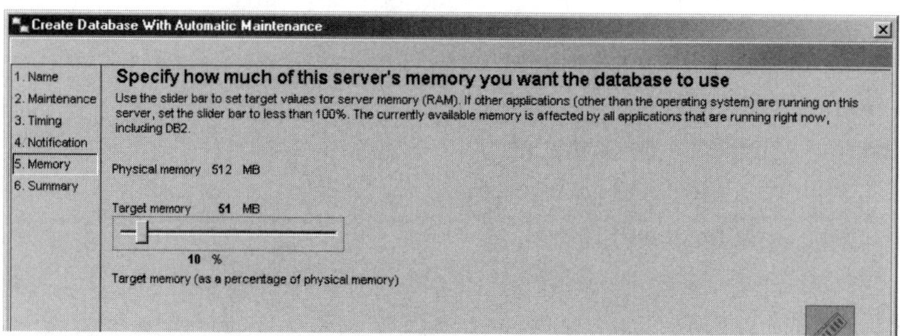

In making this decision, you should consider which other applications or databases will be running on the same system. Be sure to leave physical memory available for other applications when deciding on this value.

Consider the memory requirements for the following:

- The operating system itself
- Other applications such as Web servers and application servers
- Other databases running on this machine
- Development tools running on the same machine

Therefore, assuming you are installing DB2 on your primary development workstation, we recommend setting this value to a lower value, such as 10% or 20%. Later, in Chapter 10, Performance Tuning, you will see how DB2 can be further tuned. Select the desired memory setting and click Next.

Note: If you are not careful, you can easily overtune your database. If the system tries to use more memory than is physically available, overall system performace may degrade significantly.

Click Finish to start the database creation process. Database creation usually takes a few minutes, during which time a progress indicator will be displayed.

2.6 DB2 Command Editor

Using the Command Editor, you can execute DB2 commands and SQL, analyze the execution plan of an SQL statement, and view and update query result sets. The Command Editor offers some nice features to help you be more productive. For example:

- The built-in SQL Assist tool can help you generate SQL if you are not familiar with SQL syntax.
- A history of executed SQL statements is maintained to save retyping.
- After you execute queries, you can edit the results directly in the table, saving you the effort of writing multiple UPDATE statements.
- To help tune an SQL statement you can use a tool called Visual Explain, which graphically displays how the SQL statement will be executed. For example, Visual Explain can tell you which indexes are being used to access data, the kind of sort operations that are occurring, and the order in which tables are accessed (when multiple tables are referenced).

Within the Control Center, launch the Command Editor by right-clicking on the SAMPLE database (created earlier) and select the Query menu item. This will launch the Command Editor as an embedded tile in the Control Center (Figure 2.18).

Figure 2.18 Embedded Command Editor

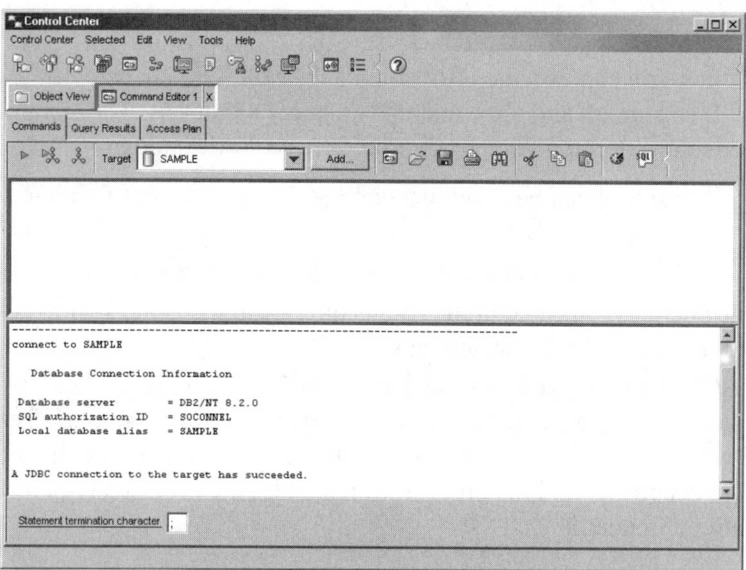

When the Command Editor is launched, it displays only an input and an output area. The input area (the top portion of the editor) is where you can submit SQL and CLP (Command Line Processor) commands. Depending on how the Command Editor is launched, a connection may be attempted automatically. After a connection has been established, two more tabs (labeled "Query Results" and "Access Plan") will appear.

You can return to the Control Center view by clicking on the Object View tile. To close the Command Editor, click the X icon associated with the tile.

The Command Editor can also be launched in other ways:

- Whenever a queryable object is selected (such as a database, table, or view), you can launch the Command Editor by clicking the Query link in the Control Center's object details panel.
- You can launch the Command Editor as a stand-alone application from the DB2 command prompt by typing db2ce, from the Control Center toolbar, or from the Windows Start menu.

You can establish a database connection by inheriting one from the Control Center (by launching the embedded Command Editor) or by using the Add button within the Command Editor to add to the list of connections made during this session.

When you press the Add button, a dialog appears (Figure 2.19), where you can select a database to connect to. Using this dialog you can provide specific authentication criteria using the User ID and Password fields. (If the database is local, you can use the implicit credentials option, which means that the Command Editor will reuse the credentials you used to log in to the operating system.)

Figure 2.19 Command Editor Add (database connection) dialog

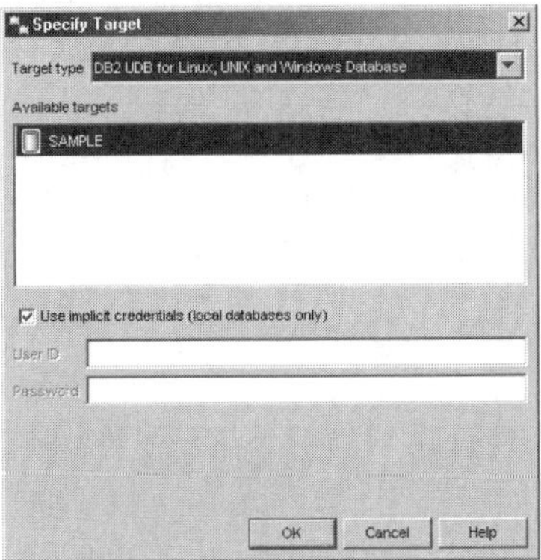

Commands Tab

When a connection is established you can submit commands and queries against the database. First, familiarize yourself with the buttons in the top-left corner of the Commands tab (Figure 2.20).

Figure 2.20 Command Editor controls

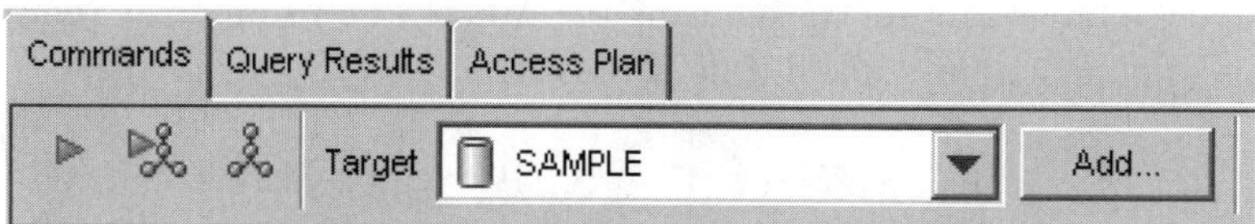

- The first button (Execute) runs the command in the input area.
- The second button (Execute and Access Plan) runs the command in the input area and generates an access plan for the query.
- The third button (Access Plan) generates an access plan for a query without executing the query. This is useful when you're troubleshooting a long-running query and you want to know what is happening internally, without actually executing the statement.

Using the SAMPLE database, we will query a table called DEPARTMENT. Type the following SQL statement in the input window.

```
SELECT * FROM DEPARTMENT;
```

Click the single green arrow button to execute the statement. You can also use the shortcut Ctrl+Enter.

Tip: You can have multiple statements in the input window as long as each statement ends with a termination character. If you press the execute button, the statements will be executed one after another. If you explicitly highlight a particular statement, only the highlighted statement will be executed.

Note: The statement here ends with a semicolon, which is the default statement terminator. You can change the statement terminator by specifying a different termination character at the bottom of each Command Editor window.

Query Results Tab

The Query Results tab (Figure 2.21) can be used to view and edit the results of your query (called the *result set*). That is, you can add, delete, or update rows of data without having to use SQL statements. (This feature is available only when you're executing a single query at a time.) If you execute multiple statements at one time, the results will be displayed in the output window rather than in the Query Results tab.

Figure 2.21 The Query Results tab of the Command Editor

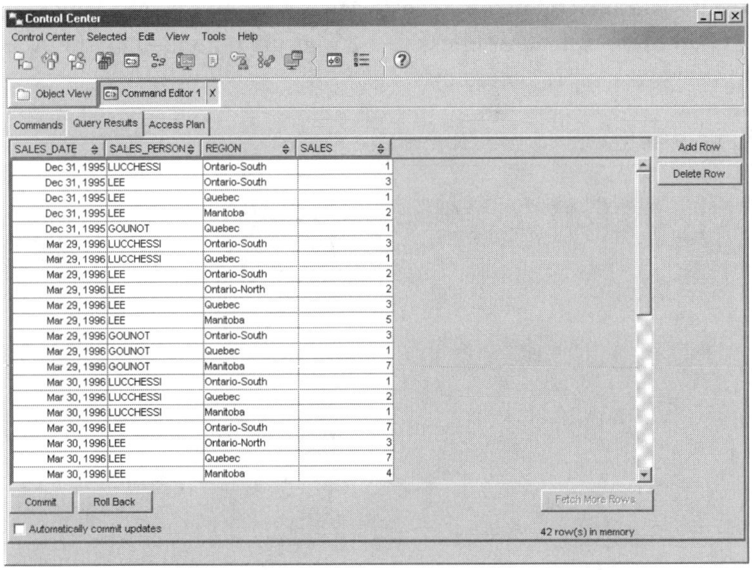

To add data to the Department table, click the Add Row button. To delete a row, select a row from the result set and click the Delete Row button. To modify data in existing rows, click on any cell and directly change the values. The changes you make are not made permanent until you click the Commit button. If you make a mistake, you can undo the changes you've made by clicking the Roll Back button. For convenience, you can also have the Command Editor automatically commit changes as you make them. To do that, select Automatically Commit Updates option.

Access Plan Tab

If you are interested in how DB2 is performing a particular SQL statement, you can use DB2's Visual Explain tool to explain the query (called an *access plan*). This tells you, among other things,

- How a table is accessed
- In what order tables are accessed
- Which sorting algorithms are employed, and so on

The access plan for the query is displayed in the Access Plan tab. Return to the Command tab of the Command Editor. This time, instead of clicking the Execute button, click the Access Plan button. Figure 2.22 shows a sample access plan.

Figure 2.22 Viewing access plans in the Command Editor

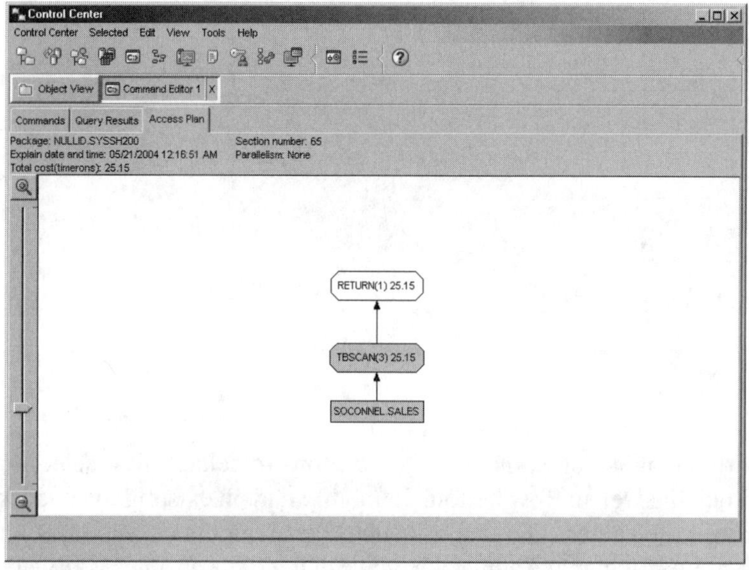

Visual Explain will be discussed in greater detail in Chapter 10, Performance Tuning.

2.7 DB2 Information Center

No getting-started chapter would be complete without a discussion of where to find more information. For most users, the primary source of official DB2 information will be the DB2 Information Center. Open a browser to

http://publib.boulder.ibm.com/infocenter/db2help/index.jsp

Bookmark this site. It is an invaluable resource that is actively maintained and updated as documentation is improved or when new DB2 features are released.

The left navigation tree organizes information by topic. If you know what you are looking for, the Reference subtree is particularly useful. For example:

- If you were looking for the syntax for any SQL statement, you can look in Reference > SQL > SQL Statements.

- For the latest information on JDBC support in DB2, navigate to Developing > Database applications > Programming applications > Java.

- For Command Line Processor commands, go to Reference > Commands > DB2 Universal Database > Command Line Processor (CLP).

If you're not quite sure where to look for something, the Search function is a great way to start. All official DB2 documentation is searched, and results are returned with rankings in order of expected relevance.

2.8 Supplemental: Installing DB2 Clients from a Server CD

In general, a DB2 client must be installed in order to communicate with a DB2 server (JDBC type 4 connections are the exception). DB2 uses a client/server architecture, even when interacting with a local database. When the database server runs on a separate physical machine from the application client, you may need to install the DB2 client software. A DB2 client comes in three forms:

- DB2 Runtime client: an installable image of the bare minimum client, providing no graphical administration or development tools
- DB2 Administration client: an installable image of the Runtime client and administration utilities
- DB2 Application Development client: an installable image of the Runtime client with application development tools.

DB2 client software can be installed from any DB2 Server CD (using a custom install) or can be download for free from http://www.software.ibm.com/data/db2/udb/support.html.

To install client software from a DB2 Server CD, use a custom installation and deselect the Server Support option, as illustrated in Figure 2.23. If you need only the basic DB2 Runtime client, deselect Application Development Tools and Administration Tools.

Figure 2.23 Using custom installation to install only a DB2 client

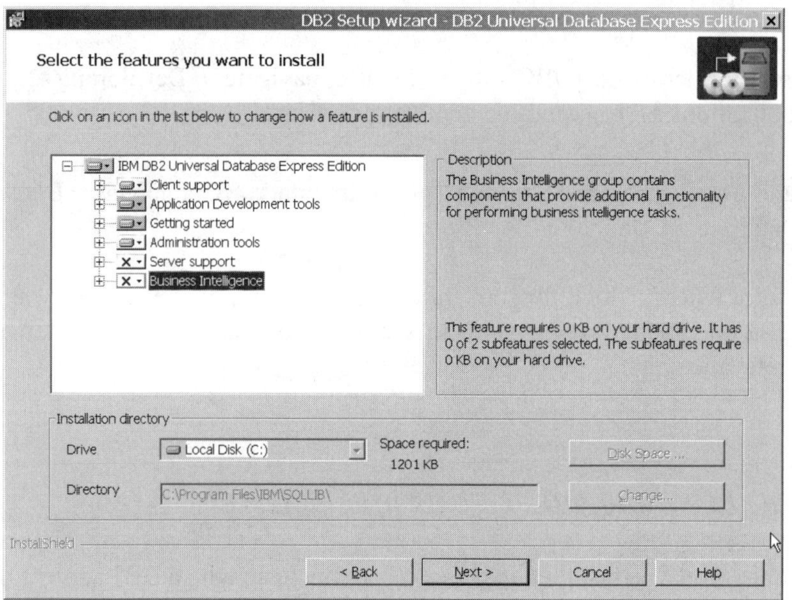

2.9 Summary

In this chapter, you got up and running with DB2 by installing the software, creating the SAMPLE database, and using the DB2 Control Center to create your own database called L8NITE which will be used later to develop an application. The Command Editor was also introduced, and you learned how to query a database table, modify its contents, and view access plans for a query. Finally, we introduced you to the DB2 Information Center, an online repository of constantly updated information on DB2.

In Chapter 3, you will prepare for developing the L8NITE sample application by overviewing the application's purpose and functionality.

CHAPTER 3

The L8NITE Database Application

In this chapter, you will learn:

- About the Late Night Convenience Store's business requirements
- About the application's data model
- How to use the sample application to be developed throughout this book

3.1 Introduction

Chapter 1 introduced DB2 Express and described the benefits of using DB2 Express for building database applications. Then in Chapter 2 we walked you through the installation process and introduced the fundamental tools for working with DB2 databases. You now have a good foundation for doing something useful with DB2.

One of the best ways to learn about database application development is to build an actual application. Throughout this book, DB2 application development concepts will be discussed, and then you will apply them to building a sample application called L8NITE.

The application is a point-of-sale (POS) terminal used for a simple convenience store called the Late Night Convenience Store, which sells a variety of products such as beer, soft drinks, chips, and diapers. A DB2 database will be used to maintain inventory records, customer records, sales transactions, and other related information to support point-of-sale services.

DB2 Express is targeted directly at the small and medium business segment, and therefore it is appropriate to demonstrate how to develop this application using the two most dominant programming languages in this market: Visual Basic .NET (VB.NET) and Java.

The full cycle for developing and deploying the application is as follows:

- Understand the functional requirements of the Late Night Convenience Store and design a graphical user interface that will meet the defined requirements (this chapter).
- Design and create database objects to support the application and its data requirements (Chapter 4).
- Create the application. In Chapter 5, we build the application using VB.NET. In Chapter 6, we demonstrate how to build the same application again using Java. The chapters have been written so that if you are interested only in one of the languages, you can read either chapter and continue with the rest of the book.
- Review the application in light of important design considerations to maximize concurrency (Chapter 7).
- Consider how application logic can be pushed down into the database for better performance using triggers, functions, and stored procedures (Chapter 8).
- Load the application with sufficiently large quantities of sample data (Chapter 9).
- Tune the database for better performance (Chapter 10).
- Design and implement a set of security policies (Chapter 11).
- Generate DDL (Data Definition Language) statements and create scripts that can be used to re-create the database, and package them for easy deployment (Chapter 12).
- Deploy the database to a production environment, leveraging DB2's autonomic self-managing capabilities (Chapter 13).
- Troubleshoot problems that may occur (Chapter 14).

Throughout the book, we will discuss DB2 application development features and apply them to the L8NITE application using a step-by-step approach. In some cases, we leave development activities as exercises to reinforce what you have learned. The activities completed in each chapter are the starting point for the next one. The application source code can be downloaded from the book Web site.

We now describe the functional requirements of the Late Night Convenience Store and design a graphical user interface to meet those requirements. You will then understand how the application should work as you progress through the chapters.

3.2 Late Night Convenience Store Requirements

The Late Night Convenience Store is a successful business that has many loyal customers. In the past, it sold only a limited variety of products, and that made managing inventory very simple. However, business has been growing and customers are starting to demand a larger selection of goods, making inventory control signficantly more difficult. Also, the current method of handling all cash in a shoebox is starting to become a concern because although the store has only one checkout counter now, the owner wants to have additional checkout counters to handle the increased customer volume. A traditional cash register may help in the short term, but the owner has a greater vision.

The owner wants to have a point-of-sale system that not only processes transactions but also has the following operational capabilities:

- Is able to support more than one checkout counter—potentially dozens or more as the store expands.
- Allows products to be picked up or returned.
- Has an awareness of the store's current inventory. It should know how much of each product remains in the store so that the owner knows which products need to be reordered.
- Always knows the most up-to-date prices to reduce transaction mistakes.
- Allows loyal customers to open accounts and handle payments using both cash and accounts. So that customers do not have to remember their account numbers or carry membership cards, account numbers should be searchable.
- Can extend the store's offerings to be sold on the Internet.

In addition to the operational capabilities, the owner wants to gather insight on the overall business based on any period of business operations. For example, the following business insights would be very valuable for maintaining a healthy and growing business:

- Which are the best- and worst-selling products
- How much money has been made for any given period of time
- Which are the best customers so that they can be rewarded for their loyalty in the future
- Which customers have not revisited recently so that marketing programs can be more targeted and efficient

Other insights might be useful, and the system should be flexible enough to allow creation of new reports when needed.

3.3 The Data Model

The term *data model* refers to the tables designed to support the application requirements. There are a variety of ways to do this. We could store everything in one giant table. Each row of this table could contain the account number, if any, of the customer, the product(s) purchased, whether the product was picked up or returned, and so on.

This design, however, is far from adequate and likely would not meet all the requirements if all the details of this model were hashed out. Also, rows would contain repeated data because many of the customers are repeat customers buying from a relatively fixed selection of products.

Entire books have been written on efficient database design, and it would be difficult to have a full discussion of the topic in one chapter. Therefore, we simply present a data model that will suit the store's requirements and build from there.

Table Descriptions

A PRODUCT table will maintain the current inventory of each product available for sale. Each product has a unique product ID. This table will also contain information about each product:

- A description
- Wholesale cost
- Retail price
- Current quantity in stock
- Minimum quantity in stock when the product should be replenished

A CUSTOMER table maintains information about regular customers who wish to purchase on account. Each customer account has a unique customer identifier. This table will also contain information about each customer:

- First and last name
- Address and zip code
- Credit card information
- Phone number

Recording sales is a little more tricky. A sale is really a collection of customer product purchases because a customer approaches the checkout counter with a basket of products to be paid for at one time.

A SALES table will be used to record each sale and a PRODUCT_PURCHASES table will be used to store the details of each sale. Each sale will have a unique sales transaction ID and the following information:

- For sales on account, the customer ID of the customer making the purchase
- Total value of the sales transaction (before taxes)
- Tax collected
- Type of transaction (sale, return)
- Date and time of the sale

The PRODUCT_PURCHASES table contains the details of each sale. For every row of data in the SALES table, there will be one or more rows of data in the PRODUCT_PURCHASES table containing the following information:

- Sales transaction ID that the product purchase belongs to
- Product ID of the product being sold
- Price of the product
- Quantity of the product

In the next section, we'll demonstrate how the application interacts with this data model to meet the requirements of the Late Night Convenience Store.

3.4 The Point-of-Sale Application Interface

In this section, you will see how the graphical user interface of the L8NITE application will work with the database. The screen shots shown here are taken from the Visual Basic .NET implementation of the application. However, the Java version of the application looks almost identical.

Login

When the application is started, the user is prompted to provide a user name and password (see Figure 3.1). During the development phase, you can use the default DB2 user ID and password we recommended during installation.

- Windows: db2admin
- Linux: db2inst1

Figure 3.1 The L8NITE application login dialog

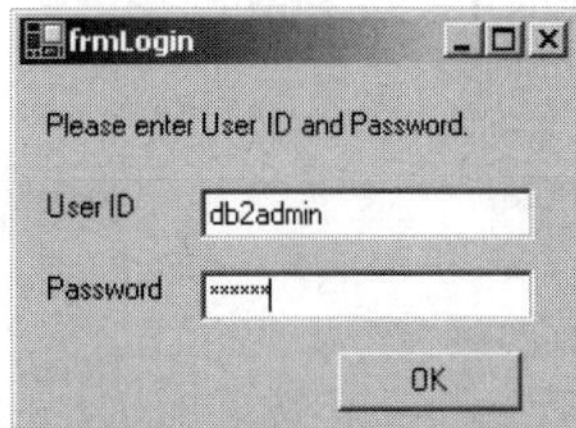

Cash Sale

The point-of-sale scenario begins with a customer walking to the cashier with items to purchase. In the simplest case, it will be a cash purchase. In the application, Sale is selected from the pull-down menu and the Cash option is selected (Figure 3.2).

Figure 3.2 Processing a cash sale

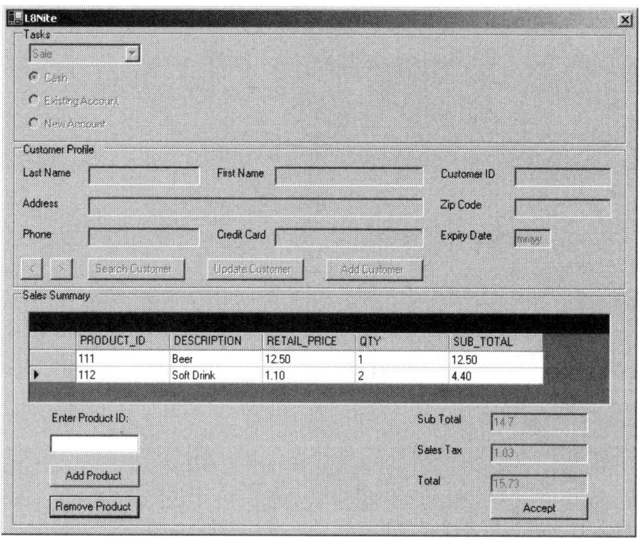

The cashier then enters products by typing the product ID (labeled on each product) followed by clicking the Add Product button. The application will then retrieve the product's description and retail price from the PRODUCT table. If a data entry error is made, the cashier can remove a product from the purchase list by selecting it and clicking the Remove Product button.

In Figure 3.2, the Add Product button was clicked twice for Product ID 112. You can see that the QTY column is 2 for that item. As products are entered, taxes, total sale amount, and amount due are calculated.

When all products have been entered, the cashier clicks the Accept button and the following sequence of database interactions occurs:

- A row is inserted into the SALES table to begin the sales transaction. A sales transaction ID is generated.

- For each unique product in the product purchase list, a row is inserted into the PRODUCT_PURCHASES table along with the sales transaction ID, which associates the product purchase information with the row in the SALES table.

- The quantity purchased is deducted from inventory in the PRODUCT table.
- The SALES table is updated with the total value of the sales transaction.
- The cashier is notified that the sales transaction was completed successfully (Figure 3.3).

Figure 3.3 Notification of successful sales transaction

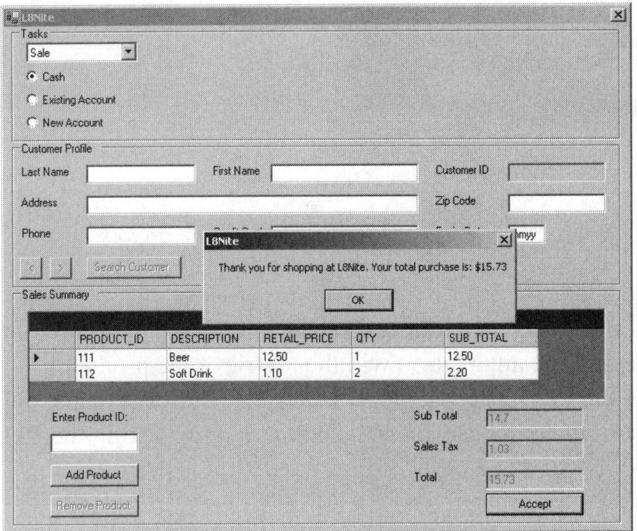

Account Purchase

Customers have the option of purchasing products on account. To do this, the clerk selects Existing Account from the Tasks panel. The customer's first and last names are used to search for the account in the CUSTOMER table. A message is displayed in the event that multiple matching customer accounts are found, as illustrated in Figure 3.4. The clerk can select the proper account by clicking the [<] and [>] record-locator buttons. The additional available customer information, such as address information, is used to differentiate one account from another.

Figure 3.4 Account search that finds more than one match

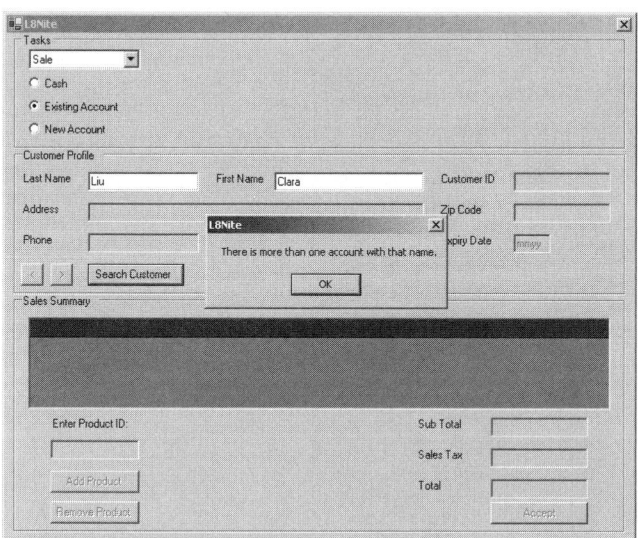

Before submitting product purchases, if the customer information is out of date, the cashier can modify the existing information as needed and click the Update Customer button to apply changes.

The remaining steps for completing an account sale are the same as for cash sales.

Processing Refunds

To process refunds, the clerk selects Refund from the Tasks pull-down menu (Figure 3.5). The refund can be processed via cash or on account. To post a return on account, the cashier searches for the account information using the customer's first and last names as before.

The clerk enters the returned product IDs by clicking the Add Product button.

Figure 3.5 Processing a product return

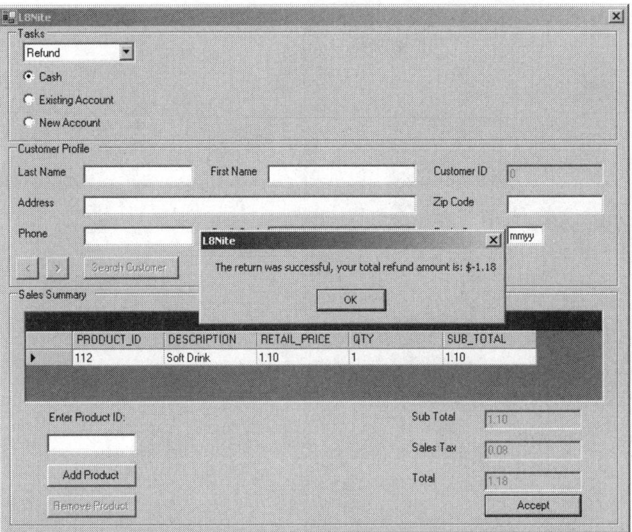

When finished, the cashier clicks the Accept button, which enters sales information into the SALES and PRODUCT_PURCHASES tables with negative retail price values to reflect a returned product. Also, product inventory is updated in the PRODUCT table to reflect the returned goods.

Creating a Customer Account

New customer accounts are also created through the application. To do so, the clerk selects the New Account option in the Tasks panel and provides the customer information.

Figure 3.6 Creating a new customer account

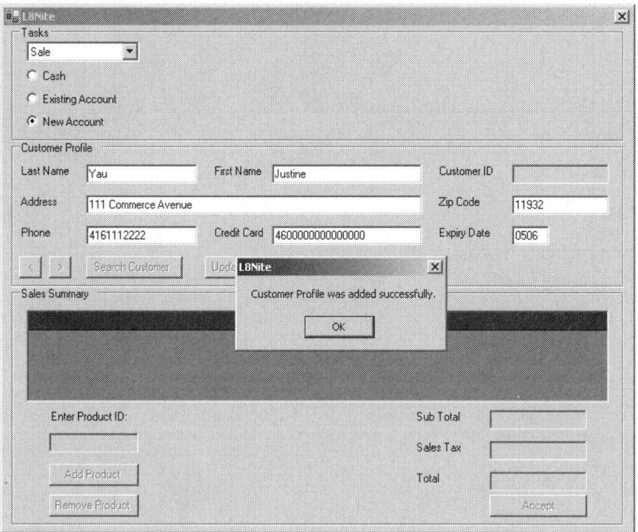

When the task is completed, the clerk clicks the Add Customer button to create a row in the CUSTOMER table (Figure 3.6). A customer ID value is automatically generated for the customer.

3.5 Summary

In this chapter, you learned about the Late Night Convenience Store and the application to be developed throughout this book. To help the store achieve its vision of rapid expansion, you learned about the business's needs, which influenced the design of the database tables. The application design was reviewed so that you can visualize how the application will eventually look and feel.

CHAPTER 4 Database Objects

In this chapter, you will learn:

- How to create fundamental database objects such as tables, views, and indexes
- How to populate and retrieve data from these objects
- More about advanced objects such as aliases and materialized query tables (MQTs)
- How to alter a previously created and populated table

4.1 Introduction

In Chapter 3, you were introduced to the L8NITE application. You also created a basic, empty database called L8NITE in Chapter 2. In this chapter, you will create the database objects used by the application to be built in Chapters 5 and 6. We will introduce data types and explain how to build tables, indexes, and views. You will also insert sample data into this database and learn how to query its contents. These are the basics needed to build yourself a DB2 database. A supplemental section discusses advanced topics such as aliases and describes how to alter a table that has already been created and filled with data.

Note: Before you begin this chapter, make sure you know how to launch the Control Center and have created an empty database named L8NITE. If you have not, please complete this task before proceeding. Details on creating the L8NITE database and launching the Control Center can be found in Chapter 2.

4.2 Schemas

Before you create database objects, it is important to understand the notion of database schemas. *Schemas* are namespaces for a collection of database objects and can be used to provide an indication of object ownership or relationship to an application. When you connect to a database and create an object (but do not specify a schema), DB2 will create the object in a schema that matches your user ID.

For example, if you create a table called T1 and you are connected to the database as user db2admin, then DB2 will create the table as DB2ADMIN.T1.

The schema used during a session is actually controlled by a DB2 special register called CURRENT SCHEMA, which defaults to your connection user ID. When you create or refer to objects without specifying a schema, DB2 uses CURRENT SCHEMA to determine the schema to use. When you refer to an object with its schema, you are using the object's *qualified name*. All objects belong to schemas, and a qualified object name must be unique. In other words, an object must be unique within its schema.

For example, the name DB2ADMIN.T1 is qualified. If the schema were not specified, DB2 would use the CURRENT SCHEMA special register value:

```
SELECT * FROM DB2ADMIN.T1
```

Schemas can also be used to group related database objects. For example, application 1 might create all its database objects in schema APP1, whereas application 2 creates its objects in schema APP2 in the same database.

In the L8NITE database application, we will create objects in the L8NITE schema. We will always use qualified names in our SQL so that the application can connect as any user and DB2 can identify specific objects to use. This is considered a best practice.

If you do not wish to qualify all object names, an alternative is to change the CURRENT SCHEMA special register value using the SQL SET SCHEMA statement:

```
SET SCHEMA L8NITE
```

4.3 Data Types

A traditional relational database is used to store structured data. The more structured the data is, the more efficiently a database can store and retrieve it. Data is stored in tables within the database, and tables are made up of columns and rows. The columns are defined when a table is created. Rows of information can then be inserted, updated, and deleted from a table. Every column of a table has a name and specifies the type of data that can be stored in it. Table 4.1 provides the full list of data types supported by DB2 and lists the kind of information they can store.

Table 4.1 All DB2 Data Types

SMALLINT	A small two-byte integer with precision of 5 digits.
INTEGER INT	A large four-byte integer with precision of 10 digits. Has a range from –2 147 483 648 to +2 147 483 647.
BIGINT	A big eight-byte integer with precision up to 19 digits.
FLOAT DOUBLE	A double-precision floating point number. An eight-byte approximation of a real number. Imprecise.
REAL	A single-precision floating point number. A four-byte approximation of a real number. Imprecise.
DECIMAL NUMERIC	Used for decimal numbers. Decimal point is determined by precision and scale.

(continues)

Table 4.1 All DB2 Data Types (Continued)

CHAR	Fixed-length storage for a sequence of characters and numbers. Generally used for smaller character strings where performance is more important than storage.
VARCHAR	Used for variable-length character strings where storage is more important than performance. Generally used for larger character strings that can vary in length. Maximum size depends on table space page size.
BLOB	Binary large object, which is used for binary data. Can be used for pictures or other types of binary files. The performance of BLOBs is not as good as structured data such as characters or integers but is used for storing unstructured data. Tip: You can use VARCHAR FOR BIT DATA for small objects if performance is a major consideration.
CLOB	Character large object. Used to store vary large strings beyond the limits of the VARCHAR data type.
DBCLOB	Double-byte character large object. Like CLOB but used to store very large multi-byte character strings (such as Chinese characters) beyond the limits of VARGRAPHIC.
GRAPHIC	Like a CHAR type, but used to store multibyte character strings (such as Chinese characters).
VARGRAPHIC	Like a VARCHAR type, but used to store multibyte character strings (such as Chinese characters).
DATE	Date data type representing year, month, and day.
TIME	Time data type representing hour, minute, and second of the time of day based on the 24-hour clock.
TIMESTAMP	A value that includes both the time and the date.
DATALINK	Contains a logical reference to a file outside the database.
Distinct type	User-defined type that shares its internal representation with an existing type.
Structured type	User-defined type that has its internal structure defined in the database.

Note: To use GRAPHIC, VARGRAPHIC, and DBCLOB data types, you must create a database to support multibyte character sets such as UTF-8. When creating databases in the Control Center, you configure this in the region/code set option of the Create Database wizard.

Some data types are used more often than others (examples are INTEGER and VARCHAR). The following data types will be used in the L8NITE database.

- INTEGER
- CHARACTER
- VARCHAR
- DECIMAL
- TIMESTAMP

Most data types have or can have some sort of attribute associated with them. Table 4.2 shows some common attributes.

Table 4.2 L8NITE Column Attributes

Length	The maximum size of the data. The greater the length, the more storage required for the data type.
Scale and Precision	Used for decimal data types. For example, DECIMAL(5,2) means that the type can store up to five digits of precision with two digits after the decimal (e.g, 123.45).
NOT NULL	Specifies whether or not a NULL value is an acceptable value. By default, NULLs are allowed.
DEFAULT	Specifies the default valuc to bc inserted into the column if no value is provided.
GENERATED ALWAYS	The value of the column is always generated by DB2 based on a formula.
IDENTITY	A special type of GENERATED ALWAYS column consisting of a numeric value that will increment or decrement automatically each time a new row is inserted into the table.

Note: NULL simply means an unknown value in DB2. The default value of any column, unless otherwise specified, is NULL.

4.4 Tables

Tables can be created within the Control Center by using the Create Table wizard. You can launch the Create Table wizard from the Tools > Wizards… menu, or you can right-click on the Table folder in the Control Center object tree. Three elements are required for every table: a name, a schema, and at least one column definition. Follow these steps:

Step 1: Launch the Create Table wizard.

As shown in Figure 4.1, from the Control Center object tree, select Control Center > All Databases > L8NITE > Tables > (right-click) Create…

Figure 4.1 Launch Create Table wizard from Control Center object tree

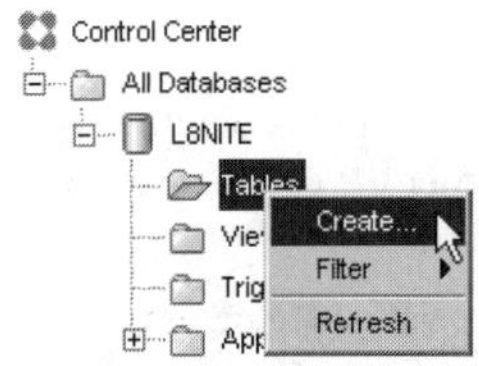

Step 2: Provide the table name and schema information.

The Create Table wizard will require a name and column definitions for the new table. Let's create the PRODUCT table for the L8NITE database (see Figure 4.2). This table will be used to store all the inventory. The table will have seven columns:

- product_id: unique identifier of the product
- description: description of the product
- cost: the wholesale cost of the product
- retail_price: the retail price of the product
- inventory: the quantity of product the store has in stock
- minimum_inventory: the minimum quantity of this product the store should maintain in stock at any given time. The default minimum is 0.
- image: a picture of the product, possibly to be used for an online store

Figure 4.2 Create Table wizard introduction page

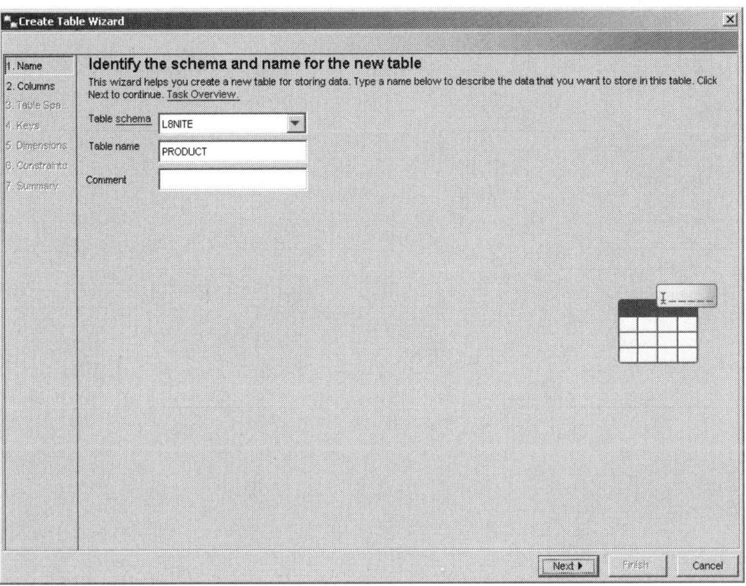

Enter the schema: L8NITE, and enter the table name: PRODUCT. Click the Next button to continue.

Step 3: Define the table columns.

From here, you can either add your own columns to the table, or you may choose to add a set of predefined columns. Select and add your own column (see Figure 4.3).

Figure 4.3 Add a column to Table

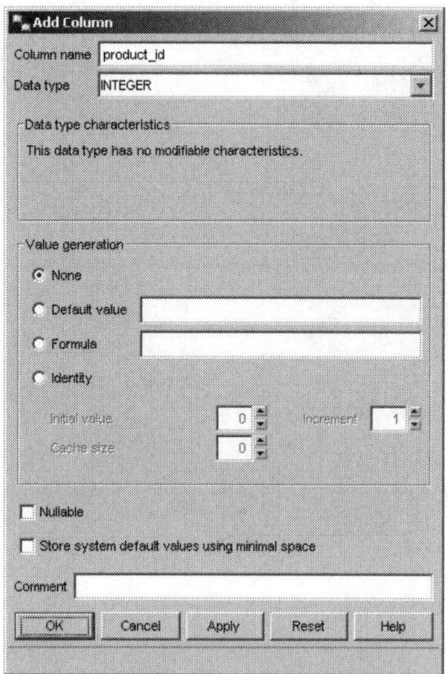

Enter the column name: product_id, and select the data type: Integer. Then uncheck Nullable, and click Apply to define the column.

Note: The Apply button is useful if you wish to define multiple columns without closing the current dialog box. Click OK when all columns have been defined.

Repeat this step for the remaining columns of the table, as shown in Table 4.3.

Table 4.3 Columns of the PRODUCT Table

Column Name	Attributes
product_id (completed)	INTEGER, NOT NULL
description	VARCHAR, Length 40, NOT NULL
cost	DECIMAL, Precision 7, Scale 2, NOT NULL
retail_price	DECIMAL, Precision 7, Scale 2, NOT NULL
inventory	INTEGER, NOT NULL
minimum_inventory	INTEGER, NOT NULL, DEFAULT 0

When you have defined all the columns, your window should look like Figure 4.4. If you've made a mistake, you can select the column to be corrected and click the Change... button.

Figure 4.4 Completed columns of the PRODUCT table

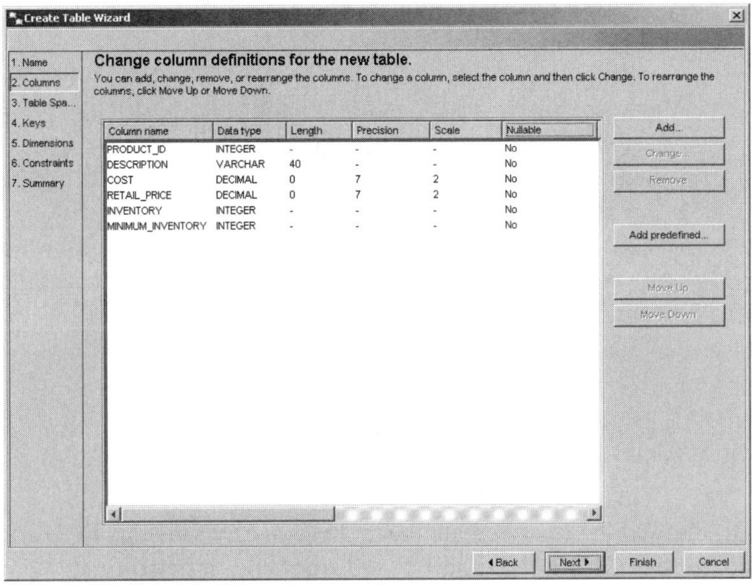

Step 4: Set optional parameters and create the table.

At this point, all the mandatory information for creating a table has been provided. You can continue going through the wizard, changing other parameters of the table. Or you can skip to the summary page, or simply click Finish to create the table.

On the summary page, you can review the SQL that will be used to create this table (see Figure 4.5). By skipping the other pages, you are choosing the default values for table space, keys, dimensions, and constraints. You can add keys and constraints after a table has been created, and we will do so later in section 4.6. After a table is created, however, you cannot change its table space. The default table space is the first user-defined table space created in the database, or USERSPACE1 if no user-defined table space exists. In our example, L8NITE.PRODUCT will be created in USERSPACE1.

Figure 4.5 Summary page for Create Table wizard

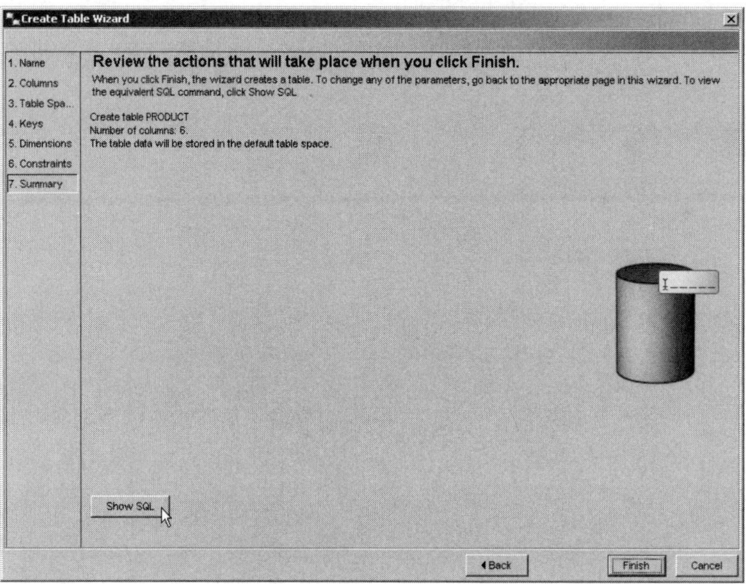

You can review the SQL that will be run to create the table. You can copy this SQL into the Command Editor of the Control Center and modify, save, and rerun it many times against different databases.

In this section, we create only the PRODUCT table. Creation of other tables for the L8NITE application has been left as an exercise at the end of this chapter. To prepare for the next section, you should perform exercises 1 and 2 now. Alternatively, you can import the files schema.ddl and sample_data.sql available from the book's Web site into the Command Editor and run it from there.

4.5 Retrieving Data from the Database

Data is retrieved from the tables through SQL queries. SQL is a very powerful language, and entire books have been written about it. We will not attempt to teach you SQL but rather will introduce its basic concepts. An SQL query can be broken into three major sections:

- The type of information you want to retrieve
- Where you want the information retrieved from
- What information you want and how it is retrieved

The following simple query will retrieve the description and retail price for all items in the PRODUCT table whose retail price is less than $5:

```
SELECT description, retail_price
FROM 18nite.product
WHERE retail_price < 5.00
```

The following more complex query will retrieve the products sold in the most recent transaction:

```
SELECT a.description, b.product_id, b.price, b.qty, b.total
  FROM 18nite.product a, 18nite.product_purchases b
 WHERE a.product_id=b.product_id AND
                 b.sales_transaction_id=identity_val_local()
```

Note: The table PRODUCT_PURCHASES has an identity column defined that automatically generates values for sales_transaction_id. When a purchase is made, the application performs an INSERT into this table without immediately knowing what the next transaction ID might be. The built-in function identity_val_local(), when called immediately after an INSERT, returns the last generated identity value.

Note: If you are curious about how a query is executed and how to tune SQL, read about DB2's Visual Explain tool in Chapter 10, Performance Tuning.

4.6 Table Relationships

In a relational database, data in tables can be related to one or more other tables to accomplish many things, including the following:

- Enforce referential integrity
- Eliminate the possibility of orphaned data
- Add business logic to the base data structure
- Increase performance through SQL engine optimizations

A table can declare restrictions on the values it can store. These restrictions, formally called *constraints,* can be very simple, such as the range of values that a column can store, or more complex, such as whether the data to be inserted must be related to data in another table (called a parent-child or foreign-key relationship). To explain how table relationships work and can be created, we first must explain the basic objects that make up table relationships (see Table 4.4).

Table 4.4 Basic Objects of Table Relationships

Parent table	A parent table is the controlling data table in which the parent key exists.
Dependent table	A dependent table, or child table, is dependent on the data within a parent table. A dependent table contains a foreign key. For a row to exist in a dependent table, a matching row must first exist within a parent table.
Primary key	A primary key defines the parent key of the parent table. Each parent key of the parent table must be unique, and the primary key enforces this uniqueness. A primary key consists of one or more columns within a table.
Foreign key	A foreign key references the primary key of a parent table.

For data to exist within a dependent table, the foreign key of the dependent table must first match an existing primary key on a parent table. If this relationship holds true for all data within the tables, it is called *referential integrity.*

Inquiring Minds: Constraints

Constraint is a general term used to define restrictions on data within a table. There are several different types of constraints within a database:

- Referential constraints
- Check constraints
- Unique constraints

Referential constraints are discussed in this section. Check constraints and unique constraints put restrictions on the data based on the content of the column itself. Unique constraints enforce uniqueness among all the data values in a given column or columns of a table. Internally, a unique index is created so that DB2 can quickly determine whether a unique constraint is violated as values are inserted or updated. Check constraints put restrictions on the values allowed within a table. For example, a check constraint may restrict the minimum retail price of an item to be greater than 0.

Constraints serve other purposes in addition to enforcing rules. Their existence also provides additional information about the nature of the data, optimizing SQL execution and thereby improving performance. Constraints can also be defined but unenforced, something that is useful when the application already guarantees the correctness of data. The overhead of checking constraints can be eliminated, while still providing information to DB2 about the nature of the data. For more information, see the DB2 Information Center > Reference > SQL for CREATE TABLE.

Let's create a referential constraint between PRODUCT (the parent table) and PRODUCT_PURCHASES (the child table). PRODUCT is the parent table because for every product purchase recorded in the PRODUCT_PURCHASES table, the item must have existed in the PRODUCT table (see Figure 4.6). The primary key will be created on the product_id column of the PRODUCT table. We also need a foreign key on the product_id column of the PRODUCT_PURCHASES table to reference the product_id column of the PRODUCT table.

Figure 4.6 Table relationship of PRODUCT and PRODUCT_PURCHASES tables

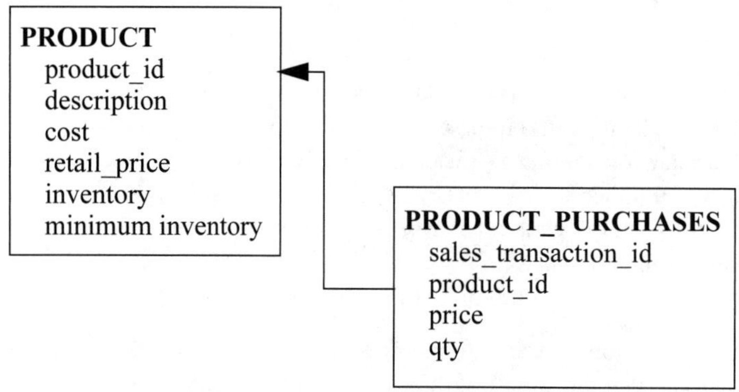

Follow these steps:

Step 1: Open the Alter Table dialog box.

From the Control Center object tree, select Control Center > All Databases > L8NITE > Tables. Then select the PRODUCT table > (right-click) Alter…

Figure 4.7 Alter Table, Add Primary Key

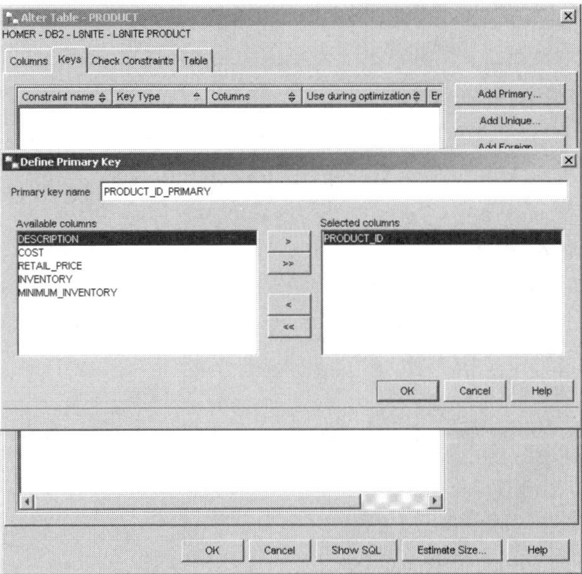

Step 2: Add a primary key.

From the Keys tab, click the Add Primary... button (see Figure 4.7). Enter the new primary key name: PRODUCT_ID_PRIMARY. Then select the PRODUCT_ID column from the left pane and move it to the right pane. Click the OK button.

Step 3: Create a foreign key.

Now create a foreign key on the PRODUCT_PURCHASES table. First, alter the PRODUCT_PURCHASES table.

Figure 4.8 Alter Table, Add Foreign Key

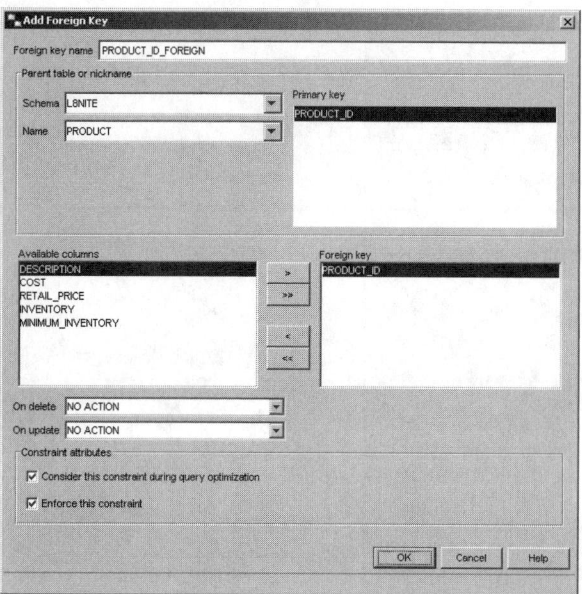

Again, from the Keys tab, select the Add Foreign... (see Figure 4.8).

Enter the new foreign key name: PRODUCT_ID_FOREIGN. For the parent table, select the schema: L8NITE. For the parent table, select the name: PRODUCT. Then verify the primary key, and select the PRODUCT_ID column from the left pane of available columns and move it to the right pane. Click the OK button.

Note that constraints can be defined at the same time as tables are created (using the Create Table wizard) or as a separate step, as just demonstrated.

The remaining relationships have been left as an exercise at the end of the chapter. Before continuing with this chapter, you should now complete exercises 3 and 4.

4.7 Views

Views in a database can be thought of as virtual tables defined by an SQL query that provide a special perspective on one or more tables.

For example, you could build a very complex view called V1 using a very complex query that uses a 10-table join. Simply performing a SELECT * FROM V1 is the same as issuing the complex query.

From the perspective of an application, views are no different from tables in that they are accessed in the same way. Whenever a view is accessed, the underlying query with which it was defined is executed automatically. Views can be used to save typing for a complex query that is used many times or as a mechanism to separate the actual organization of data from that required for business logic.

You can build tables whose columns directly correlate with business logic, but it can be wasteful and can sacrifice the benefits of relational database capabilities. In general, a properly designed database minimizes storage of repeated data values, giving you better performance, less wasted storage, and better data integrity. Although such a design may be efficient, it can sometimes be hard to understand how to get the information you need to facilitate business logic. Creating views on top of those tables can make it easier to query and understand the layout of a database.

Let's create a view that uses the query listed in section 4.4. Follow these steps:

Step 1: Launch the Create View dialog box.

From the Control Center object tree, navigate to Control Center > All Databases > L8NITE > Views.

Right-click the Views folder, and select Create… from the pop-up menu.

Step 2: Create the view.

Figure 4.9 Create View dialog box

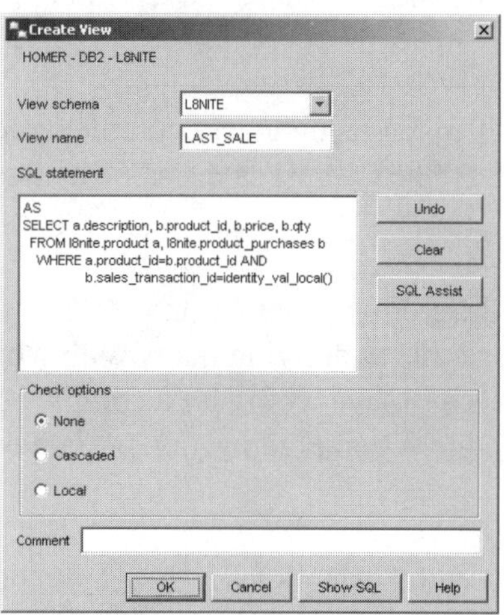

Select the schema L8NITE from the pull-down menu, and type LAST_SALE for the view name (see Figure 4.9).

Enter the following query to define the view.

```
AS
SELECT a.description, b.product_id, b.price, b.qty
 FROM l8nite.product a, l8nite.product_purchases b
  WHERE a.product_id=b.product_id AND
          b.sales_transaction_id=identity_val_local()
```

Inquiring Minds: Materialized Query Tables (MQTs)

Materialized query tables (MQTs) are very similar to views, except that they store or cache the results of the underlying query. (Views are purely logical and do not contain data themselves.) After an MQT has been built, you can query it many times without having to reexecute its underlying query, improving query response times. MQTs either can be automatically updated as the underlying data changes or can be manually refreshed. MQTs are most often used as performance-enhancing objects that are administered by a database administrator. MQTs also have a feature that allows for automatic query routing so that a query gets automatically rerouted to an MQT if the requested data has already been cached by the MQT. MQTs can be created using the Design Advisor in the Control Center. More details on the Design Advisor and performance-enhancing tips are given in Chapter 10, Performance Tuning.

4.8 Indexes

Everyone has used a book index. Book indexes are a quick way to look up a word of particular interest and skip directly to the page in which the keyword is contained. *Database indexes* are to tables as book indexes are to books. Instead of mapping words to pages, database indexes map key values to specific rows in a table.

By having indexes, the database can retrieve data from a table without having to search through the entire table (called a *table scan*). Indexes can be defined for tables to improve performance, improve concurrency, and enforce uniqueness. It is obvious how indexes can improve the performance of queries, but it may not be as clear how they help in improving concurrency and enforcing uniqueness.

Internal locks are acquired on behalf of applications as rows are inserted, updated, or deleted. If many users or applications are concurrently accessing the same table, the use of an index decreases the chance of encountering lock contention because not all applications are performing table scans. For uniqueness, indexes provide a quick way to search a table to determine whether a value exists when you are inserting or updating a value in the table. Therefore, when you create a unique constraint on a column, DB2 automatically creates a unique index to enforce the constraint.

Indexes are part of every good database design. In-depth knowledge of the workload run against a database plays a big role in the effectiveness of a particular index.

Advanced users who have a good understanding of SQL and the workload of an application can often anticipate which indexes should be created manually, and this can be done using SQL or using the Create Index dialog box in the Control Center. When a skilled database administrator is not available or the query to be performed is complex, DB2 has an industry-leading tool called the Design Advisor, which can automatically create indexes for a given SQL workload. The Design Advisor will be discussed in Chapter 10, Performance Tuning.

We will now demonstrate how to create an index using the Create Index dialog box to improve the performance of the complex query used by the view created earlier.

Note: Primary keys have unique indexes within their underlying definitions.

Step 1: Launch the Create Index dialog box.

From the Control Center object tree, navigate to Control Center > All Databases > L8NITE > Tables.

Select the PRODUCT_PURCHASES table > (right-click) Create > Index…

Note: To access the Create Index dialog box, you may need to switch to the Control Center's Advanced view by using the Control Center View dialog box as outlined in Chapter 2.

Step 2: Create the index.

Figure 4.10 Create Index dialog box

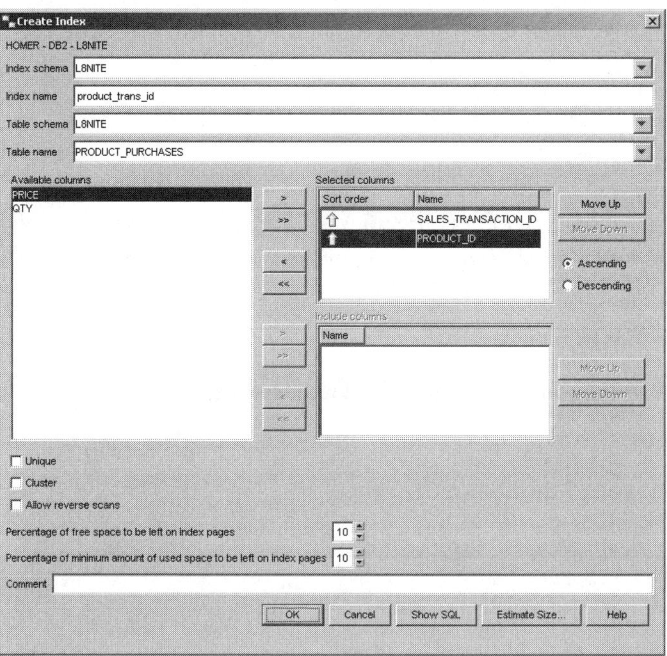

Specify the index name: product_trans_id (see Figure 4.10). Ensure that the table schema is L8NITE and the table name is PRODUCT_PURCHASES. Then move both the PRODUCT_ID and the SALES_TRANSACTION_ID column from the left pane of available columns to the right pane. Click the OK button to create the index.

4.9 Supplemental

This chapter deals primarily with creating the most commonly used database objects. This supplemental section discusses other types of objects that may be of interest. However, the discussion here is not a prerequisite for understanding topics discussed in later chapters.

Aliases

Aliases allow objects to be referred to by different names. The base object can be any table, view, or even another alias. Aliases can create a separation layer between the application and the real objects underneath, allowing the base objects to change without affecting the application.

Note: Don't confuse aliases with *nicknames,* another DB2 object. Aliases point to local objects, whereas nicknames refer to objects that are in another database (but appear local to applications). Nicknames are beyond the scope of this book.

Figure 4.11 shows an example of a completely layered database design that uses the view discussed before.

Figure 4.11 Example of layered database design

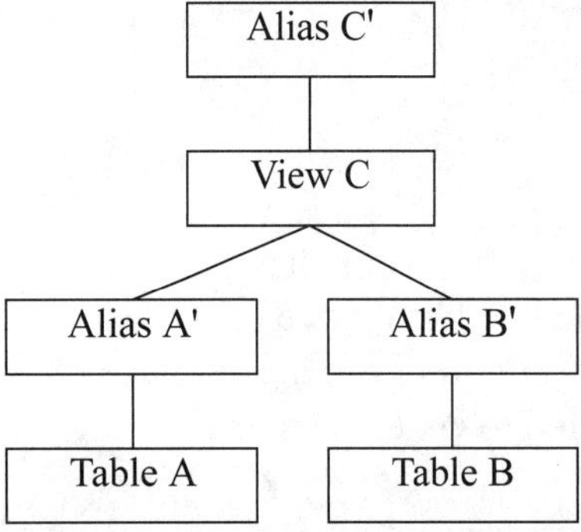

By referencing only aliases and never the objects themselves, you can switch an object with another object, modify it, and switch it back during the online hours of a database without affecting the underlying application logic or availability.

4.10 Altering the Definition of a Table

The definition of a table is usually fully specified at table-creation time. You should take care during creation to ensure that the definition is sufficient for your needs. However, cases will arise when you need to alter the definition of your table to fix a mistake or adapt to changing business needs. Some changes to a table, such as adding a column, can be very easy, but others, such as renaming or deleting a column, can be more difficult. There is added complexity when you want to alter a table in a way that may affect dependencies on it, such as views or foreign key relationships. The altered table may require further validation or altering of the data within it.

In essence, there are two types of table alterations. The first kind is very straightforward and uses the SQL statement ALTER TABLE. Making this type of change is easy and fast, and the change is effective immediately.

The second type requires consideration of your changes and how they affect objects that are dependent on the table and the data within it. The changes are not instantaneous, and the time required to perform the operation depends heavily on the size of the table. This second type of change will perform the following operations on your database:

- Delete all objects dependent on a table.
- Rename the old table.
- Create a new table.
- Re-create all objects dependent on the new table.
- Load data from the old table into the new table, transforming data if necessary.
- Delete the old table.

All this can be done by using a stored procedure, with the additional flexibility that a script can be generated if migration of a production database is required.

The Control Center can be used to perform both types of table alteration. We will guide you through an example that has both a simple and a complex table alteration: Add a column, and rename a column in the L8NITE database.

Step 1: Open the Alter Table dialog box for the CUSTOMER table.

Navigate to the Tables folder in the L8NITE database, and select the CUSTOMER table. Right-click the object, and select Alter... from the pop-up menu.

Step 2: Specify the table modifications.

Figure 4.12 Alter Table dialog box

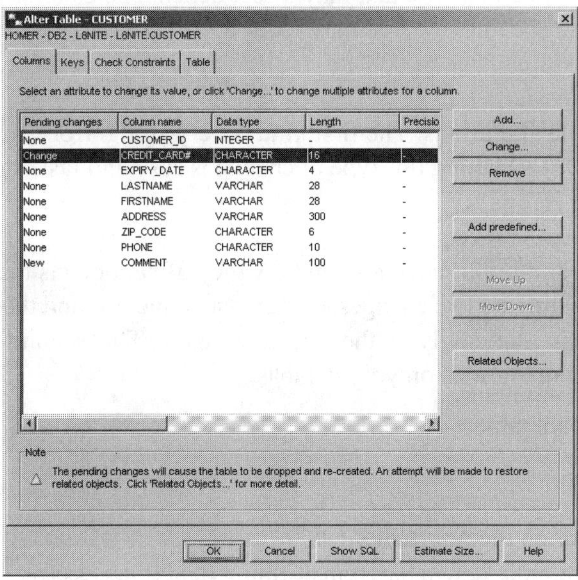

In the Alter Table dialog box (Figure 4.12), do the following:

- Click the Add... button to add a new column. Set the new column name as Comment of type VARCHAR(100).
- Modify the name of the credit_card column to credit_card#.

At this point a warning message will appear to prompt you to view related objects because changing a column name is a complex operation that requires reconstruction of the table. Click OK to close the warning message. Click the Related Objects... button to validate the proper creation of related objects, as shown in Figure 4.13.

Figure 4.13 Alter Table, Related Objects dialog box

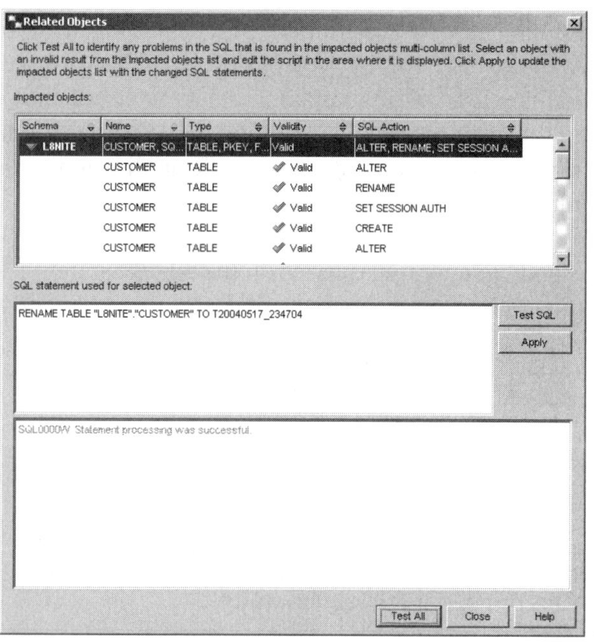

In the Related Objects window, perform the following:

- Click Test All.
- Validate that all related objects were validated and can be re-created.
- Close Related Objects, and click OK to alter the table.

The Related Objects dialog box allows you to test the statements to be run before actually committing the changes to the database. Altering a table that has dependent objects can cause dependent objects to fail during their re-creation. The Related Objects window gives you the opportunity to correct those problems before applying the changes. You can test and revalidate your changes as many times as you wish.

4.11 Summary

In this chapter, you have learned about the basic building blocks of a database: data types, tables, indexes, and views. In addition to creating objects, you have learned how to establish relationships between tables and why it is important in maintaining data integrity and improving performance. By following the examples and completing the exercises in this chapter, you will prepare the L8NITE database objects for creating the application. This database is the foundation for the application you will build in Chapters 5 and 6.

You have inserted data into the tables and have written queries on the tables. In the supplemental section, we discussed related topics such as how aliases can be used and how to alter a table after it has been created. You now have the fundamental knowledge you need for designing a database and can embark upon creating an application.

4.12 Chapter Exercises

1. Finish creating all the tables for the L8NITE database (see Figure 4.14). The tables CUSTOMER, SALES, and PRODUCT_PURCHASES definitions are as follows:

   a. Table: CUSTOMER

      customer_id INT NOT NULL GENERATED ALWAYS AS IDENTITY(start with 1 increment by 1)
      credit_card CHAR(16)
      expiry_date CHAR(4)
      lastname VARCHAR(28)
      firstname VARCHAR(28)
      address VARCHAR(300)
      zip_code CHAR(6)
      phone CHAR(10)

      (continued)

b. Table: SALES

sales_transaction_id INT GENERATED ALWAYS AS IDENTITY (start with 1 increment by 1)

customer_id INT

sub_total DECIMAL(7,2)

tax DECIMAL(7,2)

type INT NOT NULL

transaction_timestamp TIMESTAMP

c. Table: PRODUCT_PURCHASES

sales_transaction_id INT

product_id INT

price DECIMAL(5,2) NOT NULL

qty INT NOT NULL

Figure 4.14 L8NITE database table relationships

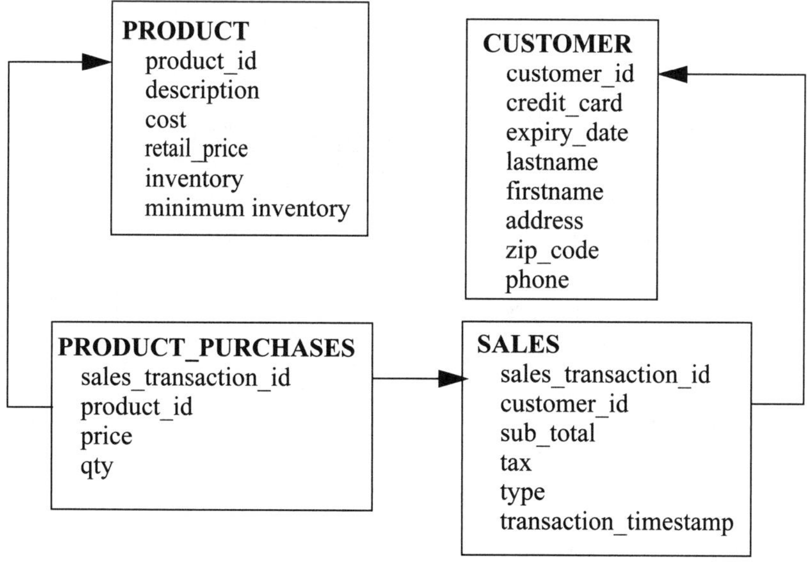

2. Download sample_data.sql from the book website and run it to populate all the tables.

3. Create a relationship between the parent table CUSTOMER and the dependent table SALES on the customer_id column.

4. Create a relationship between the parent table SALES and the dependent table PRODUCT_PURCHASES on the transaction_id column.

CHAPTER 5

Visual Basic .NET Application Development

In this chapter, you will learn:

- What .NET and ADO.NET are
- How to enable .NET support in DB2
- How to use DB2 tools from Visual Studio .NET 2003
- How to write Visual Basic .NET applications to work with DB2
- How to set up and run DB2 Call Level Interface (CLI) traces to troubleshoot .NET applications

5.1 Introduction

You have been introduced to the fundamentals of DB2 and various types of database objects. You have created a sample database, L8NITE, with step-by-step instructions. Chapters 1 to 4 set the stage for developing an actual application using Visual Basic .NET, the focus of this chapter. If you have not followed along with the previous chapters, you should at least create the L8NITE database and tables by using the script l8nite.ddl available from the book's Web site. You should also have the graphical integrated development environment (IDE) Visual Studio .NET 2002 or 2003 installed. Visual Studio .NET 2003 was used for screen shots in this book to illustrate Visual Basic .NET development.

5.2 What Are .NET and ADO.NET?

.NET is not a particular product or service. Rather, it is a brand that applies to various technologies. The development platform that these technologies are built on is called the .NET framework. There are three key components in the .NET framework:

- The Common Language Runtime (CLR)
- The framework class libraries
- .NET-compliant languages

When .NET-compliant languages such as C# .NET, J# .NET, and Visual Basic .NET are compiled, byte code known as Intermediate Language (IL) is produced. The Common Language Runtime is a runtime environment that provides code execution services to the IL code. Because all .NET-compliant languages are compiled into IL, CLR can integrate code written in various languages. For example, a Visual Basic (VB) method can access a C# method, and a class that is defined in C# can be accessed from VB.

The .NET framework libraries are classes and application programming interfaces (APIs) that developers use to build .NET applications. It provides a set of common services, such as file I/O and data source access, allowing developers to add functionality to programs regardless of the programming language. ADO.NET is an example of a programming model that is part of the .NET framework. Like Open Database Connectivity (ODBC) and Object Linking and Embedding Database (OLE DB), ActiveX Data Objects .NET (ADO.NET) is another data access application interface Microsoft provides. It is a new data access model that combines the best features of its predecessor, ActiveX Data Objects (ADO), together with traditional database access, integrated XML support, and a disconnected data architecture. In the following sections, we will look at how .NET applications interact with DB2 databases using ADO.NET.

5.3 .NET Support in DB2

To connect to a DB2 database from a .NET application via ADO.NET, three access methods are possible. As illustrated in Figure 5.1, you can use the Microsoft ODBC .NET data provider, the Microsoft OLE DB .NET data provider, or the DB2 .NET data provider.

Figure 5.1 Data access alternatives between DB2 and .NET applications

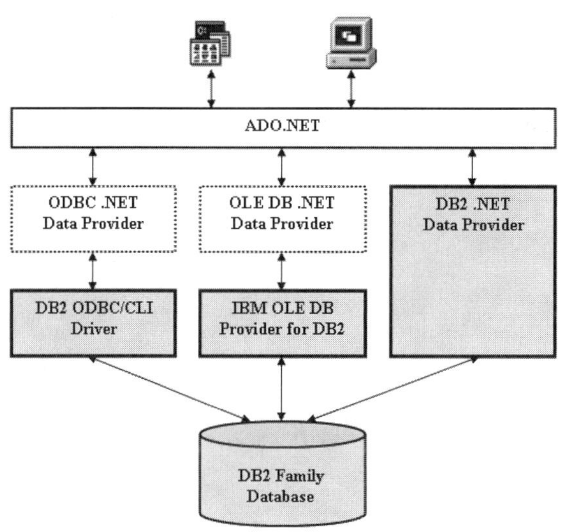

Previous versions of DB2 shipped with the DB2 ODBC/CLI driver and the IBM OLE DB provider for DB2. In DB2 v8.2, these two drivers are updated to also work with the Microsoft ODBC .NET and OLE DB .NET data providers. With the enhanced drivers, .NET applications can access DB2 family databases—such as DB2 for Linux, UNIX, and Windows and DB2 for iSeries—through the use of ODBC and OLE DB.

You can see from Figure 5.1 that both the ODBC and the OLE DB option require the application requests to be translated from the ODBC and OLE DB .NET data providers to the DB2 ODBC and OLE DB native drivers, and vice versa. This leads to longer code paths and thus impacts performance. In addition to performance considerations, the ODBC and OLE DB .NET data providers pose some restrictions because translation between the drivers is not 100 percent compatible. Therefore, the native DB2 .NET data provider is recommended.

The DB2 .NET data provider is the foundation of DB2 support for the ADO.NET model. It acts as a resource manager for DB2. This support gives .NET applications the ability to manipulate and work directly with DB2 data using the ADO.NET interface.

To comply with the ADO.NET architecture, classes supplied by the DB2 .NET data provider are categorized as belonging to one of two layers: the *connected layer* and *disconnected layer*. Operations in the connected layer work directly with data stored in the database. They must be connected to the database, and database resources (such as row locks) are acquired when needed. On the other hand, the disconnected operations allow developers to work with data that is managed and cached at the clients. No connection to the data source is required. The disconnected design offers a programming model that consumes less server load, and it works very efficiently in Web-based application environments.

The connected layer consists of four main classes:

- DB2Connection
- DB2Command
- DB2DataReader
- DB2DataAdapter

As for the disconnected layer, here are some of the main classes:

- DataSet
- DataTable
- DataRow

These classes are all part of the IBM.Data.DB2 namespace used by .NET languages. Namespaces group related classes, interfaces, and other types. You can either prefix the class names when declaring or instantiating the objects or, more conveniently, import its namespace at the beginning of the code:

```
Imports IBM.Data.DB2
```

DB2 .NET Connected Interface

A database connection must be opened before you can access its data. The DB2Connection class allows you to open or close a connection, customize the behavior of the connection using the class properties, begin and end a transaction using the class methods, and so on.

The DB2Command class is used to execute SQL. You can use its class properties and methods to set the SQL, add parameters, and prepare and execute it.

You use the DB2DataReader class to obtain results from a query after calling the execute method of the DB2Command class. DB2DataReader is a data class that retrieves one row of the result set at a time. A loop is used to iterate through the result set only in the forward direction. Note that the result set is read-only, so no positioned update or delete is allowed.

The DB2DataAdapter class is used to retrieve data from the actual data source and populate DataSet and related classes such as DataTable and DataRow. DataSet, DataTable, and DataRow are classes in the disconnected layer. They provide local cache for disconnected data and have no knowledge of the data source. In other words, the DB2DataAdapter bridges the disconnected classes (such as DataSet) with the connected world (such as the data source, DB2Connection, DB2Command, and DB2DataReader classes).

Enabling DB2 .NET Support

The DB2 .NET data provider is packaged with the DB2 application development client. Depending on the order of installation of DB2 and the .NET framework, .NET support may have been automatically enabled. If the .NET framework is installed on the machine before DB2, then DB2 .NET support is automatically enabled during DB2 installation. On the other hand, if DB2 is installed first, then you need to manually enable DB2 .NET support using the following command:

```
db2nmpreg.exe
```

The executable can be found in the sqllib\bin of the DB2 install path. To disable DB2 .NET support, use the same command with the –u option.

```
db2nmpreg.exe -u
```

5.4 A Tour of DB2 Tools in Visual Studio .NET 2003

When you enable DB2 .NET support as described in the preceding section, the DB2 development add-in is also registered in the Visual Studio .NET (VS.NET) IDE. The first thing you will probably notice about the availability of DB2 add-ins in VS.NET are the tool icons in the toolbar, as shown in Figure 5.2. They are also conveniently available under the menu Tools > IBM DB2 Tools. These are the same DB2 tools you can launch from the Start > Programs > IBM DB2 folder on Windows.

Figure 5.2 DB2 tools add-in in Visual Studio .NET

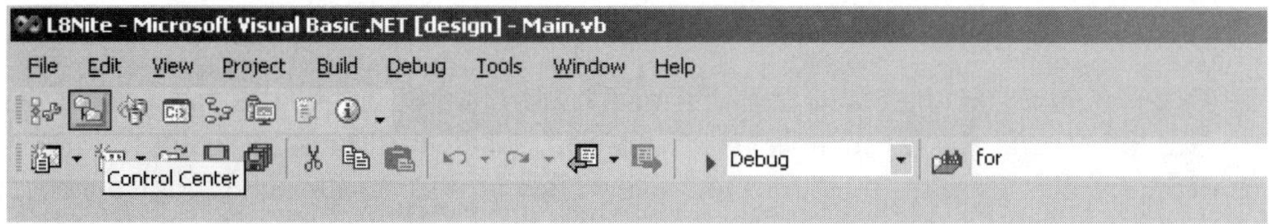

In addition to the ability to launch DB2 tools directly from VS.NET, a tool called the IBM Explorer comes with the DB2 development add-ins. It allows you to explore DB2 connections and objects (see Figure 5.3). If the IBM Explorer is not already opened, it can be launched from the menu View > IBM Explorer.

Figure 5.3 Add a DB2 connection in the IBM Explorer

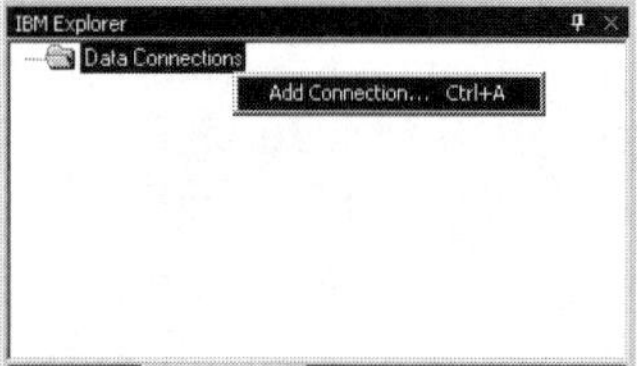

Right-click Data Connections to add a DB2 connection. Enter all the requested information shown in Figure 5.4 to configure a connection. You can also specify a schema for the database objects that you will be working on under the Options tab. To follow our examples, use L8NITE as the schema name.

Figure 5.4 Configuring a DB2 database connection

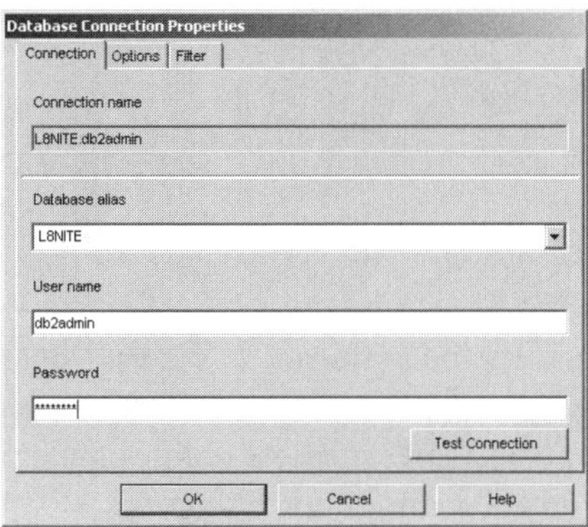

If the connection is successfully configured, you should see the objects defined in folders like those shown in Figure 5.5. Note that only L8NITE tables are displayed because all the system tables are filtered out by the schema setting. You can change this behavior in the Filter tab of the Database Connection Properties window.

Figure 5.5 DB2 objects and associated folders in the IBM Explorer

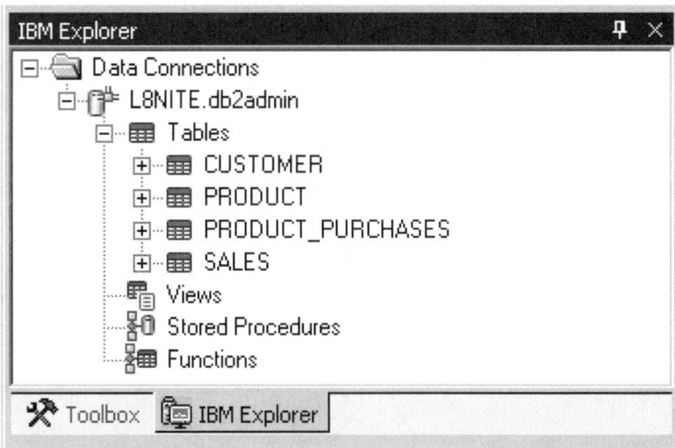

The IBM Explorer can also be used to retrieve data. See Figure 5.6 for an illustration.

Figure 5.6 Retrieving data from a table using the IBM Explorer

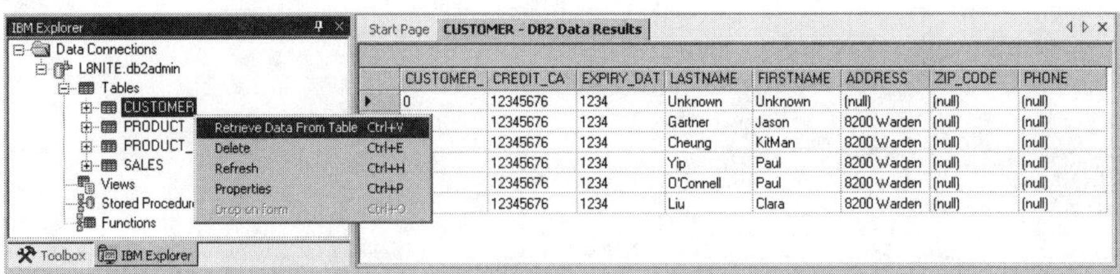

The DB2 development add-ins provide a set of templates to create tables, views, triggers, functions, procedures, queries, and scripts. These templates are available in DB2 Projects. We will look at how database objects can be created using DB2 projects in the supplemental section of Chapter 8, Working with Functions, Stored Procedures, and Triggers.

In addition to getting to know what tools are available in the VS.NET IDE, it is handy to know where to find the documentation. The DB2 .NET data provider documentation is available through the VS.NET dynamic help (see Figure 5.7). It can also be launched from the VS.NET dynamic help menu. Because DB2 .NET documentation is integrated into the IDE, you can conveniently search for information about DB2 .NET support and the VB.NET programming language without switching between tools.

Figure 5.7 DB2 .NET provider manual available in VS.NET

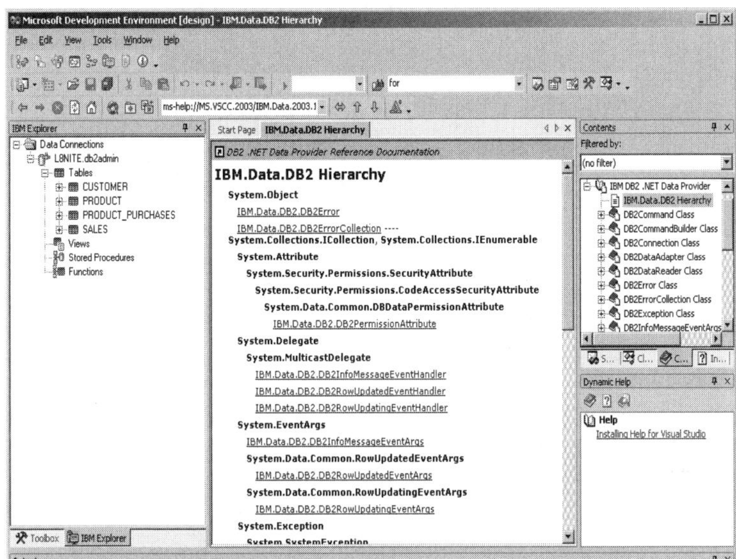

NOTE: The latest DB2 and .NET application development information can be found at

www.ibm.com/developerworks/db2/zones/vstudio
www.ibm.com/developerworks/db2/downloads/dotnetbeta/

5.5 Getting Started with the L8NITE Application

In this section, we will show you how to set up the work environment for the L8NITE application. If you prefer not to follow the steps of building the interface, you can load the Visual Basic project (which contains only the graphical interface) available from the book's Web site. The project can be found in L8NITE_GUI.zip. You can then skip to the next section and learn how to use the DB2 .NET driver. The complete application is found in L8NITE.zip.

Step 1: Create a Visual Basic project.

Create a new Windows application of the type Visual Basic Projects, and name the project L8NITE, as shown in Figure 5.8.

Figure 5.8 Creating a new Visual Basic .NET Windows application

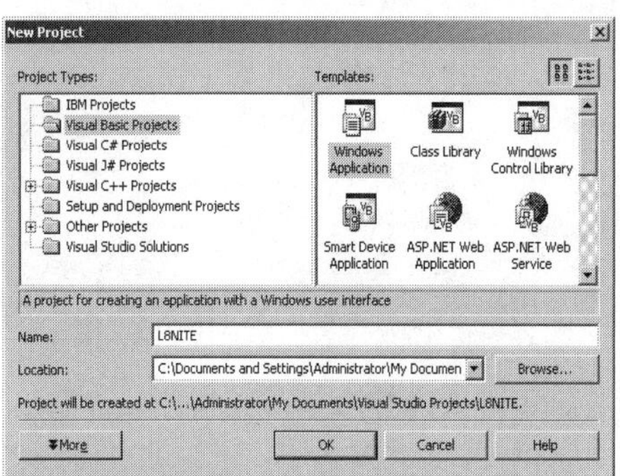

Step 2: Open the Solution Explorer.

By default, the L8NITE project will be created in a solution called L8NITE. To view the solution, open the Solution Explorer from the menu; select Tools > Solution Explorer, as shown in Figure 5.9.

Figure 5.9 The Solution Explorer

Step 3: Change the properties of the form.

You should now get a blank form, which you will use as the main form for the L8NITE application. In the Solution Explorer, locate and rename the file, changing it from Form1.vb to Main.vb. Click on Form1, and select Properties from the pop-up menu. The Properties window, as shown in Figure 5.10, is opened.

Figure 5.10 Properties window of the form

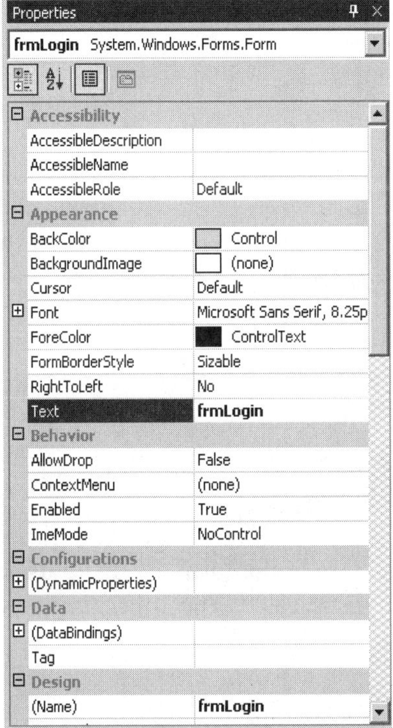

Update the following properties with these values:

Property	Value
Text	L8Nite
Name	frmL8Nite
Size	680, 552

Step 4: Create controls in the frmL8Nite form.

Use the tools in the toolbox window to create all the controls, as shown in Figure 5.11, the graphical interface design of the application. We will guide you through the creation of a few objects and then leave the rest as an exercise.

Figure 5.11 Main form of the L8NITE application

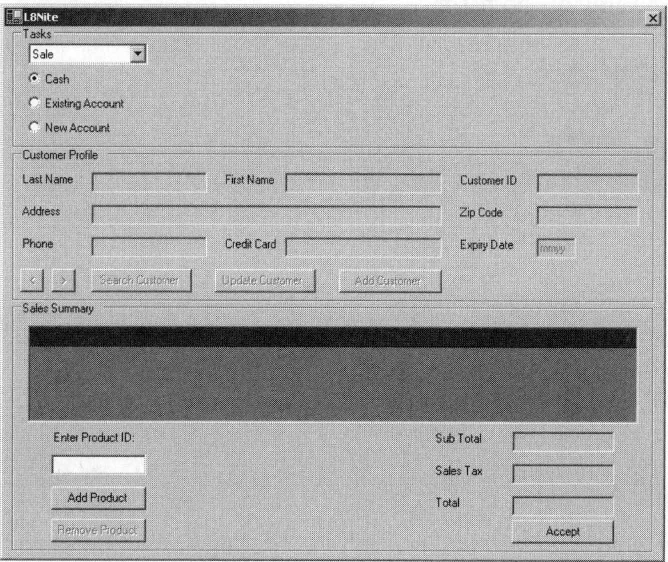

From the toolbox, click the GroupBox control and drag it onto the form. Bring up its properties window by selecting the GroupBox that you just created. The only change we will make to the GroupBox is to update the Text property to Tasks.

Next, drag three RadioButton controls onto the form. You should now have the controls as shown in Figure 5.12.

Figure 5.12 Building the graphical interface for L8NITE

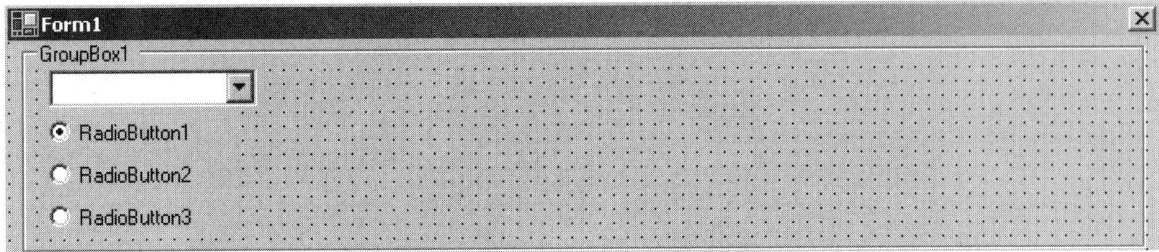

Select RadioButton1 and bring up the properties window. Set the following properties to the values specified. The Checked property is set to True because Cash Sales is the default selection when the application is invoked.

Property	Value
Text	Cash
Name	rbtnCashSales
Checked	True

You probably get the idea of how to create the controls and set their properties. It is now your turn to complete the graphical interface. Follow Figure 5.13 to lay down the rest of the controls in the form. Most controls can be easily identified by the text displayed, except that you may not be familar with the gray area inside GroupBox3 (shown in Figure 5.13). It is a DataGrid, which can be used to display query results.

Figure 5.13 Controls used in the L8NITE application

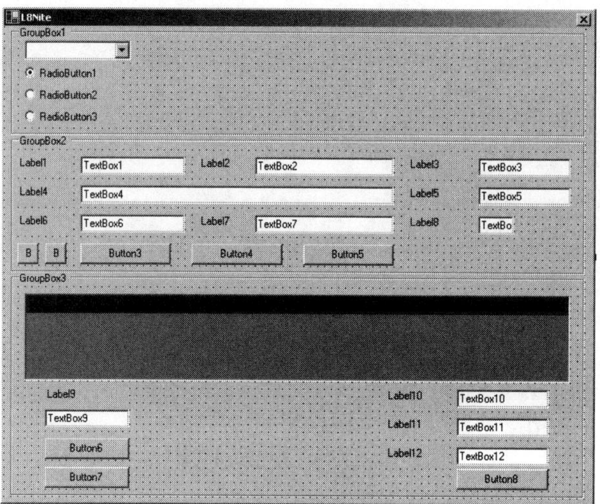

Update the control properties with the values listed in Figure 5.14. For cells that are empty, leave the default values.

Figure 5.14 Properties of controls in the L8NITE application

Control	Text	Name	Checked	Enabled	Tab Index
GroupBox1	Tasks				
GroupBox2	Customer Profile				
GroupBox3	Sales Summary				
RadioButton1	Cash	rbtnCashSales	True		2
RadioButton2	Account	rbtnSearchCust			3
RadioButton3	AddAccount	rbtnAddCust			4
ComboBox1	Sales / Refund	cBoxTask			1
Label1	Last Name				
Label2	First Name				
Label3	Customer ID				
Label4	Address				
Label5	Zip Code				
Label6	Phone				
Label7	Credit Card				
Label8	Expiry Date				
Label9	Enter Product ID:				
Label10	Total Sales				
Label11	Tax				
Label12	Amount Due				
TextBox1	[empty string]	txtLastName			5
TextBox2	[empty string]	txtFirstName			6
TextBox3	[empty string]	txtCustID			7
TextBox4	[empty string]	txtAddress			8
TextBox5	[empty string]	txtZCode			9
TextBox6	[empty string]	txtPhone			10
TextBox7	[empty string]	txtCreditCard			11
TextBox8	[empty string]	txtExpiryDt			12
TextBox9	[empty string]	txtProdID			18
TextBox10	[empty string]	txtTotal		False	
TextBox11	[empty string]	txtTax		False	
TextBox12	[empty string]	txtAmount		False	
Button1	<	btnPrev			13
Button2	>	btnNext			14
Button3	Search Customer	btnSearchCust			15
Button4	Update Customer	btnUpdateCust			16
Button5	Add Customer	btnAddCust			17
Button6	Add Product	btnAddProduct			19
Button7	Remove Product	btnRemoveProduct			20
Button8	Accept	btnCompleteSales			21

Step 5: Create the frmLogin form.

To allow only authorized personnel to use the application, we next add a login form. From the Solution Explorer, right-click on the L8Nite project, and select Add > Add Windows Form. Refer to Figure 5.15 for a demonstration.

Figure 5.15 Adding a form to the L8NITE project

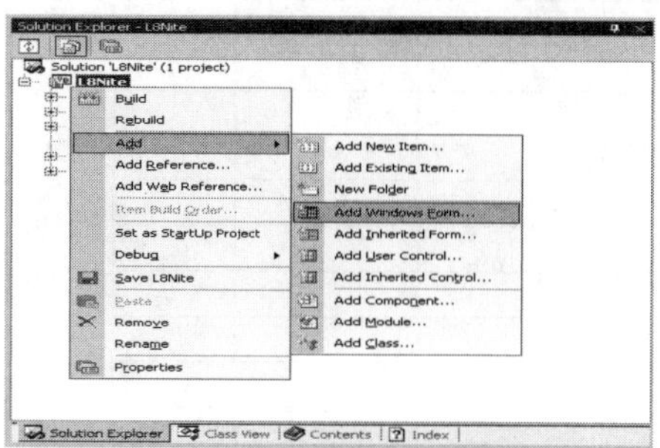

Update the new form with the following properties.

Property	Value
Text	Login
Name	frmLogin
Size	232, 168

Step 6: Create the controls in the frmLogin form.

Create all the controls in the frmLogin form as shown in Figure 5.16.

Figure 5.16 Controls in the frmLogin form

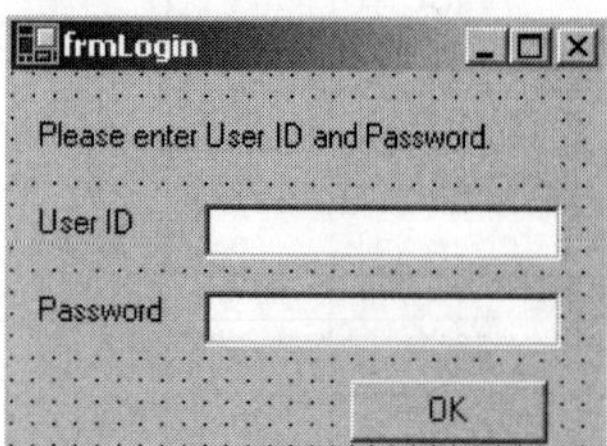

Name the controls using the following.

Control	Text	Name
TextBox1	[empty string]	txtPasswd
TextBox2	[empty string]	txtUserID
Button1	OK	btnOK

5.6 Adding the DB2 .NET Data Provider Reference

To avoid fully qualifying all DB2 .NET classes in the source code, import the DB2 namespaces at the beginning of the code. Add the following Imports statements before the definition of the public classes frmL8Nite and frmLogin. Your code should read as in Figure 5.17.

Figure 5.17 Adding Imports statements to the code

```
Imports System
Imports System.Data
Imports Microsoft.VisualBasic
Imports IBM.Data.DB2

Public Class frmL8Nite
     Inherits System.Windows.Forms.Form
     . . . . .
End Class
```

The System namespace contains fundamental classes and base classes that define common value and reference data types, events and event handlers, interfaces, attributes, and process exceptions.

The System.Data namespace consists mostly of the classes that constitute the ADO.NET architecture.

The Microsoft.VisualBasic namespace contains classes that support compilation and code generation using the Visual Basic .NET language.

The IBM.Data.DB2 namespace contains classes that deliver high-performance, and secure access to DB2 data via the ADO.NET interface.

If you try to build the project, you will probably notice that IBM.Data.DB2 is underlined. Also, the Task List shows a build error indicating that the namespace cannot be found, as shown in Figure 5.18.

Figure 5.18 Build error of IBM.Data.DB2 namespace not found

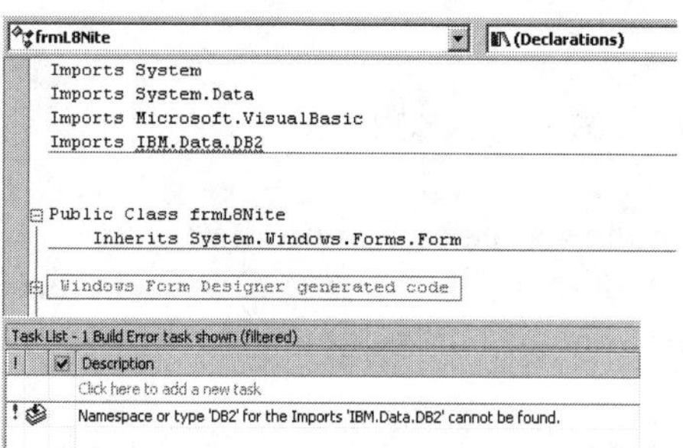

When DB2 is enabled for .NET support, it places the appropriate library files in the global assembly cache. To fix the unknown namespace error, you need to add a reference to the DB2 .NET data provider library file to the project you are working on. Open the Solution Explorer as shown in Figure 5.19. In the L8Nite project, open the References folder. Right-click References, and choose Add References. From the .NET tab, find and add the IBM.Data.DB2.dll to the project.

Figure 5.19 Add the IBM.Data.DB2.dll library to the project

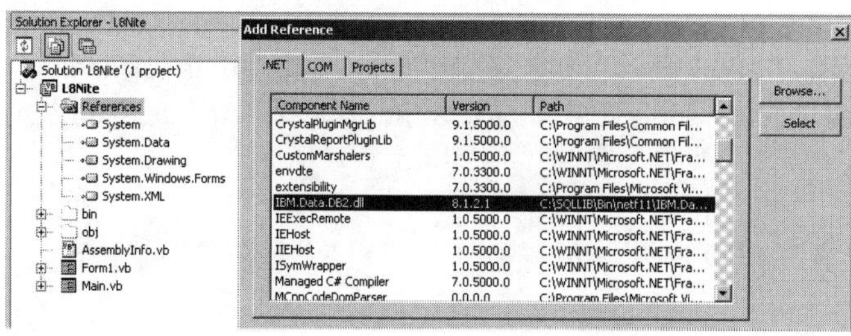

5.7 Establishing a Database Connection

When the application is started, we want frmLogin to be automatically loaded. Upon successful validation of the user ID and password, frmL8Nite will be launched. To do so, we want the application to be started with the Main subroutine. From the Solution Explorer, right-click on the L8Nite project and select Properties.

In the L8Nite Property Pages (as shown in Figure 5.20), under Startup Object, choose Sub Main.

Figure 5.20 L8Nite Property Pages

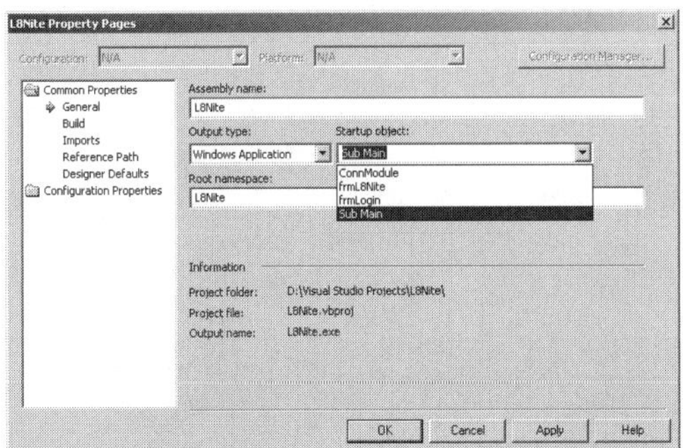

Because the Main subroutine needs to be an object accessible to both frmLogin and frmL8Nite, we will create a module and place the Main subroutine in the module. A *module* is a file that contains attributes that are accessible by other files in the same project.

From the Solution Explorer, right-click the L8Nite project and select Add > Add Module. Name the new module ConnModule.vb, as shown in Figure 5.21.

Figure 5.21 Adding a Module

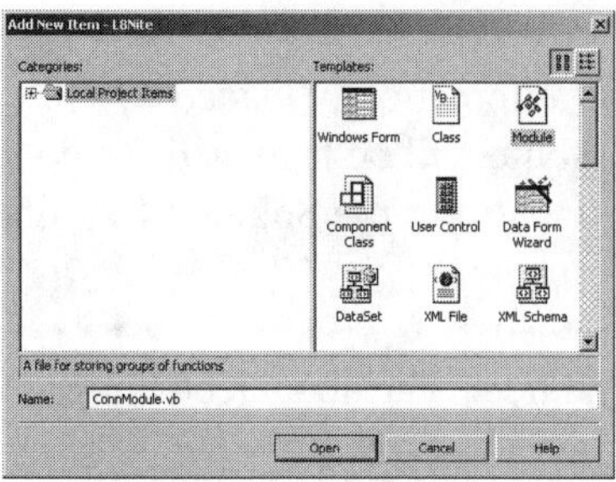

Enter the code in Figure 5.22 to the module.

Figure 5.22 Code for the ConnModule

```
Imports IBM.Data.DB2                                          (1)
Public Module ConnModule
  Public conn As DB2Connection                                (2)

  Sub Main()                                                  (3)

    Dim frmL8Nite As New frmL8Nite                            (4)
    Dim frmLogin As New frmLogin                              (5)

   ' Use ShowDialog to cause the program flow to stop until the dialog
   ' (i.e., the logon form) is closed
    If frmLogin.ShowDialog() = DialogResult.Yes Then          (6)
        Application.Run(frmL8Nite)                            (7)
    End If

  End Sub
End Module
```

In Figure 5.22, you can see that the IBM DB2 namespace IBM.Data.DB2 is imported at (1). The Main subroutine starts with Sub Main() at (3). Lines (4) and (5) instantiate the frmL8Nite and the frmLogin objects, respectively.

The frmLogin.ShowDialog() function at (6) shows the frmLogin as a dialog box. This will bring up the login form you created in Figure 5.16. In the frmLogin class (which is shown in Figure 5.23), DialogResult will be set to Yes if the user ID and password are validated.

Now back to Figure 5.22. If frmLogin returns a DialogResult of Yes (i.e., the database connection has been established), frmL8Nite will be invoked as an application (7).

Notice that there is a DB2Connection object declared at (2) so that frmL8Nite can get a handle to the connection opened in frmLogin. The database connection can then be used by subsequent requested operations, such as performing customer searches, adding new customers, and creating sale transactions.

Figure 5.23 shows a code snippet of the event when the OK button is clicked in the frmLogin.

Figure 5.23 Establish a database connection

```
Public Sub btnLoginOK_Click
   (ByVal sender As System.Object, ByVal e As System.EventArgs) Handles
btnLoginOK.Click
      ...
  ' Open a database connection
  Dim connectionString As String                                      (1)
  connectionString = "Database=L8NITE;UID=" + vUserID + ";PWD=" + vPasswd (2)
  conn = New DB2Connection(connectionString)                          (3)
  conn.Open()                                                         (4)

  DialogResult = DialogResult.Yes                                     (5)
  Me.Close()                                                          (6)
        ...
End Sub
```

In Figure 5.23, the conn object declared in the ConnModule maintains a connection to the database. At (1) and (2), we declare and set the connection string. There are other properties available to customize the behavior of a connection. Refer to the VB.NET language manual for the other options and properties. Line (3) instantiates a DB2Connection object with the connection string. The connection is opened at line (4).

If the connection is successfully established, we set the DialogResult to Yes at (5). Then we close frmLogin using Me.Close at (6).

To close a connection, we simply use the Close method of the connection, as demonstrated in Figure 5.24.

Figure 5.24 Closing a database connection

```
Private Sub frmL8Nite_Closing
        (ByVal sender As Object,
         ByVal e As System.ComponentModel.CancelEventArgs)
         Handles MyBase.Closing

        MsgBox("This cashier is now closed.")
        conn.Close()
End Sub
```

Notice that the connection was opened inside the public class frmLogin, but it is closed inside the frmL8Nite_Closing subroutine—that is, after the cashier is finished with the main form of the L8NITE application.

Inquiring Minds: Common Properties of the DB2Connection Class

Some other commonly used properties available in the DB2Connection class are as follows:

- Database: the name of the current database or database to be used after a connection is opened
- ServerType: the type of server to which the client is connected
- ServerVersion: the version of the server to which the client is connected
- State: the current state of the connection

5.8 Executing Queries

DB2Command is probably one of the most frequently used objects in a .NET application that manipulates DB2 data. You can use DB2Command to execute an SQL statement such as database definition language (DDL) statements, database manipulation language (DML) statements, and also stored procedure call statements. In the L8NITE example, we use the DB2Command object to search for customers.

First, declare a variable as a DB2Command object. Then instantiate the object using a query and a previously established database connection. Refer to Figure 5.25 for a code snippet of a command object creation.

Figure 5.25 Create a DB2Command object

```
Dim cmdCustList As DB2Command
Dim vSQLSelect As String = _
      "SELECT lastname, firstname, customer_id, address, zip_code, phone,
credit_card, expiry_date " & _
      "FROM l8nite.customer " & _
      "WHERE lastname = ? " & _
      "AND firstname LIKE ? "

cmdCustList = New DB2Command ( vSQLSelect, conn )
```

Figure 5.26 illustrates another way to create a DB2Command object. It is a matter of preference to choose one over the other.

Figure 5.26 An alternative for creating a DB2Command

```
cmdCustList = conn.CreateCommand ()
cmdCustList.CommandText = vSQLSelect
```

Notice that the FROM clause of the query in Figure 5.25 references the customer table by its qualified name (l8nite.customer). Because the application may use any user ID to connect to the database (see Figure 5.23, line 2), the default schema for all unqualified tables referenced in subsequent SQL statements will be set to the user ID currently connected to the database. If the schema l8nite is not specified explicitly here, the query will receive an error indicating that table <userID>.customer is not found. To resolve this, one option is to fully qualify the table, as demonstrated in Figure 5.25. Another option is to change the default schema globally when connecting to the database. You can do this by setting a DB2 CLI setting. Please refer to section 5.14, Troubleshooting Using DB2 CLI Tracing, for detailed discussions. For now, we will fully qualify the database objects in all the examples.

Assigning Values to Parameters of a Command

Two question marks are used in the query in Figure 5.25. When the statement is executed, the values of the last name and the first name will be substituted in place of the question marks. These question marks are known as the *parameter markers*. It is always a good practice to use parameter markers if the statement is executed repeatedly with different search values. The next execution of the same statement allows DB2 to eliminate statement compilation and simply load the previously compiled statement from the DB2 dynamic SQL cache. In the L8NITE example, because we are searching for a customer profile repeatedly based on the first and last names, it is a perfect candidate for the use of parameter markers.

To provide input values for statement parameter markers, we create a DB2Parameter object and add it to a DB2Command class property called Parameters. Figure 5.27 demonstrates one way to specify parameter values to the cmdCustList command.

Figure 5.27 Specify values to parameter markers

```
cmdCustList.Parameters.Add ( New DB2Parameter ("lastname", vLastName) )
cmdCustList.Parameters.Add ( New DB2Parameter ("firstname", vFirstName) )
```

Note that this example assigns parameters by the order of the parameter list. The name specified in the DB2Parameter method ("lastname" and "firstname" in Figure 5.27) is just to increase code readability. If you were to swap the order of the two commands, the search criteria would be incorrectly specified. In some cases, you will also receive a data type mismatch error if the parameters are defined with different data types.

Alternatively, name parameters can also be used. First, you define the parameter names in the SQL statement. The parameter names begin with the @ sign. Here is an example:

```
Dim vSQLSelect As String = _
      "SELECT lastname, firstname, customer_id, address, zip_code, phone,
credit_card, expiry_date " & _
       "FROM l8nite.customer " & _
       "WHERE lastname = @lname "  & _
       "AND firstname LIKE @fname "
```

When a parameter is added with the DB2Parameter class, you simply specify the parameter name used in the SQL statement:

```
cmdCustList.Parameters.Add ( New DB2Parameter ("@fname", vFirstName) )
```

```
cmdCustList.Parameters.Add ( New DB2Parameter ("@lname", vLastName) )
```

Note that the order of the parameters does not necessarily have to match the SQL statement for the result to be correct.

If you need to pass a NULL value to a parameter, use the System.DbNull.Value static value:

```
cmdCustList.Parameters.Add ( New DB2Parameter ("lastname",
                             SystemDbNull.Value) )
```

DB2DataReader Versus DB2DataAdapter

Now that you have established a database connection, created a command object, and assigned values to the parameters, you need to somehow execute the command against DB2. ADO.NET provides several methods to execute SQL queries. One option is to use the ExecuteReader method of the DB2Command class to instantiate a DB2DataReader object. Figure 5.28 demonstrates this.

Figure 5.28 Use of the DB2DataReader class

```
Dim drdCustList As DB2DataReader
drdCustList = cmdCustList.ExecuteReader ()
```

The DB2DataReader class stores only one row of the result set at a time and is therefore very efficient when it comes to memory usage. However, you must use a mechanism, such as a loop, to read through all the rows returned from the result set. Another characteristic of DB2DataReader is that it is a read-only and forward-only data class. It cannot navigate back to previously read rows.

In some cases, it is probably applicable to use DB2DataReader because you want to minimize memory usage and have no requirement of using backward-scrollable cursors. However, if a scrollable cursor is required, use the DB2DataAdapter class to provide this functionality. In the L8NITE application, if more than one customer profile matches the search criteria (has the same name), we want to provide the flexibility for the cashier to move back and forth in the results until the desired profile is located. In the next section, we will show you how to use the DB2DataAdapter class to obtain a multirow result.

Using a Data Adapter to Populate a Data Set

To use a data adapter, declare and instantiate a variable of the DB2DataAdapter class. Set the class's SelectCommand property to the DB2Command object you created in Figure 5.25. In case of update and delete statements, use the properties UpdateCommand and DeleteCommand accordingly. Refer to Figure 5.29 for a code snippet.

Figure 5.29 Instantiate a DB2DataAdapter class

```
Dim dadCustList As DB2DataAdapter
dadCustList = New DB2DataAdapter
dadCustList.SelectCommand = cmdCustList
```

Recall that DataSet, DataTable, and DataRow are classes in the disconnected layer. They can be used to cache data extracted from the database. In Figure 5.30, a DataSet object is declared and populated with the result set of the data adapter. A DataSet object can contain more than one result set. In ADO.NET, a returned result set is called a DataTable object. If more than one DataTable is defined in a DataSet, you can identify it by name as well as by the order in which the table is created. Figure 5.30 shows that the result of the DataAdapter is used to fill the "Customer" DataTable. Later, we will see how the table can be referenced by its name.

Figure 5.30 Instantiate a DataSet class and fill it with the result of a query

```
Dim dsCustList As DataSet
dsCustList = New DataSet
dadCustList.Fill (dsCustList, "Customer")
```

Executing a Query from Beginning to End

Let's now put together the classes, properties, and methods introduced so far. In Figure 5.31, you can see how they are used in the event of a click on the Search Customer button.

Figure 5.31 An almost complete btnSearchCust_Click subroutine

```
Private Sub btnSearchCust_Click
```

```
  (ByVal sender As System.Object, ByVal e As System.EventArgs) Handles
btnSearchCust.Click

 'Declarations of the local variables                                    (1)
  Dim vLastName As String
  Dim vFirstName As String
  Dim vSQLSelect As String
  Dim cmdCustList As DB2Command
  Dim dadCustList As DB2DataAdapter
  Dim dsCustList As DataSet

  btnUpdateCust.Enabled = True                                           (2)
  txtTotal.Text = ""
  txtTax.Text = ""
  txtAmount.Text = ""

  If txtLastName.TextLength = 0 And txtFirstName.TextLength = 0 Then    (3)
      MsgBox("Please enter customer's lastname and firstname.", & _
                    MsgBoxStyle.OKOnly, "Missing Search String")
  Else
     'Perform a customer search with the supplied search criteria
      vLastName = txtLastName.Text
      vFirstName = txtFirstName.Text + "%"
  End If

  vSQLSelect  = _                                                        (4)
    "SELECT lastname, firstname, customer_id, address, zip_code, " & _
    "phone, credit_card, expiry_date FROM l8nite.customer " & _
    "WHERE lastname = ? AND firstname LIKE ?"

  'Instantiate the command with the SQL statement and connection object(5)
   cmdCustList = New DB2Command(vSQLSelect, conn)

  'Add parameter values to the command parameter list                   (6)
   cmdCustList.Parameters.Add(New DB2Parameter("lastname", vLastName))
   cmdCustList.Parameters.Add(New DB2Parameter("firstname", vFirstName))

  'Instantiate the data adapter and set the SelectCommand               (7)
   dadCustList = New DB2DataAdapter
   dadCustList.SelectCommand = cmdCustList

  'Instantiate and populate the data set                                (8)
   dsCustList = New DataSet
   dadCustList.Fill(dsCustList, "Customer")

  'Binding result to controls - to be discussed in the next section     (9)
End Sub
```

(1) Declarations of the local variables. Note that the DB2Connection object, conn, is public and is declared at the beginning of the frmL8Nite class.

(2) Set the properities of the controls to prepare for a customer search.

(3) Ensure that the search criteria are entered.

(4) Set the query with parameter markers to vSQLSelect.

(5) Create a DB2Command object with the query text and connection associations.

(6) Assign values to the parameters of the command object.

(7) Associate the DB2Command object with the SelectCommand property of the DataAdapter object.

(8) Populate the DataSet using the Fill method of the DataAdapter.

(9) Search result in the form. Binding data to controls is discussed in the next section.

5.9 Displaying Data in the User Interface

Previous versions of Visual Basic used data binding to display data from an underlying data source on a set of controls with very little programming code. As each new version of Visual Basic was released, controls were given the ability to bind data. With the release of Visual Basic .NET, almost all controls have the data binding ability, including text boxes, data grids, radio buttons, tab controls, and buttons, to name a few. In this section, we will demonstrate how to bind data to text boxes and data grids in the L8NITE application.

Let's pick up where we left off in section 5.8, Executing Queries. The data set is now filled with one or more customer profiles, and we want to use text boxes to display the details of the retrieved records. Figure 5.32 illustrates a subroutine called AddBinding. All this routine does is to add each returned item to the Text property of the associated text box controls. Where do we obtain the data? Well, it is stored in the Customer DataTable, which is also generally known as a data member of the dsCustList DataSet.

Figure 5.32 Subroutine to bind data to text box controls

```
Private Sub AddBinding (ByVal dsCustList As DataSet)
   txtAddress.DataBindings.Add (New Binding("Text", dsCustList,
"Customer.address") )
   txtZCode.DataBindings.Add (New Binding("Text", dsCustList,
"Customer.zip_code") )
   txtPhone.DataBindings.Add (New Binding("Text", dsCustList,
"Customer.phone") )
   txtCreditCard.DataBindings.Add (New Binding("Text", dsCustList,
"Customer.credit_card") )
   txtExpiryDt.DataBindings.Add (New Binding("Text", dsCustList,
"Customer.expiry_date") )
   txtCustID.DataBindings.Add (New Binding("Text", dsCustList,
"Customer.customer_id") )
End Sub
```

The design of L8NITE is to allow a cashier to loop through the customer profiles if more than one match is found. Use the Count method to get a row count of the Customer data table. If the row count is greater than 1, then the navigation buttons "<" and ">" are enabled.

Figure 5.33 Check for multirow result

```
If dsCustList.Tables("Customer").Rows.Count = 1 Then
        EnableTextBox()
        btnPrev.Enabled = False
        btnNext.Enabled = False
        ClearBinding(dsCustList)
        AddBinding(dsCustList)

ElseIf dsCustList.Tables("Customer").Rows.Count > 1 Then
        EnableTextBox()
        btnPrev.Enabled = True
        btnNext.Enabled = True
        ClearBinding(dsCustList)
        AddBinding(dsCustList)
Else
        MsgBox("There were no records matching your search criteria.")
End If
```

Notice that in Figure 5.33 there is also a call to the ClearBinding routine. It is needed to clear any bindings to the text boxes from the previous customer search operation. Otherwise, the second customer search will fail with an error indicating that two bindings are trying to be bound to the same property. The ClearBinding subroutine is straightforward. It calls the Clear method of the DataBindings member, as shown in Figure 5.34.

Figure 5.34 Subroutine to clear text box controls' data binding

```
Private Sub ClearBinding(ByVal dsCustList As DataSet)
        txtAddress.DataBindings.Clear()
        txtZCode.DataBindings.Clear()
        txtPhone.DataBindings.Clear()
        txtCreditCard.DataBindings.Clear()
        txtExpiryDt.DataBindings.Clear()
        txtCustID.DataBindings.Clear()
End Sub
```

To display the next or the previous record of the result, we choose to use the BindingManagerBase class. It can manage all binding objects that are bound to the same data source (in this case, DataSet) and data member. The Position property of the BindingManagerBase class provides a mechanism to move forward and backward within the data member.

Because the BindingManagerBase object will be referenced by both the previous and the next navigation buttons' click events, we declare the object as public, as demonstrated in line (1) of Figure 5.35. Then at (2), we use the BindingContext class to get the BindingManagerBase for the Customer DataTable of dsCustList DataSet. In the btnNext_Click and btnPrev_Click events, we increment and decrement the Position property to move between records at line (3) and (4).

Figure 5.35 Use BindingManagerBase to navigate through the result

```
Public myBindManBase As BindingManagerBase                              (1)

' Get the BindingManagerBase for the Customer data member
myBindManBase = BindingContext (dsCustList, "Customer")                 (2)

Private Sub btnPrev_Click (ByVal sender As System.Object, ByVal e As
System.EventArgs) Handles btnPrev.Click
        myBindManBase.Position -= 1                                     (3)
End Sub

Private Sub btnNext_Click (ByVal sender As System.Object, ByVal e As
System.EventArgs) Handles btnNext.Click
```

```
        myBindManBase.Position += 1                                    (4)
End Sub
```

Another commonly used data binding technique is to bind a data set to a data grid. If you were not using text boxes to display the data but instead were providing all the data in a tabulated data grid, you could bind it to the data grid using the SetDataBinding method:

```
DataGrid1.SetDataBinding (dsCustList, "Customer")
```

5.10 Making Changes to Data in the Database

In addition to searching for customer profiles, the L8NITE application is designed to update and add new customer profiles. This section discusses two approaches to propagate changes to the database.

Executing a Command with the ExecuteNonQuery and ExecuteScalar Methods

In section 5.8, Executing Queries, we introduced the ExecuteReader class to run a query provided by the DB2Command class. For SQL that does not return any rows, such as INSERT, UPDATE, and DELETE statements, you can also use the ExecuteNonQuery class as illustrated in (1) of Figure 5.36.

Figure 5.36 Execute SQL statement with the ExecuteNonQuery method

```
Private Sub btnUpdateCust_Click
  (ByVal sender As System.Object, ByVal e As System.EventArgs) Handles
btnUpdateCust.Click
  Dim vSQLUpdate As String
  Dim cmdCustUpdate As DB2Command

  vSQLUpdate = "UPDATE l8nite.customer " _
             "SET lastname=?, firstname=?, address=?, zip_code=?, " & _
                       "phone=?, credit_card=?, expiry_date=? " & _
                       "WHERE customer_id=?"

  cmdCustUpdate = conn.CreateCommand()
  cmdCustUpdate.CommandText = vSQLUpdate
```

```
  cmdCustUpdate.Parameters.Add(New DB2Parameter ("lastname",
txtLastName.Text) )
  cmdCustUpdate.Parameters.Add(New DB2Parameter ("firstname",
txtFirstName.Text) )
  cmdCustUpdate.Parameters.Add(New DB2Parameter ("address", txtAddress.Text))
  cmdCustUpdate.Parameters.Add(New DB2Parameter ("zip_code", txtZCode.Text) )
  cmdCustUpdate.Parameters.Add(New DB2Parameter ("phone", txtPhone.Text) )
  cmdCustUpdate.Parameters.Add(New DB2Parameter ("credit_card",
txtCreditCard.Text) )
  cmdCustUpdate.Parameters.Add(New DB2Parameter ("expiry_date",
txtExpiryDt.Text) )
  cmdCustUpdate.Parameters.Add(New DB2Parameter ("customer_id",
txtCustID.Text) )

   cmdCustUpdate.ExecuteNonQuery ()                                  (1)

End Sub
```

There are also cases when you might want to return only a single scalar value. Rather than create a DataAdapter object and populate the result in a DataSet, you can use the ExecuteScalar method. Refer to Figure 5.37 for a simple example.

Figure 5.37 ExecuteScalar method to return a single value

```
Dim vSQLScalar As String
Dim vScalarResult As String
Dim cmdScalar As DB2Command
vSQLScalar = "SELECT COUNT(*) FROM customer"
cmdScalar = New DB2Command (vSQLScalar, conn)
vScalarResult = cmdScalar.ExecuteScalar()
```

Generate Update, Insert, and Delete with DB2CommandBuilder

The second approach to change data in the database is to use the DB2CommandBuilder. Objects instantiated from this class can automatically generate DeleteCommand, InsertCommand, and UpdateCommand objects based on the SelectCommand you specified for a DataAdapter. DB2CommandBuilder is useful particularly in scenarios when queries are specified at run time and subsequent INSERT, UPDATE, or DELETE statements must be dynamically created in the code by evaluating all cases. To avoid complex code to just produce SQL statements, you can take advantage of the DB2CommandBuilder object.

However, there are a few rules you must follow for the object to generate commands automatically:

- The query you specified in the DB2Command object must reference only one single table. Views composed of two or more tables are not considered a single table.
- The Command object must be set to the SelectCommand property of the DataAdapter object. The DB2CommandBuilder uses the table schema retrieved by the SelectCommand object to automatically construct the insert, update, and delete commands.
- The SelectCommand must also return at least one primary key or unique column. Otherwise, an InvalidOperation exception is generated and the commands will not be generated.

Using our L8NITE application as an example, Figure 5.38 demonstrates how DB2CommandBuilder can be used instead of the ExecuteNonQuery method described previously.

Figure 5.38 Example of DB2CommandBuilder usage

```
Dim vSQLSelect As String
Dim cmdCustList As DB2Command
Dim cbCustomer As DB2CommandBuilder

vSQLSelect = _                                                   (1)
        "SELECT lastname, firstname, customer_id, address, " & _
        "zip_code, phone, credit_card, expiry_date " & _
        "FROM l8nite.customer WHERE lastname = ? AND firstname = ?"

'Instantiate cmdCustList and add parameter values to command parameter list
cmdCustList = New DB2Command (vSQLSelect, conn)
cmdCustList.Parameters.Add(New DB2Parameter ("lastname", vLastName))
cmdCustList.Parameters.Add(New DB2Parameter ("firstname", vFirstName))

'Instantiate the data adapter and set the SelectCommand
dadCustList = New DB2DataAdapter
dadCustList.SelectCommand = cmdCustList                          (2)

'Use CommandBuilder to generate update, insert, delete statement
cbCustomer = New DB2CommandBuilder (dadCustList)                 (3)

'Populate the data set                                           (4)
dadCustList.Fill(dsCustList, "Customer")
```

```
'Modify data stored in data set                                    (5)
dsCustList.Tables ("Customer").Rows(0)("address") = txtAddress.Text
dsCustList.Tables ("Customer").Rows(0)("zip_code") = txtZCode.Text
dsCustList.Tables ("Customer").Rows(0)("phone") = txtPhone.Text
dsCustList.Tables ("Customer").Rows(0)("credit_card") = txtCreditCard.Text
dsCustList.Tables ("Customer").Rows(0)("expiry_date") = txtExpiryDt.Text
dsCustList.Tables ("Customer").Rows(0)("lastname") = txtLastName.Text
dsCustList.Tables ("Customer").Rows(0)("firstname") = txtFirstName.Text

dadCustList.Update (dsCustList, "Customer")                         (6)
```

The following summarizes usage of the DB2CommandBuilder class as shown in Figure 5.38.

(1) Specify a query that is valid for DB2CommandBuilder (one that includes a unique or primary key column in its select list and has only one table reference).

(2) Associate the DB2Command object with the DB2DataAdapter's SelectCommand property.

(3) Instantiate a DB2CommandBuilder object.

(4) Populate the results to the Customer DataTable of the dsCustList DataSet.

(5) Modify data stored in the dsCustList DataSet.

(6) The Update method generates and executes an UPDATE SQL statement against the database if changes are made to the data set.

The DB2CommandBuilder object obtains metadata of the query result from the SelectCommand class member that is being used to generate the associated UpdateCommand, InsertCommand, and DeleteCommand objects. Automatically generated code is fairly general so that it will cover all possible scenarios and is usually not very efficient. If you want to analyze the SQL being generated, refer to section 5.14, Troubleshooting Using DB2 CLI Tracing, to learn how to capture SQL.

5.11 Learning More about DataSet, DataTable, and DataRow

With L8NITE, when a cashier scans an item at checkout, the product ID, item description, and retail price are retrieved and stored in a DataSet object, dsProdFound. They are bound to a data grid on the L8NITE main form. As the cashier scans more items, we want to add the information to the existing DataSet until the last item of the sales transaction is scanned. Two methods in the DataSet class are available to archive this requirement: the Copy and the Merge methods.

The Copy method makes a copy of a specified DataSet. We use it to duplicate the structure and data of the dsProdFound DataSet. We then call the new DataSet dsProdPurchase. When we have the first scanned item cached (in the DataSet), information about subsequent scanned items will be added to dsProdPurchase. Refer to Figure 5.39 to see how the methods are used with the logic just described.

Figure 5.39 Copying and merging a data set

```
Private Sub btnAddProduct_Click
        (ByVal sender As System.Object, ByVal e As System.EventArgs) Handles
btnAddProduct.Click

    Public dsProdPurchase As DataSet
  Dim cmdProdList As DB2Command
  Dim dadProdList As DB2DataAdapter
  Dim dsProdFound As DataSet
  Dim dtProdList As DataTable

  Dim vSQLSelect As String = _
          "SELECT product_id, description, retail_price
                        , 1 AS qty, retail_price as sub_total
              FROM l8nite.product WHERE product_id = ?"

  'Instantiate the command
  cmdProdList = New DB2Command(vSQLSelect, conn)                         (1)

  'Add parameter values to the command parameter list
  cmdProdList.Parameters.Add(New DB2Parameter("product_id", vProdID)) (2)

  'Instantiate the data adapter and data set
   dadProdList = New DB2DataAdapter(cmdProdList)                         (3)
   dsProdFound = New DataSet
```

```
    'Populate the data set
      dadProdList.Fill(dsProdFound, "ProductFound")                    (4)

      dtProdList = dsProdFound.Tables("ProductFound")                  (5)
        . . .

     If dsProdPurchase Is Nothing Then                                 (6)
        dsProdPurchase = New DataSet
            dsProdPurchase = dsProdFound.Copy()                        (7)
         Else
        . . .
            dsProdPurchase.Merge(dtProdList)                           (8)
        End If
        . . .
  End Sub
```

(1) Instantiate a DB2Command object and associate it with a query and a database connection.

(2) Specify parameter values for the query.

(3) Instantiate a DataAdapter object and a DataSet dsProdFound. dsProdFound contains only product information of the one item just added.

(4) Populate the DataSet dsProdFound.

(5) Set dtProdList object equal to the only DataTable in dsProdFound.

(6) When the first item of a sales transaction is scanned, instantiate the dsProdPurchase object.

(7) Copy the dataset from dsProdFound to dsProdPurchase.

(8) If the item is not the first one being scanned, the dsProdPurchase object should already exist. Simply add (or merge) the data table dtProdList to the dProdPurchase DataSet.

For learning purposes, we also show how to merge a DataSet object with an array of DataRow objects. DataRow represents a row of data in a DataTable. In Figure 5.40, we declare drwProdFound as a DataRow object at (1). Because we are going to merge a DataSet with an array of DataRow, we also need to declare an array as a DataRow object at (2). Lines

(3) and (4) assign values to the DataRow object and the associated array. Finally, we merge the DataSet with the array of DataRow at (5).

Figure 5.40 Merging a DataSet object with an array of DataRow

```
Dim drwProdFound As DataRow                                  (1)
Dim arraydrwProdFound(0) As DataRow                          (2)

drwProdFound = dtProdList.Rows(0)                            (3)
arraydrwProdFound.SetValue(drwProdFound, 0)                  (4)
dsProdPurchase.Merge(arraydrwProdFound)                      (5)
```

5.12 Controlling a Transaction

When you develop applications that interact with databases, it is important to understand the concept of database transactions. A *transaction* groups database operations. If one operation fails, there is an opportunity to undo the entire set of changes so that the database remains consistent. Using the L8NITE application as an example, we have not worried about how to group SQL in transactions because the operations discussed so far are transactionally independent of each other. However, there are three operations that must be placed in a transaction to ensure data consistency.

When the cashier completes the transaction by clicking the Accept button, a sale transaction is created. At the same time, we also want to update the product_purchases table and update the product table to reflect the inventory change. These three operations should not be committed if any of them fails. For example, it is incorrect to decrement the product inventory if the application fails to insert an item to the product_purchases table. You can avoid this by controlling the database transaction manually.

Refer to the btnCompleteSales_Click subroutine for an example of how to begin and end a transaction. Figure 5.41 shows the code snippet.

Figure 5.41 Controlling a transaction manually

```
Private Sub btnCompleteSales_Click(ByVal sender As System.Object, ByVal e As
System.EventArgs) Handles btnCompleteSales.Click
```

```
        Dim txnSales As DB2Transaction                                  (1)
        'Create a Sales transaction
        txnSales = conn.BeginTransaction()                              (2)
        ...
           UpdateInv_InsertProdPurchases(vNewTxnID, txnSales, vType) (3)

                Try
                'Commit the transaction
                txnSales.Commit()                                       (4)
                Catch myException As DB2Exception
                    txnSales.Rollback()                                 (5)
                    DB2ExceptionHandler(myException)
                Catch
                    txnSales.Rollback()
                    UnhandledExceptionHandler()
                End Try
End Sub
```

(1) Declare txnSales as a DB2Transaction object.

(2) To begin a transaction, a valid connection must exist.

(3) Perform necessary inventory updates.

(4) Commit the transaction.

(5) If any command failed, roll back the transaction.

However, making the decision about which SQL should be grouped requires careful thinking. The reason is that if you do not complete transactions efficiently, either through commit or rollback, the database manager will hold locks on the database objects to make sure your transactions are intact. Excessive locking will decrease the concurrency of the database, and that will hinder the application's performance. On the other hand, if you commit or roll back the transactions too frequently, the database manager will spend too many resources in processing the commits or rollbacks. This also impacts performance. Therefore, it is important to understand the DB2 locking mechanism so that you can design efficient transactions as well as conform to the business requirements. Refer to Chapter 7, Maximizing Concurrency, for more information about transactions, isolation levels, and DB2's locking mechanism.

In Figure 5.41, notice the Try and Catch block, which we have not looked at. What does it do? Keep reading. We are about to show you how to catch and display DB2-specific errors in a VB.NET application.

5.13 Catching Errors with Exception Handlers

To complete any discussion of application development, a discussion of how to handle exceptions is essential. Writing code to account for every scenario is crucial if you want to build a robust application. However, there are always exceptional cases that the application code does not catch. The VB.NET language allows you to handle exceptions that occur during execution of a program by using a Try ... Catch ... Finally statement.

The Try statement contains a block of code that you want to monitor for exceptions. If a problem occurs during its execution, an exception is thrown. Immediately following the Try block is a sequence of Catch blocks. Each of these begins with the Catch keyword. An argument is passed to each Catch block. That argument is the exception object that contains information about the problem. For example, the DB2Exception object specifically contains warnings or errors returned by DB2.

Let's revisit the btnLoginOK_Click subroutine, which establishes the database connection if the user ID and password is validated. We add the appropriate Try and Catch block to handle exceptions in Figure 5.42.

Figure 5.42 Adding exception handlers to the frmL8Nite_Load subroutine

```
Private Sub btnLoginOK_Click
        (ByVal sender As System.Object, ByVal e As System.EventArgs) Handles
btnLoginOK.Click

        Try                                                                 (1)
            ' Open a database connection
            Dim connectionString As String
            connectionString="Database=L8NITE;UID="+vUserID+";PWD="+vPasswd
            conn = New DB2Connection(connectionString)
            conn.Open()
        Catch myException As DB2Exception                                   (2)
            DB2ExceptionHandler(myException)
        Catch                                                               (3)
```

```
            UnhandledExceptionHandler()
        Finally                                                  (4)
            'some cleanup tasks
        End Try
End Sub
Private Sub DB2ExceptionHandler(ByVal myException As DB2Exception) (5)
    Dim i As Integer
    For i = 0 To myException.Errors.Count - 1                      (6)
      If (myException.Errors(i).SQLState = "08001" ) Then
            MessageBox.Show("Invalid User ID or Password. Please try again.")
      Else
        MessageBox.Show("Index #" + i.ToString() + ControlChars.Cr _
       + "Message: " + myException.Errors(i).Message + ControlChars.Cr _
       + "Native: "+ myException.Errors(i).NativeError.ToString() +
ControlChars.Cr _
       + "Source: " + myException.Errors(i).Source + ControlChars.Cr _
       + "SQL: " + myException.Errors(i).SQLState + ControlChars.Cr)
      End if
    Next i
End Sub
Private Sub UnhandledExceptionHandler()                          (7)
    'Display an error to the user
    MsgBox("An Error Occurred. Error Number: " & Err.Number & _
        " Description: " & Err.Description & " Source: " & Err.Source)
End Sub
```

The Try statement at (1) specifies the beginning of the Try block. Any error occurring within the block will be captured by the exceptions at (2) or (3). DB2Exception captures all DB2 errors and warnings. Other errors will be captured by the following catch-all block. In line (5), the DB2Exception object is used to evaluate the error or print the error descriptions, SQLSTATE, and so on. A DB2Exception object contains at least one instance of DB2Error, a class that collects information relevant to a DB2 warning or error.

Line (6) uses a For statement to loop through the DB2Error instances and display their contents in a message box. There are four public properties in the DB2Error member: Message, NativeError, Source, and SQLState. The Message property provides a short description of the error. The NativeError gets the DB2 SQLCODE information. The Source property contains the name of the driver that generated the error. In this case, the value is IBM.Data.DB2. The SQLState property provides the five-character SQLSTATE, which follows the ANSI SQL database standard.

Any other exceptions will be caught at (7). Error numbers and messages are printed in the UnhandledExceptionHandler routine.

The Finally block at (4) will always be executed, whether or not the execution was successful. Therefore, it is a perfect place for cleanup code, such as resetting DataSet objects, closing DB2Connection objects, and so on.

5.14 Troubleshooting Using DB2 CLI Tracing

DB2 provides an integrated set of monitoring tools and trace facilities to help you identify various types of problems. When it comes to troubleshooting .NET applications, the DB2 CLI trace facility plays a very important role. CLI is a programming interface that is based on the Microsoft ODBC specification. All database operations requested by the .NET application are mapped to CLI calls and are executed against the database.

Before CLI tracing can be turned on for a particular database, it must be registered as an ODBC data source (see Figure 5.43). On Windows, you open the ODBC Data Source Administrator from the Control Panel. Go to the System DSN tab, and click Add. In the next window, choose IBM DB2 ODBC Driver. Enter the database name and its alias name when prompted. As an example, enter L8NITE for both entries.

Figure 5.43 Register a data source for ODBC

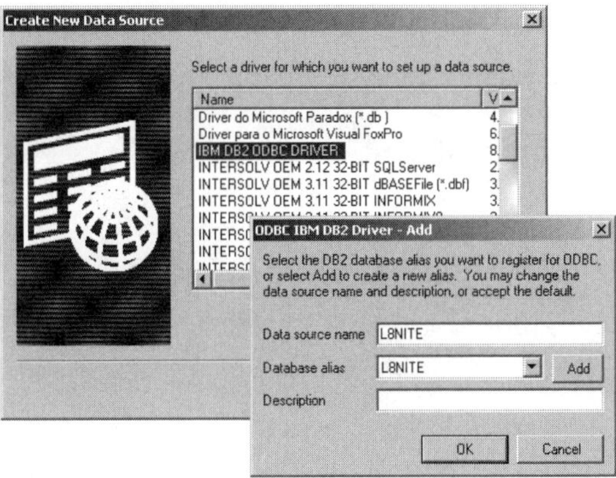

DB2 CLI settings, including CLI trace, can be specified in the DB2 Configuration Assistant. Open it from the Windows folder IBM DB2 > Set-up Tools > Configuration Assistant.

Follow these steps to enable DB2 CLI tracing for a database.

Step 1: Select the database to configure.

Right-click the database you want to trace, and select CLI Settings (see Figure 5.44).

Figure 5.44 DB2 Configuration Assistant, 1

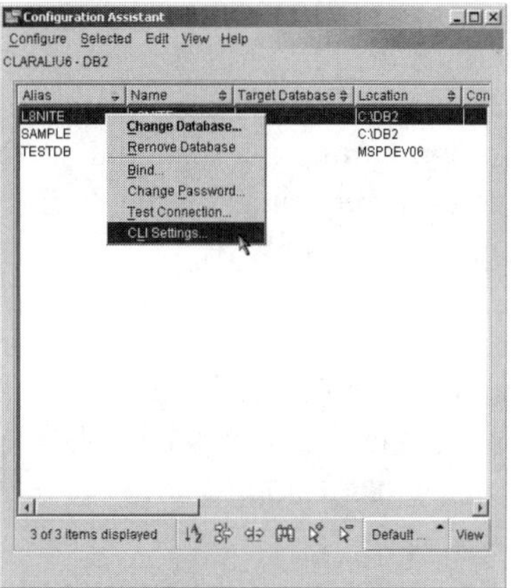

Step 2: Add a CLI parameter.

From the Settings tab, click Add to add a CLI parameter (Figure 5.45).

Figure 5.45 Configuration Assistant, 2

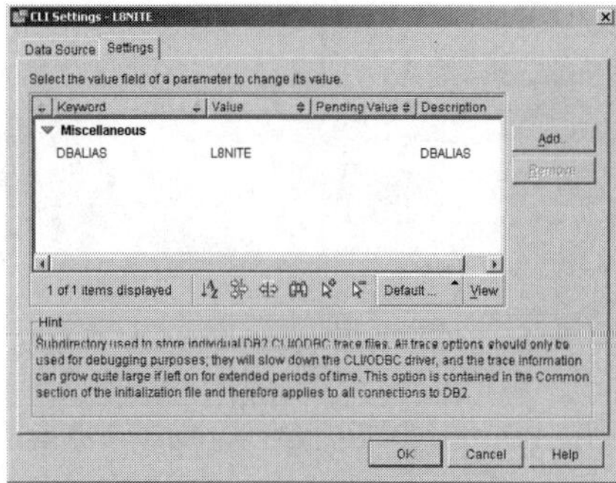

Step 3: Enable trace.

Under the list of CLI keywords, select Trace. Check the Enable trace check box, and enter the path where you want the trace files to be kept. Check the Flush After Each Entry check box. Click OK. DB2 CLI trace is now enabled for the L8NITE database.

There are a few other trace-related keywords that allow you to customize the amount or type of information that the utility will collect. Refer to Figure 5.46 for the keywords and their descriptions.

Figure 5.46 DB2 CLI keywords related to trace

DB2 CLI Trace Keywords	Descriptions
Trace	Turn on the DB2 CLI/ODBC trace facility.
TraceComm	Include information about each network request in the trace file.
TraceFileName	Specify the file name where the CLI/ODBC trace information will be recorded.
TraceFlush	Force the collected information to be written to disk after **n** CLI/ODBC trace entries.
TraceLocks	Trace only lock timeouts in the CLI/ODBC trace.
TracePIDList	Trace only the process IDs specified when CLI/ODBC trace is enabled.
TracePIDTID	Capture the process ID and thread ID for each item being traced.
TracePathName	Specify the sub-directory used to store individual DB2 CLI/ODBC trace files.
TraceRefreshInterval	Set the interval (in seconds) at which the TRACE and TRACEPIDLIST keywords are read from the db2cli.ini file. Allow you to dynamically turn off the CLI/ODBC trace within **n** seconds.
TraceStmtOnly	Trace only dynamic SQL statements in the CLI/ODBC trace.
TraceTime	Capture elapsed time counters in the trace file.
TraceTimestamp	Capture different types of timestamp information in the CLI/ODBC trace.

Notice that in the CLI keyword list, many other settings are available. A brief description for each keyword is provided under Hint. For more information, refer to the DB2 CLI Guide and Reference.

There is one other option we want to set for the L8NITE application. Recall that in section 5.8, Executing Queries, we mentioned that all the tables referenced in the SQL are qualified because the schema of the tables is different from the user ID connected to the database. There is one easy way to change the schema globally so that objects do not have to be fully qualified in the application code.

In the list of CLI keywords (see Figure 5.47), locate two settings called CurrentSchema and CurrentFunctionPath. If an application is connected and manipulating DB2 via CLI, CurrentSchema allows you to specify a schema name as the default for any unqualified database object references of the specified database. Similarly, CurrentFunctionPath specifies a list of schemas that DB2 will search to resolve functions, stored procedures, and data types referenced in the SQL.

Note that the settings apply only to the client machine you are working on. In other words, any other client machine without these settings will use the user ID connected to the database as its default schema and function path.

Figure 5.47 Adding CLI parameters, 1

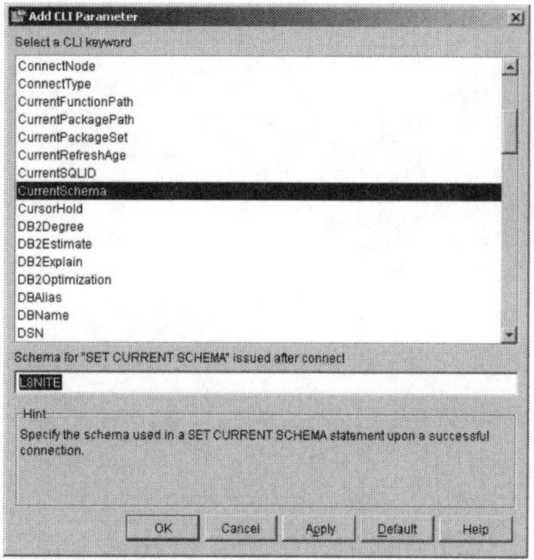

Step 4: Verify parameters.

You should see three keywords that have been added under Services and one keyword under Enterprise (see Figure 5.48).

Figure 5.48 Adding CLI parameters, 2

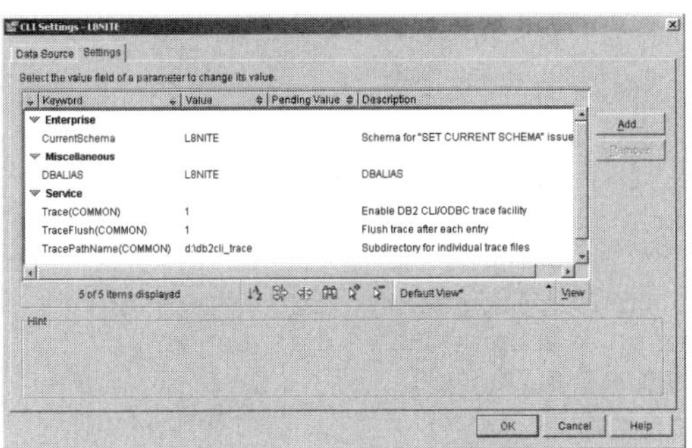

Now let's see what kind of information the trace facility will capture. Run the L8NITE application and perform a customer search. Then close the application. In the trace path that you specified in step 3, you should find a few files with the extension .cli. Each file name is based on the process and thread ID of the application instance just invoked. One of the files contains the CLI calls for the commands executed, such as making a connection to the database, executing the query with parameter markers for the last and first names, fetching data from the query result, and finally closing the database connection. Figure 5.49 shows a portion of the trace file with some key operations identified.

Figure 5.49 Sample DB2 CLI trace output

```
[ Process: 2568, Thread: 2248 ]                                         (1)
[ Date & Time:             11-26-2003 00:41:39.000004 ]
[ Product:                 QDB2/NT DB2 v8.1.3.132 ]
[ Level Identifier:        02040106 ]
[ CLI Driver Version:      08.01.0000 ]
[ Informational Tokens: "DB2 v8.1.3.132","s030728","WR21324","Fixpack 3" ]

SQLAllocHandle( fHandleType=SQL_HANDLE_ENV, hInput=0:0, phOutput=&007f82ac )
    ---> Time elapsed - 0 seconds                                       (2)

SQLAllocHandle( phOutput=0:1 )
    <--- SQL_SUCCESS   Time elapsed - +1.149200E-002 seconds

SQLSetEnvAttr( hEnv=0:1, fAttribute=Unknown value 2473, vParam=4, cbParam=0 )
    ---> Time elapsed - +1.407000E-003 seconds

SQLSetEnvAttr( )
```

```
    <--- SQL_SUCCESS   Time elapsed - +1.164300E-002 seconds

SQLInitializeADONET( )
    <--- SQL_SUCCESS   Time elapsed - +2.180100E-002 seconds

SQLDriverConnectW( hDbc=0:1, hwnd=0:0,
szConnStrIn="dsn=L8NITE;uid=db2admin;pwd=******;", cbConnStrIn=35,
szConnStrOut=NULL, cbConnStrOutMax=0, pcbConnStrOut=NULL,
fDriverCompletion=SQL_DRIVER_NOPROMPT )                                (3)
    ---> Time elapsed - +2.193000E-003 seconds
( DBMS NAME="DB2/NT", Version="08.01.0003", Fixpack="0x22040106" )
( Application Codepage=1252, Database  Codepage=1252, Char Send/Recv
Codepage=1208, Graphic Send/Recv Codepage=1200 )

SQLDriverConnectW( )
    <--- SQL_SUCCESS   Time elapsed - +6.110900E-002 seconds
( DSN="L8NITE" )
( UID="db2admin" )
( PWD="******" )
( DBALIAS="L8NITE" )
( CURRENTSCHEMA="L8NITE" )

SQLConnectADONET( )
    <--- SQL_SUCCESS   Time elapsed - +1.795000E-003 seconds
. . .

SQLBindParameter( hStmt=1:1, iPar=1, fParamType=SQL_PARAM_INPUT,
fCType=SQL_C_WCHAR, fSQLType=SQL_VARCHAR, cbColDef=3, ibScale=0,
rgbValue=&087a69d8, cbValueMax=520, pcbValue=&087a69c0 )              (4)
    ---> Time elapsed - +1.334200E-002 seconds

SQLBindParameter( )
    <--- SQL_SUCCESS   Time elapsed - +3.342500E-002 seconds

SQLBindParameter( hStmt=1:1, iPar=2, fParamType=SQL_PARAM_INPUT,
fCType=SQL_C_WCHAR, fSQLType=SQL_VARCHAR, cbColDef=5, ibScale=0,
rgbValue=&087a6bf8, cbValueMax=520, pcbValue=&087a6be0 )
    ---> Time elapsed - +2.637000E-003 seconds

SQLBindParameter( )
    <--- SQL_SUCCESS   Time elapsed - +3.384000E-002 seconds

SQLExecDirectW( hStmt=1:1, pszSqlStr="SELECT lastname, firstname,
customer_id, address, zip_code, phone, credit_card, expiry_date FROM
l8nite.customer WHERE lastname = ? AND firstname = ?" - X"530045004C004. . .
20003F00", cbSqlStr=-3 )                                               (5)
    ---> Time elapsed - +4.042000E-003 seconds
```

```
( StmtOut="SELECT lastname, firstname, customer_id, address, zip_code, phone,
credit_card, expiry_date FROM l8nite.customer WHERE lastname=? AND firstname=
?")
( Package="SYSSH200          ", Section=4 )
( Row=1, iPar=1, fCType=SQL_C_WCHAR, rgbValue="Liu" -  - X"4C0069007500",
pcbValue=6, piIndicatorPtr=6 )
( Row=1, iPar=2, fCType=SQL_C_WCHAR, rgbValue="Clara" -  -
X"43006C00610072006100", pcbValue=10, piIndicatorPtr=10 )

SQLExecDirectW( )
    <--- SQL_SUCCESS   Time elapsed - +2.674620E-001 seconds
. . .

SQLFetch( hStmt=1:1 )                                                 (6)
    ---> Time elapsed - +8.484000E-003 seconds

SQLFetch( )
    <--- SQL_SUCCESS   Time elapsed - +1.625200E-002 seconds

SQLGetData( hStmt=1:1, iCol=1, fCType=SQL_C_WCHAR, rgbValue=&094a8f20,
cbValueMax=4094, pcbValue=&0012e96c )
    ---> Time elapsed - +7.761000E-003 seconds

SQLGetData( rgbValue="Liu" -  - X"4C006900002000200020002000", pcbValue=56 )
    <--- SQL_SUCCESS   Time elapsed - +4.574900E-002 seconds

SQLGetData( hStmt=1:1, iCol=2, fCType=SQL_C_WCHAR, rgbValue=&094a8f20,
cbValueMax=4094, pcbValue=&0012e96c )
    ---> Time elapsed - +4.292000E-003 seconds

SQLGetData( rgbValue="Clara" -  - X"43006C00002000200020002000", pcbValue=56 )
    <--- SQL_SUCCESS   Time elapsed - +4.764700E-002 seconds
. . .

SQLFetch( hStmt=1:1 )
    ---> Time elapsed - +2.192500E-002 seconds

SQLFetch( )
    <--- SQL_NO_DATA_FOUND   Time elapsed - +1.587900E-002 seconds

SQLMoreResults( hStmt=1:1 )
    ---> Time elapsed - +9.333000E-003 seconds
( COMMIT REQUESTED=1 )
( COMMIT REPLY RECEIVED=1 )

SQLMoreResults( )
    <--- SQL_NO_DATA_FOUND   Time elapsed - +4.102700E-002 seconds
```

```
SQLFreeStmt( hStmt=1:1, fOption=SQL_CLOSE )                          (7)
    ---> Time elapsed - +4.918000E-003 seconds

SQLFreeStmt( )
    <--- SQL_SUCCESS   Time elapsed - +1.975200E-002 seconds

SQLDisconnect( hDbc=0:1 )                                            (8)
    ---> Time elapsed - 0 seconds

SQLDisconnect( )
    <--- SQL_SUCCESS   Time elapsed - +2.917100E-002 seconds

SQLFreeHandle( fHandleType=SQL_HANDLE_DBC, hHandle=0:1 )
    ---> Time elapsed - +1.255000E-003 seconds

SQLFreeHandle( )
    <--- SQL_SUCCESS   Time elapsed - +6.511000E-003 seconds

SQLFreeHandle( fHandleType=SQL_HANDLE_ENV, hHandle=0:1 )
    ---> Time elapsed - +2.829000E-003 seconds

SQLFreeHandle( )
    <--- SQL_SUCCESS   Time elapsed - +7.621000E-003 seconds
```

Note the following about Figure 5.49.

(1) Information about the client process, CLI API, and DB2 server version are recorded.

(2) Allocate an environment handle and initialize the ADO.NET environment.

(3) Establish a connection to the L8NITE database using the user ID, password, database alias name, and schema name.

(4) Bind values to the parameter markers specified in the query.

(5) Execute the query.

(6) After the query is executed successfully, fetch the result and get the data from each column of the result set.

(7) Stop fetching if the last row is fetched.

(8) Disconnect from the database and free the environment handle.

5.15 Summary

This chapter covered quite a number of topics. First, you were introduced to the .NET framework, which is made up of three key components: CLR, the framework class libraries, and .NET-compliant languages. To access DB2 from .NET applications, the ADO.NET API is used. DB2 provides .NET support via three access methods. The native DB2 .NET data provider method is recommended because it is efficient and because the database calls generated are most compatible with DB2.

After DB2 is enabled with .NET support, you can also take advantage of the add-ins added to the Visual Studio .NET IDE, such as the IBM Explorer and the ability to launch DB2 tools from within the IDE.

We then used VS.NET to develop the L8NITE application from beginning to end. The application starts by establishing a database connection via the DB2Connection class. Other classes in the .NET connected layer are DB2Command, DB2DataReader, and DB2DataAdapter. After a DB2Command object is set, you can use the DB2DataAdapter's Fill method to execute the query and populate a DataSet. DataSet, DataTable, and DataRow are all classes defined in the .NET disconnected layer. Through the L8NITE application, we looked at how these classes can be used to provide application functionality.

To write robust applications, you must not omit exception handling. We demonstrated how to catch and display errors and warnings using the Try ... Catch ... Finally statement.

You can use the DB2 CLI trace utility to capture all SQL statements being executed from the .NET application. This is very handy when it comes to troubleshooting problems or monitoring SQL statements.

5.16 Exercises

In this chapter, you have learned how to write a VB.NET application from beginning to end. Code snippets were presented. To get complete working source code of the L8NITE application, you can download and open the project from the book's Web site. The VB.NET source code is contained in the compressed file L8NITE.zip.

You may notice that a few operations in the L8NITE application were not discussed in the chapter. They are left for you to do as an exercise. Implementation of the two functions is also included in the source code.

1. When a cashier enters a product for checkout, the application currently can add only products to the checkout list. We would like to implement a Remove Product function so that items can be removed from the list should the customer decide not to take them. Here are some hints to help you in coding the Remove Product function:
   - Obtain the item selected by using the DataGrid's CurrentCell property.
   - Cast the current cell to a DataSet.
   - Obtain the DataTable ProductFound from the DataSet.
   - Obtain the DataRow from the DataTable.
   - Obtain the product ID from the selected row.
   - Remove the DataRow from the DataTable.
   - Refresh the DataGrid binding so that the removed row is not displayed.
   - Update the PRODUCT table to reflect the inventory changes.
   - Delete the selected item from the PRODUCT_PURCHASES table.
   - Update the subtotal, tax, and amount due values.

2. Notice that the drop-down box has two values: Sales and Refund. All the code demonstrated in the chapter is to implement a Sales operation. Use or modify some of the subroutines to also support a Refund transaction.

   There is a column called Type defined in the SALES table. It is used to record a Sales or Refund transaction. Note that 0 stands for sales, and 3 stands for Refund.

   Keep these considerations in mind when coding the Refund function:
   - Insert an item into the sales table with type of 3 to indicate a refund transaction.
   - When an item is returned, the product table is updated to show the inventory changes.
   - Insert an item into the product_purchases table to keep a record of what is being returned.

CHAPTER 6

Java Application Development

In this chapter, you will learn:

- What Java is and its key advantages
- Which JDBC drivers are provided with DB2
- How to design and code a Java-based point-of-sale terminal application
- How to use Java SDK classes designed to work with a JDBC data source
- How to use a JDBC connection to retrieve and update data
- How to work with SQL for Java (SQLJ) to provide connectivity for your Java application

6.1 Introduction

In this chapter, you will learn to implement the same point-of-sale terminal application developed in Chapter 5, this time with Java technologies. Because the aim of this book is for you to learn about using DB2, this chapter will concentrate on accessing data through JDBC and, to a lesser extent, SQLJ. We will also briefly touch on topics such as designing a Java application and creating a graphical interface using Swing. Swing is a library of GUI components (buttons, checkboxes, etc.) provided as part of the Java Software Developer Kit (SDK). This chapter is designed to be hands-on, giving you the opportunity to develop your own Java database application.

6.2 Why Java?

Java is an object-oriented programming language developed by Sun Microsystems. Since its initial public release in May 1995, it has been widely adopted by the software development community. Java offers a great many advantages over other programming languages. For starters, Java provides *garbage collection* to clean up objects that are no longer in use and thereby free up memory. It is also standards-based and supported by a wealth of online resources to help resolve problems during the development cycle.

One of the most attractive features of Java is its cross-platform capability. An application written in Java is compiled to byte code that is executed on a Java virtual machine (JVM). This means that any computer with a JVM installed can run that application without the need to recompile the source code. Currently JVMs are available for a wide variety of UNIX-based operating systems as well as for Microsoft Windows. This makes Java an ideal programming language for the development of any application that will be deployed on a variety of computer systems.

Another major reason for using Java is related to the ease of achieving database connectivity using the JDBC API. JDBC provides classes and interfaces that make it easy to connect to a database and retrieve data. DB2 provides implementations of the JDBC API in its driver classes. This means that you don't have to know any more about connecting to a database than simply how to call various methods defined by the JDBC interfaces.

To write the point-of-sale terminal application in Java, you need the following:

- Java Software Development Kit (SDK) version 1.4.1
- IBM DB2 JDBC driver

Both of these are available as part of your standard DB2 installation. To access the Java SDK and JDBC driver, you simply add them to your PATH and CLASSPATH environment variables, respectively.

6.3 JDBC in DB2

JDBC is the industry standard for database connectivity between a Java application and a database. As a standard, JDBC is independent of the database vendor. The JDBC API is supported by all major database products on the market, including DB2.

The JDBC API can be divided into two main categories: application programming and driver programming. The application programming API provides three major functions:

- Connecting to the database
- Submitting SQL
- Processing query results

JDBC drivers provide these functions and are included as part of a DB2 installation. In this chapter, we will look at how you can use the application programming API to create a Java application.

The JDBC specification defines four types of drivers (type 1 through type 4). It is sufficient to know that a type 2 and a type 4 driver are provided with DB2 (a type 3 driver is also available but is deprecated). We will briefly discuss the differences between the two driver types.

Type 2 Driver: Partly Native Java Code

The type 2 JDBC driver uses a combination of Java code and data-source-specific native code to provide database connectivity (see Figure 6.1). Therefore, this driver requires installation of a database-vendor-specific binary on the client.

Note: The supplemental section of Chapter 2, Getting Started, demonstrates how to install the minimal DB2 client binaries from a DB2 server CD.

Figure 6.1 Type 2 JDBC driver overview

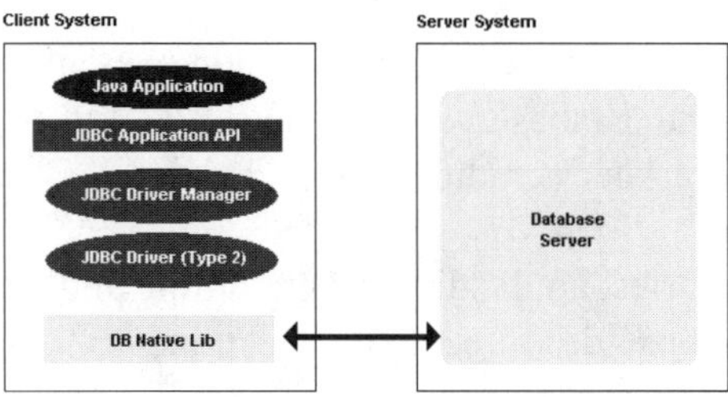

Type 4 Driver: Direct to Database, Pure Java Driver

Using a type 4 driver, JDBC implements the network protocol for a specific data source (see Figure 6.2). Clients connect directly to the data source server. Because type 4 drivers are implemented in Java, the driver does not use any native binary library.

Figure 6.2 Type 4 driver overview

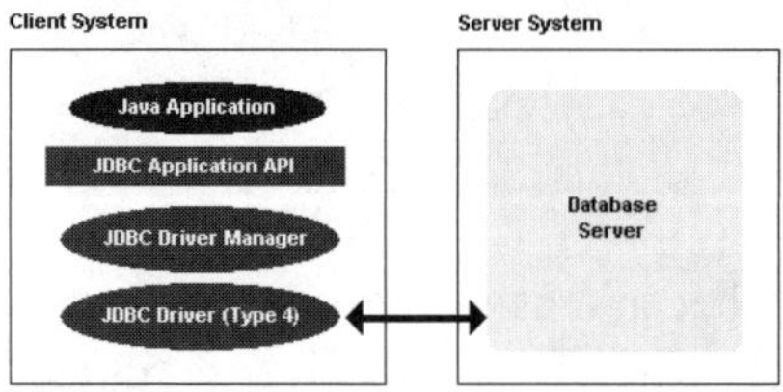

Selecting a DB2 JDBC Driver

From the application deployment point of view, a type 2 driver requires some installation processing on the client system. Because a type 4 driver is a pure Java implementation, it simply requires a Java archive (JAR) file to be copied onto the client system. Because the JAR file contains Java byte code, it does not require an installation process.

Depending on the type of database application you are writing, the impact of the choice of JDBC driver may vary. Both types of driver provide support for standard SQL. For the L8NITE sample application, either driver will provide the required connectivity features. The type 2 driver provided with DB2 can be used to access DB2 administration APIs that are not available with the type 4 driver. The administration APIs are used to support DB2 administration tasks.

6.4 Designing a Java Application

There are many ways to design and implement a software application to achieve the same goal. The implementation differences are as much the result of different constraints as of the developer's personal preference. In this section, we will not dwell on the exact implementation details of the entire point-of-sale application. Instead, we will discuss a few general programming guidelines.

Identifying Required Functions

To design an application, you need to identify the necessary functionality to achieve your task. In our L8NITE convenience store example, we are designing a point-of-sale terminal application to process customer purchases. This high-level task can be broken into a set of smaller tasks:

- Process both cash and account sales.
- Create a detailed record of transactions.
- Update inventory.
- In case of an account sale, retrieve customer information based on first and last names.
- Create new user accounts.

Object-Oriented Application Design

After you identify the functions that you need to implement, the next step is to think about how the application is to be written. Java is an object-oriented programming language, and having a good object design can greatly reduce the effort needed during development and maintenance. In general, for this type of application, you can divide it into its interface components and its data model. In Java, you can put groups of related classes into separate packages. For the L8NITE application, we will create two separate Java packages: *gui* and *model.*

The *gui* package will contain all the panels and dialog boxes needed to create the user interface. The *model* package will contain classes that represent various objects that your application will deal with. The following classes are used in the L8NITE application.

- CustomerInformation: This class encapsulates information about a customer.
- Product: This class contains information about a particular product.
- PurchaseTableModel: This class stores a list of product purchases listed in the application.

The model package will also contain helper classes that facilitate various actions, such as retrieving customer information and recording a purchase.

The key advantage of separating the model from the interface is that it lets you easily change the interface implementation without interfering with the business logic (for example, if you were to change the application to be Web-based). The reverse is also true: Changing the implementation of the data access will not affect the graphical user interface. Later in this chapter, we will replace the JDBC part of the application with an SQLJ implementation.

6.5 Building the Application Using JDBC

In this section, you will learn more about coding Java to connect to a database and accessing and updating a DB2 database using JDBC. We will use the type 4 driver provided with your DB2 installation. You will learn how to use the following JDBC components to build the L8NITE application:

- Driver: The Driver interface is implemented by the type 4 JDBC driver provided with DB2. In Java, all JDBC drivers must implement the java.sql package Driver interface. The full class name for the type 4 driver is com.ibm.db2.jcc.DB2Driver. This class can be found in the db2jcc JAR file in the SQLLIB/java directory. To deploy your application on a client system, you must make sure that a copy of this JAR file, along with appropriate license files, is available on the client system. This class contains code for building a database connection. An instance of the driver is loaded at run time and registered with the DriverManager class. You will not need to interact directly with the driver class programmatically except for loading and registering it with the DriverManager. You will learn how to do that later in this section.

- DriverManager: The Java DriverManager class is provided as part of the standard Java SDK installation. Many different JDBC drivers can be loaded at run time. When a connection request to a database is made, the DriverManager tries requesting a connection to the required database with each driver currently registered. The main feature provided by the DriverManager is the getConnection method. You will learn how to request a connection by identifying a database using a uniform resource locator, or URL.
- Connection: Each driver has its own implementation of a database connection. To ensure consistency between various implementations, all connections must adhere to the same Java *Connection* interface. Connection provides a great many interesting functions. You will learn to use these to make your Java application programming easier. In particular, we are interested in the various types of statements created by the Connection, methods for controlling a transaction, and methods for controlling isolation level.
- Statement: In the examples, you will learn about how to use the Statement class to execute queries and manipulate data. The executeQuery method is used to submit queries and returns a single result set. The executeUpdate method is used to execute INSERT, UPDATE, and DELETE statements. The method returns the number of rows affected by the statement. You create a statement by calling the createStatement method of a Connection.
- PreparedStatement: As with Statement, you can retrieve an object implementing the PreparedStatement interface by invoking the prepareStatement method of the Connection object. You will see how a prepared statement can be used to execute queries and statements. The key difference between a statement and a prepared statement is that a prepared statement offers some performance advantage if the SQL is executed repeatedly. When a prepared statement is used, the SQL is parameterized and its access plan can be reused. Values for each parameter are passed in just before the SQL is executed.
- ResultSet: A ResultSet object encapsulates a query result. The result set provides both read and write access to the data in your tables.

To isolate the code needed for database connectivity and data retrieval from the rest of the application, the JDBC code is grouped into one class (the DataAccessor class) in the sample application. This is advantageous because you can change the design and driver for connectivity without rebuilding other parts of the application.

Establishing a Database Connection

The first task in building an application using JDBC is to establish a connection to the database. Figure 6.3 is a segment of code taken from part of the sample application's DataAccessor class. A URL string is declared in the file at (1) to identify the database that we will connect to. For our application, the database is on the local machine. The URL contains three separate parts: the driver type, the database vendor protocol, and the database name. If the database is located on a different server, the URL must also identify the host system. It might look something like this:

```
jdbc:db2://<remote-host>:<port-number>/<database-name>
```

The method for getting a connection, at (2), has three parameters: URL, user ID, and password. The method allows this class to be used to build connections to other databases. The user ID and password information at (3) and (4) are used by DriverManager to build the connection. In the *try* block at (5), the DB2Driver is registered with DriverManager. After the driver is loaded, a request for a connection is made using the getConnection method of DriverManager. DriverManager then establishes a connection using the provided input parameters; to do this, it requests a connection to the specified database URL using each of the registered drivers. If a suitable driver is found, the connection will be established by the driver class as requested by the DriverManager.

The connection is then returned and ready for use. When the application is started, the user will be prompted to enter a user ID and password. The information is used to call the connect method at (6) to connect to the L8NITE database. The connection is static because only one connection is necessary for the point-of-sale application. The connection to the database is intentionally maintained as long as the application is running, because establishing a new connection requires considerable overhead.

Figure 6.3 Establishing a JDBC Connection

```
Public class DataAccessor() {

  Public static final String DB_URL = "jdbc:db2:L8NITE";              (1)
  private static Connection connection = null;

  ... source code...
  /**
   *  This method tries to get a connection to a database with the
```

```
  *  specified user ID and password.
  *  @param url - database url as a string.
  *  @param userid - User ID
  *  @param password - password
  *  @return Connection - connection to the specified database url
  *                       using the specified userid and password.
  *  @throws Exception - SQL Exception.
  */
 public static Connection getConnection(String url,                  (2)
                   String uid, String pswd) throws Exception{
   Connection connection = null;

   Properties connectProperties = new Properties();
   connectProperties.put("user", uid);                               (3)
   connectProperties.put("password", pswd);                          (4)

   try {
     Class.forName("com.ibm.db2.jcc.DB2Driver").newInstance();
     connection = DriverManager.getConnection(url,
                                         connectProperties);   (5)

   } catch (Exception e) {
     throw e;
   }
   return connection;
 }

  ... source code...
 /**
  *  Establish a connection to the L8NITE database. This method
  *  will connect to the database with the specified User ID and
  *  Password. It allows the application to have different
  *  access privileges based on user ID.
  *  @param userid - user ID use for connection.
  *  @param password - password for authentication.
  *  @throws Exception - SQL exception can be thrown if connect fails.
  */
 public void connect(String userid, String password) throws Exception {
   connection = getConnection(DB_URL, userid, password);               (6)
 }
}
```

Inquiring Minds: Java Connection Interface

A Connection provided by different drivers can vary in functions, but all drivers must provide a base set of features as defined by the Java Connection interface. Here are a few useful features that can be helpful in this and future application development projects.

- commit ( ) method: By calling commit, you are confirming that the changes you have made since the last commit call are correct and that the changes will be written to the database.
- rollback ( ) method: Use this method to "undo" any uncommitted changes you have made to the data in your database.
- setAutoCommit (boolean auto_commit) method: Use this method to enable automatic commit. This means that each SQL statement is committed automatically after its execution without any explicit commit call.
- createStatement ( ) method: This method creates and returns an object that implements the Statement interface.
- prepareStatement (String sql_stmt) method: Use this method to obtain a PreparedStatement object. We will go over the usage of a prepared statement later in this chapter.
- setTransactionIsolation (int iso_level) method: This method tries to change the isolation level of transactions executed through this connection. Changing isolation level during a transaction may have different results based on different vendor implementations. Isolation levels are discussed in Chapter 7, Maximizing Concurrency.

Executing Queries

After you are connected to the database, your application can retrieve and update data using SQL. In this section, we will go over the source code used to retrieve customer information needed to start a sales transaction. Figure 6.4 is another code segment found in the DataAccessor class.

The basic part of the SQL for retrieving customer account information is declared as a final static String at (1). It is generally good coding practice to declare constants near the top of your source file. It makes reviewing and changing the code easier. The retrieveCustomersUsingStatement method expects two input parameters: the customer's last name and partial first name. At (2), these parameters are combined with the String constants to complete the query. Because the application is maintaining a connection to the database, there is no need to build a new connection to run this query.

At (3), a new Statement is created, and the query is then executed at (4) by a call to the executeQuery method on that Statement object. After executing the query, the routine returns a reference to the result set as the output. The ResultSet object provides a series of simple-to-use methods to parse through this data. At (5), these methods are used to initialize a new CustomerInformation object to represent a customer account. You might want to take a quick look at the CustomerInformation class for this method. Because it is possible to have more than one customer with information matching the search criteria, the method returns a list of CustomerInformation objects. After all the data from the result set is processed, the result set and statement are closed and cleaned up at (6) and (7), respectively.

Figure 6.4 Retrieving customer information from the database

```
Public class DataAccessor() {

  public static final String RETRIEVE_CUSTOMER_INFO_SQL =                (1)
   "SELECT CUSTOMER_ID, LASTNAME, FIRSTNAME, " +
   "ADDRESS, ZIP_CODE, PHONE, CREDIT_CARD, EXPIRY_DATE " +
   "FROM L8NITE.CUSTOMER WHERE LASTNAME = ";

  public static final String FIRSTNAME_LIKE_CLAUSE =
   " AND FIRSTNAME LIKE ";

  ... source code...
  /**
   *  This method will retrieve information on customers whose last name
   *  and first name match the search criteria.
   *  @param lname - string, customer's complete last name.
   *  @param fname - string, customer's partial or complete first name.
   *  @return Vector - contains CustomerInformation
   *  objects for customer who matches the search.
   *  @throws Exception - SQL Exception.
   */
  public Vector retrieveCustomersUsingStatement
                (String lname, String fname) throws Exception{
    Vector customerVector = new Vector();
    try {
      StringBuffer sqlBuffer = new StringBuffer();                        (2)
      sqlBuffer.append(RETRIEVE_CUSTOMER_INFO_SQL)
               .append("'").append(lname).append("'");
      if (fname != null && fname.length() > 0) {
        sqlBuffer.append(FIRSTNAME_LIKE_CLAUSE).append("'")
                 .append(fname).append("%'");
      }
      Statement statement = connection.createStatement();                 (3)

      ResultSet resultSet =
                       statement.executeQuery(sqlBuffer.toString());     (4)
```

```
      CustomerInformation customerInfo = null;
      while (resultSet.next()) {
        customerInfo = new CustomerInformation();
        customerInfo.quickInitialize(                              (5)
                    resultSet.getInt(CUSTOMER_ID_COL),
                    ...list of parameters...
                    );
        customerVector.add(customerInfo);
      }
      resultSet.close();                                           (6)
      statement.close();                                           (7)
      connection.commit();
    } catch (Exception e) {
      e.printStackTrace();
      throw e;
    }
    return customerVector;
  }
  ...more source code...
}
```

Inquiring Minds: Java Statement Interface

Here are a few useful features that you might find helpful in this and future application development projects.

- executeQuery (String sql_stmt) method: Execute a query (SELECT) using this method. A single result set will be returned when the execution is completed.
- executeUpdate (String sql_stmt) method: Execute SQL statements (such as INSERT, UPDATE, and DELETE) that modify database data. The total number of rows affected by the statement will be returned by the method call.
- execute (String sql_stmt) method: Execute an SQL statement, which may return more than one result.
- addBatch, clearBatch, executeBatch methods: You can use these methods to execute multiple SQL operations as a single batch. The addBatch method lets you add SQL to the batch, and the clearBatch method empties all entries currently in the batch. The executeBatch method returns a set of integers. Each number represents the number of rows affected by each statement in the batch.

In the example, the query is built as a string and is executed directly. This code can be implemented differently by using the prepareStatement method provided by the Connection interface. You should consider using a prepared statement when a query is executed repeatedly. It can be helpful in improving the performance of your application. In our current example, the customer retrieval query is reused.

The code segment in Figure 6.5 shows how you can use a prepared statement to retrieve customer data. At (1), the query is prepared by a call to the prepareStatement method of the Connection interface. In the query, parameters to be passed in at a later time are denoted with "?". You should also note that prepareStatement is called only the first time the retrieveCustomers method is used. To actually execute the prepared statement, you must set the parameters to the appropriate values. This is done by invoking set<type> methods of the PreparedStatement interface. In our example, the query requires two string values. We can set these values using the setString method shown at (2) and (3). After the parameters are set, you can execute the query and process the result set as you did in the preceding example.

Figure 6.5 Retrieving customer information using PreparedStatement

```
Public class DataAccessor() {

  private PreparedStatement getCustomerInfoSQL = null;
  public static final String RETRIEVE_CUSTOMER_INFO_FULL_SQL =
    "SELECT CUSTOMER_ID, LASTNAME, FIRSTNAME, ADDRESS, ZIP_CODE, " +
    "CREDIT_CARD, EXPIRY_DATE, PHONE FROM L8NITE.CUSTOMER " +
    "WHERE LASTNAME = ? AND FIRSTNAME LIKE ?";

  ... source code...

  /**
   *  This method will retrieve information on customers whose last name
   *  and first name match the search criteria.
   *  @param lname - string, customer's complete last name.
   *  @param fname - string, customer's partial or complete first name.
   *  @return Vector - contains CustomerInformation objects for customer
   *                   who matches the search.
   *  @throws Exception - SQL Exception.
   */
  public Vector retrieveCustomers
       (String lname, String fname) throws Exception{
    Vector customerVector = new Vector();
    try {
      if (getCustomerInfoSQL == null) {
        getCustomerInfoSQL =
           connection.prepareStatement(RETRIEVE_CUSTOMER_INFO_FULL_SQL); (1)
      }
      getCustomerInfoSQL.setString(1, lname);                            (2)
```

```
      getCustomerInfoSQL.setString(2, fname);                                    (3)
      ResultSet resultSet = getCustomerInfoSQL.executeQuery();
      CustomerInformation customerInfo = null;
      while (resultSet.next()) {
        customerInfo = new CustomerInformation();
        customerInfo.quickInitialize(...list of parameters...);
        customerVector.add(customerInfo);
      }
      resultSet.close();
      connection.commit();
    } catch (Exception e) {
      throw e;
    }
    return customerVector;
  }
}
```

Inquiring Minds: JDBC PreparedStatement Interface

A PreparedStatement object is very similar to a Statement object. You create a PreparedStatement by passing a parameterized SQL statement to a Connection's prepareStatement method. The SQL is compiled, and in some cases optimized, by the database server. Once this is done, the execution of the statement will no longer include compilation and optimization. For statements that are often reused with different values, this technique can provide a significant performance boost. Methods are available to set values for each of the parameters in the statement. The execute, executeQuery, and executeUpdate methods have identical behavior to their counterparts for a regular Statement.

- set<objType> (int param_index, <obj type> <obj value>) method: A series of set methods are provided to input values to the PreparedStatement. If the first parameter in the SQL is of integer type and has a value of 5, you can set the value of the parameter using the following call:

  preparedStatement.setInt(1, 5); // where 1 is the parameter index and 5 is the value.

Making Changes to Data in the Database

In addition to retrieving data from the database, the application also needs to insert information into the database. In this section, we will spend a few moments going over the method of the DataAccessor class used to create a new customer account. The code is listed in Figure 6.6.

At (1), the actual SQL is declared as a constant near the top of the source file. As in the preceding section, a PreparedStatement is created at (2). At (3), the returned value is a result set containing the value of the generated customer ID number. This is necessary because CUSTOMER_ID is a generated value, and it is also important to make sure that the CustomerInformation object contains the generated ID so that it can be displayed in the GUI.

Figure 6.6 Creating a new customer account

```
Public class DataAccessor() {

  private PreparedStatement createCustomerSQL = null;
  public static final String INSERT_CUSTOMER_FULL_SQL =
  "SELECT CUSTOMER_ID FROM NEW TABLE " +                                (1)
  "(INSERT INTO L8NITE.CUSTOMER " +
  "(CUSTOMER_ID, LASTNAME, FIRSTNAME, ADDRESS, ZIP_CODE, " +
  "PHONE, CREDIT_CARD, EXPIRY_DATE) " +
  "VALUES (DEFAULT, ?, ?, ?, ?, ?, ?, ?))";

  ... source code...

  /**
   *  This method will create a new customer account entry in
   *  the CUSTOMER table.
   *  @param customer - CustomerInformation object containing
   *                    info on new customer.
   *  @throws Exception - SQL Exception.
   */
  public void createCustomer(CustomerInformation customer) throws Exception {
    try {
      if (createCustomerSQL == null) {
        createCustomerSQL =
           connection.prepareStatement(INSERT_CUSTOMER_FULL_SQL);       (2)
      }

      createCustomerSQL.setString(1, customer.getLastname().trim());
```

```
        createCustomerSQL.setString(2, customer.getFirstname().trim());
        createCustomerSQL.setString(3, customer.getAddress().trim());
        createCustomerSQL.setString(4, customer.getZipCode().trim());
        createCustomerSQL.setString(5, customer.getPhoneNum().trim());
        createCustomerSQL.setString(6, customer.getCreditCardNum().trim());
        createCustomerSQL.setString(7, customer.getExpiryDate().trim());

        ResultSet rs = createCustomerSQL.executeQuery();                (3)
        while (rs.next()) {
          customer.setCustomerID(rs.getInt(CUSTOMER_ID_COL));
        }

        rs.close();
        connection.commit();
      } catch (Exception e) {
        throw e;
      }
    }
  }
```

Controlling a Transaction

In developing a database application, it is crucial that you have a good understanding of transactions. A transaction groups database operations so that if one fails, they all fail. In most development projects, the data in a database is usually shared among many applications. For the data to remain consistent and correct, it is crucial to maintain control over database transactions.

In our application, when a customer proceeds to the cashier to purchase a product, the application will need to complete the following steps as a single transaction:

1. Create a sales record in the SALES table.
2. For each item purchased, record the individual purchases in the PRODUCT_PURCHASES table.
3. For each item, update the inventory in the PRODUCT table.

Only when all these operations are completed correctly can the transaction then be committed to the database. Failure of any of the operations should result in the entire transaction being canceled, or rolled back.

Let's take a moment to see why this transaction control is so important. Let's say the operations to insert a new sales record and to update a product purchase are completed successfully, but the operation to decrement the inventory fails. Without transaction control, this error will result in income that is unaccounted for and inventory that has gone missing. Over time, with transactions failing at different points, it will become impossible to keep an accurate record of the business's progress and successfully control the store's inventory. Figure 6.7 lists sample code taken from the L8NITE application.

Figure 6.7 Controlling transactions in the L8NITE application

```
Public class DataAccessor() {

  private PreparedStatement salesSQL = null;
  public static final String SALES_FULL_SQL =                          (1)
  "SELECT SALES_TRANSACTION_ID FROM NEW TABLE ("
  + "INSERT INTO L8NITE.SALES (CUSTOMER_ID, SUB_TOTAL, TYPE,
     TRANSACTION_TIMESTAMP ,"
  + " SALES_TRANSACTION_ID) VALUES (?, ?, ?, ?, default))";


  private PreparedStatement productPurchaseSQL = null;
  public static final String PRODUCT_PURCHASE_FULL_SALE =
  "INSERT INTO L8NITE.PRODUCT_PURCHASES (SALES_TRANSACTION_ID, PRODUCT_ID,"
  + " PRICE, QTY) VALUES (?, ?, ?, ?)";

  private PreparedStatement inventorySelectSQL = null;
  public static final String INVENTORY_SELECT_FULL_SALE =
  "SELECT INVENTORY FROM L8NITE.PRODUCT WHERE PRODUCT_ID = ? "
  + " FOR UPDATE OF INVENTORY";

  private PreparedStatement inventoryUpdateSQL = null;
  public static final String INVENTORY_UPDATE_FULL_SALE =
  "UPDATE L8NITE.PRODUCT SET INVENTORY = ? WHERE PRODUCT_ID = ?";

  ... source code...

 /**
   *  This method will process the entries in the product purchase table
   *  and charge it to a customer with the CustomerInformation object.
   *  @param customer - CustomerInformation object containing
   *                    info for update.
   *  @throws Exception - SQL Exception.
   */
  public void processPurchaseTable(
```

```
                 PurchaseTableModel purTableModel,
                 CustomerInformation customer,
                 float subTotal,
                 int type)
     throws Exception{

  Timestamp ts = new Timestamp(
                (new GregorianCalendar()).getTime().getTime());
  int transactionID = 0;

  int multiplier = 1;
  if (type == RETURN_TYPE) {
    multiplier = -1;
  }

  float tax = (multiplier * (float)0.07 * subTotal);

  try {

    if (salesSQL == null) {
      salesSQL = connection.prepareStatement(SALES_FULL_SQL);          (2)
    }

    if (productPurchaseSQL == null) {
      productPurchaseSQL =
        connection.prepareStatement(PRODUCT_PURCHASE_FULL_SALE);
    }

    if (inventorySelectSQL == null) {
      inventorySelectSQL =
        connection.prepareStatement(INVENTORY_SELECT_FULL_SALE);
    }

    if (inventoryUpdateSQL == null) {
      inventoryUpdateSQL =
        connection.prepareStatement(INVENTORY_UPDATE_FULL_SALE);
    }

    int cID = CASH_PURCHASE_ID;
    if (customer != null) {
      cID = customer.getCustomerID();
    }

    salesSQL.setInt(1, cID);
    salesSQL.setFloat(2, (multiplier * subTotal));
    salesSQL.setInt(3, type);
    salesSQL.setInt(4, type);
```

```
salesSQL.setTimestamp(5, ts);

ResultSet rs1 = salesSQL.executeQuery();                    (3)
while (rs1.next()) {
  transactionID = rs1.getInt(SALES_TRANSACTION_ID_COL);     (4)
}

rs1.close();


int prodID = 0;
float price = 0;
int quantity = 0;
int inventory = 0;
for (int rowIndex = 0; rowIndex < purTableModel.getRowCount();
     rowIndex++) {
  prodID = Integer.parseInt(
    (String) purTableModel.getValueAt(rowIndex,
          PurchaseTableModel.COL_NUM_PRODUCT_ID));
  price = ((Float) purTableModel.getValueAt(rowIndex,
          PurchaseTableModel.COL_NUM_UNIT_PRICE)).floatValue();
  quantity = ((Integer)purTableModel.getValueAt(rowIndex,
          PurchaseTableModel.COL_NUM_QUANTITY)).intValue();

  productPurchaseSQL.setInt(1, transactionID);
  productPurchaseSQL.setInt(2, prodID);
  productPurchaseSQL.setFloat(3, price);
  productPurchaseSQL.setFloat(4, quantity);

  productPurchaseSQL.executeUpdate();                       (5)

  inventorySelectSQL.setInt(1, prodID);

  ResultSet rs2 = inventorySelectSQL.executeQuery();        (6)

  while (rs2.next()) {
    inventory = rs2.getInt(INVENTORY_COL);
  }

  rs2.close();

  inventory = inventory - (multiplier * quantity);

  inventoryUpdateSQL.setInt(1, inventory);
  inventoryUpdateSQL.setInt(2, prodID);

  inventoryUpdateSQL.executeUpdate();                       (7)
```

```
        }
        connection.commit();                                          (8)
      } catch (Exception ex) {
        try {
          connection.rollback();                                      (9)
        } catch (Exception ex2) {
          throw ex2;
        }
        throw ex;
      }
    }
  }
```

The automatic commit feature of the connection is switched off. This means that the updates made to the database will not be final until they are explicitly committed. The first INSERT statement is used to create a new sales transaction by inserting a row into the SALES table (1). The transaction ID is reused in the PRODUCT_PURCHASES table to record each item sold in this sales transaction. To do this, your application must retrieve the generated value from this insert.

Let's take a moment to look at two ways to accomplish this. The first is based on a new SQL syntax that was also used to create a new customer account in the preceding section. Let's take a look at this method.

```
SELECT SALES_TRANSACTION_ID FROM NEW TABLE (
    INSERT INTO L8NITE.SALES (CUSTOMER_ID, SUB_TOTAL,
           TYPE, TRANSACTION_TIMESTAMP,
           SALES_TRANSACTION_ID)
           VALUES (?, ?, ?, ?, ?, DEFAULT))
```

This query uses a new feature supported by DB2 to retrieve a value generated by an INSERT statement without using a second query. The row created by the INSERT statement is made available through the use of the FROM NEW TABLE feature. You can think of this "NEW TABLE" as a temporary table in your database created to contain the single row that was inserted into the SALES table. The transaction ID can then be retrieved from the result set generated by this query.

At (2), PreparedStatement objects are created from the JDBC connection. To begin a sales transaction, a sales record must first be created in the SALES table (3). After the row is inserted, the transaction ID number is retrieved at (4). For each of the product entries in the GUI, a new entry is created in PRODUCT_PURCHASES referencing the TRANSACTION_ID from the SALES table at (5). The latest inventory status is retrieved at (6) and then updated at (7). When all operations are executed without any exception, the update can then be committed to the database using the commit method at (8). If any of the statements fails, an SQLException will be thrown by the PreparedStatement object, causing the catch block to be executed. In the catch block, the rollback method is executed at (9) and no changes are made to the data in the database.

A second method can be used to retrieve the generated sale transaction ID. With Java SDK version 1.4, you can use the getGeneratedKeys method to retrieve a result set containing the set of generated keys from executing the query. Figure 6.8 shows how you can modify the source code to use this new Java feature.

Figure 6.8 How to use the getGeneratedKeys feature

```
Statement salesStatement2 = connection.createStatement();

String sqlString =
     "INSERT INTO L8NITE.SALES (CUSTOMER_ID, SUB_TOTAL, TYPE, TIME "
      + ") VALUES ("
      + customer.getCustomerID() + ", "
      + subTotal + ", "
      + tax + ", "
      + type + ", "
      + "\'" + ts + "\')";

salesStatement2.executeUpdate(sqlString,
                              Statement.RETURN_GENERATED_KEYS);

ResultSet rs_gk = salesStatement2.getGeneratedKeys();
while (rs_gk.next()) {
  transactionID = rs_gk.getInt(1);
}

rs_gk.close();
```

Exception Handling

Even the best-planned application can run into unanticipated conditions after it is deployed. It is important to include error-handling capabilities in your application programs to gracefully recover from unexpected events. When handling errors, you should try to

- Prevent the program from crashing
- Protect the integrity of your data
- Provide helpful messages as to what the problem might be

All JDBC methods related to accessing data can throw SQLException exceptions. For a Java program, all undeclared checked exceptions must be caught. This forces the developer to consider and process possible errors. In the sample code you have seen in this chapter, the SQL calls are made in a try block. If an exception is thrown during execution, a generic handler is called to process the exception. Figure 6.9 shows the code for a simple error-handling method. The error message is extracted from SQLException and displayed in a small dialog box.

Figure 6.9 Handling error conditions

```
public class POSTerminal {

  ... source code...


  /**
   *  This method will be invoked when an exception occurs. The
   *  purpose of this method is to create a message dialog and
   *  display the information regarding the exception to the user.
   *  As an added feature, the Java method in which the exception
   *  has occurred is also added.
   *  @param ex - Java Exception
   *  @param methodName - the String name of the offending method.
   */
  private static void handleException(Exception ex, String methodName) {
    String msgs = ex.getMessage();
    StringBuffer msgBuffer = new StringBuffer();
    msgBuffer.append(ex);
    msgBuffer.append("\n\n");
    if (msgs != null) msgBuffer.append(msgs).append("\n\n");;
    msgBuffer.append("An error occurred in: ").append(methodName);
```

```
        msgBuffer.append("\n\n");
        ex.printStackTrace();
        MessageDialog msgDialog =
            new MessageDialog(pos, msgBuffer.toString());
        msgDialog.setVisible(true);
    }
}
```

In the exception handler highlighted here, all exceptions are treated the same way. Most exceptions you will encounter in a JDBC application will be instances of the SQLException class. SQLException is a subclass of Exception that provides a few extra features specific to SQL execution. The getErrorCode method, for example, allows you to retrieve the error code programmatically to implement "smarter" error handling. For example, if your database server is not started, you will receive an error code of -1013. To recover, you can simply display the error message, as we did in the sample application, or attempt to start the server programmatically.

JDBC Tracing

Any application that accesses DB2 using JDBC can use the CLI and JDBC trace facility to record all JDBC calls made by the DB2 JDBC driver. With the tracing option turned on, the trace information is written to a directory on the disk that you specify. The log files can be used to help with debugging your application.

By default, the JDBC tracing is turned off to prevent any impact on system performance. To turn tracing on, you alter the configuration of the JDBC trace facility in the db2cli.ini file. The file is located in the SQLLIB directory on Windows operating systems, and in the sqllib/cfg directory on Linux. You can turn on JDBC tracing by adding the following entries to the db2cli.ini file:

```
[COMMON]
jdbctrace=1
JdbcTracePathName=<file path>
JDBCTraceFlush=1
```

The jdbctrace parameter is set to 1 to enable the tracing. The second parameter is used to specify a directory on the file system to keep the log files. There is no default location for JDBC log files. If this variable is not set, no trace information will be produced even if jdbctrace is set to 1. The JDBCTraceFlush parameter is used to control how the trace information is to be written. If flush is turned off, a trace file is written when a thread has completed executing its JDBC operations. If the thread is terminated unexpectedly, the trace information will be lost. Switching the option to 1 tells DB2 to write an entry to disk as soon as a JDBC call is made (but this incurs a greater performance penalty). If your application terminates unexpectedly, the trace information will not be lost.

To try out the JDBC trace facility, we will deliberately introduce an error into our L8NITE application. In the DatabaseAccessor, let's make a change to the query that is used to retrieve customer information. We will change the table name from CUSTOMER to BOB. Because the BOB table does not exist in the database, this will result in an error when the application tries to retrieve customer information from the L8NITE database.

After adding the four lines to the db2cli.ini file, you can go ahead and launch the application. After you have entered a last name and clicked on the search button, an error message will be displayed stating that the table was not found. If you take a look in the directory specified in the db2cli.ini file, you will find some new files that look something like this:

```
WSDB::D:\SQLLIB\jdbcTrace>dir
 Volume in drive D has no label.
 Volume Serial Number is ACC5-7D92

 Directory of D:\SQLLIB\jdbcTrace

03/29/2004  12:25a      <DIR>          .
03/29/2004  12:25a      <DIR>          ..
03/28/2004  10:30p               2,039 2076_1_AWT-EventQueue-0.trc
03/28/2004  10:30p                 728 2076_1_main.trc
```

The first few digits of the trace file name is the ID of the process that is making the JDBC call. Each Java thread is tracked separately in its own file. If you open the AWT-EventQueue file, you will see entries similar to those in Figure 6.10. The first part of the trace shows the successful creation of a statement. The second part shows the query failing, with an SQL0204 error stating that the table BOB is not defined.

Figure 6.10 Sample JDBC trace file

```
jdbc.app.DB2Connection -> createStatement() (2004-03-28 22:30:29.579)
| jdbc.app.DB2Statement -> DB2Statement( con, 1003, 1007 ) (2004-03-28
22:30:29.609)
| | jdbc.app.DB2Statement -> checkResultSetType( 1003, 1007 ) (2004-03-28
22:30:29.619)
```

```
| | jdbc.app.DB2Statement <- checkResultSetType() [Time Elapsed = 0.0] (2004-
03-28 22:30:29.619)
| | 10: Peak statements = 1
| | 10: Statement Handle = 1:1
| jdbc.app.DB2Statement <- DB2Statement() [Time Elapsed = 0.02] (2004-03-28
22:30:29.619)
jdbc.app.DB2Connection <- createStatement() [Time Elapsed = 0.08] (2004-03-28
22:30:29.619)

jdbc.app.DB2Statement -> executeQuery( SELECT CUSTOMER_ID, LASTNAME, FIRST-
NAME, ADDRESS, ZIP_CODE, CREDIT_CARD, EXPIRY_DATE, USERID, PASSWORD FROM
L8NITE.BOB WHERE LASTNAME = 'Chan' ) (2004-03-28 22:30:29.619)
| 10: Statement Handle = 1:1
| jdbc.app.DB2Statement -> getStatementType( SELECT CUSTOMER_ID, LASTNAME,
FIRSTNAME, ADDRESS, ZIP_CODE, CREDIT_CARD, EXPIRY_DATE, USERID, PASSWORD FROM
L8NITE.BOB WHERE LASTNAME = 'Chan' ) (2004-03-28 22:30:29.619)
| jdbc.app.DB2Statement <- getStatementType() returns STMT_TYPE_QUERY (24)
[Time Elapsed = 0.0] (2004-03-28 22:30:29.619)
| jdbc.app.DB2Statement -> execute2( SELECT CUSTOMER_ID, LASTNAME, FIRSTNAME,
ADDRESS, ZIP_CODE, CREDIT_CARD, EXPIRY_DATE, USERID, PASSWORD FROM L8NITE.BOB
WHERE LASTNAME = 'Chan' ) (2004-03-28 22:30:29.619)
| | 10: StatementHandle  = 1:1
| | 10: SQLExecDirect - returnCode  = -1
| | jdbc.DB2Exception -> DB2Exception() (2004-03-28 22:30:30.22)
| | | 10: SQLError = [IBM][CLI Driver][DB2/NT] SQL0204N  "L8NITE.BOB" is an
undefined name. SQLSTATE=42704
| | |     SQLState = 42S02
| | |     SQLNativeCode = -204
| | |     LineNumber = 0
| | |     SQLerrmc = L8NITE.BOB
| | jdbc.DB2Exception <- DB2Exception() [Time Elapsed = 0.02] (2004-03-28
22:30:30.23)
| | 10: rowCount = 0
| jdbc.app.DB2Statement <- execute2() [Time Elapsed = 0.262] (2004-03-28
22:30:30.25)
jdbc.app.DB2Statement <- executeQuery() [Time Elapsed = 0.262] (2004-03-28
22:30:30.25)
```

6.6 Retrieving Data Using SQLJ

In addition to using JDBC and the Java classes in the java.sql package, there is yet another method to programmatically retrieve data from a database called SQLJ. In an application written in SQLJ, the data retrieval is still done through a JDBC connection. The main difference here is that the SQL is statically coded in your application. This makes the program considerably easier to read.

Figure 6.11 shows the SQLJ code segment (found in DatabaseAccessor2.sqlj) for retrieving product information from the database. The import declaration at (1) identifies the necessary Java packages. Before any statement is executed, there must be a connection to the database. A JDBC connection is established at (2) by using the code in the ConnectionBuilder class. At (3), a DefaultContext is created to link any SQL executed in this application to the connection. From this point forward, any SQL delimited by #sql {} will be executed via the default context. At (4), you can see that the actual variable names (preceded by the ":" character) are integrated into the SQL. After the query is executed, the results can be accessed through the application variables (5).

To build the application Java objects, the SQLJ source file must be translated to standard Java classes using the command sqlj. The sqlj utility is provided with your DB2 installation. You can type the following command from a command prompt to find out about the various options provided:

```
C:\> sqlj -help
```

SQLJ also requires application code to be bound to the database. To simplify the process of building and binding your SQLJ program, DB2 provides the bldsqlj batch utility in the SQLLIB/samples/java/sqlj directory. The usage of the batch file is shown in Figure 6.12. To successfully build and bind the SQLJ program, you must change one line of the bldsqlj.bat file. Open the batch file and locate the line "DB=sample", replace sample with L8NITE as the target database. After making the change, you can save the file and exit.

Figure 6.11 Retrieving product information using SQLJ

```
package sqljSample;

import sqlj.runtime.*;                                           (1)
import sqlj.runtime.ref.*;

public class DatabaseAccessor {

  public DatabaseAccessor() {
    try{
      connection = ConnectionBuilder.getConnection();            (2)
      connection.setAutoCommit(false);
```

```
      ctx = new DefaultContext(connection);
      DefaultContext.setDefaultContext(ctx);                           (3)
    } catch (Exception e){
      handleException(e);
    }
  }
  ... some source code ...
  public Product retrieveProductInfo(int prodID) {
    String description = null;
    float retailPrice = 0;
    int inventory = 0;

    Product prod = new Product();
    try {
      #sql {SELECT DESCRIPTION, RETAIL_PRICE, INVENTORY                (4)
            INTO :description, :retailPrice, :inventory
            FROM L8NITE.PRODUCT
            WHERE PRODUCT_ID = :prodID };

      prod.initialize(prodID, description, retailPrice, inventory); (5)
    } catch (SQLException ex) {
      handleException(ex);
    }
    return prod;
  }
}
```

Figure 6.12 bldsqlj usage

```
Usage: bldsqlj prog_name (requires hardcoding user ID and password)
       bldsqlj prog_name userid password
       bldsqlj prog_name userid password server_name
       bldsqlj prog_name userid password server_name port_number
       bldsqlj prog_name userid password server_name port_number db_name

       Defaults:
         userid      = %USR%
         password    = %PSWD%
         server_name = %SERVER%
         port_number = %PORTNUM%
         db_name     = %DB%
```

6.7 Online Resources

There is a wealth of resources available online to help you develop applications using DB2. The following are a few major starting points for the latest information:

- IBM DeveloperWorks for DB2: A good site to find postings from other DB2 developers as well as information on tools and fix packs.
  http://www-136.ibm.com/developerworks/db2/
- IBM DB2 Universal Database V8 Application Development.
  http://www-306.ibm.com/software/data/db2/udb/ad/v8/java/
- DB2 Information Center: Online DB2 documentation.
  http://www-306.ibm.com/cgi-bin/db2www/data/db2/udb/winos2unix/support/v8infocenter.d2w/report?target=mainFrame&fn=c0008880.htm
- Sun Java Developer, JDBC download site: JDBC API documentation available for download.
  http://java.sun.com/products/jdbc/download.html

6.8 Summary

The focus of this chapter is writing a Java application that uses a DB2 database as its data source. We covered the various types of JDBC drivers currently available and explained how you can choose the one that is right for your application. We looked briefly at designing a GUI application so that it can be easily upgraded and maintained. Through the sample code and some of the exercises, you have built an application to serve as a point-of-sale terminal for a convenience store using JDBC to provide database connectivity. We also discussed implementing the same capability using SQLJ.

6.9 Exercises

1. For the L8NITE convenience store, create a method called returnPurchases to process customers' returns using JDBC. The method is as follows:

```
public void returnPurchases(PurchaseTableModel dataModel,
                            CustomerInformation customer)
```

   where dataModel is the TableModel from the list of puchases table and customer is the CustomerInformation representing the customer account to credit. (For cash returns, set customer to null.)

2. Implement the createCustomer method using SQLJ.

CHAPTER 7

Maximizing Concurrency

In this chapter, you will learn:

- What a transaction is
- How to design transactions for better concurrency
- How DB2 manages concurrent access to data
- How to provide better, more consistent end-user experiences

7.1 Introduction

At this point, you should have created a working DB2 application from scratch using either Visual Basic .NET or Java. You are currently the only user of this application. Although the application functions properly with reasonable performance in a single-user environment, characteristics of the application may change when you promote your application to a multi-user environment. *Concurrency*—the ability for multiple users to read and modify data in the same database—is the focus of this chapter.

DB2 was designed from the ground up as a multiuser database system. The key benefit of using databases as opposed to simple flat files for applications, after all, is to provide an organized and efficient data store to be shared among many users. Moreover, the access to this data store must be coordinated properly and transparently using a mechanism to ensure data integrity. For example, without coordinated access to data, two applications may try to update the same row at the same time. Although coordinated access is provided transparently regardless of how your application is designed, there are still general rules that you should adhere to for the highest degree of concurrency.

When you design interactive applications, it is important to understand how transaction design can impact the end-user experience. Poorly designed transactions, for example, may result in applications that run perfectly fine for a single user but crawl or hang in multiuser environments. DB2 has features that allow you to ensure more positive and consistent user experiences.

7.2 Transactions

A *transaction* is a sequence of one or more SQL statements that must complete in its entirety or not at all. It is also referred to as a *unit of work* (UOW).

The application issues each SQL statement of the transaction one after another. Upon completion of the entire set, the application requests a COMMIT from the database. If DB2 can guarantee that the changes to the database have been written to disk, DB2 responds with a success code.

Under normal circumstances, transactions should always commit—but it isn't always desired or possible. The application may start a transaction but enounter an unexpected condition or event such that changes to the data should be undone. A ROLLBACK statement can be used to undo changes made to a database since the start of the transaction. A transaction interrupted by a system failure will also be rolled back so that the database returns to a consistent state.

Lets consider an example. Banks use transactions for almost everything they do. The great bulk of bank operations is the transfer of funds from one account to another. For example, if you wanted to transfer $100 from your checking account to your savings account, the transaction could be described as follows:

- Debit $100 from checking account.
- Credit $100 to savings account.
- COMMIT.

You can see why such an operation should be performed as a single unit of work. Both the debit and the credit operation must complete successfully or not at all. If a power failure occurred after $100 was deducted but before the credit operation, $100 would have suddenly disappeared from the monetary system—at your expense.

In DB2 a new transaction begins with the first SQL statement after connection or the COMMIT or ROLLBACK of a previous transaction. Most application interfaces also provide an ability to run in auto-commit mode—that is, a COMMIT is automatically issued by the application interface driver after each database operation.

How DB2 Handles Transactions

Transaction information is kept in a set of files that DB2 maintains called the *transaction log*. Whenever changes occur in a database, information is recorded in the log files so that DB2 can undo the changes if necessary. The location of the transaction log is defined in the database configuration file. In this chapter, we will focus on the three main SQL statements that cause logging of data: INSERT, UPDATE, and DELETE.

When you INSERT a row into a table, DB2 must keep a record of the row data in the transaction log. If you have any indexes on that table, additional information related to the index changes must also be logged.

When you UPDATE an existing row in a table, DB2 must keep a record of both the old values and the new values of the row. Of course, if you update only a single column of a row, only the old and new value of the column are logged. Special techniques are used to minimize the number of bytes required to represent changed data. If you have any indexes on the changed column, additional information related to the index must also be logged.

When you DELETE an existing row in a table, DB2 must keep a record of the entire row that was deleted. If you have any indexes on the table, additional information related to the indexes must also be logged.

7.3 DB2's Concurrency Model

DB2 can be thought of as a data storage service that provides coordinated access to shared data. To do this, DB2 automatically applies a locking scheme based on your application's requirements to ensure that applications do not read data at the *wrong time*. The wrong time can be defined in two ways: from an operational perspective and from a business logic perspective.

For example, if you were in the middle of loading new data into a table using the LOAD utility (discussed in Chapter 9, Working with Data) and an application wanted to query the same table, DB2 would not allow an application to see the new data until the operation was complete, because it would be the wrong time.

When you're using electronic bill payment, it is theoretically possible that the bill payment transaction would read the balance of your bank account at the wrong time—for example, right in the middle of your other transactions. By using internal locking mechanisms, DB2 can ensure that data is read only at the *right time*.

A discussion of the full breadth of DB2's internal locking mechanisms can get quite drawn out and complex. If you are interested in a full discussion of the topic, see the *DB2 Administration Guide*. Essentially, locks are acquired as needed to support a transaction and are released when the transaction commits or rolls back. For most people, it is sufficient to understand conceptually that

- Locks can be acquired on individual tables and rows
- Locks are acquired on behalf of applications automatically as transactions are executed
- *Share locks* (S locks) are acquired on rows when an application wishes to prevent others from updating (but not to prevent them from reading) the same row
- *Exclusive locks* (X locks) are acquired on rows to indicate to other applications that the row is being updated, deleted, or is a new row

The Four Concurrent Situations

There is no absolute right and wrong time to read data. The concurrency needs of one application may differ from those of another. Even within an application, transactions may have different concurrency needs. In a multiuser environment, there are four concurrent situations that might occur:

- Lost update
- Uncommitted read
- Nonrepeatable read
- Phantom read

Each concurrent situation can be illustrated using two applications—App1 and App2—which share data in the same database. DB2 provides a solution for each of these situations. Before we discuss the solutions, you first must understand the concurrent situations.

Lost Update

A lost update situation occurs when the following occur:

- App1 updates a row of the table.
- App2 updates the same row of the table.
- App1 commits.
- App2 commits.

In this situation, the update performed by App1 is lost. In any reliable data management system, this certainly should never be allowed.

For example, an airline seat is free and App1 assigns it to Donald. At the same moment, App2 finds the same seat and assigns it to Paul. App1 commits and thinks that the seat has been confirmed for Donald when in fact Paul has it. Donald arrives at the airport but is left frustrated at the gate. By locking updated rows exclusively, DB2 never allows lost updates.

Uncommitted Read

- App1 updates a row.
- App2 reads the new value from the same row.
- App1 issues a ROLLBACK.

In this situation, App2 performed what is commonly known as a *dirty read* (a row that has been changed but not committed). The danger of performing dirty reads is that the row may become invalid if the transaction that modified the data performs a rollback, as illustrated here. App1's rollback invalidates the data read by App2. Dirty reads are sometimes useful, however, for improving concurrency (and hence performance) when the risk of reading dirty data is manageable and acceptable.

For example, App1 books the last available airline seat on behalf of Paul, but the transaction has not yet committed because Paul is a very indecisive person. At the same time, Donald urgently needs a seat but App2 has indicated to him that no seats are available, and he gives up. Soon after, Paul decides not to take the seat, and App1 performs a ROLLBACK. Had the transaction been designed differently, Donald might not have missed out.

Nonrepeatable Read

- App1 opens a cursor for a query and fetches all the rows.
- App2 modifies a row that also qualifies for App1's query, and App2 commits.
- App1 closes and reopens the cursor.

In this situation, one must ask whether App1's business logic requires that the results of the second query return the same results as the first. It may or may not be; it depends on business requirements. When needed, DB2 has mechanisms to prohibit App2 from changing rows required by App1 so that repeatable reads are possible.

For example, Donald uses App1 to check for available airline seats and finds exactly one available. At that very moment, Paul books the same seat. Donald tries to book the seat, but the application tells him the seat is no longer available. This situation could have been prevented if the seat were somehow held at the moment it was selected by the application.

Phantom Read

- App1 opens a cursor for a query and fetches all the rows.
- App2 inserts a new row into a table that qualifies for App1's cursor, and App2 commits.
- App1 opens the same cursor again.

As in the nonrepeatable read situation, one must ask whether App1's business logic requires that the second query return the same results as the first. Because of App2's INSERT, a *phantom row,* which was not there the first time, will appear the second time App1 opens the cursor. When needed, DB2 has mechanisms to prohibit App2 from adding rows that would modify the result set required by App1.

For example, Donald tries to search for available seats again. Paul, indecisive as always, has just canceled his reservation. Donald is incredibly annoyed now because the seat appears available! Donald is finally able to book a seat. In this case, the appearance of a phantom row benefits Donald.

The situations described here are not specific to DB2. They are inherent in any concurrent environment where data must be shared among multiple independent users. Now that you understand the various classes of concurrency problems, we can discuss the solutions that DB2 provides for them.

Isolation Levels

Although it may be desirable to prevent all four situations all the time, in reality it is not possible to do so without sacrificing concurrency. DB2 uses the concept of *isolation levels* to manage concurrency. Each isolation level defines which concurrent situations are prevented and which are allowed.

When an application connects, it chooses an isolation level at which to operate. The choice of isolation level has implications for the degree of concurrency that is possible. The concept of isolation levels is not specific to DB2. Depending on the technology you use, it may be referred to by another name. In Table 7.1, DB2's four isolation levels are listed in order of increasing restrictiveness. Also shown are their equivalents according to the JDBC and .NET specifications.

Table 7.1 A Comparison of Terms Used by DB2, JDBC, and .NET for Isolation Levels

DB2	JDBC	.NET
Uncommitted Read (UR)	TRANSACTION_READ_UNCOMMITTED	ReadUncommitted
Cursor Stability (CS)	TRANSACTION_READ_COMMITTED	ReadCommitted
Read Stability (RS)	TRANSACTION_REPEATABLE_READ	RepeatableRead
Repeatable Read (RR)	TRANSACTION_SERIALIZABLE	Serializable

Note: Cursor stability is the default and the most commonly used isolation level in high-concurrency environments.

A common misconception is that the isolation level is defined at the database level and that all applications must use the same isolation level. This is not true. Rather, each database connection selects its own isolation level. For example, it is possible for one application to connect using the repeatable read isolation level while another uses cursor stability. Each application has its own data integrity requirements, and the isolation level is selected to meet those requirements. The following explains each DB2 isolation level in more detail.

Uncommitted Read

The uncommitted read (UR) isolation level, sometimes referred to as dirty read, is the lowest isolation level and provides the highest degree of concurrency. An application using UR ignores most table and row locks and does not acquire any row locks when reading. If an application using this isolation level attempts to modify table data, DB2 automatically escalates its isolation level to cursor stability. UR allows three of the four concurrent situations to occur (see Table 7.2). As you can see and would expect, lost updates can never occur in DB2.

Table 7.2 Uncommitted Read Concurrent Situations

Situations Allowed	Situations Disallowed
	Lost Update
Uncommitted Read	
Nonrepeatable Read	
Phantom Rows	

Cursor Stability

The cursor stability (CS) isolation level (sometimes referred to as read-committed) is the default isolation level and provides standard row-level locking. CS is by far the most common isolation level used by applications, because it provides a good balance of data consistency and allows for high transaction concurrency.

As an application fetches rows from a cursor, a row lock is held on the current row. If the row is only being read, the lock is released after the fetch operation is complete. Any rows in the cursor that are modified or deleted are locked using an exclusive (X) lock until the transaction is completed. The exclusive lock lets other applications know that the row has been changed, and only applications using uncommitted read isolation will ignore this lock. Cursor stability allows two of the four concurrent situations to occur (see Table 7.3). Essentially, an application using cursor stability will never read uncommitted (dirty) data.

Table 7.3 Cursor Stability Concurrent Situations

Situations Allowed	Situations Disallowed
	Lost Update
	Uncommitted Read
Nonrepeatable Read	
Phantom Rows	

Read Stability

The read stability (RS) isolation level is more restrictive than CS. Rather than lock the current row being referenced by a cursor, all rows returned by a query in the same transaction are locked. An application using RS is guaranteed to be able to retrieve the same rows between two subsequent queries within the same transaction. Other applications cannot delete or modify any rows of result sets referenced. RS isolates applications from all concurrent situations except for phantom rows (see Table 7.4).

Table 7.4 Read Stability Concurrent Situations

Situations Allowed	Situations Disallowed
	Lost Update
	Uncommitted Read
	Nonrepeatable Read
Phantom Rows	

Repeatable Read

The repeatable read (RR) isolation level is the most restrictive isolation level possible. RR guarantees that the exact same data will be returned by two invocations of a given query in the same unit of work. To achieve this, locks are held on all rows that are processed to build the result set, whether or not they actually qualify for the final result set. In this way, no other applications can update, delete, or insert new rows that might affect the result. The RR isolation level isolates applications from all concurrent situations (see Table 7.5).

Table 7.5 Repeatable Read Concurrent Situations

Situations Allowed	Situations Disallowed
	Lost Update
	Uncommitted Read
	Nonrepeatable Read
	Phantom Rows

An Introduction to Visualizing Locks

It often helps to visualize how locking works under different isolation levels. The topic of locking in DB2 is vast, and a full treatment would be unnecessarily detailed for new users. The *DB2 Administration Guide—Performance* is the best place to get full details on the various locks used by DB2—when they are acquired and when they are released. However, we will introduce the topic here.

Let us start with a table called TAB1 that contains several rows of data (Figure 7.1).

Figure 7.1 Visualization of table TAB1

TAB1

	A	1
	B	2
	C	3
	D	4
	E	5
	F	6

An application (App1) connects to the database and performs an update to row C so that the new row value is (C,0). A COMMIT is not yet performed, so an exclusive lock (X) is acquired on the row for App1 (Figure 7.2).

Figure 7.2 Row C is X-locked after UPDATE until COMMIT

App1

TAB1

	A	1
	B	2
X	C	0 ~~3~~
	D	4
	E	5
	F	6

Next, a second application (App2) tries to query TAB1 to retrieve all the rows. To select all rows, a table scan is required. App2 uses the cursor stability isolation level. To fetch a row using cursor stability, a share lock must be acquired on the row to be fetched. App2 successfully fetches rows A and B. The share locks are released after the fetch is successful on each of these rows. To fetch row C, App2 must acquire a share lock on the row, but App1's existing X lock forces App2 to wait on App1 to complete its transaction (Figure 7.3).

Figure 7.3 Visualizing lock-wait

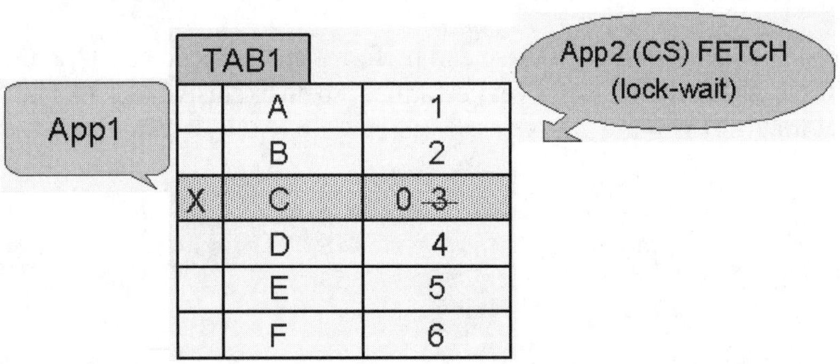

When App1 issues a COMMIT, the X lock is released, and App2 can fetch row C and its new updated value.

If App2 were instead using the uncommitted read isolation, a lock-wait would not occur because App2 would ignore the exclusive lock. Also, whether a lock-wait occurs depends on how the rows are retrieved. In this example, we demonstrated a simple case where TAB1 has no index and App2's query required that all rows be fetched. Had there been an index on the first column and App2 requested only row E, no lock contention would have occurred.

Note: The term *deadlock* is often incorrectly used to describe a lock-wait. A deadlock is a situation where two applications are in lock-wait and are waiting on each other. One application must be forced to roll back to break the deadlock. DB2 has a background process that automatically detects and resolves deadlocks by forcing one transaction to roll back.

We'll finish this discussion with one more short example. An application performs the following query:

```
SELECT * FROM TAB1 WITH RS
```

Recall that when RS is used, share locks are acquired on all rows that qualify for the result set (Figure 7.4). This prevents others from modifying the selected rows.

Figure 7.4 Share locks acquired under RS isolation

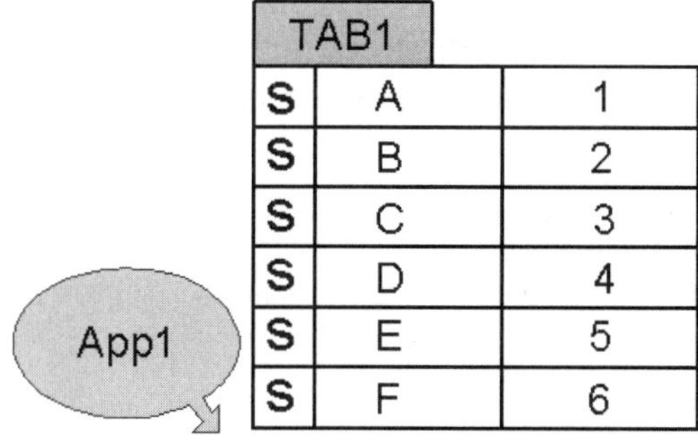

In Figure 7.4, a share lock is acquired on every row that qualifies for the result set. However, each row lock requires memory. Therefore, DB2 may decide it is more efficient to hold a single table-level share lock rather than hold one lock for each row. This is called a *lock escalation* and is controlled by two parameters in the database configuration file:

- LOCKLIST: the amount of memory, in units of 4K pages, a database can use to manage locks for all connected applications. The default value is 50 x 4K pages (200K).
- MAXLOCKS: the maximum percentage of the entire locklist a single application may use up. The default value is 22 percent.

Using the default values as an example, lock escalation will occur when a single application requires more than about 44K of memory for locks (22 percent of 200K). Lock escalations should generally be avoided in normal day-to-day operations. If you notice that lock escalation is occurring, you can simply increase the value of LOCKLIST, MAXLOCKS, or both. Setting MAXLOCKS to 100 will allow an application to consume the entire locklist before escalation, but this is not recommended.

Note: To determine if lock escalations are occurring, you can check the DB2 diagnostic log file in the C:\Program Files\SQLLIB\DB2 directory on windows, or /home/db2inst1/sqllib/db2dump directory on Linux.

Specifying Isolation Level

Isolation level can be specified either at the connection level or at the statement level. If you specify a database connection to use RS, for example, all SQL issued through that connection will use RS locking semantics.

The sample code in Figures 7.5 and 7.6 does not perform any useful tasks. It serves only to demonstrate the syntax for changing isolation levels.

Note: In DB2, the isolation level for JDBC and VB.NET remains in effect until explicitly changed and can be changed at any time. However, this may not be the case for other database vendors.

Specifying Isolation Level in Java

Figure 7.5 provides sample code for connecting to the L8NITE database followed by a series of isolation level changes.

Figure 7.5 Java code to set isolation level

```
import java.sql.*;

public class DB2Isolations {
  public static void main (String[] args) throws Exception {
    Class.forName("com.ibm.db2.jdbc.jcc.DB2Driver");
    Connection con = DriverManager.getConnection("jdbc:db2:l8nite");

    //DB2 Uncommitted Read(UR)
    con.setTransactionIsolation(Connection.TRANSACTION_READ_UNCOMMITTED);

    //DB2 Cursor Stability(CS)
    con.setTransactionIsolation(Connection.TRANSACTION_READ_COMMITTED);

    //DB2 Read Stability (RS)
    con.setTransactionIsolation(Connection.TRANSACTION_REPEATABLE_READ);

    //DB2 Repeatable Read (RR)
    con.setTransactionIsolation(Connection.TRANSACTION_SERIALIZABLE);
    con.close();
  }
}
```

Specifying Isolation Level in Visual Basic .NET

Figure 7.6 VB.NET code to set isolation level

```
Imports System
Imports System.Data
Imports IBM.Data.DB2
Imports Microsoft.VisualBasic

Public Class DB2Isolations
  Public Shared Sub Main(ByVal args() As String)
```

```
      Dim conn As DB2Connection = _
        New DB2Connection("Database=l8nite;UID=db2admin;PWD=ibmdb2")

      Dim trans As DB2Transaction
      conn.Open()

      'DB2 Uncommitted Read (UR)
      trans = conn.BeginTransaction(IsolationLevel.ReadUncommitted)
      trans.Commit()

      'DB2 CursorStability (CS)
      trans = conn.BeginTransaction(IsolationLevel.ReadCommitted)
      trans.Commit()

      'DB2 Read Stability (RS)
      trans = conn.BeginTransaction(IsolationLevel.RepeatableRead)
      trans.Commit()

      'DB2 Repeatable Read (RR)
      trans = conn.BeginTransaction(IsolationLevel.Serializable)
      trans.Commit()

    End Sub
  End Class
```

Statement-Level Isolation Level

Statement-level isolation is most commonly used when an application requires one isolation level most of the time but uses another level for a specific statement. For example, your application may use cursor stability most of the time, but a point of lock contention is known to exist when SELECT is performed on a particular table. Assuming that the functional requirement allows for reading uncommitted data, the query can be modified to use a UR isolation level so that the query can bypass any exclusive locks held by other applications.

```
SELECT * FROM T1 WHERE ….. WITH UR
```

Another example of using the WITH clause is to issue a query to get a value but ensuring that no other applications can change it while you perform some other operation.

To do this, you can use:

```
SELECT * FROM T1 WHERE ..... WITH RS
```

In general, you always want to use the lowest isolation possible to meet your business requirements. For most applications, the default level (cursor stability) will work just fine. Reporting applications that must have a steady state for a given point in time of data may require repeatable read. On the other hand, for quick report queries where the data does not have to be 100 percent correct, the uncommitted read isolation level may be all that's required. Your design may also mix both connection-level isolation with statement-level isolation.

Note: The WITH *isolation* clause cannot be used in subqueries. The WITH UR modifier applies only to read-only operations.

7.4 Transaction Design

We can now leverage our understanding of transactions and isolation levels to discuss some transaction design best practices.

There are two important rules to follow when designing transactions.

- Keep transactions as short as possible.
- Log transaction information only when required.

Short Transactions

By far the most important transaction design consideration to maximize concurrency is to keep transactions as short as possible.

For example, Hugo designs an application that performs SQL operations based on user actions. User actions cause rows to be immediately inserted, updated, or deleted. To give users a chance to undo their changes, the application does not issue a COMMIT until the user clicks a special COMMIT button. Hugo tested the application himself, and everything worked and performed well. Hugo's boss and others in the company were then instructed on how to use the new application. One day, Hugo's boss was using the application but was running late for an important lunch meeting and left without clicking the COMMIT button. Soon after, the other users complained of the application hanging. Some users even rebooted their computers, to no avail.

This story perhaps describes the worst way to design database applications: to let transactions be controlled by the user. When Hugo's boss left for lunch without committing changes, the transaction was still in progress. Modified rows of data were still locked, and that affected others' ability to share the data.

Locks are automatically acquired on behalf of applications that are performing transactions. Shorter transactions mean holding locks for shorter times. A better way to design such an application would be to track and batch the set of SQL operations required so that when the user is ready to apply the changes, the transaction starts when the user clicks a SUBMIT button and completes as quickly as it can. The user should have no control over when a transaction begins and ends.

The symptom of the application hanging was incorporated into the illustration for a very good reason. The situation encountered by the other users is called a *lock-wait*. That is, they performed operations that had to wait for locks to be released by the boss's application. Lock-waits can cause applications to hang until the lock conflict is resolved. Therefore, especially in user-interactive applications, you should ensure that transactions are designed to execute quickly.

In later sections, we will discuss other techniques and database settings that can be employed to improve the end-user experience. In Chapter 14, Troubleshooting Tools, you will learn how to detect and diagnose locking problems.

Log Transactions Only When Required

The second important rule is to log transactions only when required. For example, let's say that you wish to delete all the rows from a particular table. A novice database programmer's first inclination is probably to issue an SQL statement as follows:

```
DELETE FROM T1
```

The statement performs just fine if the table has only a few rows, or even a few thousand rows. Keep in mind, however, that all INSERT, UPDATE, and DELETE SQL statements require a database log write so that the operation is recoverable by DB2 in the event of an explicit ROLLBACK or system failure. In other words, if the table were very large, having millions of rows, the DELETE operation could take several hours or days. Even worse, DB2 could attempt the DELETE for several hours, only to run out of log space and perform a rollback of the entire operation.

In the case of purging data, we really do not care about the recoverability of the data and would therefore never issue a rollback. Furthermore, in the event of a system crash, we would not care if the data in the table were consistent. So how can we quickly purge table data without logging the transaction?

In the simplest case, you could drop the table and re-create it. However, this is often impractical because you may have indexes and other constraints defined. Re-creating them can be a hassle and error-prone. A better solution is to use the ALTER TABLE statement with the EMPTY TABLE option. For example:

```
ALTER TABLE T1 ACTIVATE NOT LOGGED INITIALLY
    WITH EMPTY TABLE
```

The ALTER TABLE ... WITH EMPTY TABLE statement activates table T1's not-logged mode and replaces the existing data with an empty table. It is a very effective way to quickly truncate a table's data if the data does not need to be recoverable.

If you want to purge only a subset of data from the table (using a WHERE clause), the DELETE statement is required, and logging must be performed. However, you can still shorten the transaction by deleting rows in groups. For example, you can repeat the following SQL statement (followed by a COMMIT) as many times as needed until all the rows have been deleted.

```
DELETE FROM ( SELECT * FROM T1 WHERE C1= ....
                FETCH FIRST 5000 ROWS ONLY )
```

Now that you know how to quickly purge data, what can you use to quickly load data? If you need to bulk-load thousands of rows, you generally have three options:

- Insert one or a few rows at a time, followed by a commit.
- Insert all rows at once, followed by a commit.
- Load data using DB2 tools.

In the first case, the insert can be performed with little impact on concurrency. The inserts would easily interleave with the database operations of others. This method, however, is the slowest of the three.

Alternatively, you can insert all rows at once, followed by a single commit. The insert statement can decrease concurrency if other applications need to access this table at the same time. As more rows are added, row locks may exceed the maximum allowed (as determined by the MAXLOCKS and LOCKLIST database parameters), and a lock escalation can occur. Moreover, if your transaction log is not defined large enough, you could run out of log space, forcing you to roll back before you can increase your transaction logs for another attempt.

Finally, you have the option of using DB2's data-loading tools. DB2 provides two tools: IMPORT and LOAD. These tools are discussed in Chapter 9, Working with Data, where we show you how to load data into the L8NITE database. These tools have features that promote concurrency during a data load and can load data from flat files very quickly without sacrificing concurrency.

7.5 Improving the User Experience

Interactive applications have some special considerations. Here, we discuss some best practices to provide more consistent user experiences.

The best practices for interactive applications are as follows:

- Set a lock timeout value.
- Do not show more data than is required.
- Optimize queries for initial result size.

Database Lock Timeout

As described earlier, transactions should be designed to minimize the duration of time that locks are held. However, even if all your transactions are fully optimized, there may still be situations when locking problems are unavoidable. Therefore, we recommend, as a best practice, to take advantage of specifying a lock-wait time limit (the maximum time that an application will wait for other applications to release their locks). Lock-wait time limits can be configured at the session level or globally for a database.

To set a lock timeout globally, modify the LOCKTIMEOUT parameter in the database configuration file (database configuration parameters are discussed further in Chapter 10, Performance Tuning) . This value is set to -1 by default, and this means that there is no timeout; that is, it allows applications to wait for locks forever. Leaving LOCKTIMEOUT at its default value may be useful for catching and identifying concurrency problems during development. But after your application is deployed to production, you'll want to set this parameter to the maximum number of seconds an application should be allowed to wait for locks (usually 30 to 120 seconds). If a lock-wait occurs and the application times out, DB2 will return an SQL0911N error with reason code 68.

In our L8NITE application, a user should wait for no longer than 60 seconds on locks for a response. To configure this, follow these steps:

Step 1: Switch to the Control Center's Advanced View.

In the Control Center, select the topmost object in the object tree (labeled "Control Center"). Then, in the object details panel, click on the Customize Control Center link.

A dialog box will appear that allows you to change the current Control Center view (Figure 7.7).

Figure 7.7 The Control Center View dialog

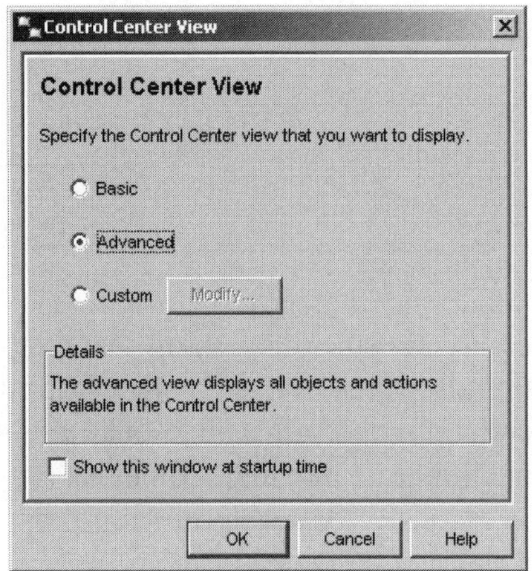

In the Control Center View dialog box, select Advanced View. Click OK.

Step 2: Open the database configuration file.

Expand the Control Center object tree to All Databases > L8NITE.

Right-click on the L8NITE database and select Configure Parameters from the pop-up menu (Figure 7.8).

Figure 7.8 Opening the database configuration file

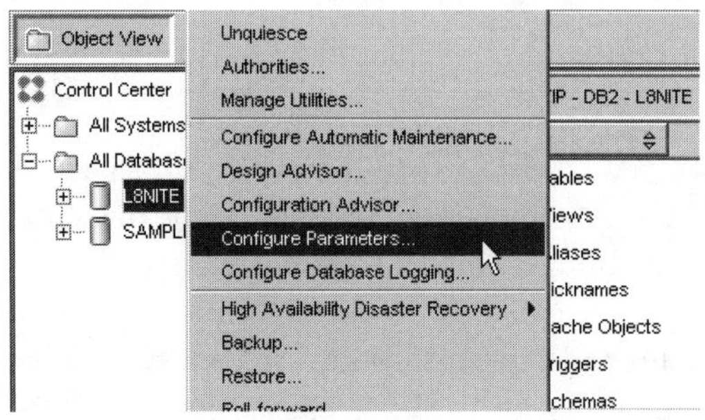

Step 3: Change the LOCKTIMEOUT parameter.

The LOCKTIMEOUT parameter is located in the Applications section of the configuration window. Click on the current value (None), and update the value to 60. Notice that the change does not happen immediately. The value 60 appears under the Pending Value column and takes effect after a database restart (Figure 7.9).

Figure 7.9 Changing the LOCKTIMEOUT database parameter

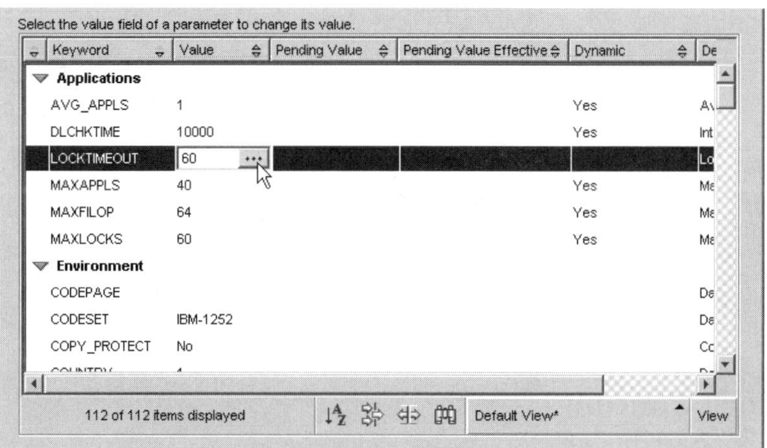

Click OK to close all dialog boxes and return to the Control Center.

Step 4: Restart the database.

Back in the Control Center, ensure that the L8NITE database is selected in the object tree.

Right-click the database and select Stop from the pop-up menu. You are then asked to confirm the database stop (Figure 7.10). Be sure to select the Disconnect all applications option. Otherwise, the database stop will fail if the database is still in use.

Figure 7.10 Stopping DB2 and disconnecting all users

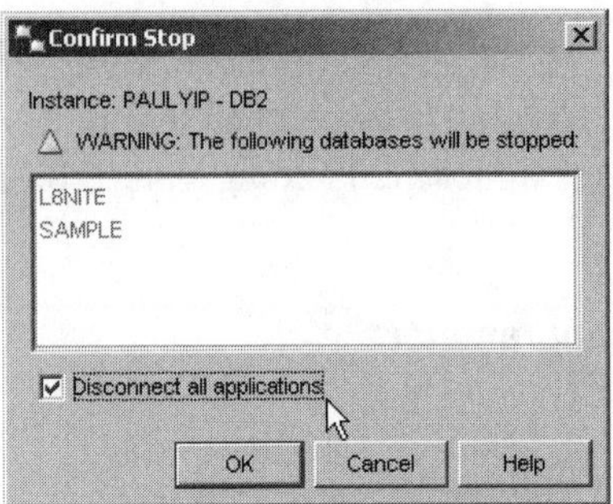

Click OK and wait for a confirmation message.

To start up DB2 again, right-click on the L8NITE database object and select Start from the pop-up menu.

You may want to switch back to the Basic view of Control Center (see Step 1).

Session-Based Lock Timeout

Every database session also has a user-settable CURRENT LOCK TIMEOUT special register. By default, it inherits its value from the database configuration parameter (DB CFG) LOCKTIMEOUT identified in the preceding section.

The SET CURRENT LOCK TIMEOUT statement changes the value of the CURRENT LOCK TIMEOUT special register. It is not under transaction control, meaning that you can set it once during a connection and the value will persist across transactions.

For example:

```
SET LOCK TIMEOUT=WAIT,     wait indefinitely for locks
SET LOCK TIMEOUT=WAIT n,   wait up to 32767 seconds for locks
SET LOCK TIMEOUT=NOT WAIT, do not wait for locks
SET LOCK TIMEOUT=NULL,     use the value in DB CFG
```

Do Not Retrieve More Data than Required

In most cases, you should not show more data than is required. It sounds simple enough but is sometimes difficult to manage.

Imagine that you are adding search functionality to your application. The user is allowed to perform any type of search, and the result can be hundreds of thousands of matches, or more.

In an ideal world, all user searches will return only the most meaningful and useful matches—those that are easily consumable by the user. However, searches that match on hundreds of thousands of rows may take a long time to complete. When a query is submitted, the application must wait for the query to complete before it returns control to the user. Therefore, long-running queries can make applications appear to hang. If your queries are inherently long running, consider executing the query under a separate thread so that it can be executed in the background, allowing the user to perform other tasks.

If a query matches more than a few dozen rows, you'll probably want to display them in a series of pages. In many cases, displaying the first page as quickly as possible is the most important for the user experience. Users do not know in advance how many matches there may ultimately be, but they want to see the best matches as quickly as possible.

Whenever you cannot anticipate how many rows will be returned by a query, it is a best practice to limit the number of rows explicitly to minimize query response time. Simply append a FETCH FIRST n ROWS ONLY clause (where n is the number of rows) at the end of any query.

```
SELECT * FROM EMPLOYEE WHERE … FETCH FIRST 100 ROWS ONLY
```

In this example, if there happen to be fewer than 100 employees, the clause has no impact on the result.

Optimize Queries for Initial Result Size

Usually, there are more ways than one to resolve a query. For example, a query may use an access plan that takes the least amount of time overall but cannot determine what the first row of the result will be until the very end. Alternatively, an index can also be used to resolve the first few rows quickly, but the overall query performance time for the rest of the result is less than optimal.

By default DB2 chooses the access plan that minimizes overall query time. For interactive applications, however, this may not be ideal. You can imagine a query that can return thousands of rows and takes a long time to complete. For the best user experience, you want to return the first few rows as quickly as possible, while DB2 continues to process the remaining rows in the background. To do this, append the OPTIMIZE FOR n ROWS clause at the end of your query. Note that this is only an indicator to DB2 and does not guarantee that such access plans for returning rows early are available.

```
SELECT * FROM T1 OPTIMIZE FOR 100 ROWS
```

You can also combine all the query clauses we have discussed in this chapter.

```
SELECT * FROM T1
FETCH FIRST 100 ROWS ONLY
OPTIMIZE FOR 100 ROWS
WITH UR
```

7.6 Summary

This chapter explained the concept of transactions and described how DB2 uses the transaction log to ensure data consistency. In any multiuser environment, concurrency problems can arise. Four concurrent situations were described, and you learned how isolation levels are used to isolate individual applications from each of them. Isolation levels can be set by an application at either a connection level or a statement level, and we showed you how to do both using Java and VB.NET code and extensions to SQL query syntax.

To maximize concurrency, you learned why it's important to design transactions so that they are kept as short as possible and to log information only when needed. Efficient transactions, along with SQL extensions and tuning of lock-wait behavior, can result in a better overall user experience.

7.7 Exercises

1. Familiarize yourself with a log-full error by running the following SQL PL code block in the DB2 Command Editor. Before you do this, change the end-of-statement delimeter to @ in the Command Editor.

```
CREATE TABLE T1 (C1 CHAR(100)) @

BEGIN ATOMIC
    WHILE (1=1)
         INSERT INTO T1 VALUES ('hello');
    END WHILE;
END@
```

2. Write two simple applications in either Java or Visual Basic .NET to demonstrate a deadlock.

   Application1:
   Connect to L8NITE and INSERT a row into the CUSTOMER table without committing.

   Application2:
   Connect to L8NITE and INSERT a row into the CUSTOMER table without committing.

   Application1:
   SELECT all rows from the CUSTOMER table. It should lock-wait on Application2.

   Application2:
   SELECT all rows from the CUSTOMER table. It will lock-wait on Application1, resulting in a deadlock.

   After about 10 seconds, DB2 should return an SQL0911N error with reason code 2. To learn how to troubleshoot deadlocks, see Chapter 14, Troubleshooting Tools.

CHAPTER 8

Working with Functions, Stored Procedures, and Triggers

In this chapter, you will learn:

- How to encapsulate application logic into user-defined functions (UDFs) and stored procedures
- How to use triggers to automatically perform business logic in the database
- How to use various tools to create triggers, UDFs, and stored procedures

8.1 Introduction

In previous chapters, we showed you how to create fundamental database objects and demonstrated how to work with them by using DB2 tools and the Java and ADO.NET application programming interfaces. In this chapter, we introduce a few other types of advanced database objects collectively known as *database application objects:* user-defined functions (UDFs), stored procedures, and triggers. Database application objects can be used to simplify your application code, improve performance, and increase code reusability and portability. We will extend the L8NITE application to demonstrate how to use these objects. If you have not created the L8NITE database, you can load the script tables.sql available from the book's Web site.

NOTE: DB2 SQL Procedural Language (DB2 SQL PL) is more powerful than what we can demonstrate in this chapter. You can find a complete discussion and lots of examples in the book, *DB2 SQL PL Essential Guide for DB2 on Linux, UNIX, Windows, i5/OS, and z/OS*; Janmohamed, Liu, Bradstock, Chong, Gao, McArthur, Yip; IBM Press; October 2004.

8.2 The DB2 Development Center

The DB2 Development Center is a graphical tool for developers and database administrators to use in creating and building UDFs and stored procedures. A comprehensive discussion of how to use the Development Center can be found in Appendix A, Development Center. In this chapter, we will use the Development Center to introduce the concept of database application objects.

Getting Started

Launch the Development Center from the Control Center's Tools menu. By default, the Development Center launchpad is loaded to guide you through creating your first object. Rather than use the launchpad (demonstrated in Appendix A, Development Center) to create an application object, here we'll show you another way to

- Create a project
- Add a connection to the project

Both steps are required before objects can be created.

Step 1: Create a project.

In the Development Center, create a new project by selecting New Project from the Project menu. Specify the name and location of the project as demonstrated in Figure 8.1. A new Project folder will appear in the Development Center object tree.

Figure 8.1 Create a project in the DB2 Development Center

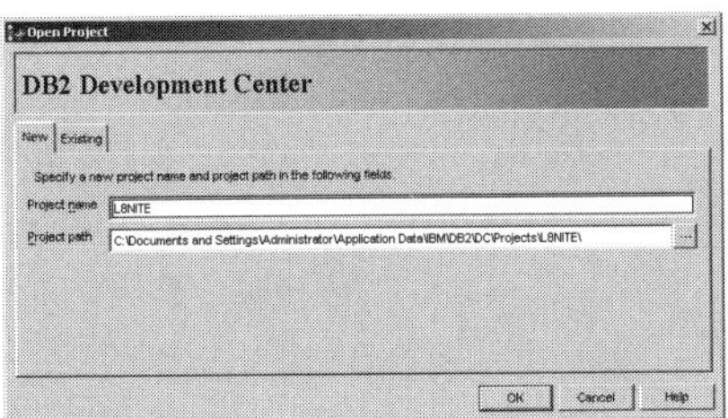

Step 2: Add a connection.

Each project requires a connection to a database. Under the Project folder just created is a Database Connections subfolder. Right-click on the Database Connections folder and select Add Connection from the pop-up menu to launch the Add Database Connection wizard.

In the first step of the wizard, select the Online connection type and click Next.

In the Connection panel, enter the database and user information as you see in Figure 8.2. Note that the user ID you specify will be used to create and manage the UDFs and stored procedures. Verify that the connection information is correct using the Test Connection button, and click Next.

Figure 8.2 Add Database Connection Wizard: Connections

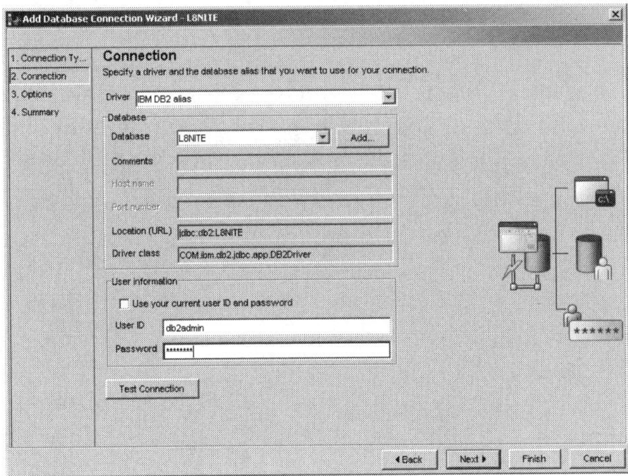

In the Options panel of the wizard, specify the schema and authorization ID options. Because all our tables are created in the L8NITE schema, enter L8NITE in the SQL Schema or SQL ID field, as illustrated in Figure 8.3. You can click Finish to add the connection, or click Next to view the connection summary before closing the wizard.

Figure 8.3 Add Database Connection wizard: Options

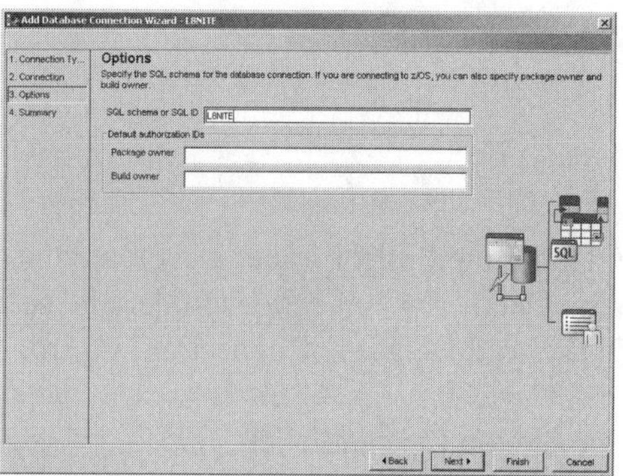

8.3 User-Defined Functions

A database function is an object that maps a set of input data values to a set of output values. For example, a function may take as input a decimal value as euros and output (return) its equivalent value in U.S. dollars.

Functions can be either built-in or user-defined. Out of the box, DB2 has many useful built-in functions to manipulate strings, dates, and data values. In Chapter 9, Working with Data, you will see some of these built-in functions, such as DIGITS, RAND, and COALESCE. Some of these functions are similar to those available in other database systems and programming languages, although their names may be different.

TIP: A list of built-in functions can be found in the online DB2 Information Center at

http://publib.boulder.ibm.com/infocenter/db2help/index.jsp

Navigate to Reference > SQL > Scalar functions.

In addition to built-in functions, DB2 supports user-defined functions that allow you to encapsulate frequently used logic to reduce the complexity of applications. You can create UDFs using SQL, C/C++, Java, CLR (Common Language Runtime), and OLE (Object Linking and Embedding). Only SQL UDFs are covered in this book.

There are four different types of functions: column, scalar, row, and table. Table 8.1 summarizes their characteristics.

Table 8.1 Four Types of DB2 Functions

Function Type	Description
Scalar functions	Take input values and return a single value. The built-in function UCASE() is an example of a scalar function that, given a string, returns the same string in uppercase form. User-defined scalar functions are supported and will be covered in this chapter.
Table functions	Return values in a table format. These functions are called in the FROM clause of a query. User-defined table functions are supported and will be covered later in this chapter.
Row functions	Return a row of data. This is a special type of function designed to disassemble a user-defined structured type into a row form. This feature is part of DB2's object-relational features, which are beyond the scope of this book. Therefore, row functions will not be discussed here.
Column functions	Operate on the values of an entire column, such as SUM() and AVG(), which return the sum and average of the values in a column, respectively. There is currently no support to build external user-defined column functions.

Creating a Basic UDF

The first SQL UDF we will create is fairly simple. It is a scalar function called tax that calculates the tax amount for a given input value.

Right-click the User-Defined Functions folder and select New > SQL User-Defined Function.

A basic template for creating a UDF is provided in an editor. Modify the code so that it appears similar to that in Figure 8.4.

Figure 8.4 Editor View of the TAX SQL UDF

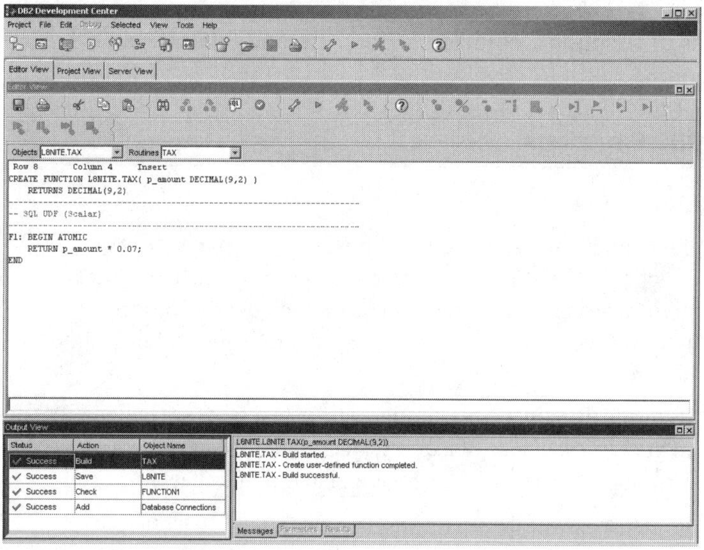

The CREATE FUNCTION statement is composed of several mandatory and optional clauses. It must start with CREATE FUNCTION, followed by the name of the function. Within the parentheses, you can specify parameters and their associated data types. In this example, we have only one parameter, called p_amount and its data type is DECIMAL(9,2). The parameter represents the total amount of a sale. The application will call this function, and the function will return the amount of tax to be applied to the sale. The RETURNS clause indicates that a scalar value of type DECIMAL(9,2) will be returned.

The function body is wrapped inside a BEGIN ATOMIC ... END SQL block. The function contains only one statement:

```
RETURN p_amount * 0.07
```

From the Development Center, you can also test the UDF by clicking the Run button. As demonstrated in Figure 8.5, a window pops up requesting the value of the input parameter, p_amount. Use a sample value such as 100, and click OK to run it.

Figure 8.5 Testing the TAX UDF

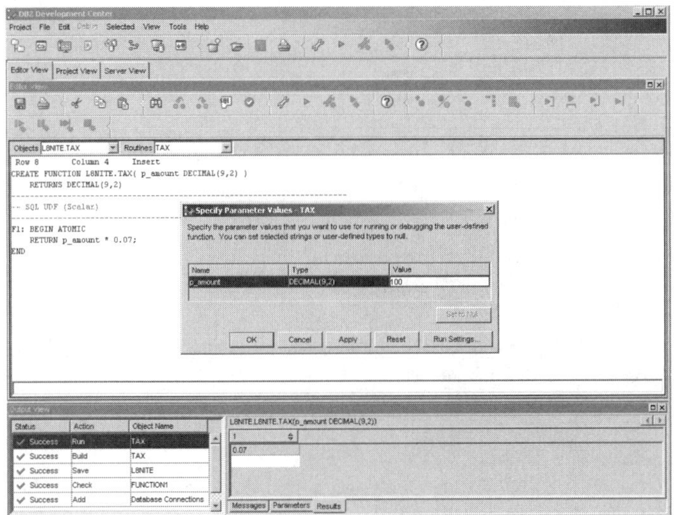

If the UDF runs successfully, you will see the result in the Output view, similar to the one shown in Figure 8.6.

Figure 8.6 Output view of the TAX UDF

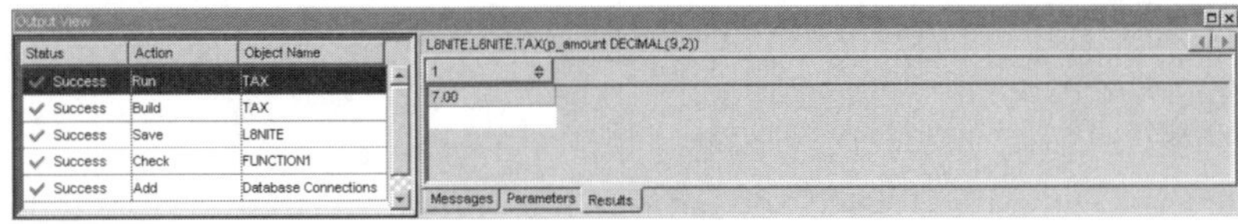

As a quick exercise, let's apply the function to our L8NITE example. Issue the following query in the Command Editor:

```
SELECT product_id, retail_price, L8NITE.TAX(retail_price) AS tax FROM product
```

You will receive the result in the Query Results tab, as illustrated in Figure 8.7.

Figure 8.7 Query result of a query with TAX UDF

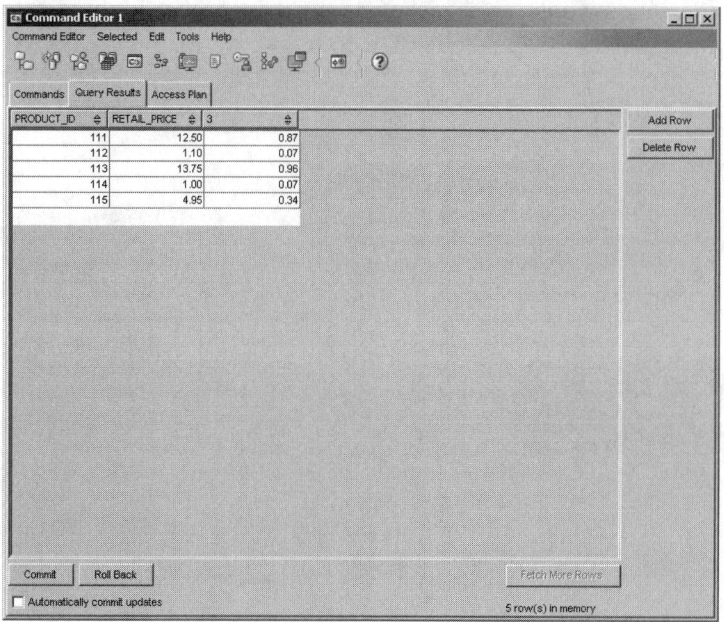

Notice that the foregoing query qualifies the TAX function. To eliminate the schema name, you can edit the DB2 CURRENT PATH, which is a DB2 special register similar to CURRENT SCHEMA discussed in Chapter 4, Database Objects. CURRENT PATH works just like the PATH environment variable except that it applies to resolving function calls within a DB2 session.

From a DB2 command line, you can obtain the current path using the following query:

```
VALUES CURRENT PATH
```

If you are connected to the database as user ID db2admin, the output will look similar to this:

```
"SYSIBM","SYSFUN","SYSPROC","DB2ADMIN"
```

As you can see, the default CURRENT PATH is a list of schemas (also known as SYSTEM PATH), followed by the schema of the connected user (or technically, the DB2 special register USER). When resolving unqualified function names, DB2 uses the CURRENT PATH register variable to resolve the function. The order of the schema names determines the order in which schemas will be searched to look for functions.

To update the current path, use the SET CURRENT PATH statement. Figure 8.8 illustrates some examples.

Figure 8.8 Display and update the CURRENT PATH special register

```
SET CURRENT PATH = CURRENT PATH,"L8NITE"                                   (1)
VALUES CURRENT PATH
----------------------------------------------------------
"SYSIBM","SYSFUN","SYSPROC","DB2ADMIN","L8NITE"
  1 record(s) selected.

SET CURRENT PATH = SYSTEM PATH, "L8NITE"                                   (2)
VALUES CURRENT PATH
----------------------------------------------------------
"SYSIBM","SYSFUN","SYSPROC","L8NITE"
  1 record(s) selected.

SET CURRENT PATH = USER, "L8NITE"                                          (3)
VALUES CURRENT PATH
----------------------------------------------------------
"DB2ADMIN","L8NITE"
  1 record(s) selected.

SET CURRENT PATH = "DB2ADMIN", "SYSIBM", "SYSFUN", "SYSPROC", "L8NITE" (4)
VALUES CURRENT PATH
----------------------------------------------------------
"DB2ADMIN","SYSIBM","SYSFUN","SYSPROC","L8NITE"
  1 record(s) selected.
```

Line (1) adds the schema L8NITE to the existing CURRENT PATH.

Line (2) resets the CURRENT PATH to the SYSTEM PATH and L8NITE schemas.

Line (3) uses another special register called USER, which contains the current user ID.

Line (4) explicitly specifies every schema name for CURRENT PATH.

Complex Scalar UDFs

Now that you have a feel for UDFs, here is a more complex example. Suppose the L8NITE application frequently calculates the profit percentage of a particular product sold over a given time period. However, the required information is spread across three tables:

- The PRODUCT_PURCHASES table has the retail price of each product.
- The cost of the product is stored in the PRODUCT table.
- The date and time of the sales transaction are stored in the SALES table.

Therefore, to determine profit for a given time period, you would have to join these three tables every time the profit percentage is needed. To simplify this task, a UDF can be written that takes as input parameters the product ID, start date, and end date of the desired period and returns the profit as a percentage.

Using the Editor view in the Development Center, let's create a UDF called PROD_PROFIT. Figure 8.9 shows the code of such a UDF.

Figure 8.9 A more complex example of a scalar UDF

```
CREATE FUNCTION L8NITE.PROD_PROFIT                                          (1)
     (p_pid INTEGER, p_sdate DATE, p_edate DATE)                            (2)
RETURNS DECIMAL(5,2)                                                        (3)
BEGIN ATOMIC                                                                (4)
   DECLARE v_retail_price DECIMAL(9,2);                                     (5)
   DECLARE v_cost DECIMAL(9,2);
   DECLARE v_err VARCHAR(70);

   SET (v_retail_price, v_cost) = (                                         (6)
         SELECT SUM(retail_price), SUM(cost)
            FROM product p, product_purchases pp, sales s
          WHERE p.product_id = pp.product_id
               AND pp.sales_transaction_id = s.sales_transaction_id
               AND p.product_id = p_pid
               AND DATE(s.transaction_timestmp) BETWEEN
                       p_sdate AND p_edate);                                (7)

   SET v_err = 'Error: product ID' || CHAR(p_pid) || ' was not found.';    (8)
   IF (v_retail_price IS NULL OR v_cost IS NULL) THEN                       (9)
       SIGNAL SQLSTATE '80000' SET MESSAGE_TEXT = v_err;
   END IF;
   RETURN (v_retail_price - v_cost) / v_cost * 100;                        (10)
END                                                                        (11)
```

(1) The function being created is called l8nite.prod_profit.

(2) prod_profit has three parameters:

- p_pid is the product ID.
- p_sdate is the beginning of the desired time period.
- p_edate is the end of the desired time period.

(3) The UDF is defined to return the profit percentage of type DECIMAL(9,2). Because this function returns a single value, it is a scalar function.

(4) In the previous UDF example, the function body was a single line. To use multiple lines of code in the UDF, you must wrap the body of the function with BEGIN ATOMIC (4) and END (11).

(5) Three variables are declared to store the retail price and the cost of the product, and for the error message if the specified product is not found.

(6) A query that joins data from PRODUCT, PRODUCT_PURCHASES, and SALES is used to determine the revenue attributed to that product and the cost of the product. The SET statement is used to store the retrieved values.

(7) Because the transaction_timestamp is stored as a TIMESTAMP in the database and because we are concerned only with a date range, the date is extracted from the timestamp by using the DATE() function so that it can be compared with the p_sdate and p_edate input parameters.

(8) Create an error message in case the product ID is not found.

(9) If the product ID does not exist, the UDF signals an error. This will terminate the execution of the function and return the error to the calling application. Note that the variable v_err was defined as VARCHAR(70). The limit for custom error text for SIGNAL SQLSTATE (used in line 9) is 70 characters. If you have a message that exceeds this limit, the message will be truncated without warning.

(10) This line calculates the profit percentage by using the variables that store the retail price and the cost of the product.

Build and run the UDF from the Development Center. Because the UDF has parameters, a window pops up requesting parameter values (Figure 8.10).

Figure 8.10 Specify parameter values for the PROD_PROFIT UDF

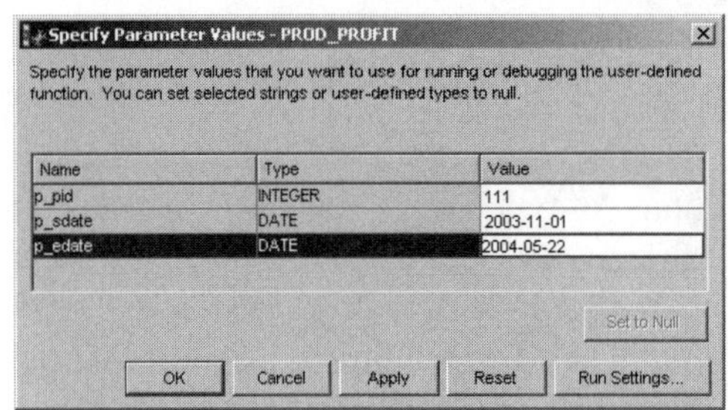

If the UDF executes successfully, you will get a result similar to that in Figure 8.11.

Figure 8.11 Output of a successful execution of the PROD_PROFIT UDF

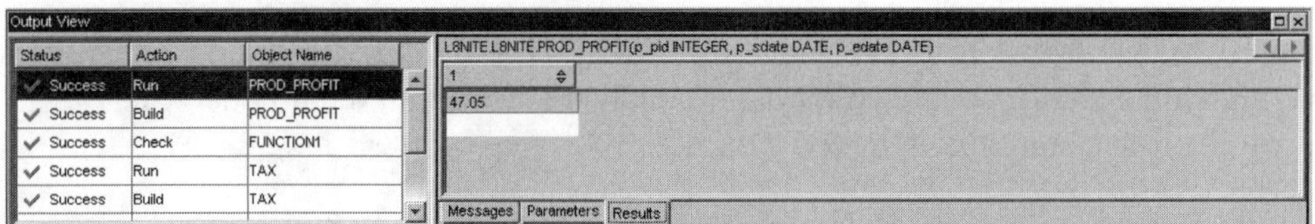

Run the UDF again, but this time enter an invalid product ID, such as 9999. The customized error message coded in the function will be signaled and captured in the Output view (Figure 8.12).

Figure 8.12 Output of the PROD_PROFIT UDF execution with an invalid product ID

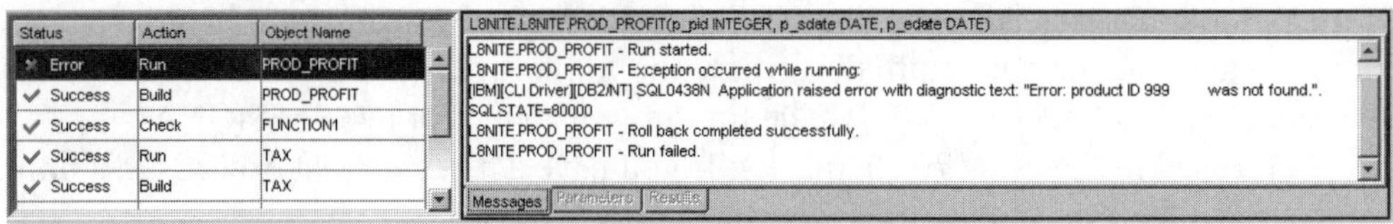

Table UDFs

Table functions return an entire table of rows and are used in the FROM clause of a query. Suppose you want to have a table function that determines all products that need to be restocked in the L8NITE store. A view could be used for this, except that the owner has a special requirement to keep a record of when the stock was checked and the staff who checked it. It is an employee responsibility, and the owner wants to make sure the employees are checking regularly. To do so, we use a new table called AUDIT_STOCKCHK (Figure 8.13). Use the Command Editor to create such a table. The CREATE TABLE statement is as simple as the following.

```
CREATE TABLE audit_stockchk (staff VARCHAR(50), checktime TIMESTAMP )
```

You are now ready to create the sample table SQL UDF. From the Development Center, right-click the User-Defined Functions folder and select New > SQL User-Defined Function.

Figure 8.13 An example of a table UDF: STOCKCHK

```
CREATE FUNCTION L8NITE.STOCKCHK( )                                     (1)
    RETURNS TABLE ( product_id INTEGER                                 (2)
                             , description VARCHAR(40)
                             , inventory INTEGER
                             , minimum_inventory INTEGER )
    MODIFIES SQL DATA                                                  (3)
------------------------------------------------------------------
-- SQL UDF (Table)
------------------------------------------------------------------
F1: BEGIN ATOMIC

    INSERT INTO audit_stockchk VALUES (USER, CURRENT TIMESTAMP);       (4)

    RETURN
        SELECT product_id, description, inventory, minimum_inventory
         FROM product
        WHERE inventory < minimum_inventory;

END
```

(1) The table UDF is called STOCKCHK and has no parameters.

(2) The RETURNS clause of the table functions specifies all the columns and their types for the table structure to be returned.

(3) Table UDFs by default can execute only queries. Specifying the MODIFIES SQL DATA option allows the use of INSERT, UPDATE, and DELETE statements within table functions. However, MODIFIES SQL DATA is not allowed in scalar UDFs.

(4) To keep track of who checked the stock and when, the function inserts a record in the AUDIT_STOCKCHK table. The USER and CURRENT TIMESTAMP special registers provide the value of the current user ID connected to the database and the current timestamp, respectively.

After the UDF has been created, test the function using the Run button in the Development Center.

Invoking a table UDF is slightly different from invoking a scalar UDF. You must cast the result of the table UDF to a table type by using the keyword TABLE. Furthermore, you must use a *correlation name* for the table returned by the table function (Figure 8.14).

Figure 8.14 Using the STOCKCHK table function in a query

```
SELECT * FROM TABLE (STOCKCHK( )) AS stockCheck

PRODUCT_ID  DESCRIPTION  INVENTORY  MINIMUM_INVENTORY
----------  ------------ ---------- -----------------
111         Beer                  0                 2
113         Diapers               1                 2
114         Chips                 3                 5

  3 record(s) selected.
```

8.4 Stored Procedures

Stored procedures are database objects that usually contain one or more SQL statements to access and modify data in the database. They are executed and managed under the control of DB2. You can write stored procedures using SQL PL, C/C++, Java, COBOL, CLR, and OLE. SQL procedures are very popular because of their simplicity. In this book, we will cover SQL stored procedures (i.e., those written in SQL) only.

There are many benefits of using SQL stored procedures. They include the following:

- Centralized business logic that promotes code reuse
- Improved security
- Improved performance

Stored procedures are stored in the database and encapsulate SQL statements and business logic. Any client application (with proper privileges) can invoke a stored procedure. In other words, stored procedures also promote code reusability. Maintenance effort is also reduced because changes can be made at the stored procedure level without the need to propagate changes to every affected application or client.

Users do not require explicit privileges to the tables or views they access through stored procedures. You just need to grant sufficient privilege to the users to invoke the stored procedures. The only way the users can access the tables or views is through the stored procedures. This is an extremely powerful method for locking down the server and keeping users from accessing information they aren't supposed to.

Finally, stored procedures keep SQL and business logic close to the database. Network traffic between the application and the database can be significantly reduced. SQL can also be precompiled for improved performance.

Preparing the L8NITE Database for Stored Procedure Development

In the next few sections, we will show you examples of what stored procedures can do. To set up the stage for the discussion, we will alter definitions of two tables in the L8NITE database.

Because Internet online purchases are getting more popular, the L8NIGHT convenience store owner wants to implement a Web site to accept online orders. Assume that a Web-based application has already been created. As the application takes online orders, it populates the SALES and PRODUCT_PURCHASES tables just like point-of-sale purchases. However, to keep track of the status of the orders, an additional column is required in each of the two tables.

Add a column called ORDER_STATUS to the SALES table. The ORDER_STATUS column is used to keep track of the status of orders. A check constraint is defined to make sure that only the letters *N*, *C*, *P*, and *I* are used to represent certain statuses:

- *N* stands for new order.
- *C* stands for completed order.
- *P* stands for order partially filled.
- *I* stands for incomplete customer profile.

Similarly, the column STATUS is added to the PRODUCT_PURCHASES table and is used to keep track of the status of the ordered products. A check constraint is defined to make sure that only the letters *N*, *C*, and *O* are used to represent its unique status.

- *N* stands for new order.
- *C* stands for completed order.
- *O* stands for out of stock.

To add a column to a table, you issue the ALTER TABLE statement. Scripts can be found on the book's Web site (L8NITECh8.sql). Alternatively, launch the Control Center. Right-click on the table you want to alter, and select Alter (Figure 8.15).

Figure 8.15 Altering a table using the Control Center

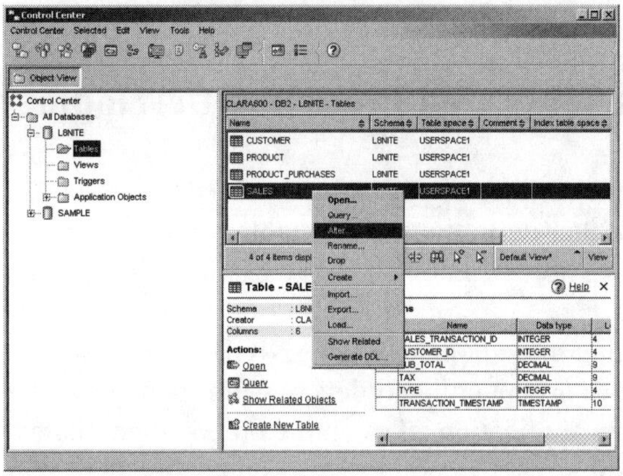

From the ALTER Table dialog box, click Add to add a new column. As you can see in Figure 8.16, the Add Column dialog box is launched, and here you can customize the column definition.

Figure 8.16 Adding a column to the SALES table

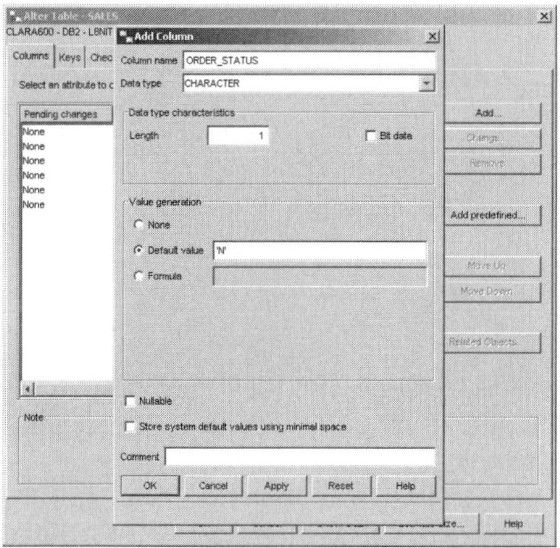

Enter the following information in the Add Column dialog box to indicate that the column order_status is of the CHAR(1) data type. It has a default value of 'N'.

- Column name: ORDER_STATUS
- Data type: CHARACTER
- Length: 1
- Default value: 'N'

Click OK to confirm the definition of the new column. Next, we need to define the check constraint so that only certain values are allowed in the order_status column. In the Alter Table dialog box, there is a Check Constraints tab. From the tab, click Add. This brings up the Add Check Constraint dialog box, as shown in Figure 8.17.

Figure 8.17 Adding a check constraint to the SALES table

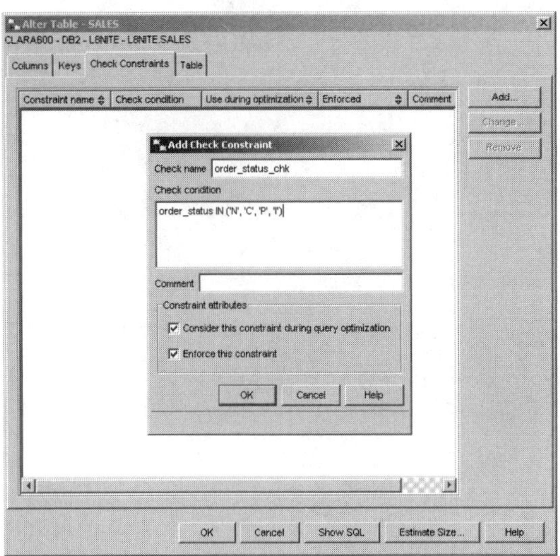

In this dialog box, enter the following information:

- Constraint name: ORDER_STATUS_CHK
- Check condition: ORDER_STATUS IN ('N', 'C', 'P', 'I')

Click OK to complete the operation. Perform the same steps for the PRODUCT_PURCHASES table, but with the following column and check constraint definitions:

- Column name: STATUS
- Data type: CHARACTER
- Length: 1
- Default value: 'N'
- Constraint name: status_chk
- Check condition: status IN ('N', 'C', 'O')

Before you start to create the stored procedures described in the next section, let's populate the tables with useful data to use the new columns we just added to the table. Use the Command Editor to execute the script l8niteCh8_data.sql which is available from the book's Web site.

Creating a Simple Stored Procedure

Assume that we want to create a new task in the L8NITE application to obtain a list of new orders and the customers who placed the orders. Using the Development Center, let's use the code presented in Figure 8.18 to introduce the structure of a stored procedure.

Figure 8.18 An example of a simple stored procedure

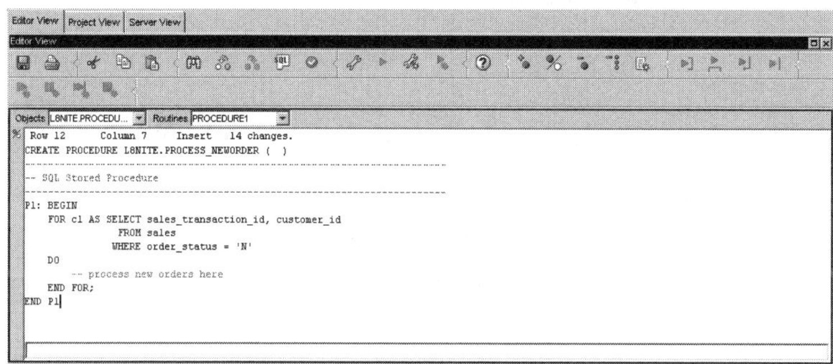

The procedure PROCESS_NEWORDER is defined with an empty parameter list. The procedure body is implemented inside the BEGIN and END block. In the body, a FOR loop is defined to process the result of the query:

```
SELECT sales_transaction_id, customer_id
   FROM sales
 WHERE order_status = 'N'
```

Inside the FOR loop, you can implement some logic to process the new orders (this will be demonstrated in the next section).

Build the PROCESS_NEWORDER procedure in the Development Center. Make sure that it is successfully built before proceeding to the next section.

Unleashing the Power of Stored Procedures

You have just seen how to create a simple stored procedure. In the preceding example, the procedure body is actually too simple. In fact, it is costly to make a stored procedure call to execute only a single query. In this section, we will expand on the example and show you how to unleash the power of stored procedures.

Let's return to the online order example. The L8NITE store owner wants to also process orders received from the new Web application. Because the previous version of the process_neworder procedure already retrieves all the new orders, we can use the same logic to loop through the result. For each order, the following is performed:

- Information for the customer who ordered the product is validated.
- If the customer's address or credit card information is incomplete or missing, the order will not be processed.
- Orders with valid information will then go through the rest of the processing.

Figure 8.19 presents the modified PROCESS_NEWORDER stored procedure code.

Figure 8.19 Modified PROCESS_NEWORDER stored procedure

```
CREATE PROCEDURE L8NITE.PROCESS_NEWORDER ()
------------------------------------------------------------------------
-- SQL Stored Procedure
------------------------------------------------------------------------
P1: BEGIN
  -- Declare variables
  DECLARE v_orderNo, v_custId INTEGER;
  DECLARE v_creditCard CHAR(16);
  DECLARE v_expiryDate CHAR(4);
  DECLARE v_address VARCHAR(300);
  DECLARE v_err VARCHAR(70);

  FOR c1 AS SELECT sales_transaction_id, customer_id                   (1)
              FROM sales
             WHERE order_status = 'N'
  DO
    SELECT credit_card, expiry_date, address                           (2)
      INTO v_creditCard, v_expiryDate, v_address
      FROM customer
     WHERE customer_id = v_custId;

    IF (v_creditCard IS NULL AND v_expiryDate IS NULL) OR
       (v_address IS NULL) THEN                                        (3)
      SET v_err =
        'The customer information is not complete to process the order no ' ||
         CHAR(v_orderNo);
      SIGNAL SQLSTATE'80000' SET MESSAGE_TEXT = v_err;                 (4)
```

```
        END IF;

        -- Call another stored procedure to process the valid orders
              CALL L8NITE.FILLORDER(v_orderNo, v_custId);                (5)
           END FOR;
    END P1
```

The procedure starts with the variable declaration section. No default values are assigned to the variables, and hence they are all initialized to NULL.

As in the previous example, a FOR loop is defined to process the result of a query (1). It obtains a list of orders with a status of N. Column values of order_no and customer_id are stored in the local variables v_orderNo and v_custId (2).

As the FOR statement loops through the result set, it checks whether the credit card and address information are complete (3).

If any of the required information is not complete, an SQLSTATE 80000 error is signaled (4). Otherwise, the procedure will process the order (5).

DB2 supports the nesting of SQL procedures. In the example presented here, this concept was introduced. At line (5), a CALL statement is made to the FILLORDER stored procedure. It further processes the order, creates a sales transaction, updates the product inventory, and so on.

Calling Stored Procedures from a VB.NET Application

Making stored procedure calls from a VB.NET application is very similar to executing an SQL CALL statement. Code snippets will be presented in this section. For detailed discussions of classes and methods used, refer to Chapter 5, Visual Basic .NET Application Development.

Figure 8.20 VB.NET code that calls stored procedure PROCESS_NEWORDER

```
Try
     ' Create a DB2Command to run the stored procedure PROCESS_NEWORDER
     Dim procName As String = "PROCESS_NEWORDER"
     Dim cmd As DB2Command = conn.CreateCommand()                        (1)
     cmd.CommandType = CommandType.StoredProcedure                       (2)
```

```
        cmd.CommandText = procName                                        (3)

        ' If input and output parameters are used, register them for the DB2Command
        ' parm = cmd.Parameters.Add("p_staffId", DB2Type.VarChar)         (4)
        ' parm.Direction = ParameterDirection.Input
        ' parm.Value = staffId
        ' parm = cmd.Parameters.Add("p_msg", DB2Type.VarChar)             (5)
        ' parm.Direction = ParameterDirection.Output

        ' Call the stored procedure
        Dim reader As DB2DataReader = cmd.ExecuteReader()                 (6)

        Catch myException As DB2Exception
        DB2ExceptionHandler(myException)
    Catch
        UnhandledExceptionHandler()
    End Try
```

Based on the definition of the procedure PROCESS_NEWORDER created in the preceding section, Figure 8.20 shows how to call such a procedure. As with any normal SQL statement, the stored procedure is called using the DB2Command class. A DB2Command object is created in line (1). To identify this command object as a stored procedure call, the CommandType must be set as CommandType.StoredProcedure, as shown in line (2). Line (3) specifies the name of the stored procedure.

For each input and output parameter, the associated data type, the value (if it is an input parameter), and the parameter direction must be provided. Lines (4) and (5) illustrate the methods and properties used to accomplish this.

A couple of options are possible in executing a stored procedure. You use the DataReader object and the ExecuteReader method if result sets are returned from the stored procedure. If the stored procedure returns only a single value, you can choose to use the ExecuteNonQuery method instead.

Calling Stored Procedures from a Java Application

To call a stored procedure from a Java application, you use the CallableStatement class. After a CallableStatement is prepared as shown in line (1) of Figure 8.21, you can execute it with the execute() method at line (2).

Figure 8.21 Java code snippet that calls stored procedure process_neworder

```
try {
            // Connect to L8NITE database
            String url = "jdbc:db2:l8nite";
            con = DriverManager.getConnection(url);

            CallableStatement cs = con.prepareCall("CALL process_neworder()");  (1)
            cs.execute();                                                        (2)
            con.close ();

} catch (Exception e) {
            /* code to handle exception */
```

8.5 Triggers

Triggers are database objects associated with a table to define operations that should occur automatically upon an INSERT, UPDATE, or DELETE operation on that table. Operations that cause triggers to be invoked are called *triggering* SQL statements. You can choose to have a trigger activated before or after a triggering SQL statement executes. There are basically three types of triggers, and they are summarized in Table 8.2.

Table 8.2 Three Types of Triggers in DB2

Trigger Types	Description
BEFORE trigger	Trigger is activated before any table data is affected by the triggering SQL statement. A BEFORE trigger is always defined in a way that operations performed by this trigger cannot activate other triggers in the database.
AFTER trigger	Trigger is activated after the triggering SQL statement has executed to successful completion. Depending on the trigger action, an AFTER trigger may cause other triggers to be invoked. DB2 allows this cascade effect for a maximum of 16 levels.
INSTEAD OF trigger	Trigger is defined on database views rather than tables. Instead of executing the trigger event against the subject view, the triggered actions defined in the trigger are executed. They are useful, particularly in cases when the view is too complex to support update operations natively. Masking SQL statements in INSTEAD OF triggers can also simplify application interfaces.

Triggers are particularly useful when certain business rules should always be enforced across applications. These rules may exist because data in one table is related to data in other tables. If there is ever a change in the rules, you need only change the trigger definitions at the database, and all applications will follow the new rules without any additional changes required.

A very good example of such a rule was demonstrated in the L8NITE application. Recall that when the cashier scans and adds a product at customer checkout, the product information is inserted into the PRODUCT_PURCHASES table. In the same transaction, the product inventory is also updated. Similarly, for a refund request, the same business rule applies. The information for the product being returned is inserted into the PRODUCT_PURCHASES table. The application updates the product inventory to reflect this change. Rather than code such logic repeatedly in different parts of the application, we can move it to a trigger, allowing the trigger action to take care of the product inventory updates.

Creating Your First Trigger Using the Control Center

Several tools are supported in DB2 for trigger creation. Using the CREATE TRIGGER command is one option. If you search the "DB2 SQL Reference Guide" for the syntax diagram of the command, it may seem fairly complex. When you understand the various options, you will find that the command is quite straightforward. Here, however, we will show you a simpler way to create triggers by using the Control Center.

In this section, we will use the L8NITE application to show you how to simplify your application by using a trigger. Consider the trigger in Figure 8.22.

Figure 8.22 Example of a trigger: UPD_PRODINV_TRIG

```
CREATE TRIGGER L8NITE.UPD_PRODINV_TRIG
    AFTER INSERT ON L8NITE.PRODUCT_PURCHASES
    REFERENCING NEW AS newrow
    FOR EACH ROW  MODE DB2SQL

BEGIN ATOMIC
    IF ( newrow.qty > 0 ) THEN
        UPDATE product
               SET inventory = inventory - newrow.qty
         WHERE product_id = newrow.product_id;
    ELSEIF ( newrow.qty < 0 ) THEN
        UPDATE product
               SET inventory = inventory + newrow.qty
         WHERE product_id = newrow.product_id;
    END IF;
END
```

The UPD_PRODINV_TRIG trigger will be activated when an insert operation is performed against the product_purchases table. If the quantity being inserted is greater than 0 (a sale transaction), the inventory will be decremented. On the other hand, if the quantity being inserted is less than 0 (a refund transaction), the inventory will be increased.

Let's now look at how to create a trigger from the Control Center. Navigate to the L8NITE database folder and right-click on the PRODUCT_PURCHASES table. Select Create > Triggers. See Figure 8.23 for a demonstration.

Figure 8.23 Create triggers using the Control Center

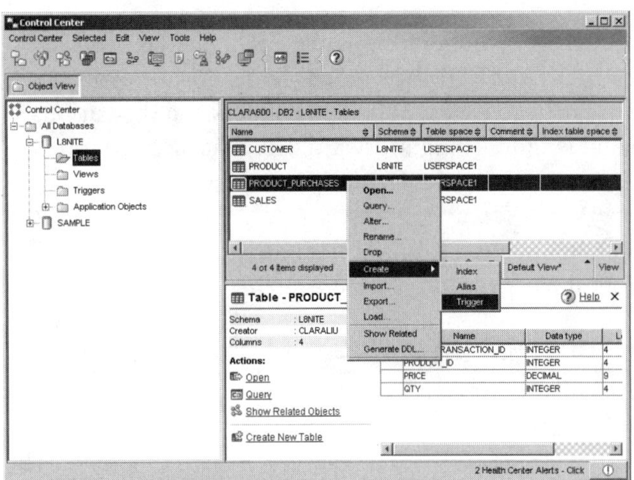

This brings up the Create Trigger dialog box, where you can specify the definition of the trigger. The window is divided into two tabs: Trigger and Triggered Action. All the options in the Trigger tab are mandatory except for the Comment entry. Let's examine each option here.

Trigger schema: Specify the schema of the trigger. In our example, choose L8NITE from the drop-down menu.

Trigger name: Specify the name of the trigger. Note that the longest trigger name allowed is 18 characters. In our example, call it UPT_PRODINV_TRIG.

Table or view schema: This should be preselected with the schema L8NITE.

Table or view name: This should be preselected with the table PRODUCT_PURCHASES.

Time to trigger action: Specify when the trigger will be activated. In our example, we will create an AFTER trigger.

Operation that causes the trigger to be executed: Specify whether the trigger will be activated because of an INSERT, a DELETE, or an UPDATE of a table, or an UPDATE of any column(s). In our example, we want the trigger to be fired on INSERTs into the PRODUCT_PURCHASES table. Therefore, select the Insert radio button.

Figure 8.24 shows the options we have chosen for the example. You can also click the Show SQL button to take a look at the CREATE TRIGGER command generated so far.

Figure 8.24 Create Trigger: Trigger tab

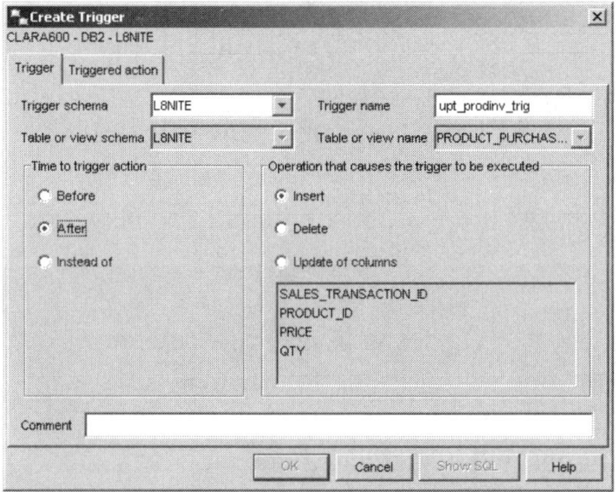

Next, go to the Triggered Action tab to specify the SQL statements and define when they will be executed.

Figure 8.25 Create Trigger: Triggered Action tab

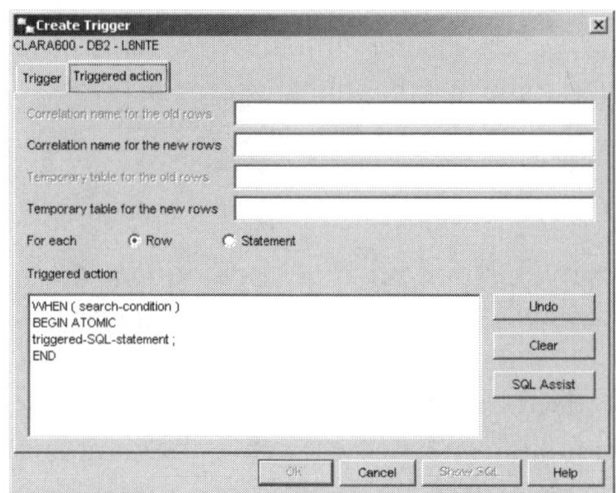

In Figure 8.25, the first few entries allow you to make a reference to the old or new rows of the data being inserted, updated, or deleted. Known as the *transition variables,* they can be used in the triggered action. Old transition variables will be populated with data from the affected rows before an insert or delete statement is executed. On the other hand, when an update or insert statement is executed and triggers a trigger, the new transition variables will contain data being updated or inserted.

Here is a summary of the rules for using transition variables:

- For triggering SQL statements that are DELETE operations, only old values are available.
- For triggering SQL statements that are INSERT operations, only new values are available.
- For triggering SQL statements that are UPDATE operations, both old and new values are available.

Because we are creating an insert trigger, only the two entries with new row references are enabled. In our example, we enter newrow as the correlation name for the new rows.

The next option lets you choose whether the trigger will be activated once for each row affected by the triggering SQL statement, or for each statement regardless of the number of rows affected. In our example we want the trigger to be activated for every row inserted into the PRODUCT_PURCHASES table. Therefore, we check the Row button.

Finally, we specify in the Triggered Action text area the SQL operations to be performed when the trigger is fired. Notice that a template of the triggered action is already provided. The optional WHEN clause defines the conditions for trigger activation. You could, for example, define the trigger to activate only if certain data is inserted into the base table of the trigger. The following example of a search condition indicates that the triggered action will be executed only if the new row data column price multiplied by qty is greater than 100.

```
WHEN ( newrow.price * newrow.qty > 100 )
```

In the L8NITE example, we want the trigger to be invoked for any insert operation performed on the product_purchase table. Hence, we will not use the WHEN condition.

As shown in Figure 8.25, the WHEN clause is followed by a dynamic atomic compound statement. It must be atomic so that the trigger will fail if any statement inside the compound block fails. When writing the triggered SQL statement, you must follow a few rules. One of them indicates that a BEFORE trigger does not allow INSERT, UPDATE, or DELETE statements in the trigger body. If you wish to perform data modification operations, you must define AFTER triggers. The other rules are not covered in this book. Refer to the "DB2 SQL Reference Guide" for more detail.

Back to our example. Figure 8.26 demonstrates that the triggered SQL statement decrements the product inventory if the quantity amount of the sales transaction is a positive number, indicating a normal sale transaction. It will increment the product inventory when the quantity is negative, indicating a refund transaction. Note that you need the semicolon (;) at the end of each triggered SQL statement.

Figure 8.26 Triggered action of the trigger UPD_PRODINV_TRIG

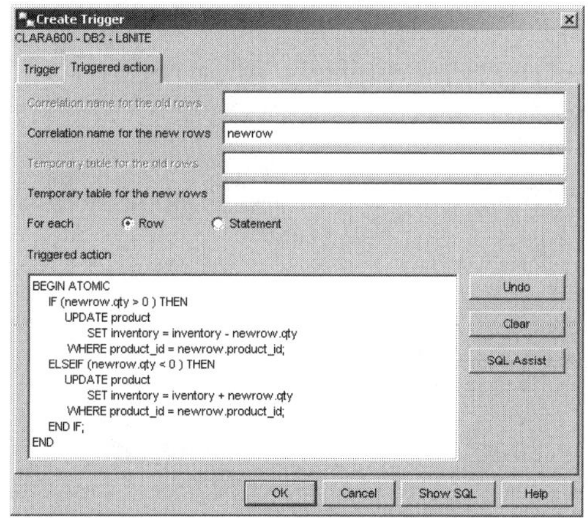

To examine the CREATE TRIGGER command generated by the tool, simply click Show SQL. See Figure 8.27 for the complete command.

Figure 8.27 Complete CREATE TRIGGER command

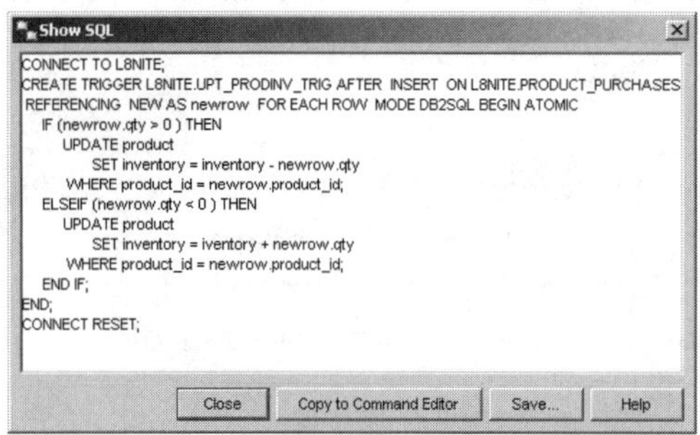

In the same window, you can also choose to copy the command to the Command Editor or save it to a file or to the Task Center. If a task is created, the trigger is created at a later scheduled time. In this example, we will create the trigger immediately. Click OK to proceed.

Note that with this trigger, you should change the VB.NET and Java L8NITE application so that the inventory update is now handled by the trigger.

Calling Stored Procedures from Triggers and UDFs

With DB2 v8.2, you can call stored procedures from triggers and UDFs. This further increases code reusability. The syntax for calling stored procedures from triggers is the same as calling stored procedures from UDFs. In this section, we will demonstrate an example of a trigger calling a stored procedure.

Refer to the stored procedure example (process_neworder) presented in Figure 8.20. Assume that we want to automate the online order processing the instant the orders are inserted into the sales table. Based on this requirement, a trigger can be used to fire on any INSERT into the SALES table. The trigger is very straightforward, and the CREATE TRIGGER statement is demonstrated in Figure 8.28. Notice that if the called stored procedure is defined with MODIFIES SQL (the default behavior), the NEW SAVEPOINT LEVEL clause must also be specified. Refer to the earlier section Unleashing the Power of SQL Stored Procedures for information about the types of SQL access stored procedures allowed.

Figure 8.28 Trigger that calls the PROCESS_NEWORDER stored procedure

```
CREATE TRIGGER tr_autoproc_order
     AFTER INSERT ON sales
     FOR EACH ROW MODE DB2SQL
     BEGIN
          CALL l8nite.process_neworder();
     END
```

8.6 Supplemental: Creating UDFs, Stored Procedures, and Triggers Using VS.NET

As introduced in Chapter 5, Visual Basic .NET Application Development, DB2 v8.2 is now also engineered with .NET support. In addition to the key feature—native DB2 for .NET data provider—described in the earlier chapter, DB2 v8.2 also extends the power of Visual Studio .NET through the DB2 administration and development add-ins. The DB2 database project template included in the add-ins lets you use scripts for developing server-side objects such as UDFs, stored procedures, triggers, tables, views, indexes, and so on. These DB2 scripts may contain DB2 data definition language (DDL) and data manipulation language (DML) SQL statements.

You can create a DB2-specific database project for your Visual Studio solution by adding a new project (Figure 8.29).

Figure 8.29 Creating a DB2 database project

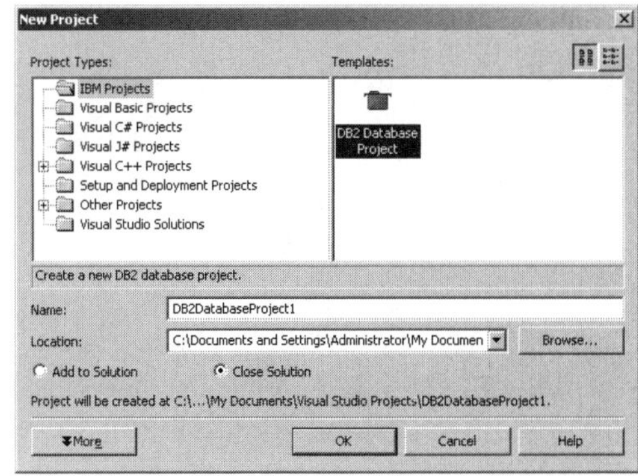

In the Solution Explorer, you will now find the DB2 project just created. Right-click on the project, and choose to add a new item (Figure 8.30). A DB2 *project item* is the general term for DB2 scripts in VS.

Figure 8.30 Adding a new DB2 project item

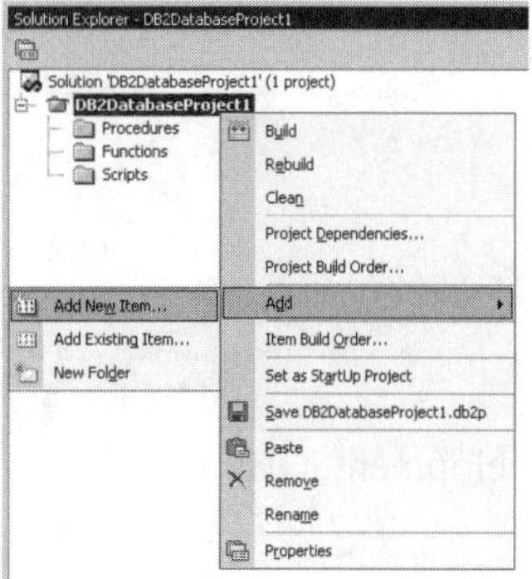

You can see that in Figure 8.31, a few templates are available for creating stored procedures, UDFs, triggers, tables, views, queries, and scripts.

Figure 8.31 DB2 project item templates

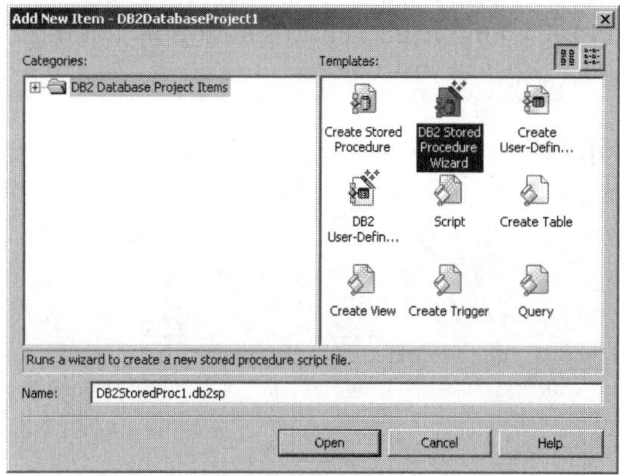

If you choose the Create Stored Procedure project item template, a default DB2 create stored procedure script file is added to your project and is shown in the editor (Figure 8.32). You can modify the script to include additional supporting DDL, such as granting access for the procedure, altering the procedure, and so on. Similarly, creation of other database objects is supported in the same way through templates.

Figure 8.32 Default stored procedure script template

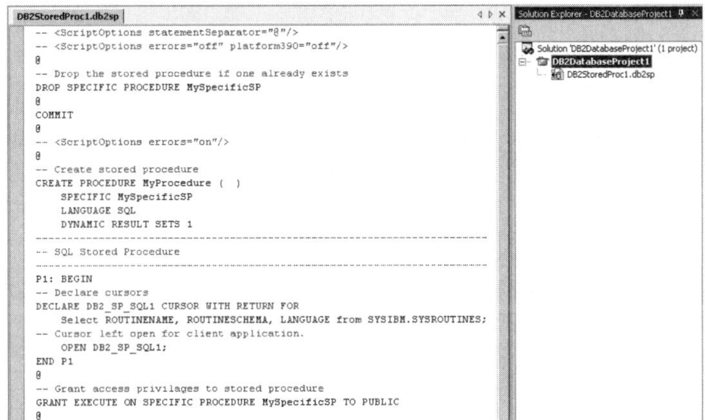

8.7 Summary

In this chapter, three types of database application objects were introduced. User-defined functions are database objects that can be used to extend and customize SQL. Using the DB2 Development Center, you can quickly create UDFs. You created two sample UDFs to calculate the tax amount on a given sale and the profit for a given period.

Stored procedures are database objects that can encapsulate application logic. In many cases, stored procedures improve performance, enhance code reusability, and tighten database security. You can write stored procedures in quite a few programming languages, but SQL stored procedures are the most popular ones. They can easily be created and tested using the Development Center. The examples presented in this chapter got you started quickly using stored procedures and demonstrated some best practices.

Triggers can be used to automatically perform some SQL operations based on the operations performed on the tables and views on which the triggers are defined. They are particularly useful for keeping related data logically synchronized to conform with the business rules. A few examples were demonstrated in the chapter.

8.8 Exercises

1. Create a scalar function to calculate the total number of refund transactions.

2. Create a stored procedure to obtain a list of products for which its inventory falls under the minimum inventory required. The list of products will be used for reordering.

3. Create a trigger to automate the reordering process. The trigger is an UPDATE trigger on the PRODUCT table. If the inventory is less than the minimum inventory, the product will be reordered.

CHAPTER 9

Working with Data

In this chapter, you will learn:

- How to create and manipulate data through the Command Editor
- How to load data using the LOAD and IMPORT utilities
- How to generate random data to populate a development database
- How to extract data from DB2 using the EXPORT utility
- How to import data from DB2 into a spreadsheet

9.1 Introduction

To facilitate application development, the data loaded into the L8NITE database in Chapter 4, Database Objects (in the exercises) contained only a few rows of data. Before deploying your application to production, you need to determine whether it will continue to perform as the database grows. In this chapter we will discuss the IMPORT and LOAD utilities, describe how they differ, and explain how they can be used to import data from flat files into tables.

For new applications, however, significant amounts of sample data do not exist in files because they never existed before. Therefore, we'll demonstrate some tricks for creating large amounts of sample data using only SQL statements.

After you have generated significant amounts of sample data, you'll probably want to unload the data into files so that they can be reused in the future. The EXPORT utility is used to extract data from a table into a text file. The generated data will serve two purposes:

- Business insight reporting
- Performance tuning

First, recall from Chapter 3, The L8NITE Database Application, that in addition to the operational requirements of the L8NITE application (supporting day-to-day transactions), there were several requirements related to business insight. We need to have sufficient data to test correctness and performance of these reports (generated by queries). You will also learn the basics of directly extracting data from DB2 databases using Microsoft Excel.

Second, performance tuning will be discussed in Chapter 10. To ensure that the database will sustain good performance as it grows, performance tuning should be conducted with a populated database to simulate a real environment.

9.2 The LOAD and IMPORT Utilities

Loading data into a DB2 database using INSERT statements for large amounts of data can be very clumsy, especially if the data are already in a structured format, such as a spreadsheet. DB2 has two tools to rapidly import data from files into DB2 tables: IMPORT and LOAD. Here is a quick summary.

- The IMPORT utility reads structured data from a file and uses SQL to insert the data into a table. Constraints are checked immediately as rows are inserted. Where triggers are defined, they will be activated.

- The LOAD utility also reads structured data, but it does not use SQL. It uses lower-level techniques to load data directly into the internal table structure. This enables LOAD to be much faster than IMPORT. Constraint checking can be deferred, and triggers are not activated. LOAD has the added capability of using a query as an input source. As you will see in the next section, this is a valuable feature for generating very large amounts of data.

Structured File Formats

The IMPORT and LOAD utilities can read the same kinds of files:

- IXF (Integrated Exchange Format): This file format was designed to enable the exchange of relational database structures and data between any systems that support this format. This data format is ideal for loading into DB2 databases. Information about column names and data types is also contained within IXF files. This file format can be created using the EXPORT utility discussed in section 9.4.

- DEL (Delimited ASCII): This is a generic format supported by most database vendors. Special characters are used to indicate the beginning and end of a column value and the end of a row. Delimited data can come from any source. You could, for example, save spreadsheet data in text-delimited format and use it to populate a table in DB2. The following is an example of text-delimited data that could be used to populate the PRODUCT table:

```
10,"beer", 1.00, 1.40, 144,24
11,"diapers",10.00,14.00,100,0
1234,"chips",0.85,1.99,144,24
144,"magazines",2.40,3.00,144,24
```

- ASC (Non-delimited ASCII): This is a generic format supported by most database vendors. Rather than have special characters denote the start and end of column data, this format uses the character position to indicate where column data begins and ends. The following is an example of ASCII positional data that could be used to populate the PRODUCT table:

```
10   beer        1.00  1.40 144 24
11   diapers    10.00 14.00 100 20
1234 chips       0.85  1.99 144 24
144  magazines  2.40   3.00 144 24
```

- WSF (Worksheet Format): Outputs a file in native Lotus 1-2-3 or Lotus Symphony format. Unless you are using these products, you likely will not use this format.

The IMPORT Utility

The IMPORT utility has many options and features. Rather than list them all here, we'll point out its more useful capabilities. For more information on IMPORT, consult the online DB2 Information Center:

> http://publib.boulder.ibm.com/infocenter/db2help/
> Navigate to Reference > Commands > DB2 Universal Database > Command Line Processor (CLP) > IMPORT.

Here are some interesting capabilities of IMPORT:

- The target table can be created automatically if the input file is an IXF file.
- New rows can be appended to the table or can be used to replace the existing contents of the target table.
- The source data can be merged with existing data. That is, the key values in the input file are compared to existing primary key values in the table. If the row being imported matches a row already in the table, the row is updated. Otherwise, the row is inserted.
- Rather than issue a COMMIT after each row is inserted, it can optionally COMMIT in groups for better performance.
- If an IMPORT operation fails midway through reading a file (usually because of improperly formatted input), data that has been committed remains in the database. When the problem is fixed, IMPORT can be resumed from the middle of the file by providing the row number of the last successfully committed row (available in the utility's log file).

Let's assume for the moment that you have some data files that could be used in the application (we've provided some on the book's Web site). In the following example, we'll demonstrate how to use the IMPORT utility.

NOTE: Because IMPORT uses SQL to insert data, the factors that most affect IMPORT performance are the size of the buffer pool used, the I/O throughput of the disk(s) used for the transaction log files, and the log buffer size (LOGBUFSIZ parameter in DB CFG). See Chapter 10, Performance Tuning, for more details.

Step 1: Launch the IMPORT utility.

From the Control Center object tree, go to Control Center > All Databases > L8NITE > Tables

Select the PRODUCT table > (right-click) Import (Figure 9.1)

Figure 9.1 Launch of the Import dialog box

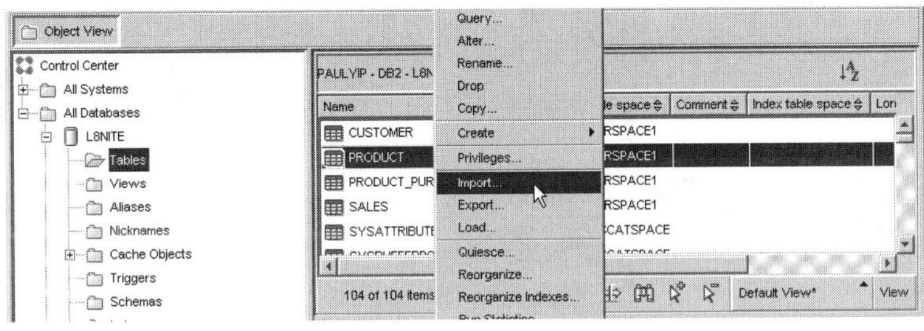

Step 2: Specify data source details.

The IMPORT utility will request the source file for your data (Figure 9.2). A file called product.del can be downloaded from the book's Web site. Specify this file in the Import File field.

A message file is optionally created by IMPORT to record messages associated with the import process. Enter a file name to be used as a message file. A common practice is to use the same name as the input file but with an .msg extension.

The file type being imported is a DEL file. For import mode, use INSERT.

Figure 9.2 The IMPORT dialog box

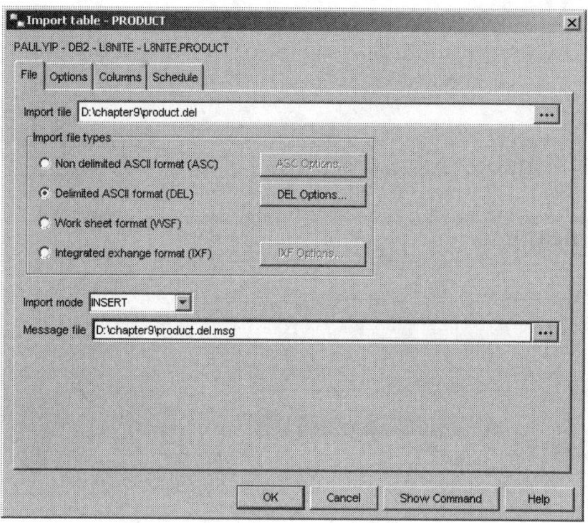

Step 3: Validate options.

File tab: Before importing any file, you should ensure that the proper delimiter options are set. The file you are about to import actually uses default delimiters:

- The character string delimiter is a double quote (").
- The column delimiter is a comma (,).
- The decimal delimiter for decimal points is a period (.).

Options tab: For larger files, it is recommended that you increase the value for Commit Frequency. (Don't be afraid to raise this value to hundreds or even thousands of rows as long as you do not run out of primary log space.) If you want to stop importing rows when warnings or errors are encountered, set Maximum Warnings to 1, which will cause IMPORT to stop immediately after the first problem is encountered. (The default of 0 means to allow warnings.)

Step 4: Start the import.

Click OK to begin the data import. When the import is complete, use the Control Center to validate that the import was successful.

Select the PRODUCT table > (right-click) Open.

Be sure to check the message file to determine whether any warnings or errors occurred. Loading from a non-delimited ASCII file has been left as an exercise.

The LOAD Utility

The LOAD utility works in three phases:

- The LOAD phase: Rows are loaded as quickly as possible without checking constraints or unique or primary key violations.
- The BUILD phase: The indexes are built. After the unique indexes are built, DB2 can efficiently determine whether primary key or unique key violations exist.
- The DELETE phase: Rows that violate primary key or unique constraints are deleted from the target table.

An additional phase, although not part of the LOAD phase, is called SET INTEGRITY. In the foregoing three phases, foreign key and check constraints are not validated. This is useful if the database is very large and you know that the data contained in the file is already "clean." The SET INTEGRITY statement has two modes: IMMEDIATE CHECKED and IMMEDIATE UNCHECKED. In the following example, you will see how this feature is used.

The LOAD utility has too many options and features to mention here (more so than IMPORT). However, we'll describe the more interesting and useful capabilities here so that you can have an idea of its capabilities. For more information on LOAD, consult the online DB2 Information Center:

> http://publib.boulder.ibm.com/infocenter/db2help/
>
> Navigate to Reference > Commands > DB2 Universal Database > Command Line Processor (CLP) > LOAD.

Here are some interesting capabilities of LOAD:

- As data is loaded, triggers will not be activated and constraint checking is deferred.
- No transaction logging occurs.
- The LOAD utility can operate online. Users can continue to have read access to data as new data is being loaded. When all the phases of LOAD have completed, the new

rows will be available to users.

- New rows can be appended to the table or can be used to replace the existing contents of the target table.
- During the DELETE phase, rows that violate unique and primary key constraints can be copied to something called an *exception table* for later analysis.

NOTE: Because LOAD uses low-level methods to populate a table, unlike IMPORT, the sizes of the buffer pool and transaction log I/O throughput do not affect its performance. The factors that affect LOAD performance most are the size of the utility heap and sort heap (UTIL_HEAP_SZ and SORTHEAP in DB CFG; see Chapter 10, Performance Tuning for more details). In fact, if LOAD performance is of primary concern, you may reallocate memory from buffer pools to the utility heap.

In the following example, we'll demonstrate how to use the LOAD utility.

Step 1: Launch the LOAD utility.

From the Control Center object tree, go to Control Center > All Databases > L8NITE > Tables

Select the PRODUCT table > (right-click) Load.

Step 2: Select append or replace mode.

The first step of the LOAD wizard is to specify whether you wish to replace the data in the existing table or append data. Select Replace Table Data.

Step 3: Specify the input file details.

For the input file type, specify IXF (Figure 9.3). A file called customers2500.ixf is available from the book's Web site. Download it and specify it here.

A message file is optionally created by LOAD to record messages associated with the LOAD process. Enter a file name to be used as a message file. A common practice is to use the same name as the input file, but with an .msg extension.

Figure 9.3 Specify input file

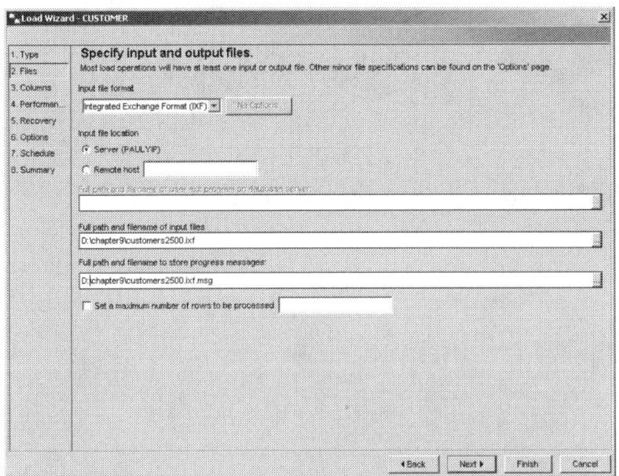

Step 4: Specify target columns.

The data in the IXF file may not align exactly with the columns in the target table. In this step, you can specify how the columns will line up. Select Map Columns Based on Column Positions Found in the File.

It is also important to note that the CUSTOMER table's customer_id column is a GENERATED ALWAYS identity column. However, the file contains explicit values for this column. To get around this, LOAD has an option called IDENTITY OVERRIDE (values in the file will override identity values normally generated by DB2). In this dialog box, specify IDENTITY OVERRIDE for Identity Column Behavior.

Step 5: Examine available LOAD options.

For steps 4 (Performance) and 5 (Recovery) of the LOAD wizard, no changes are required at this time. These are more advanced options that are explained in detail in the LOAD documentation. Skip ahead to step 6 (Options) of the wizard (Figure 9.4).

Of particular interest is the Exception table setting: Exceptions > Exception table. As mentioned earlier, during the DELETE phase, rows that violate primary or unique keys are deleted from the target table. If you specify this option, rows that are deleted are placed in the exception table specified here. However, you must create this table manually. For example, you might create it as follows:

```
CREATE TABLE L8NITE.CUSTOMER_EX LIKE L8NITE.CUSTOMER
```

Then, in the Exception Table setting, specify L8NITE.CUSTOMER_EX.

Figure 9.4 LOAD options

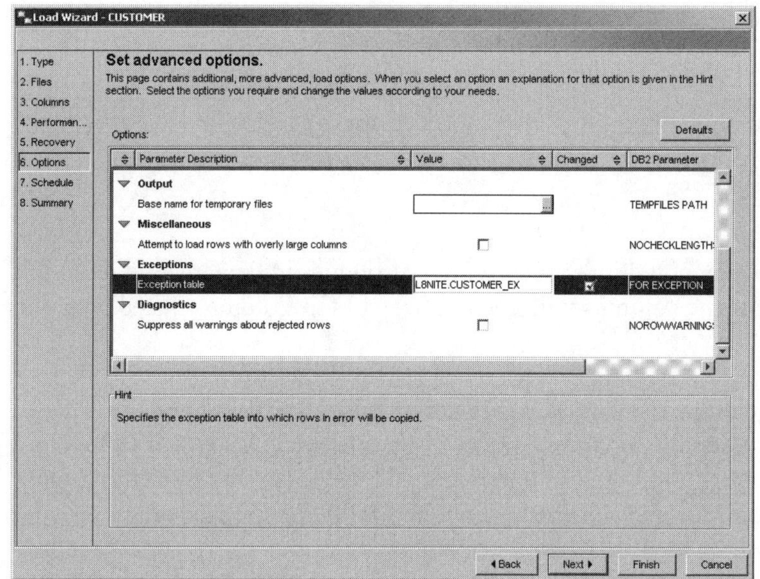

Step 6: Start LOAD.

Click Finish to begin loading data. From the Control Center, open the CUSTOMER table to validate that rows were loaded successfully into the table.

Step 7: SET INTEGRITY.

If you try to access the CUSTOMER table after the LOAD has finished, you will receive the following error:

```
SQL0668N  Operation not allowed for reason code "1"
on table "L8NITE.CUSTOMER".  SQLSTATE=57016
```

This error is returned because DB2 cannot yet determine the correctness of the data. Recall that only primary and unique keys are verified as part of the DELETE phase of LOAD. Check constraints, referential constraints, and values for generated columns are not checked, and therefore a table using any of these features is placed into *check pending state*. The customer table contains an identity column (which is a generated column) and therefore has been placed in this state. At this stage, you have three options:

- Immediately validate table data.
- Do not validate data and allow access to the table.
- Validate some subset of value types.

In the Control Center, right-click the CUSTOMER table, and select Set Integrity from the pop-up menu to launch the Set Integrity dialog box (Figure 9.5).

Figure 9.5 SET INTEGRITY dialog box

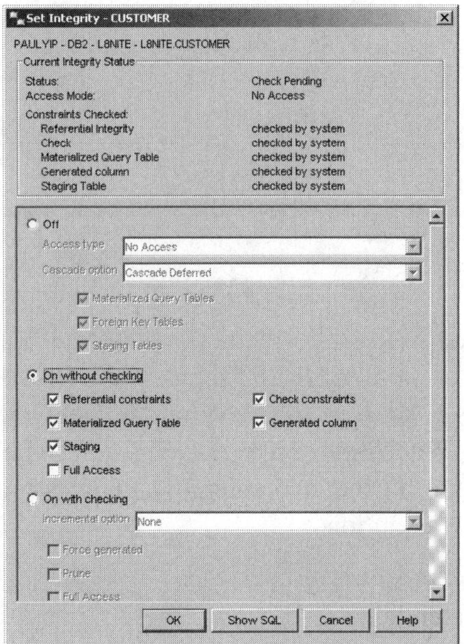

For more infomation on SET INTEGRITY, consult the online DB2 Information Center:

http://publib.boulder.ibm.com/infocenter/db2help/
Navigate to Reference > SQL > SQL Statements > SET INTEGRITY

In this case, the data is known to be good and we replaced the entire table data. Therefore, to save time, select On Without Checking.

The CUSTOMER table is now accessible, and you can validate that the data has been loaded.

9.3 Generating Sample Data

To populate the database with sample data, you must keep in mind any relationships that exist between tables. In the L8NITE example, you must populate the tables in this order:

- CUSTOMER and PRODUCT (either order)
- SALES
- PRODUCT_PURCHASES

The CUSTOMER and PRODUCT tables contain data that is used in foreign key relationships. (A sale to a customer on account cannot be completed if the customer does not exist, and a product cannot be purchased if it does not exist.)

To create sample data, it is often useful to use existing rows in other tables. Consider the following example.

Step 1: Create a basic table and populate it.

Create a table T1 with one column, c1, which holds integer values:

```
CREATE TABLE T1 (C1 INT);
```

Then populate the table by using an INSERT statement:

```
INSERT INTO T1 VALUES (1);
INSERT INTO T1 VALUES (2);
INSERT INTO T1 VALUES (3);
```

Or simply:

```
INSERT INTO T1 VALUES (1), (2),(3);
```

Step 2: Generate data.

First, validate that the rows inserted in step 1 were inserted successfully.

```
SELECT * FROM T1;

C1
-----------
          1
          2
          3

   3 record(s) selected.
```

Next, use SQL and table T1 to see the words “hello world” three times.

```
SELECT 'hello world' FROM T1;

1
-----------
hello world
hello world
hello world

      3 record(s) selected.
```

The key observation is that just because you SELECT from a table doesn’t mean you must retrieve data from it. In this case, we are simply using the fact that a table contains rows to repeat a string of characters (“hello world”) many times.

We mentioned before that every DB2 database has system catalog tables created for every database. These tables already contain many rows that can be used to help generate data, as we did in the preceeding example. The system view SYSCAT.COLUMNS is quite large by default (it has one row for every column in every table in the database, including the system catalog tables) and will be used in the following examples.

In the following examples, you will use this technique to create CUSTOMER and PRODUCT data. But before you begin, you should delete all current sample data from the tables and reset identity columns to restart at 1. This will allow better alignment of generated data with ID values. In the Command Editor, connect to the L8NITE database and execute the following commands:

```
DELETE FROM L8NITE.PRODUCT_PURCHASES;
DELETE FROM L8NITE.SALES;
DELETE FROM L8NITE.CUSTOMER;
DELETE FROM L8NITE.PRODUCT;
```

Then reset the identity column values for CUSTOMER and SALES so that they start at 1 again.

```
ALTER TABLE L8NITE.SALES ALTER COLUMN
      SALES_TRANSACTION_ID RESTART WITH 1;

ALTER TABLE L8NITE.CUSTOMER ALTER COLUMN
      CUSTOMER_ID RESTART WITH 0;
```

The CUSTOMER Table

To create sample data for the CUSTOMER table, we want to ensure that the generated data is meaningful so that we can easily differentiate one customer from another to facilitate testing. The INSERT statement in Figure 9.3 demonstrates how this can be achieved.

The INSERT statement in Figure 9.6 creates 2500 sample customers using the SYSCAT.COLUMNS table.

Figure 9.6 SQL statement to generate 2500 sample customers

```
INSERT INTO L8NITE.CUSTOMER (
    credit_card,
    expiry_date,
    lastname,
    firstname,
    address,
    zip_code)
SELECT
    right(digits (rownumber() over()-1),16),
    '0406',
    'lname' || char(row_number() over() -1),
    'fname' || char(row_number() over() -1),
    'address' || char(row_number() over() -1),
    right (digits(row_number() over() -1), 6)
FROM syscat.columns FETCH FIRST 2500 ROWS ONLY;
```

The customer_id column value is not included in the INSERT column list because customer_id is a GENERATED ALWAYS identity column (you are not allowed to provide values explicitly for it). Auto-incrementing values will be generated as the rows are inserted.

The row_number() and over() functions are used together to enumerate each row returned by the query. That is, for the first row returned, the value 1 is generated. For the second, 2 is generated, and so on. The row number calculation starts with 1 but customer IDs start with 0, so we subtract 1 from the expression. This function sequence is used to generate values for lastname, firstname, address, and zip code. For example, first names are generated as follows:

```
'fname' || char(row_number() over() -1)
```

The double bar (||) is used to concatenate character strings. row_number() and over() are converted to a character type using the char() function so that it can be concatenated with the constant fname. Therefore, first names are generated as follows:

```
fname0
fname1
fname2
fname3
... and so on...
```

Generated values for lastname and address are generated in the same way.

NOTE: Be careful when using the concatenation operator (||) because concatenating a character string with a null value (in a variable or column) will result in a null return value. This is because an unknown value (null) concatenated with anything is still considered unknown. If you are concatenating a column value that may potentially be null and want to retain nonnull values, use the COALESCE function to turn a null value into an empty string before concatenation.

```
SELECT 'string' || coalesce (col1, '') FROM T1
```

The function sequence that generates credit_card numbers and zip codes probably requires further clarification. The full expression for credit_card numbers, which is almost identical to that used for zip codes, is

```
right(digits (rownumber() over() -1),16)
```

The digits() function converts a numeric value into a string of characters and prefixes the number with zeros. The right(*str*, *n*) function keeps the rightmost *n* character substring of *str*.

This expression can be explained in parts as follows. If row_number() over() returns

```
1,2,..,99,100,101...
```

then digits (rownumber() over()) returns

```
0000000000000000001
0000000000000000002
...
0000000000000000099
0000000000000000100
0000000000000000101
```

and right(digits (rownumber() over() –1),16) returns

```
0000000000000000
0000000000000001
...
0000000000000099
0000000000000100
0000000000000101
```

If varying credit card numbers are not important, you could use a static value. All credit card expiration dates are the same (0406).

Finally, you can see that the SYSCAT.COLUMNS table is used to help generate values. The clause FETCH FIRST ... ROWS ONLY was used to limit the number of rows generated so that we have a nice round number of 2500 total customers.

Here is an example of what the generated CUSTOMER data will look like.

```
0 0000000000000000 0406        lname0   fname0   address0   000000
1 0000000000000001 0406        lname1   fname1   address1   000001
2 0000000000000002 0406        lname2   fname2   address2   000002
3 0000000000000003 0406        lname3   fname3   address3   000003
4 0000000000000004 0406        lname4   fname4   address4   000004
etc.
```

Create this sample of 2500 customers before continuing to the next example.

The PRODUCT Table

The INSERT statement in Figure 9.7 creates 100 sample products.

Figure 9.7 INSERT statement to generate 100 sample products

```
INSERT INTO l8nite.PRODUCT (
  PRODUCT_ID,
  DESCRIPTION,
  COST,
  RETAIL_PRICE,
  INVENTORY,
  MINIMUM_INVENTORY
)
SELECT row_number() over(),
'description' || char(row_number() over()),
0,
cast(rand() * 100 as decimal(5,2)),
cast(rand() * 100 as INT),
cast(rand() * 10 as INT)
 from syscat.columns fetch first 100 rows only;

UPDATE l8nite.product SET cost = retail_price*0.6;
```

This example is similar to the INSERT statement used to generate data for the CUSTOMER table except for a few things. Two additional operations are involved: casting and rand().

The rand() function returns a random floating point number beween 0 and 1. When this number is multiplied by 100, as is the case for the RETAIL_PRICE and INVENTORY columns, the number returned will be in the range of 0 and 100. Similarly, the minimum inventory value will be between 0 and 10.

The cast operation is used to convert (*cast*) a value from one type (in this case, a floating point number) to another. The value generated for the RETAIL_PRICE column is converted into decimal(5,2) to match the type of the table column. The values generated for INVENTORY and MINIMUM_INVENTORY are cast to integer type for the same reason.

The values for COST are created as a secondary step (the UPDATE statement) because we do not know what the random values for RETAIL_PRICE will be but want to ensure that the COST value is less than the retail value. Therefore, the COST column is updated using a separate SQL statement. Assuming that the owner always maintains a 40 percent margin for retail price, the cost value is simply the retail price discounted by 40 percent.

Here is an example of what the generated PRODUCT data will look like:

```
1 description1    26.17  36.64    76     9
2 description2    60.59  84.83     2     9
3 description3    18.42  25.80    29     0
4 description4    22.85  31.99    25     0
5 description5    64.55  90.37    93     3
```

The Sales and Product_Purchases Tables

Generating data for the SALES and PRODUCT_PURCHASES tables is a little more complex because there is a relationship between these tables. Furthermore, there are additional relationships between SALES and CUSTOMER as well as between PRODUCT and PRODUCT_PURCHASES.

Although it is possible to write some very advanced SQL to take all this into account, we take this opportunity to demonstrate the use of a DB2 SQL PL stored procedure to generate data for these tables. The flow of the procedure will be as follows:

1. Randomly select one of the 2500 customers (created earlier) to create this transaction. Insert a row into the SALES table. The table has an IDENTITY column called sales_transaction_id. The auto-generated sales transaction ID is retrieved for later use.
2. Determine at random how many products (N) will be sold as part of this sales transaction.
3. Determine at random which of the available 100 products (created earlier) will be selected, and retrieve the retail price of these products from the PRODUCT table.
4. The randomly selected products along with sales_transaction_id (from the SALES table) and retail_price (from the PRODUCT table) are inserted into the PRODUCT_PURCHASES table.
5. Update the TOTAL column of the SALES table as the sum of product purchases made for each sales_transaction.

Figure 9.8 lists the full source code for this stored procedure. The full code is shown first, followed by a detailed discussion of each section.

Figure 9.8 SQL procedure to generate sales and product purchases

```
create procedure l8nite.create_sales (in total_sales int)
begin
    declare new_sales_txn_id, random_prod_id, num_prods int;
    declare sales_counter, product_purchase_counter int default 0;

    while (sales_counter < total_sales) do
        insert into l8nite.sales
                (sales_transaction_id, customer_id,
                 type, transaction_timestamp)
        values ( default,                   -- generated always identity
                 int(rand() * 2499),         -- random customer id
                 0,
                 current timestamp - int(rand()*100) days );
        set new_sales_txn_id = identity_val_local();

        -- randomly determine the # of products in this sale
        set num_prods = int(rand() * 9) + 1;
        set product_purchase_counter=1;

        while (product_purchase_counter < num_prods) do
            -- get a random product id
            set random_prod_id =int(rand() * 99)+1;

            insert into l8nite.product_purchases (
                sales_transaction_id, product_id, price, qty)
            values ( new_sales_txn_id,
                     random_prod_id,
                     (select retail_price from l8nite.product
                       where product_id = random_prod_id),
                     int(rand() * 9) +1);

            set product_purchase_counter = product_purchase_counter + 1;
        end while;
        commit;

        set sales_counter = sales_counter +1;
    end while;
```

```
    update l8nite.sales s
       set sub_total=(
          select sum(price*qty)
            from l8nite.product_purchases p
           where s.sales_transaction_id=p.sales_transaction_id);
end
```

The stored procedure is called create_sales and takes an input parameter of type INTEGER. This value simply dictates how many times the main logic will loop. The local variable sales_counter starts at 0 and is incremented with each loop of the main logic until it equals the parameter value, total_sales.

```
create procedure l8nite.create_sales (in total_sales int)
begin
    declare new_sales_txn_id, random_prod_id, num_prods int;
    declare sales_counter, product_purchase_counter int default 0;

    while (sales_counter < total_sales) do
       .............
       commit;
       set sales_counter = sales_counter +1;
   end while;
   .............
end
```

As described earlier, the first step is to SELECT a random customer and perform an INSERT into the SALES table.

```
        insert into l8nite.sales
                (sales_transaction_id, customer_id,
                 type, transaction_timestamp)
        values ( default,                    -- generated always identity
                int(rand() * 2499),      -- random customer id
                0,
                current timestamp - int(rand()*100) days );

        set new_sales_txn_id = identity_val_local();
```

The SALES table has an IDENTITY column, so we use the keyword DEFAULT when inserting into that column. The function sequence `int(rand() * 2499)` is used to randomly select a customer ID value between 0 and 2499 (there are 2500 customers, starting with customer ID 0 for cash sales). For sales type, we always default to zero (although we could just as easily randomize that). The sales date is interesting. To simulate sales occurring over a period of time we randomly deduct up to 100 days from the current timestamp for the sales transaction date. After a row has been created in the SALES table, the IDENTITY_VAL_LOCAL() function is used to retrieve the identity column value used for the INSERT statement. This value is later inserted into the PRODUCT_PURCHASES table along with other information.

After the SALES row has been created, we need to create the products purchased as part of this sale. We'll assume that a customer may buy from 1 to 10 products in a given sale and call this num_prods.

```
-- randomly determine the # of products in this sale
set num_prods = int(rand() * 9) + 1;
set product_purchase_counter=1;
```

A loop will then repeat num_prods times. With each iteration, a random product_id is selected from 0 to 100. Because there is no product with product_id 0, we manually change the product_id to 1 in the rare case that the random number is 0. The retail_price of the product is then retrieved from the PRODUCT table in the form of a scalar subselect, as part of the VALUES clause of the INSERT statement.

```
        while (product_purchase_counter < num_prods) do
            -- get a random product id
            set random_prod_id =int(rand() * 99)+1;

            insert into l8nite.product_purchases (
                sales_transaction_id, product_id, price, qty)
            values ( new_sales_txn_id,
                     random_prod_id,
                     (select retail_price from l8nite.product
                       where product_id = random_prod_id),
                     int(rand() * 9) +1);

            set product_purchase_counter = product_purchase_counter + 1;
        end while;
        commit;
        set sales_counter = sales_counter +1;
    end while;
```

When all the sales transactions have been generated, an UPDATE statement is used to update the TOTAL column of the SALES table with the sum of all product purchases per sales transaction.

```
update l8nite.sales s
   set sub_total=(
      select sum(price*qty)
```

```
  from l8nite.product_purchases p
where s.sales_transaction_id=p.sales_transaction_id);
```

You can call the stored procedure to generate any number of sample sales transactions. For example, to create 5000 sample sales (and one or more product purchases with each sale), issue the following SQL statement from the Command Editor:

```
CALL L8NITE.create_sales (5000)
```

Here is an example of what the generated SALES data will look like:

Table: SALES (sales_transaction_id, customer_id, total, type, time, image)

```
1      396    549.96  0   2003-12-27-22.22.50.008000
2      557   1236.50  0   2003-12-24-22.22.50.238000
3     2404    949.46  0   2003-12-14-22.22.50.238001
```

Here is an example of what the generated PRODUCT_PURCHASES data will look like:

Table: PRODUCT_PURCHASES (sales_transaction_id, product_id, price, qty, total)

```
1      34   91.66    6  549.96
2      71   48.25    9  434.25
2      77   53.26    0    0.00
2      56   80.45    6  482.70
2      63   27.43    5  137.15
2      23    1.40    2    2.80
2      72   22.45    8  179.60
3      19   78.20    3  234.60
3      31   57.14    5  285.70
3      41   76.33    1   76.33
3      12   99.79    3  299.37
3      47    5.94    9   53.46
```

9.4 Generating Large Data Sets Using LOAD FROM CURSOR

A stored procedure was used to load data into the SALES and PRODUCT_PURCHASES tables. The stored procedure has a COMMIT statement after each sale is processed, making it very scalable for inserting any number of rows into those tables.

On the other hand, the PRODUCT and CUSTOMER tables were populated using INSERT statements. When trying to insert very large amounts of data using this method, you can run out of transaction log space because all rows must be inserted as one giant transaction.

Another consideration is that SYSCAT.COLUMNS has only about 2500 rows. Using the techniques presented so far, one might think that the maximum number of generated rows is limited by the number of rows in the largest existing table.

In this section, both problems are addressed. You will learn how to generate very large data sets and load them without transaction log contention.

Generating Large Data Sets

In the earlier examples, the SYSCAT.COLUMNS table was used to generate rows. This table contains about 2500 rows by default. If you need more rows, however, you can modify the query to use the Cartesian product of the SYSCAT.COLUMNS table with itself.

For example, to generate 10,000 rows, you can use the Cartesian product of two tables—one with 100 rows, another with 1000 rows (100 * 1000 = 10,000):

```
SELECT count(*) from
   (SELECT 1 FROM syscat.columns FETCH FIRST 100 ROWS ONLY) as A,
   (SELECT 1 FROM syscat.columns FETCH FIRST 1000 ROWS ONLY) as B
1
-----------
      10000

  1 record(s) selected.
```

With more than 2500 rows in SYSCAT.COLUMNS, you can generate up to 6.25 million rows (2500 * 2500 = 6,250,000).

Loading 6 million rows using a single INSERT statement would cause some serious transaction log contention. A better way to load large data sets is to use the LOAD utility, which does not use transaction logging. Using an option of LOAD—called LOAD FROM *cursorname*—loading large amounts of data is a simple extension of our previous examples.

Step 1: Launch the LOAD utility.

From the Control Center, navigate to All Databases > L8NITE > Tables > Product.

Right-click the PRODUCT table, and select Load from the pop-up menu.

Step 2: Select APPEND or REPLACE mode.

If you select APPEND, then new data will be added to the table. If you select REPLACE, the existing data will be deleted before new data is inserted. For this example, select REPLACE.

Step 3: Select the input format.

The LOAD utility can accept various file formats. For this example, we will actually demonstrate a method called LOAD FROM *cursorname*. That is, LOAD works by reading from the result set of a query. From the pull-down menu, select Load From Cursor.

In the text box, specify the following query (Figure 9.9):

```
SELECT row_number() over(),
'description' || char(row_number() over()),
0,
cast(rand() * 100 as decimal(5,2)),
cast(rand() * 100 as INT),
cast(rand() * 10 as INT)
 from
(select 1 from syscat.columns fetch first 100 rows only) as A,
(select 1 from syscat.columns fetch first 100 rows only) as B
```

Then specify a file name for LOAD utility generated messages. For example, use c:\product_load.msg. This file can be used for troubleshooting if LOAD fails.

Figure 9.9 Specify query for cursor

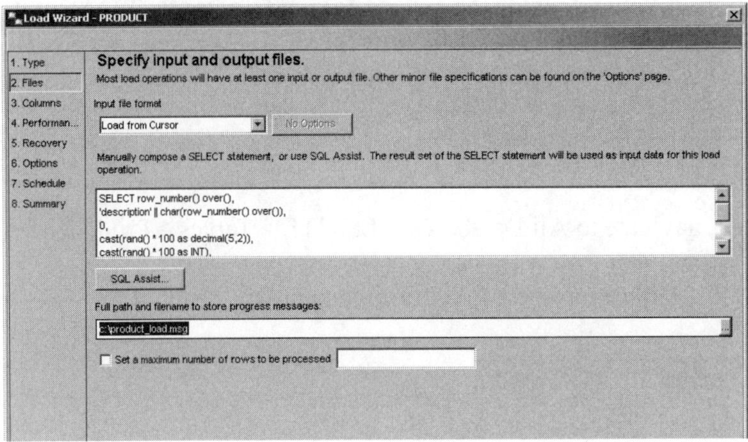

Step 4: Align the SQL input columns with the target table columns.

In this step, you have the opportunity to specify how the columns returned by the query statement align with columns in the target table.

Select Map Columns Based on Column Positions Found in the Input File (Figure 9.10).

Figure 9.10 Specify column mappings

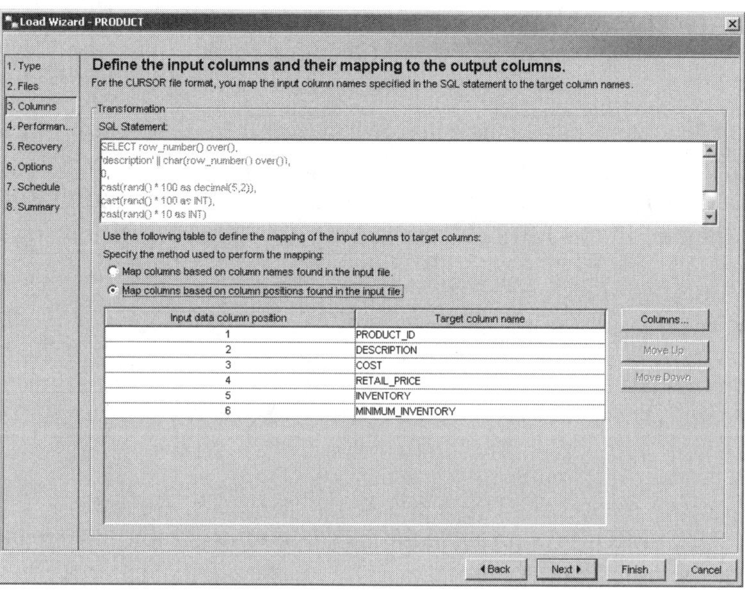

In this case, you can see that because we have provided data for all columns, no changes are required. For the remaining options, the defaults are sufficient. Click Finish.

Step 5: Validate the loaded data.

After the data load is complete, validate that the rows were loaded as expected. Run SET INTEGRITY on the PRODUCT table as described in section 9.2. Open the Command Editor and execute the following queries:

```
SELECT count(*) FROM PRODUCT;
SELECT * FROM PRODUCT FETCH FIRST 10 ROWS ONLY;
```

You should see that 10,000 rows were loaded. As in the earlier example, update the cost column as the retail price discounted 40 percent.

```
UPDATE l8nite.product SET cost = retail_price*0.6;
```

Note that a single UPDATE statement to update all rows may also cause an out-of-log space condition if the table is exceptionally large. For very large tables (millions of rows), you can update the table in chunks by repeatedly issuing UPDATE statements between COMMITs. You can use any value for the FETCH FIRST clause as long as you have sufficient log space.

```
UPDATE (SELECT cost, retail_price
        FROM l8nite.product WHERE where cost=0
        FETCH FIRST 5000 ROWS ONLY)
SET cost=retail_price*0.6;
```

Generating data using LOAD FROM *cursorname* for the CUSTOMER table has been left as an exercise. You can use the procedure l8nite.create_sales to insert any number of rows without running out of transaction log space. However, its performance is not optimal for very large data sets. Improving its performance has been left as an exercise, with guidance on how to do it in the exercise itself.

9.5 Exporting Data

After you have generated lots of random data, it is probably a good idea to export it into reusable data files so that you can use them later in other databases for repeatable and automated test cases.

DB2 has a utility called EXPORT to export data from DB2 into files. In the following example, we'll demonstrate how to export the SALES table into a delimited ASCII file.

Step 1: Launch the Export wizard from the Control Center.

Navigate to All Databases > L8NITE > Tables.

Right-click on the SALES table, and select Export from the pop-up menu to launch the Export Table dialog box (Figure 9.11).

Step 2: Specify EXPORT options.

In the Target tab, specify

- The output file name (such as sales.del)
- The file format as DEL (delimited ASCII). You can specify additional options, such as overriding the default delimiters and data formats, by clicking the Options button.

EXPORT will optionally create a file to write messages. Specify a name for this file, such as sales.del.msg.

Click the Finish button to begin the data export.

Figure 9.11 Specify export options

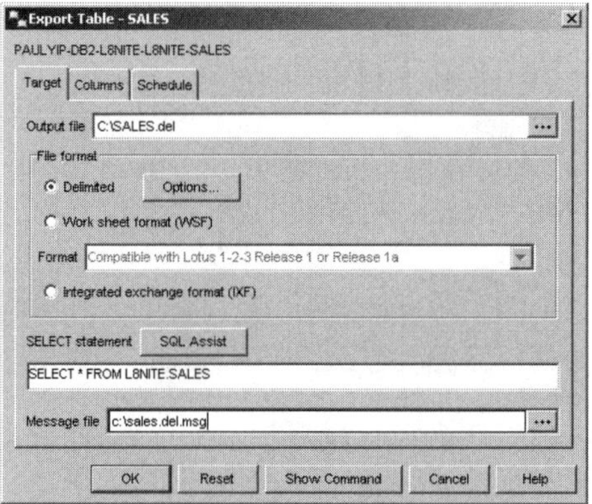

NOTE: In the SELECT statement text area, you can actually specify any valid query. For example, you can specify a FETCH FIRST n ROWS ONLY clause. You can even change the query completely to be a join of many tables.

9.6 Importing DB2 Data into Spreadsheets

Now that lots of sample data has been created, you can create some interesting reports using a spreadsheet application such as Microsoft Excel XP.

Recall that the owner of the Late Night Convenience Store wanted to gain business insight from the history of transactions. In the preceeding section, we created 5000 transactions from 2500 customers for 100 products spread over 100 days. We can now simulate answering valuable business questions such as these:

- Which are the 10 best- and 10 worst-selling products?
- How much money has been made in the past 30 days?
- Who are the best customers (so that they may be rewarded for their loyalty in the future)?

It is generally a good practice to create database views to encapsulate reporting queries. It is much easier to tell from a view name what information is being reported than to determine this from a query alone.

The Best- and Worst-Selling Products

To find out the best- or worst-selling products, you need to sum the quantities sold of all products in the SALES table and then order the rows.

```
CREATE VIEW L8NITE.product_sales_ranking AS
SELECT p.product_id, p.description,
       sum(pp.qty) as total_sold
  FROM L8NITE.product p
       LEFT OUTER JOIN L8NITE.product_purchases pp
                 ON p.product_id = pp.product_id
 GROUP BY p.product_id, p.description;
```

Then, to discover the top 10 products, use this query:

```
SELECT * FROM L8NITE.product_sales_ranking
 ORDER BY total_sold DESC
 FETCH FIRST 10 ROWS ONLY
```

To discover the worst 10 products, use this:

```
SELECT * FROM L8NITE.product_sales_ranking
 ORDER BY total_sold ASC
 FETCH FIRST 10 ROWS ONLY
```

Which Customers Have Not Revisited in the Past 30 Days?

The following query will look in the SALES table to see which customers have not completed a transaction in the past 30 days.

```
CREATE VIEW L8NITE.no_visit_30_days AS
 SELECT customer_id, firstname, lastname, address
   FROM L8NITE.CUSTOMER c
  WHERE NOT EXISTS (
         SELECT 1 FROM L8NITE.SALES s
          WHERE s.customer_id = c.customer_id
             AND s.transaction_timestamp >=
                          current timestamp - 30 DAYS)
```

9.7 Creating Reports Using Microsoft Excel

After you have created views to encapsulate useful business reports, you can extend the usability of the data by creating spreadsheets to pull data directly from DB2 using its OLE DB interface.

Step 1: Initiate data import.

Launch Microsoft Excel (Figure 9.12). From the Data menu, select: Data > Import External Data > Import Data.

Figure 9.12 Initiating data import within Excel

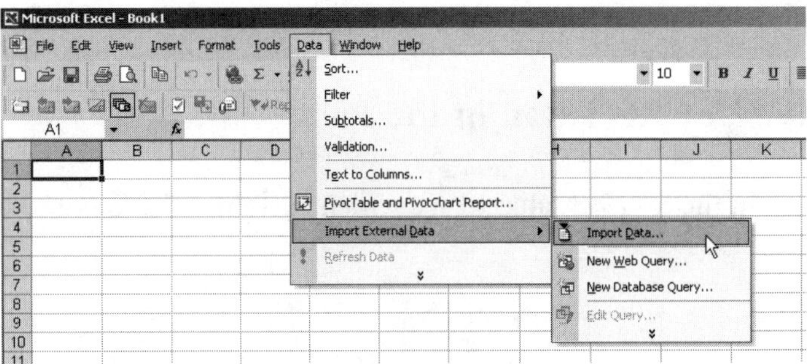

Step 2: Create a new data source.

A Select Data Source dialog box will appear. Select Connect to New Data Source.odc, and click the Open button.

This will open a Data Connection wizard dialog box. Select Other/Advanced, and click Next.

This will open a Data Links dialog box that has four tabs:

- Provider
- Connection
- Advanced
- All

In the Provider tab, select IBM OLE DB Data Provider for DB2. In the Connection tab, select L8NITE from the Data Source pull-down menu. In the All tab, change the mode from Read/Write to Read. This will prevent any changes in the spreadsheet from being applied to the database.

Step 3: Connect to the database.

In the Connect to DB2 Database dialog box, select the L8NITE database. Then provide the user name and password for user db2admin, set the connection mode to Share, and click OK (Figure 9.13).

Figure 9.13 Connect to L8NITE database

Step 4: Select the report view.

Select the PRODUCT_SALES_RANKING view from the list, and click Next (Figure 9.14). The query used to select from this table will be SELECT * FROM

PRODUCT_SALES_RANKING. However, we do not want to use this default and will change it in the next step.

Figure 9.14 Select a report view

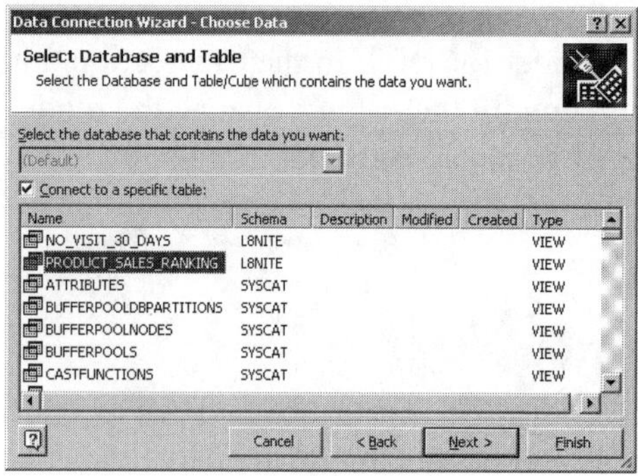

Step 5: Customize the default query.

In the Import Data dialog box, click Edit Query (Figure 9.15).

Figure 9.15 Edit the default query for data import

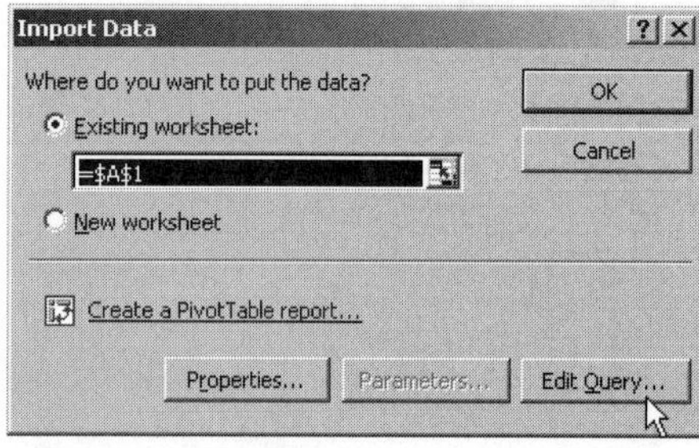

The command type should be changed from Table to SQL and modified as you see in Figure 9.16. We add SQL clauses to customize exactly what we wish to import into Excel. The following query clauses were discussed in Chapter 7, Maximizing Concurrency.

- ORDER BY total_orders, so that we can see the top sellers
- FETCH FIRST 10 ROWS ONLY, so that we can see the top 10
- WITH UR, to avoid lock contention. Including a few uncommitted sales in the report is acceptable given the concurrency benefits, especially because point-of-sale transactions tend to COMMIT successfully.

Figure 9.16 Modify OLE DB query

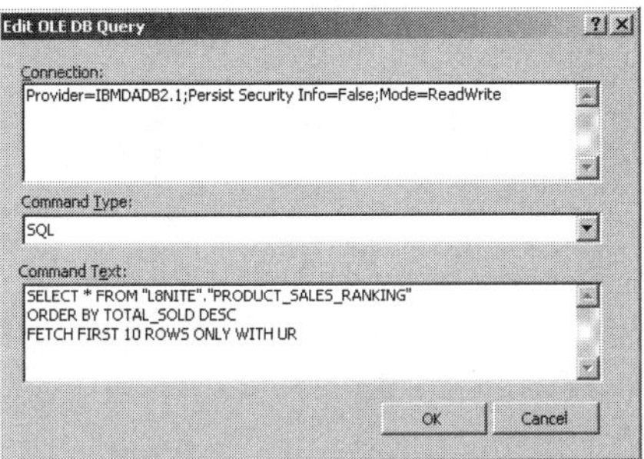

After the query has been modified, click OK. This returns you to the Import Data dialog box. Click OK to import data into the Excel spreadsheet.

NOTE: If you save this spreadsheet, you can easily reimport the latest data from the database by selecting Refresh Data from the Excel Data menu.

9.8 Summary

In this chapter, you learned how to work with data using the DB2 IMPORT, LOAD, and EXPORT utilities. You also learned about various data file formats supported by DB2.

Using some fancy SQL, you have seen how to quickly populate a database with sample random data and an SQL PL procedure. To randomize structured data, the built-in functions row_number(), over(), rand(), and digits(), as well as the cast operation, were demonstrated.

After the tables were loaded with significant data, reporting queries were demonstrated to meet the business insight requirement of the Late Night Convenience Store. For each reporting query, you saw why it's convenient to encapsulate each report.

After the views were created, access to these reports was further simplified by using Microsoft Excel to connect to DB2 via its OLE DB interface to extract data directly from these views. By default, Excel imports all rows from a table or view, but you learned how to customize the queries used by Excel to suit your data extraction and concurrency needs.

9.9 Exercises

1. Use a spreadsheet program such as Microsoft Excel to create sample rows of data for the customer data. Save the file as a comma-separated values file (.csv) and load it as a DEL file using IMPORT.

2. Delete all the products from the PRODUCT table. (You may have to delete the contents of PRODUCT_PURCHASES first because of foreign key constraints.) Download the file products.asc from the book website and use the IMPORT utility to import this data. The file uses nondelimited ASCII format.

3. Populate the CUSTOMER table with 5000 rows of random data using the LOAD FROM *cursorname* method.

4. The procedure L8NITE.CREATE_SALES can be used to simulate any number of sales. However, you can improve the performance of this procedure by using COMMIT on every 5000 sales (or more) rather than after every sale. This will reduce the frequency of flushing the log buffer to disk. Modify the L8NITE.CREATE_SALES procedure so that

    - The frequency of COMMIT is provided by a second parameter called p_commitcount
    - The algorithm issues COMMITs only after p_commitcount transactions have been created

CHAPTER 10 *Performance Tuning*

In this chapter, you will learn:

- About configuration parameters in DB2
- How to configure DB2 parameters automatically using the Configuration Advisor
- How to configure DB2 parameters manually using the Configuration Parameter dialog box
- About SQL access plans DB2 uses to retrieve data
- The basics of tuning SQL using Visual Explain
- How to tune a database schema automatically using Design Advisor

10.1 Introduction

If you have followed the exercises in this book, you have now completed the development phase of the L8NITE convenience store application. The remaining chapters will be devoted to tuning, deploying, and troubleshooting your application. This chapter describes how to pretune your database's performance before you go to production. You will be introduced to a suite of graphical tools included with DB2 that will make all these tasks quick and simple.

10.2 Performance Tuning

In previous chapters, we guided you through the process of creating a database, database objects such as tables and indexes, and a sample application. We have not discussed performance tuning at all. The L8NITE database is still using the default configuration parameter values.

Before you deploy the application, it is extremely important to establish a baseline configuration that is specific to the operational characteristics of your application and the typical environment for which it will be deployed. You should never deploy DB2 in production with the default configuration. A default DB2 database is configured for minimal resource consumption and cannot efficiently leverage modestly powered machines (and certainly not modern server-class hardware).

There are two main areas of interest in improving the overall performance of your database:

- System resource exploitation: Given the characteristics and workload requirements of the application, configure DB2 to optimally leverage system resources.
- Workload efficiency: Given the typical data access patterns of the application, modify the database design (by adding indexes or other database objects) for better performance.

Manually tuning these two areas can be an iterative and time-consuming process. Fortunately, DB2 provides two intelligent graphical administration tools: the Configuration Advisor and the Design Advisor. These tools take the guesswork out of database parameter configuration and schema tuning. To tune specific SQL, we will also explore a third graphical tool called Visual Explain, which lets you visualize how data is being accessed for a given query.

10.3 Optimizing Configuration Using the Configuration Advisor

DB2 has more than 100 configuration parameters that affect either the behavior or the performance of the database. These configuration parameters are divided into two main sets:

- Database manager configuration (DBM CFG): This lets you control the behavior of the database instance. When these parameters are changed, each database created in the instance is affected.

- Database configuration (DB CFG): This lets you control the behavior and performance of a specific database within an instance.

TIP: For detailed information about each parameter, refer to the online DB2 Information Center at:

http://publib.boulder.ibm.com/infocenter/db2help/index.jsp

Recall that you can have more than one database in an instance. If you have two databases, there will be one DBM CFG and two DB CFGs (one per database). The parameters exist so that you can configure DB2 to perform optimally for your business requirements. However, the large number of parameters that makes DB2 flexible also makes it intimidating for first-time DB2 users to tune databases. Two graphical tools are available for tuning configuration parameters:

- The Configuration Advisor
- The Configure Parameter dialog box

Configuration Advisor

Understanding how to tune all the configuration parameters can be a daunting task. Tuning the DBM CFG and DB CFG is really an art, in which you increase resource consumption in some areas at the expense of others for better overall resource exploitation. Tuning performance parameters one by one and making the correct trade-offs can be very time-consuming.

The DB2 Configuration Advisor is a graphical tool that simplifies tuning DBM and DB parameters by identifying the resources available, asking a few questions, and recommending how DB2 should tune itself. The Configuration Advisor makes its decisions based on heuristics used by expert database administrators. One of the keys to the Configuration Advisor's success is that no relevant parameter is omitted. This self-tuning capability is part of DB2's autonomic feature set.

We'll now show you how to automatically tune the L8NITE database. Expand the object tree in the Control Center, and locate the L8NITE database. Launch the Configuration Advisor by right-clicking the database object and selecting Configuration Advisor in the pop-up menu. You'll notice that the Configuration Advisor has 10 steps, and that may seem a little complicated at first glance. However, you are required to answer only one or two simple questions for each step.

Step 1: Introduction page.

The Introduction page of the advisor is mainly informational. It verifies again that the correct database is selected for tuning and provides a brief description of what the advisor will do. You can get to a more detailed discussion of the task by clicking on the Task Overview hyperlink near the top of the page. Click Next to continue.

Step 2: Server page.

The advisor has examined your computer system and has determined how much memory and how many processors are currently installed. All you are required to provide is the percentage of the resources that can be used for the target database. The advisor will keep the consumption of memory resources within this limit. In making this decision, you should consider which other applications or databases will be running on the same system. Here are some factors to consider:

- Memory requirements of the operating system itself
- Other applications such as Web servers, application servers, or similar types of applications running on the same system
- Other databases running on this machine
- Development tools running on the same machine

For example, if you are using the database on a dedicated server with no other applications running, you can devote 80 percent of the system resources to the Configuration Advisor. However, if you are tuning a database that shares your development environment, you probably want to reduce the memory constraint to much lower levels (such as 10 or 20 percent). If you are not careful, you can easily overtune your database, causing the system to try to use more memory than is physically available. Overall system performance will degrade while various processes compete for memory resources.

Because the L8NITE database exercise is a simple application, you should reduce the memory usage to a percentage that is equivalent to about 128Mb of memory (or less, depending on how much total memory you have available). Select the appropriate memory percentage for tuning, and click Next to proceed.

Step 3: Workload page.

Here, the advisor asks about the type of SQL or workload expected from the applications connecting to this database. If most of the SQL issued against the database consists of UPDATE, INSERT, or DELETE statements, then your database workload is primarily transactions. On the other hand, if the SQL is mostly SELECTs, then your database's workload is primarily query reporting.

On this page of the advisor, you will need to specify the primary client of your database. Let's use an example to see how the recommended value would change based on your answer. If you ask the advisor to tune for a queries-type workload, the memory threshold for sort operations will be increased. This decision is based on the assumption that most data-mining-type applications require complex sorts and joins.

Although we have discussed many interesting queries you can use to retrieve data for managing the store, the primary purpose of our application and database will likely be to process sales. Processing sales will require many inserts and updates, so we should consider the workload for our L8NITE database to be primarily transactional. Selecting the mixed or transactional option will add the Transaction page to the advisor. Click Next to continue.

Note: When you are looking at the workload of your next application, remember to take the frequency of each type of SQL statement into account. For example, even if you have only one UPDATE statement, your workload can still be considered transactional if this update is used significantly more often than other statements.

Step 4: Transaction page.

A transaction is a set of related SQL statements that must be executed successfully as a unit before the changes are committed (or saved). If you do not have a clear understanding of transactions, refer to Chapter 7, Maximizing Concurrency.

On this page, you tell the Configuration Advisor about the general nature of the transactions issued by the application. With this information, the advisor makes recommendations on how to allocate resources related to transaction logging and lock management. The advisor will require information about the number of transactions you expect the database to process within one minute.

The transactions for the L8NITE application are considered short (fewer than 10 SQL operations per transaction). As for transactions per minute, it would depend on how many checkout counters are in a store. For example, if we have two checkout terminals and it takes a clerk 20 seconds to process a sale, then we will have approximately 6 transactions per minute. It is recommended that you add some margin of safety, so we will set our target to 10 transactions per minute. Click Next to continue.

Step 5: Priority page.

When tuning a database, you must take an inherent trade-off between tuning for runtime performance versus database recovery in the event of a system crash. To process transactions faster, you can tune DB2 to take greater advantage of asynchronous (delayed) writing of modified data pages to disk because the transaction log, which is always flushed to disk on COMMIT, already guarantees that transactions are recoverable in the event of a crash. Under a heavy transaction workload, there can be a large number of transactions in the log that have not been propagated to the tables. In the event of a crash, the recovery time depends on how much of the transaction log must be replayed to bring the database back to a consistent state.

On this page, you will specify which is more of a priority for your business. You can choose for the configuration to favor faster transaction processing, or quicker recovery, or you can try to achieve a balance of both.

Because we do not expect an extremely high transaction rate and because a speedy recovery is desirable to avoid long delays, we will assign equal importance to both runtime performance and recovery. Click Next to continue.

Step 6: Populated page.

The advisor can further optimize resource allocation if the database is already populated. To clarify, if your database already contains real data (e.g., when you are tuning an actual database that is in production) or data that is representative of the production environment, then your answer to this question is yes.

Over time, as the size of the database grows, you may want to run the advisor periodically to fine-tune its configuration. For the initial deployment of the L8NITE database, we can populate its tables with sample data. If you did not do the load exercise in Chapter 9, you may want to review the material relating to data movement. Click Next to continue.

Step 7: Connection page.

The expected number of connections to the database will impact the allocation of resources available in your system. Depending on the number of applications expected, the maximum number of agents allowed and the application heap size are some of the parameters affected.

On this page, the Configuration Advisor asks about the number of concurrent connections you expect the database to handle. In its recommendation, the advisor will reserve resources to service these connections. A *remote* connection means that the application is connecting over a network to the database server. A *local* connection implies that the application is running on the same machine as the database server.

For example, if we expect two point-of-sale terminals at our store, we can expect two remote connections on average. Again, you should increase this number to provide a margin of safety. Underallocating resources can cause DB2 to refuse additional connection requests. To be safe, let's set the number of connections to 5. Click Next to continue.

Step 8: Isolation page.

One of the key sets of configuration parameters affected by isolation is the one related to managing locks. For a more complete explanation of the various types of locks in DB2, you can review the material in Chapter 7. In your database, locks are used to manage access to your data. DB2 provides locking at the row level. That is, if you are updating a row in a table, there is no need to lock out other applications from accessing other rows in that table.

The isolation level required by the application is related to the type of access control needed. In most sales-related applications, isolation is important to ensure that the inventory retrieved from the database is correct. For our application, the duration of each transaction is very short, and the number of locks acquired may depend on the type of inventory control that is needed by the convenience store. For now, we can select Cursor Stability as the level of isolation needed for our application. For more information on isolation levels, see Chapter 7, Maximizing Concurrency.

Step 9: Schedule page.

Because the recommendations made by the advisor can affect the ongoing operations of a live database and because some parameter changes require the database manager to be restarted, it may be convenient to schedule the configuration changes for a later time. On the schedule page of the advisor, you can choose such a schedule. If the scheduler is not enabled for the database manager, you will need to enable the scheduler by creating a *tools catalog* in a database. The catalog is simply a set of tables used to store the scripts (or tasks) that are scheduled to run and the result of their execution. If you choose to save the task to the tools catalog, you can view the task script at any time using the Task Center.

For our example, we will select the Save and Run Task Now option. With this option, the changes will be applied immediately, and a copy of the script will be stored in the tools catalog for future reference.

Step 10: Result page.

Figure 10.1 Configuration Advisor: Summary of recommended changes.

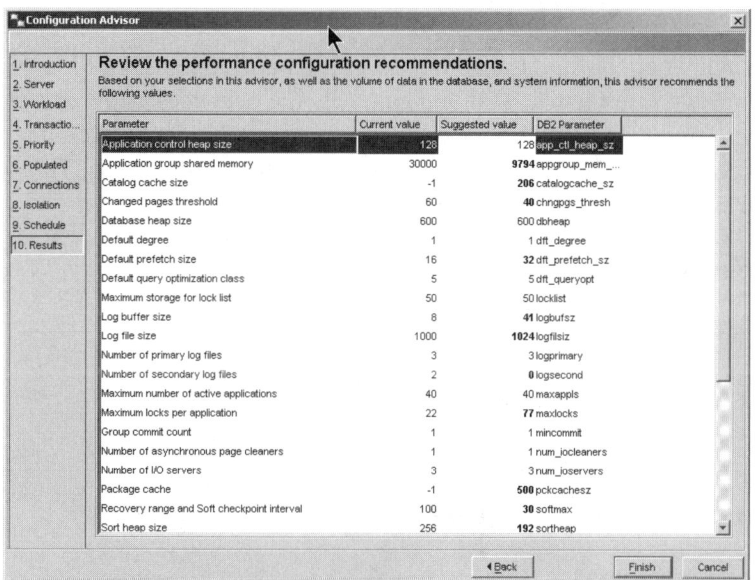

When you enter this page, the Configuration Advisor takes all the information provided on the previous pages and recommends a set of parameter changes to improve performance (see Figure 10.1). The advisor will highlight any recommended changes using bold text in the Suggested Value column so that it is easy to see what will be changed. Take a quick look at the recommendations, and click the Finish button to apply these changes. You may have to restart the DB2 database manager for all the changes to take effect.

After the parameters have taken effect, the database should have a fairly good baseline performance configuration. Every application has unique workload characteristics, however, and there may be room for improvement. The other tool available for changing parameters is the Configure Parameters dialog box, which is discussed in the next section.

Configure Parameters Dialog box

The Configuration Parameters dialog box is a graphical tool for manually changing database manager (DBM CFG) and database (DB CFG) configuration files.

To access the database manager configuration (DBM CFG) parameters, you need to switch to the Control Center's Advanced view so that you can view the instances in the object tree. Expand the object tree to find the DB2 instance under the Instances folder. Right-click the instance object and select the Configure Parameters item from the pop-up menu. This will launch the Configure Parameter dialog box (Figure 10.2).

Figure 10.2 Configure Parameters dialog box

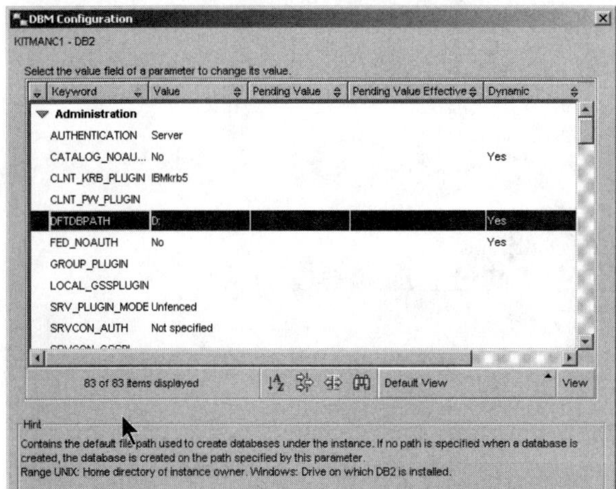

From the Configure Parameters dialog box, you can view and make changes to any of the parameters. In its Hint area the tool provides you with helpful tips as you select each parameter.

To access the database configuration parameters, you must expand the navigation tree further to the databases folder. Right-click the database you wish to configure, and select Configure Parameters from the pop-up menu. The Configure Parameters dialog box is launched.

NOTE: Many users confuse the Configure Parameters dialog box and Configuration Advisor. In general, an advisor-type tool in DB2 will provide you with recommended actions. In this case, the Configuration Advisor recommends a set of configuration parameter changes. In contrast, the Configuration Parameters dialog box provides a graphical interface to manually modify parameters, with hints for each parameter. The Configure Parameters dialog box is helpful in fine-tuning each parameter.

Final Notes on Tuning Database Configuration

The Configure Parameters dialog box and Configuration Advisor are complementary. The Configuration Advisor should be considered the starting point for performance tuning. The standard practice is to use the Configuration Advisor to establish a baseline configuration from which you can start testing the performance of the database and application. You may very well find that the recommended configuration works great without modification. However, if you need to tweak individual parameters, use the Configure Parameters dialog box.

Over time, if the size of your database or connection requirements changes dramatically, you may need to retune the database by running the advisor again. In Chapter 13, you will be introduced to a monitoring tool called the Health Center. The Health Monitor and Health Center monitor the performance of your database and make recommendations to remedy any potential problems. Some of these recommendations will require additional changes to various configuration parameters to fix specific problems. This is another DB2 autonomic feature that can help you fine-tune your database over time.

10.4 Analyzing SQL Using Visual Explain

The database configuration is now tuned for your hardware usage, but there are other ways to further improve application performance. One of the best ways is to increase the speed of data access in the database. To do that, you can use a tool called Visual Explain to better understand how data is accessed when DB2 processes SQL queries.

When an SQL query is submitted to the database, the DB2 *optimizer* (a component of the database engine) determines the optimal way to access the data. For example, for each table referenced in any SQL query, it considers the following:

- The size of the table
- The availability of indexes
- Data placement
- The organization and degree of fragmentation of the table on disk
- The database and database manager configuration parameters
- Other useful statistics known about the data

The final decision on how to retrieve the data is called an access plan. Visual Explain provides a graphical representation of the access plan created by the DB2 optimizer.

In Chapter 2 you were introduced to the Command Editor tool. Visual Explain is one of the tools available in the DB2 Command Editor. You can launch the Command Editor by selecting the icon shown in Figure 10.3.

Figure 10.3 Command Editor launch icon.

The Command Editor is shown in Figure 10.4. To start, you add a connection to the editor by selecting the Add button and selecting the L8NITE database in the Add Database dialog box.

Figure 10.4 Command Editor

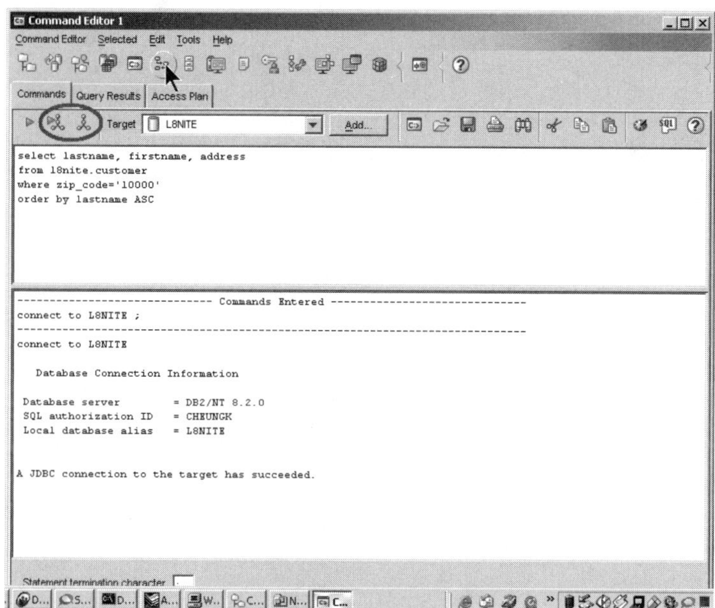

The Command Editor is now connected to the L8NITE database. Let's explore the Visual Explain tool by working through an example. Before we start, you must fill the CUSTOMER table with a significant amount of data. This will make the result of the analysis more realistic. To fill the table with data, we will use one of the techniques outlined in Chapter 9 for filling tables with random data. We can use one of the SQL statements from section 9.3:

```
INSERT INTO L8NITE.CUSTOMER (
    CREDIT_CARD,
    EXPIRY_DATE,
    LASTNAME,
    FIRSTNAME,
    ADDRESS,
    ZIP_CODE)
(SELECT
    RIGHT(DIGITS (ROW_NUMBER() OVER() -1),16),
    '0406',
    'FNAME' || CHAR(ROW_NUMBER() OVER() -1),
    'LNAME' || CHAR(ROW_NUMBER() OVER() -1),
    'ADDRESS' || CHAR(ROW_NUMBER() OVER() -1),
    RIGHT(DIGITS (ROW_NUMBER() OVER() -1),6)
    FROM SYSCAT.COLUMNS FETCH FIRST 2500 ROWS ONLY)
```

The CUSTOMER table is now filled with 2500 entries and we must select an SQL query to analyze. A reasonable query might be one that generates a mailing list for customers living in a particular zip code. Let's consider the following simple query to generate an alphabetical mailing list for customers living within zip code 10001:

```
SELECT LASTNAME, FIRSTNAME, ADDRESS, ZIP_CODE
    FROM L8NITE.CUSTOMER
    WHERE ZIP_CODE='10001'
    ORDER BY LASTNAME ASC, FIRSTNME ASC
```

Enter this query in the SQL text area of the dialog box, and click one of the two buttons highlighted in Figure 10.4. The first button (with the small green arrow) runs the SQL query and computes the access plan. The second button (the one without the green arrow) computes the access plan without executing the query. This second option is useful when you wish to analyze and tune a query having a large result set. The result of the analysis is shown graphically on the Access Plan tab of the Command Editor (Figure 10.5). Let's spend a few moments looking at the result and exploring some of the features Visual Explain has to offer.

The first thing you will notice is that the result is presented in two different windows: a larger window with a close-up view of the plan, and a smaller window labeled Overview. The sample query is relatively simple, and the Overview window may seem redundant. However, for larger queries that use complex joins and reference dozens of tables, it would be difficult to see everything all at once in one window. Using two windows allows you to look at a portion of the access plan in detail while referencing the Overview window to provide additional context.

Visual Explain can accept multiple queries as input. The result of analyzing all the statements will be displayed in the overview. You can move the detail view to another area of the access plan by dragging the blue rectangle. You can also change the magnification level by moving the slider control to the left of the detailed view.

Figure 10.5 Visual Explain

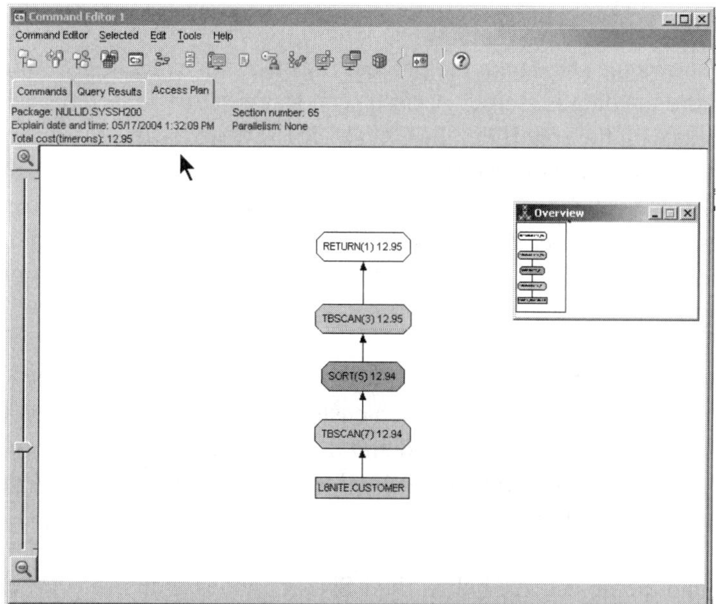

Now let's look at how to interpret the output shown in Figure 10.5. First, the total cost of processing this query can be found at the upper-left portion of the dialog box. For this SELECT query, the cost is 12.95 timerons.

Inquiring Minds: What Is a timeron?

A *timeron* is a unit of measurement that is used to give a rough relative estimate of the resources, or cost, required by the database server to execute two plans for the same query. The resources calculated in the estimate include weighted processor and I/O costs. It is very similar to a unit of time, but this concept provides a more system-neutral measurement of the cost to process a query. Although this unit does not give an absolute measurement of query performance, it provides a good comparison of queries. It also provides a good indication of changes in performance when the design of the database is altered.

To complete this particular query, DB2 had to perform a table scan (indicated by the TBSCAN box) and one sort (indicated by the SORT box). In general, it is a good idea to avoid sorts and table scans whenever possible. The cost of table scans increases linearly with the size of the table, and sorting can be an expensive operation that can sometimes (but not always) be avoided by creation of additional indexes.

In Figure 10.5, the diagram shows the steps taken to process the query. Starting at the bottom is the actual source table where the data is stored. A table scan was performed to retrieve all the required information along with the row ID in the CUSTOMER table to find entries with a zip code of 10001. The total cost of this operation was 12.94 timerons. The result was then sorted by last name and first name. The cumulative cost for operations up to this step was 12.95 timerons. Another table scan was performed over the input plan to build the output result set. You can right-click on any object in the diagram to get additional details about the operation.

According to the access plan, much of the total cost of processing this query is from the initial table scan to retrieve the data. For DB2 to get each customer living in zip code 10001, every row in the CUSTOMER table was first retrieved and then compared with the search criteria. One way to reduce this cost is to eliminate the need to read all rows in the table by creating an index on the ZIP_CODE column of the CUSTOMER table.

To create an index, you expand the object tree below the L8NITE database and select the Tables folder. In the details view, right-click the CUSTOMER table and select CREATE > INDEX from the pop-up menu (Figure 10.6).

Figure 10.6 Launching the Create Index dialog box

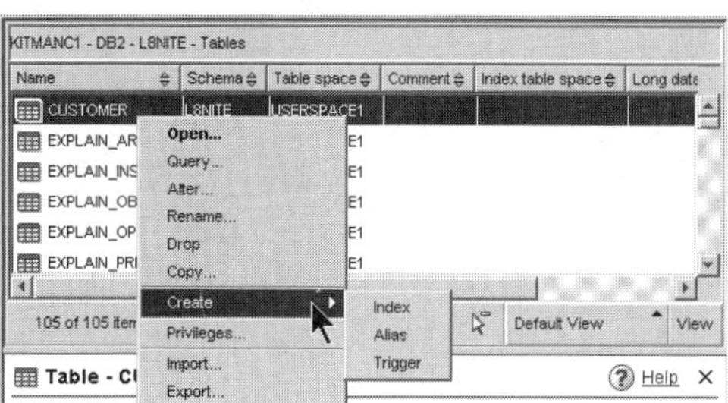

This will launch the Create Index dialog box. Fill in the required information as illustrated in Figure 10.7:

1. From the schema drop-down, select the L8NITE entry.
2. Enter ZIPCODE as the name of the new index.
3. Select the ZIP_CODE and LASTNAME columns in the column list and click the > button to use these as the index key.
4. Select the Allow Reverse Scan option.
5. Click OK to create the index.

Figure 10.7 Creating an index on the ZIP_CODE and LASTNAME columns of the CUSTOMER table

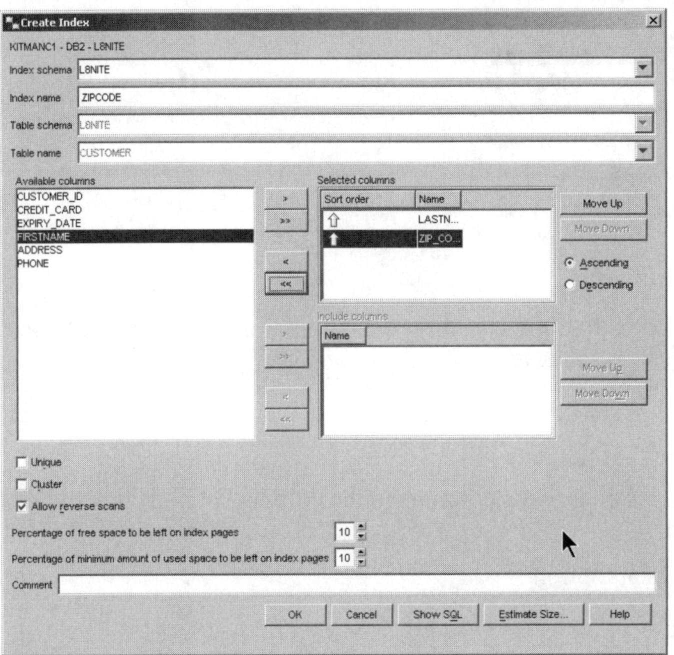

With the new ZIPCODE index created, we can look at the access plan again to see whether anything has changed. To recompute the access plan, click on the access plan button (without the green arrow) at the upper-left corner of the Command Editor. The access plan will be recomputed and the Access Plan view will be refreshed. The new access plan is shown in Figure 10.8.

Figure 10.8 Access plan after creating index ZIPCODE on table CUSTOMER

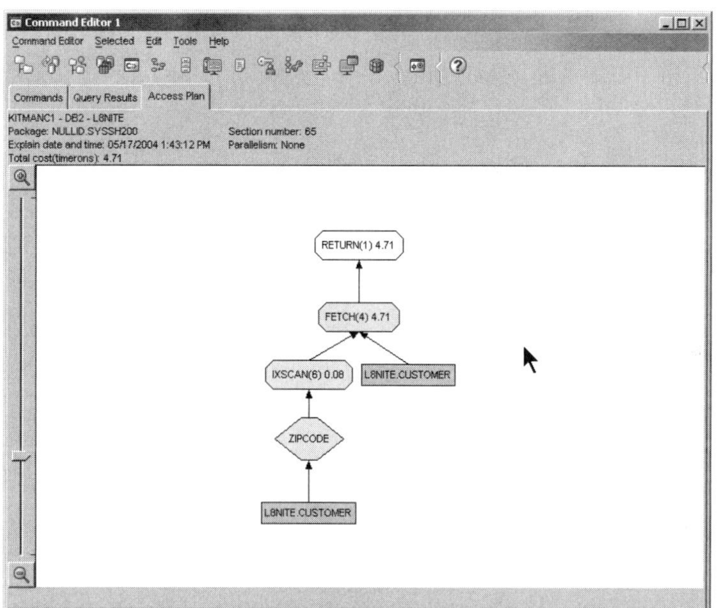

Using the new index ZIPCODE, the estimated cost of processing the query is reduced to 4.71 timerons. This represents a significant reduction from the original cost without the index. Instead of performing a table scan of the CUSTOMER table, the new access plan uses the index to fetch (IXSCAN) the records directly.

There are a few exercises at the end of this chapter on Visual Explain that may be of interest to you. Be sure to give them a try. Visual Explain is a valuable tool for tuning individual queries.

You have seen the potential for increasing database performance by adding indexes. However, it can be impractical to analyze and tune each query one by one. Also, an index that is useful for one search query may negatively impact the performance of INSERT, UPDATE, or DELETE (because of the additional overhead of maintaining the index). Therefore, before you hand-tune individual SQL queries, we recommend using the DB2 Design Advisor to automatically tune a database schema. The Design Advisor is part of DB2's autonomic self-tuning feature set.

10.5 Optimizing SQL Performance with the Design Advisor

The preceding section showed how you can improve the performance of a query by creating an index. However, the sample query was very simple. Consider the access plan for a more complex query such as the one used by the product sales ranking view from Chapter 9:

```
CREATE VIEW PRODUCT_SALES_RANKING AS
SELECT P.PRODUCT_ID, P.DESCRIPTION, SUM(PP.QTY) AS
TOTAL_SOLD
   FROM L8NITE.PRODUCT P LEFT OUTER JOIN
        L8NITE.PRODUCT_PURCHASES PP
   ON P.PRODUCT_ID = PP.PRODUCT_ID
   GROUP BY P.PRODUCT_ID, P.DESCRIPTION

SELECT * FROM PRODUCT_SALES_RANKING
ORDER BY TOTAL_SOLD DESC
FETCH FIRST 10 ROWS ONLY
```

To analyze the query for top 10 products, you must first create the PRODUCT_SALES_RANKING view. The access plan for the query is shown in Figure 10.9. The access plan is more complex, and several new indexes may be beneficial. To further complicate the problem, the access plan is highly dependent on the size of the database. All this must be taken into consideration when you tune for a single query. The problem is even more complex and time-consuming when you have more than one query in your SQL workload. An index that favors the processing of one query may slow down another. Furthermore, you will have to consider the disk space cost when more objects are created.

For our L8NITE database, the layout of the database is relatively simple and the SQL workload is also quite small. SQL tuning can be done by hand if needed. For larger databases that process a wider variety of queries, however, the problem becomes exponentially more difficult. The Design Advisor, as its name suggests, advises you on the design of your database to optimize it for a given SQL workload.

To launch the Design Advisor, expand the object tree to the L8NITE database in the Control Center. The first time the Design Advisor is launched, DB2 creates a set of predefined tables needed to analyze your SQL workload and store the result. It might take a little longer the first time, but it is a one-time cost. Subsequent launches of the Design Advisor will be much faster.

Figure 10.9 Visual Explain: A more complex example

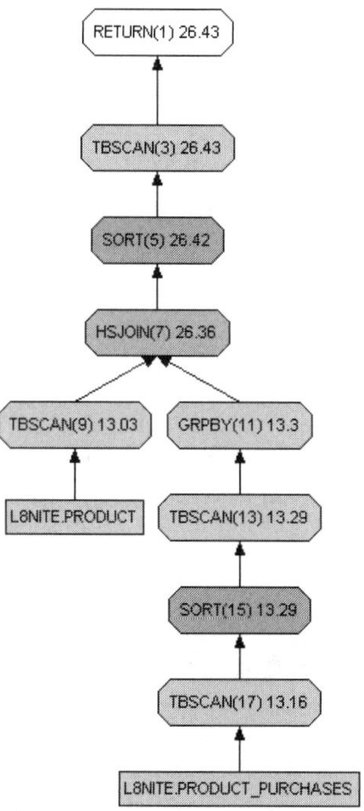

The Design Advisor is a 10-page wizard that takes advantage of the same optimizer technology used by Visual Explain to customize the design of your database. Using Visual Explain, you can tune your database for the SQL queries in your workload. The Design Advisor can do the same thing at far greater speed. It can try more variations of indexes in less time. It can also choose among various types of objects that can improve query performance. An index is only one type of DB2 object that can be used to improve query performance. Two other types of objects are available:

- Materialized query tables (MQTs)
- Multidimensional clustering tables (MDCs)

There are different reasons to use each of these objects, and the Design Advisor can help you decide by asking you a few simple operational questions about your database. Let's walk through the Design Advisor.

Inquiring Minds: What Are MQTs and MDCs?

When a query is issued, the database engine retrieves the data from the tables and arranges it into a virtual table (or view) in memory. The information is then returned as output. DB2 creates a materialized query table (MQT) by writing the result to disk in the form of a table that can be reused by multiple queries requiring the same preaggregated data. With an MQT, similar queries do not have to recalculate the same information every time, and this can dramatically improve overall query performance time.

An index allows data to be clustered based on a single dimension: one column (or a combination of columns that take part in a single index). A multidimensional clustered (MDC) table uses block indexes and organizes data grouped by multiple dimensions. Every row of data within a block of pages satisfies the clustering criteria completely. Using MDC tables promotes the possibility of data prefetching to further improve data access speed.

To use the Design Advisor, follow these steps:

Step 1: Introduction page.

The introduction page of the Design Advisor explains the advisor's capabilities. In the introductory paragraph, you can select any blue hyperlink to get an explanation of various concepts related to the advisor.

Step 2: Features page.

On this page, you can select the kind of optimizations the Design Advisor should consider in its analysis. Which options you select depends on the requirements of your database.

The first selection is which types of objects should be included in the Design Advisor's analysis. You can select up to three object types: indexes, MQTs, and MDC tables.

Regular indexes and MDC tables are safe to use in almost all databases. The user of MQTs, however, may not be appropriate depending on the type of database workload expected. MQTs derive their state based on a set of base tables. Any changes to these base tables must be reflected in the MQT by refreshing the data in the MQT, a process that can be costly. For this reason, a database workload with frequent INSERT, UPDATE, and DELETE activity and the use of MQTs may actually slow down the average SQL performance of the database.

Figure 10.10 Design Advisor: Features page

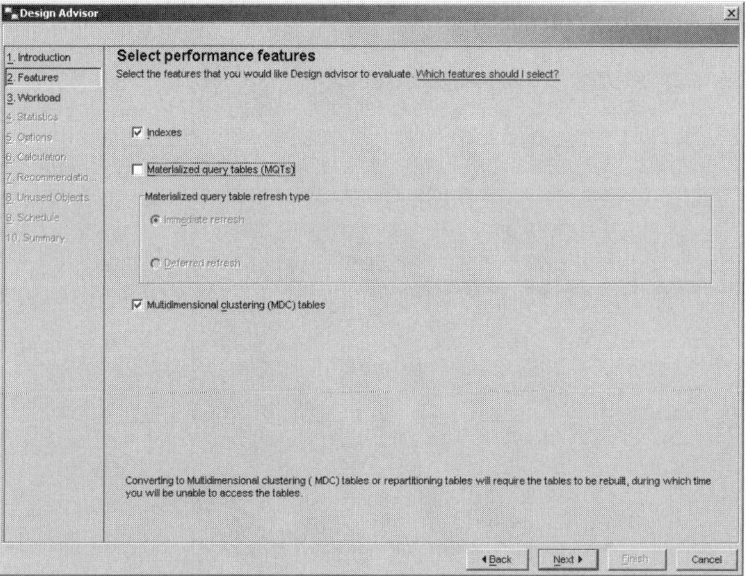

However, if the SQL workload is primarily query based, MQTs are very helpful. For a transaction-intensive workload, such as our L8NITE database, the refresh cost of MQTs outweighs it benefits. Therefore, deselect the check box for Materialized Query Table (see Figure 10.10) before proceeding.

Inquiring Minds: Keeping MQTs Up-to-Date

DB2 lets you control how a materialized query table is refreshed. You can choose to have any changes in the base tables be reflected in the MQT immediately. This is ideal if you know that the base tables are modified infrequently. In contrast, if your database application does not require up-to-the-moment data for queries that use

MQTs, you can choose to refresh the tables manually. If you choose to create a deferred MQT, you will need to set the CURRENT REFRESH AGE special register to control the tolerance allowed for old data. This register tells the optimizer whether an MQT is available for use based on its last refresh. If the data in the MQT is older than the age specified by the register, the MQT will not be used. Instead, DB2 will retrieve the data directly from the base tables.

Step 3: Workload page.

Figure 10.11 Design Advisor: Workload page

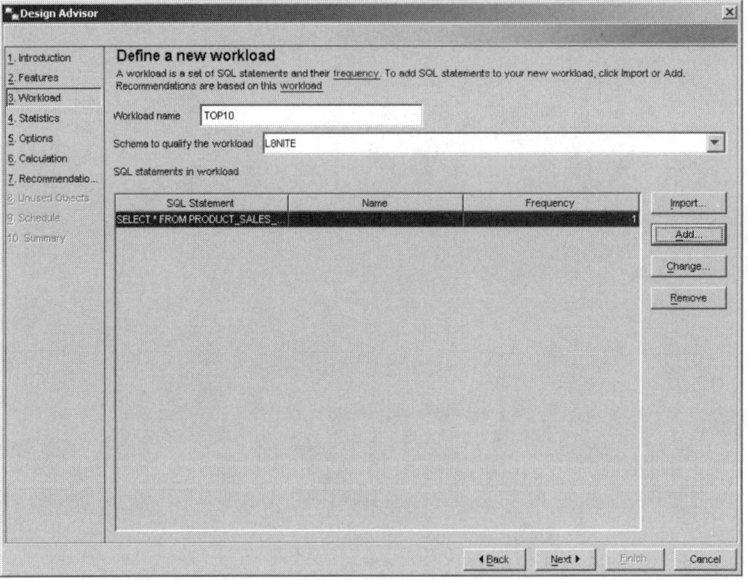

The term *workload* means the SQL used by your application. On the Workload page of the advisor (Figure 10.11), you will be asked to provide a workload. It is important to make your workload as complete as possible. This will allow the advisor to choose database objects by considering all the processing requirements on the database. The workload will be saved for reuse if needed when you run the advisor again. It also requires that you use a default schema for any table names in the workload that are not qualified.

There are a few ways to gather SQL queries for the workload. One way is to select the Add button to bring up the Add SQL dialog box and type all the SQL manually. This method can be quite tedious.

Another way to gather SQL queries is by importing them from another source. Clicking the Import button will bring up a secondary dialog box (shown in Figure 10.12) to specify the source of input. These sources include

- A workload text file
- The DB2 dynamic SQL cache (recent dynamic SQL)
- SQL that was explained using the Visual Explain tool.

For now, you can enter the SQL manually with the following steps:

1. Enter TOP10 as the workload name.
2. Select L8NITE as the default schema.
3. Click the Add button to launch the Add Statement dialog box.
4. In the Add Statement dialog box, enter

```
SELECT * FROM PRODUCT_SALES_RANKING
ORDER BY TOTAL_SOLD DESC
FETCH FIRST 10 ROWS ONLY
```

   Click OK.

5. Click Next to continue to the next page.

Figure 10.12 Import SQL Statements dialog box

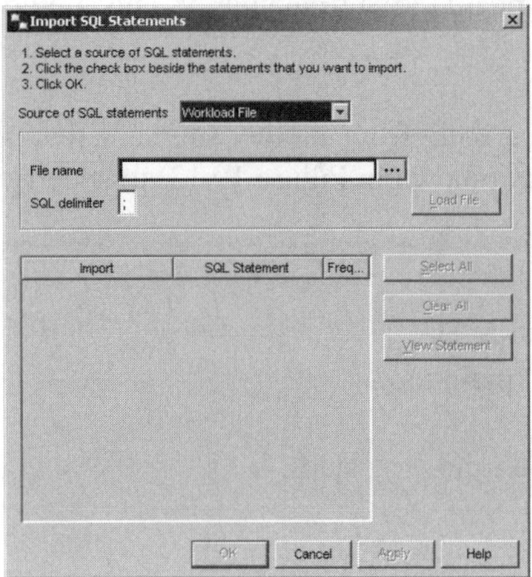

Step 4: Statistics page.

Recall from the section on Visual Explain that the optimizer uses statistics about tables and indexes, among other things, to decide on the most efficient access plan for the data. Database statistics are also used by the Design Advisor to provide accurate recommendations. The quality of the recommendations depends on the accuracy of the database statistics.

If you think that the statistics for a particular table may be out of date, select that table and click the > button to move it into the selected column (Figure 10.13). The statistics for that table will be updated and stored in the database catalog before the Design Advisor evaluates the workload.

For very large tables, statistics can be gathered by the Advisor using sampling. We will discuss that further in the next step.

Note: There are other ways of keeping table statistics up-to-date using the Automatic RUNSTATS feature. This feature monitors the tables in your database and automatically updates database statistics when needed. Automatic Maintenance will be discussed in Chapter 13.

Figure 10.13 Design Advisor: Updating table statistics

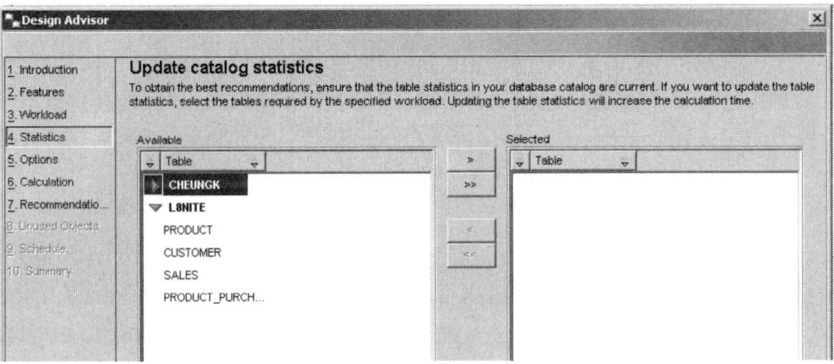

Step 5: Options page.

Several additional options are provided by the advisor to allow you to fine-tune the recommendations. All the settings on this page are optional. You can skip ahead if you like, but you may be interested in the available options.

On this page, you can choose to limit the combined amount of disk space used by the recommendations. If you use this setting, the advisor will pick the set of objects that yields the largest performance improvement and still fits within the space constraint. Simply put, the advisor will recommend objects that provide you with "the most bang for the buck."

If you have checked the option to consider materialized query tables, you can select a default table space and a default schema for all the recommended objects. If you choose to set these two options, all recommended MQTs will be created in the specified table space with the default schema.

Finally, you can choose to use a sampling algorithm to improve the accuracy of the recommendations and reduce the time needed to gather statistics. With this option, the Design Advisor will sample the base tables from the SQL workload and use the new statistics to generate its recommendations.

Step 6: Calculation page.

Because the Design Advisor will require considerable system resources to search for the appropriate recommendation, it may slow database performance during this period. To minimize the impact on your system (which may be live in production), the Design Advisor provides two additional mechanisms that allow you to schedule the start time of the search and control its duration. On the Calculate page of the advisor, you can select to run the calculation immediately or to schedule it for a later time when your database is less busy. Select the latter option. The number of pages in the Design Advisor will change.

Because you have selected to calculate later, the pages for presenting the recommendations (the Recommendation page) and the list of objects that are not used (the Unused Objects page) will not be needed. Instead, the Schedule page will be the next page in the advisor. If you decide to run the calculation later, you will have to review the result later from within the Journal. You can access the Journal from the Control Center by clicking on the Journal icon on the toolbar (Figure 10.14). The result of the analysis will be available in plain-text format similar to that found in Figure 10.15. Note that the result is actually a script that can be executed to create all the recommended objects.

Figure 10.14 Launching the Journal

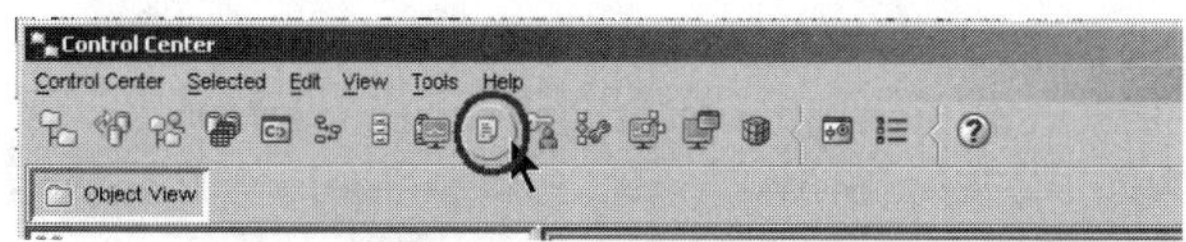

Figure 10.15 Text output from a scheduled calculation

```
Using user id as default schema name. Use -n option to specify schema
execution started at timestamp 2004-03-30-00.10.02.725000
found 1 statements in the ADVISE_WORKLOAD table
```

```
Recommending indexes...
total disk space needed for initial set [    0.018] MB
total disk space constrained to         [    4.502] MB

Trying variations of the solution set.
Optimization finished.
  2  indexes in current solution
 [ 26.0000] timerons  (without recommendations)
 [  0.1435] timerons  (with current solution)
 [99.45%] improvement

--
--
-- LIST OF RECOMMENDED INDEXES
-- ===========================
-- index[1],     0.009MB
   CREATE UNIQUE INDEX "CHEUNGK ". "IDX403300510560000" ON "L8NITE  "."PRODUCT"
("PRODUCT_ID" ASC) INCLUDE ("DESCRIPTION") ALLOW REVERSE SCANS ;
   COMMIT WORK ;
   RUNSTATS ON TABLE "L8NITE"."PRODUCT" FOR INDEX
"CHEUNGK"."IDX403300510560000";
   COMMIT WORK ;
-- index[2],     0.009MB
   CREATE INDEX "CHEUNGK "."IDX403300510240000" ON
"L8NITE"."PRODUCT_PURCHASES" ("PRODUCT_ID" ASC, "PRICE" ASC, "TOTAL" ASC,
"QTY" ASC) ALLOW REVERSE SCANS ;
   COMMIT WORK ;
   RUNSTATS ON TABLE "L8NITE  "."PRODUCT_PURCHASES" FOR INDEX "CHEUNGK
"."IDX403300510240000" ;
   COMMIT WORK ;

--
--
-- RECOMMENDED EXISTING INDEXES
-- ============================
-- ===========================
--

14 solutions were evaluated by the advisor
DB2 Workload Performance Advisor tool is finished. COMMIT WORK ;
-- ===========================
--
4 solutions were evaluated by the advisor
DB2 Workload Performance Advisor tool is finished.
```

For now, switch back to the Calculate Now option. This means that the Design Advisor will perform its analysis as soon as you click Next. But before you do that, take a look at the final option on this page. As mentioned before, you can control the maximum time that is allowed to perform the analysis. (This setting is useful if you want to try out the Design Advisor but you only have a trial window of a few minutes or hours before heavy database activity begins again.) Imposing a time limit on the advisor will cause it to report the best solution available given the time constraint. With more (or unlimited) time, the advisor can be more thorough in its analysis.

Step 7: Recommendations page.

This page will appear to take a little longer to bring up than the others because the advisor is searching for the recommendation set based on your input in the earlier pages. When the analysis is complete, the page will look similar to Figure 10.16. Near the top of the page, you will find the total performance improvement if the recommended objects are created. This figure is calculated by comparing the resources needed to run all the SQL in the workload with and without the recommended new objects. Immediately below the improvement estimate, you will find estimated disk space requirement for the new objects.

To the right of this information, you will find a button labeled Show Workload Detail. Clicking on this button will bring up a dialog box showing all the SQL in the workload and the improvement in processing speed for each operation using the recommended objects.

The Design Advisor recommendations are listed in the table near the middle of the page. The recommendations are grouped based on the type of operation required to create the recommended database objects. These actions include creating indexes, creating materialized query tables, and altering existing tables for multidimensional clustering.

This view can assist you in differentiating the recommendations by organizing them based on the action required for creating them. Here are a few rules of thumb to help you in deciding which recommendations you should accept:

- Indexes will improve search and sort performance. They are also relatively cheap to create and maintain, so you can accept Create Index recommendations in general.
- MQTs can provide performance improvement in systems in which the data is relatively static, such as databases used for data-mining-type applications. MQTs are quite costly to update if the tables referenced by the MQTs experience many

INSERTs, UPDATEs, or DELETEs.

- MDCs are good recommendations to take in most cases, provided that the workload is complete and the overhead of altering the table is acceptable. There are some additional considerations for accepting MDC recommendations. First, rebuilding large tables can take considerable time and may impact database performance. Second, it is also important to make sure that the database is populated with sufficient data. If the data is not representative of the actual production environment, the recommended clustering dimensions may be incorrect. This can cause a large increase in disk space usage and can slow data access performance.

Figure 10.16 Design Advisor: Recommendation page

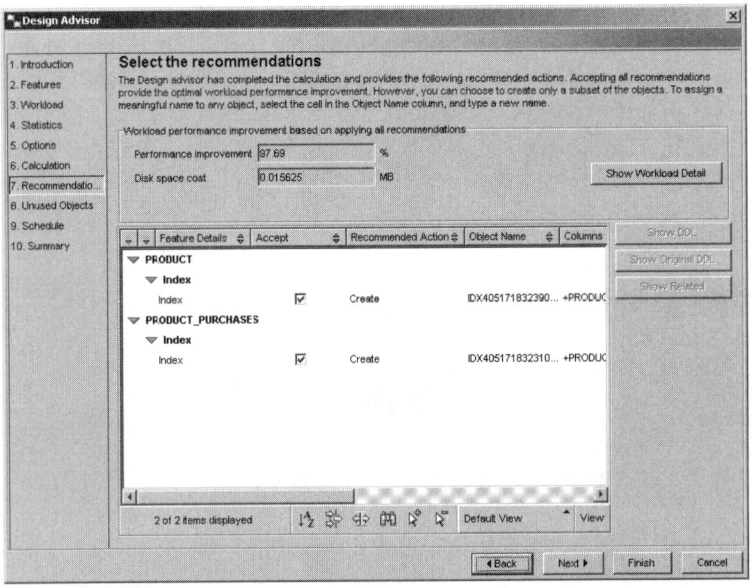

Step 8: Unused Objects page.

The Unused Objects page of the Design Advisor provides a summary of existing database objects (indexes and MQTs) that were not accessed by DB2 to process the queries in your workload (Figure 10.17). This page provides a consolidated view of what may not be needed so that you can drop these objects and recover disk space. It is important to realize that the

Design Advisor is not recommending that you remove these objects. They may still be used by SQL queries that were not included in the workload you defined. Consider dropping these objects only if you are certain that

- The workload used for the analysis contains a complete set of the SQL to be processed by the database
- The database objects are not created by someone else to support another client application for your database

Note: In Figure 10.17, the index we created in section 10.4 is listed as an unused object. This is because we did not include the SQL we used in that section as part of our workload. If the statements were included, the Design Advisor would list this index on the Recommendation page and would recommend that this index be kept. This is why it is important to make sure that the workload contains a complete set of SQL.

Figure 10.17 Design Advisor: Unused Objects page

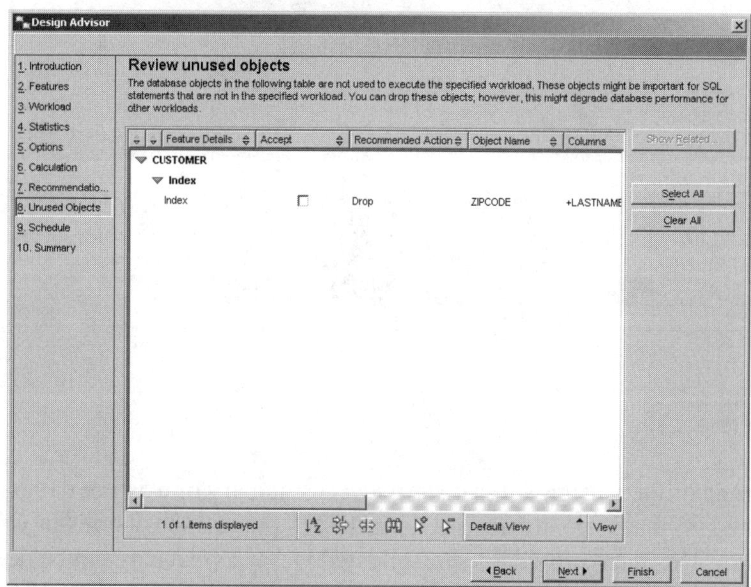

Step 9: Schedule page (Design Advisor-specific).

The Schedule page of the Design Advisor is different from that found in other parts of the graphical tools (Figure 10.18). It provides a Generate Recommendation Report function that is specific to the Design Advisor. In many companies where a database is a centralized storage of data for several applications, it is sometimes important that the various teams in charge of each application be satisfied with the recommended database objects. The report generation function allows you to write the recommendations to a text file on the file system. The report will contain crucial information—such as total performance improvement, size estimate, and all relevant SQL—so that the recommendations can be reviewed and approved. To make the creation of these objects more convenient after they are approved, the report is also a script that can be executed through the DB2 Command Editor.

From the Command Editor menu bar, select Command Editor > Open.

1. From the Open dialog box, select the report file from your file system and click Open.

2. Run the commands by clicking on the button in the Command Editor window.

Figure 10.18 Design Advisor: Schedule page

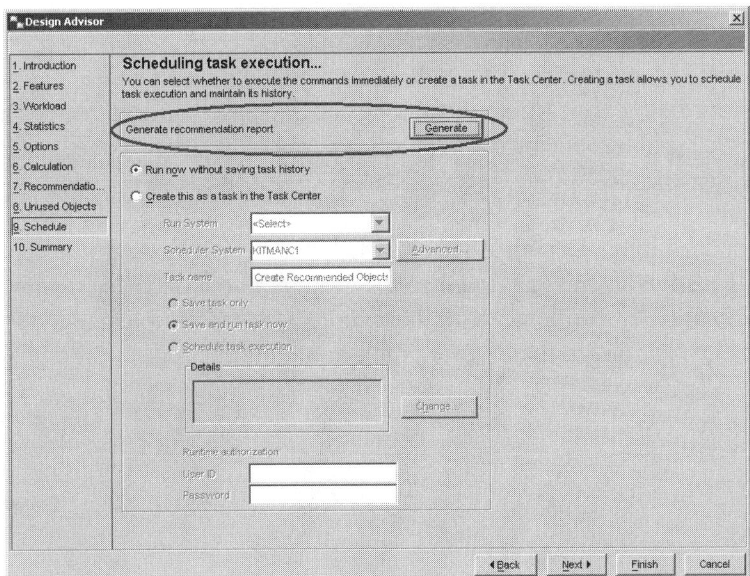

Because implementing the recommendations can consume a great deal of system resources, you may wish to create the recommended objects at a later time when system utilization is lower. You can accomplish this by selecting the Schedule Task Execution option and clicking the Change button to specify a schedule.

Step 10: Summary page.

The main purpose of this page is to provide a summary of the actions you have chosen. If you are satisfied with your choices, you can apply them to the database by clicking Finish. At any given time, you can go back to the Recommendation page, the Unused Objects page, or the Schedule page to change your choices. Note that if you move to a page prior to the Recommendations page and make a change to an option that may affect the results of the advisor's analysis, the pages after the Recommendation page will be disabled. When you enter the Recommendation page, a new analysis will take place based on the new options you have selected.

10.6 Summary

In this chapter, you have learned how to establish a baseline DB2 configuration using the Configuration Advisor and how to further tweak database parameters using the Configuration Parameters dialog box. After configuring the database you can troubleshoot specific SQL performance problems using Visual Explain. You have learned about SQL access plans and the basics of how to tune SQL.

Finally, you were introduced to the Design Advisor, which simplifies the task of schema tuning. Using the Design Advisor, you can optimize the design of your database to maximize its performance for a given SQL workload. With these tools, you can establish a good configuration baseline for your database before sending it into production.

10.7 Chapter Exercises

1. How many table scans are required to process this query for the SAMPLE database? (The SAMPLE database is provided as part of your DB2 installation. You can create this database by issuing the *db2sampl* command at a command prompt.)

```
SELECT *
  FROM EMPLOYEE, DEPARTMENT, PROJECT
  WHERE EMPLOYEE.WORKDEPT = DEPARTMENT.DEPTNO
    AND DEPARTMENT.DEPTNO LIKE 'E%'
    AND PROJECT.DEPTNO = DEPARTMENT.DEPTNO
  ORDER BY EMPLOYEE.LASTNAME ASC,
    EMPLOYEE.FIRSTNME ASC
```

2. Analyze one of the report queries used in the sample application using Visual Explain. Try to reduce the cost (in timerons) for processing this query by introducing indexes.

3. View and update DBM or DB CFG through the CLP. To retrieve the database manager configuration, open a DB2 Command Window and type

   db2 GET DBM CFG

   To update any parameters on this list, type

   db2 UPDATE DBM CFG USING *<parameter>* *<value>*

   What do you think the commands are for viewing and changing database configuration parameters?

4. Using the Design Advisor, optimize the L8NITE database for our point-of-sale terminal application.

CHAPTER 11

Implementing Security

In this chapter, you will learn:

- About DB2 authorities and privileges
- How to manage privileges for users and user groups
- About the various authentication methods available
- How to use DB2's built-in functions to perform data encryption
- How to configure DB2 servers and clients to perform encrypted communications

11.1 Introduction

Although our L8NITE database application is now fully functional, we have not discussed security very much. To accommodate new DB2 users, we developed the L8NITE application using an instance system administrator (SYSADM) user. The SYSADM user, by default, is db2admin on Windows and db2inst1 on Linux.

In this way, security issues did not complicate the learning environment. As you can imagine, it would probably be a bad idea to use the SYSADM user for everyday operations especially if your application is a multiuser application. Data in the database could become corrupted because of abuse or accident. The SYSADM user ID and password should be guarded carefully.

In the following sections, you'll learn to use DB2 to manage users, groups, and privileges. You will see how a DB2 server can be configured to use various authentication and encrypted communication modes. Also, we will look at how to leverage DB2's built-in data encryption functionality.

11.2 Database Users

Perhaps the first concept to grasp is that DB2 does not actually have database users. Instead, DB2 relies on an external security facility, such as the operating system, for user management and authentication. There are several benefits to this.

- System administrators do not have to manage additional user IDs and passwords for every user of every database.
- Companies often enforce security policies that include changing network passwords every few months. When a network password is changed, DB2 will use the latest password for greater consistency.

If you want to add a new database user, simply use an existing operating system user to authenticate, or create a new operating system user.

A user with full instance authority is called a SYSADM user. For example, a SYSADM user for a given instance can

- Stop and start the instance
- Create and drop databases
- Create and drop any database object
- Access and manipulate any data in any database
- Grant and revoke privileges to any user
- Back up and restore any database
- Force users off a database

Three other types of instance-level authority exist for every instance: SYSCTRL, SYSMAINT, and SYSMON. DB2 was designed to meet the needs of large enterprises that may have hundreds of databases managed by many database administrators. You can imagine how a company might have not just one database administrator but teams of them—one team that focuses on maintenance (e.g., backup and restore), another for performance tuning, another acting as senior DBAs. To protect information, the SYSCTRL, SYSMAINT, and SYSMON group definitions define users who can perform a subset of the SYSADM functions but without the power to view data. The groups are defined by the database manager configuration (DBM CFG) parameters SYSCTRL_GROUP, SYSMAINT_GROUP, and SYSMON_GROUP.

Note: The DBM CFG and DB CFG are discussed in Chapter 10, Performance Tuning.

For applications that do not require such fine-grained control, all four parameters are usually set to the same value. You should define separate groups for SYSCTRL, SYSMAINT, and SYSMON only if you have a clear requirement to do so.

11.3 Defining the SYSADM Authority

The SYSADM authority is defined by group membership in the DBM configuration. The DBM CFG parameter is SYSADM_GROUP, and the value of this parameter is the operating system group of users who should have SYSADM authority for that instance.

When you installed DB2, you were prompted to identify a SYSADM user for the default instance. On Windows, the user db2admin was created and added as a member of the Windows local system administrators group. The default value of SYSADM_GROUP is blank, implying that local Windows administrators are DB2 SYSADM users.

On Linux, the user db2inst1 was created, and the default value of SYSADM_GROUP is db2grp1 (the primary group of the db2inst1 user). The db2inst1 user, for example, has no special privileges on the operating system other than SYSADM authority.

Inquiring Minds: DBADM and LOAD Authority

DB2 defines two other types of authority: DBADM and LOAD. We do not use them in our application, but we discuss them briefly here.

A user granted DBADM authority has full database privileges, whereas SYSADM is an instance administrator authority. In other words, if two databases have been created in the same instance, the SYSADM would have all privileges on both databases because the authority is defined at the instance level. A user granted DBADM authority on one database, however, would not necessarily have the same privileges on another database. A user who creates a database (usually a SYSADM user) is automatically granted DBADM authority on the database. Therefore, you generally do not need to define DBADM authorities unless you have multiple databases within the same instance and require unique database administrators for each one. On production systems, we generally recommend having only one database per instance, a practice that further reduces the need to define additional DBADM authorities.

The LOAD authority is another database authority that, when combined with the INSERT privilege on a table, allows a user to use the LOAD utility (discussed in Chapter 9, Working with Data). SYSADM and DBADM can use the LOAD utility without additional authority. Therefore, you need to grant LOAD authority only if users other than SYSADM or DBADM need to use the LOAD utility.

In the following sections, we show you how to change the SYSADM on Windows so that db2admin is not also a local administrator.

Considerations for DB2 for Windows

Often, you don't want the SYSADM user to also be the operating system administrator (as is the default case for Windows). For example, your network administrator may be different from your DB2 administrator. As you would expect, it is possible to change the definition of SYSADM users. We consider it a best practice to separate these two roles, but it is optional. The considerations described here do not apply to Linux because db2inst1 does not have root authority.

Changing the SYSADM definition is a four-step process.

1. Create a new operating system group called SYSADM (or whatever you like), and make the db2admin user a member of this group.
2. Remove db2admin from the Windows local administrators group.
3. Change the SYSADM_GROUP parameter in the DBM CFG to SYSADM.
4. Restart the DB2 instance.

Now let's look at this process in more detail.

Step 1: Create a new operating system group SYSADM.

On your Windows desktop, right-click on My Computer and select the Manage menu item (Figure 11.1).

Figure 11.1 Launching the Windows Computer Management console

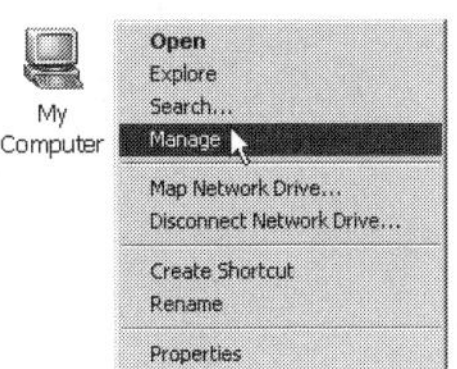

From the Windows Computer Management console, expand the object tree to the Groups folder.

Right-click on the Groups folder, and select New Group from the pop-up menu (Figure 11.2).

Figure 11.2 Creating a new group

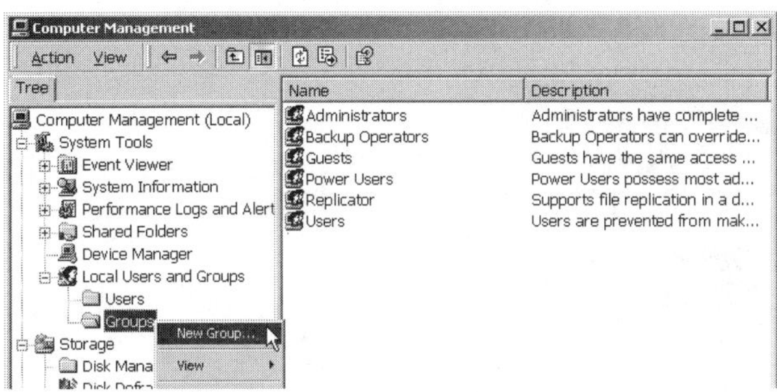

In the New Group dialog box, provide details of the new group as you see in Figure 11.3. Be sure to add the db2admin user to this group.

We decided to create a group called SYSADM. You can, of course, use any group name you want. You can also use any existing operating system groups.

Figure 11.3 Defining the SYSADM group

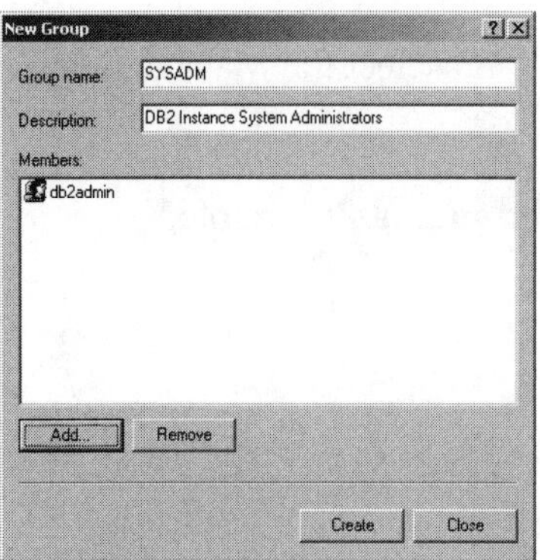

Step 2: Remove db2admin from the Windows local administrator group.

Right-click on the Administrators group, and select the Properties menu item (Figure 11.4).

Figure 11.4 Changing Administrators group members

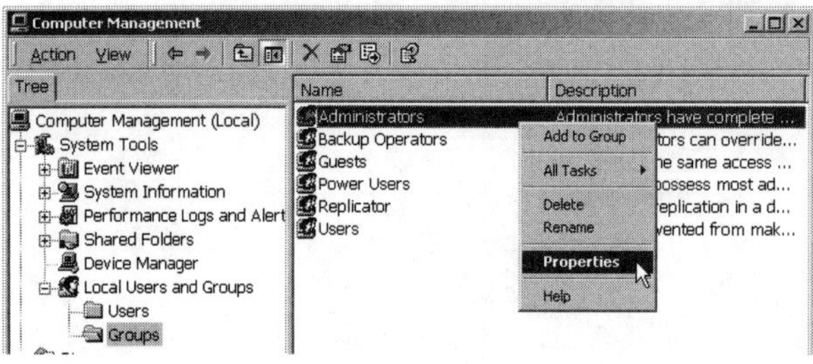

Figure 11.5 Removing db2admin from the Administrators group

In the Administrators Properties dialog box, select the db2admin user and click the Remove button (Figure 11.5).

Step 3: Change the SYSADM_GROUP parameter to SYSADM.

If you are using the Control Center's Basic view, change the Control Center view to Advanced Mode. From the Control Center Tools menu, select Customize Control Center.

Select the Advanced view and click OK.

In the DB2 Control Center object tree, navigate to All Systems > (hostname) > Instances > DB2 (or db2inst1 on Linux).

Right-click on the DB2 instance object, and select Configure Parameters from the pop-up menu (Figure 11.6).

Figure 11.6 Changing SYSADM_GROUP

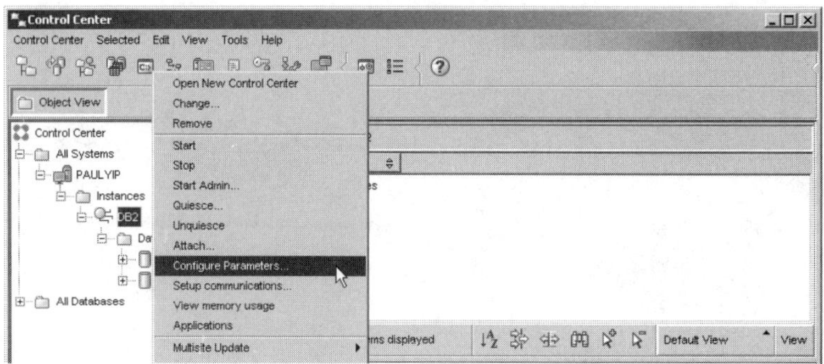

Locate the configuration parameter SYSADM_GROUP (in the Administration parameters group). This parameter identifies the operating system group of users who will have SYSADM authority. By default, this value is blank on Windows, and this means that the local Windows administrators group will have this privilege. A single click on the blank value will reveal a dotted button (Figure 11.7).

Figure 11.7 Changing the SYSADM_GROUP parameter

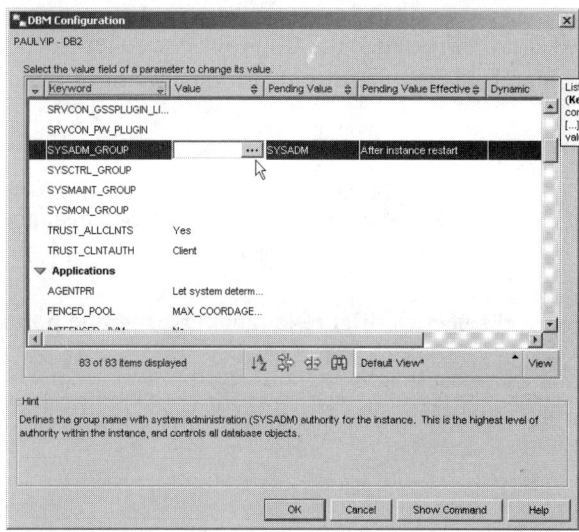

Clicking on the dotted button will allow you to change the value.

Repeat this step for the SYSCTRL, SYSMAINT, and SYSMON groups. After you complete this step, SYSADM_GROUP, SYSCTRL_GROUP, SYSMAINT_GROUP, and SYSMON_GROUP should all have the value SYSADM.

Step 4: Restart the instance.

After you click OK and close the DBM Configuration window, you should see a message like this: “The DBM configuration settings were updated successfully. If a running application is accessing DB2, some of the changes will not be reflected in that application until DB2 is re-started.”

Therefore, the last step is to restart the database for the new security policy to take effect.

Stop the database by right-clicking on the L8NITE database object and selecting the Stop menu item (Figure 11.8).

Figure 11.8 Stopping the instance

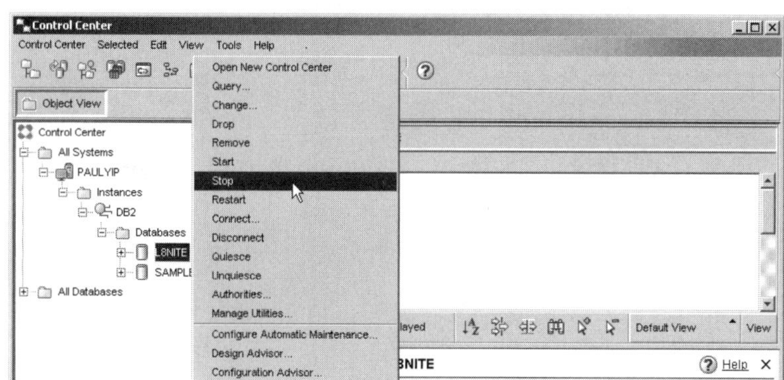

A dialog box will pop up to confirm that the instance should be stopped. You may also want to ensure that the Disconnect All Applications option is selected. The stop will fail if any database connections still exist.

Wait for a confirmation that the instance has been successfully stopped. This may take a few moments. When you have confirmation that the instance was stopped successfully, start the instance by right-clicking on the DB2 instance object and selecting the Start menu item.

Using the Local System Account for DB2 Services

On Windows, DB2 services are run using the SYSADM user ID provided during installation (for example, db2admin). A copy of the password is saved as a logon property of each DB2 service. This can cause a problem if the password for the SYSADM user is changed in the future.

To view the DB2 Service logon property, follow these steps:

Step 1: View Windows Services applet.

Right-click My Computer and select Manage from the pop-up menu.

Navigate to: Computer Management (Local) > Services and Applications > Services.

Step 2: View DB2 Service properties.

Right-click DB2 Service and select properties from the pop-up menu.

Figure 11.9 DB2 Service login properties

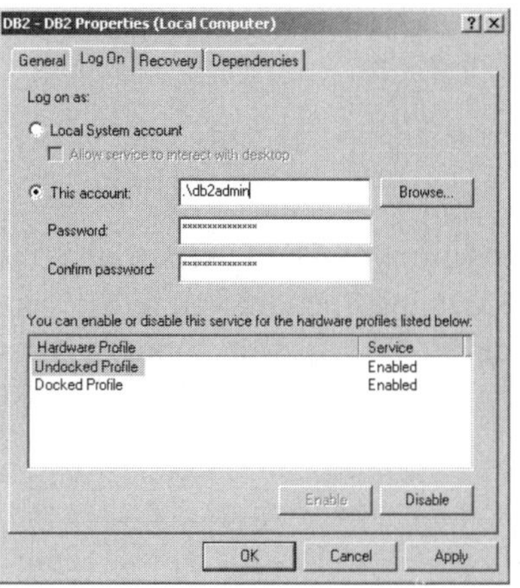

As you can see in Figure 11.9, the user ID and password are stored as part of the service. If the SYSADM password is changed, you must also remember to update the DB2 services properties to use the new password. Unfortunately, most novice users do not know about this. Therefore, we recommend changing DB2 services to run as a Windows Local System account. DB2 will then run as a local system service (Figure 11.2). It also virtually guarantees that DB2 will not have authentication problems if passwords are changed in the future.

Figure 11.10 Configuring DB2 to use the Local System account

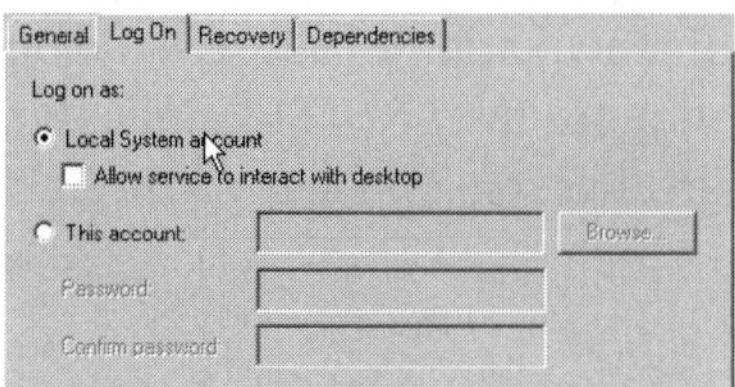

Be sure to change this setting for all DB2 services. In the Windows Services dialog box, all DB2-related service names start with "DB2." For example:

- DB2 JDBC Applet Server
- DB2 License Server

- DB2DAS
- DB2 Security Server

11.4 Application Users

In the preceding section, we showed you how to reconfigure SYSADM users so that they are not also operating system administrators (on Windows). In this section, you will see how to go further to secure the database using object-level security. Consider the types of users who may use the L8NITE application (Table 11.1).

Table 11.1 Application Users

User Type	Description
DB2 Administrator (SYSADM)	Manages the operational aspects of the database such as configuration, performance tuning, security, and backup/recovery
Manager	Needs full access to data, but because he or she may not be technical, we want to protect the system from accidental damage or corruption by this person
Employee	Daily user of the L8NITE application who should have tightly controlled access to database objects required for day-to-day operations

We already have a user to act as SYSADM. We now define two additional users—manager and employee—to implement a fine-grained security policy for the L8NITE application. As mentioned earlier, DB2 does not manage any database-level users. All users are defined at the operating system level.

Creating Users on Windows

Open the Windows Computer Management console. Right-click on My Computer, and select the Manage menu item.

In the Windows Computer Management console, navigate to Computer Management > System Tools > Local Users and Groups > Users.

Right-click on the User folder, and select the New User menu item (Figure 11.11).

Figure 11.11 Creating new Windows users

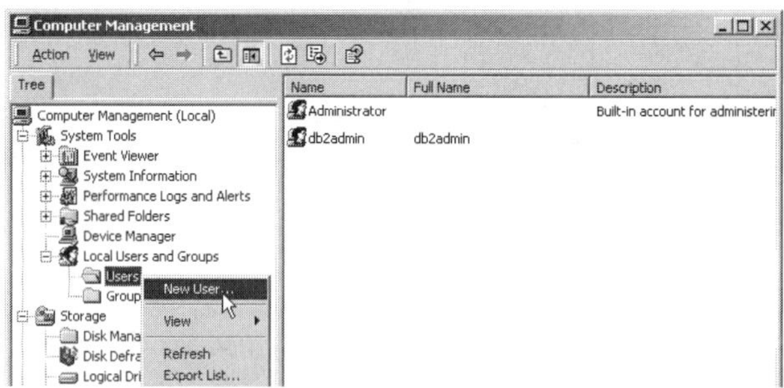

Specify the user name, full name, and description as you see in Figure 11.12. We will use the password ibmdb2 for simplicity.

Deselect the User must change password on next logon option, and click the Create button.

Figure 11.12 The Manager user

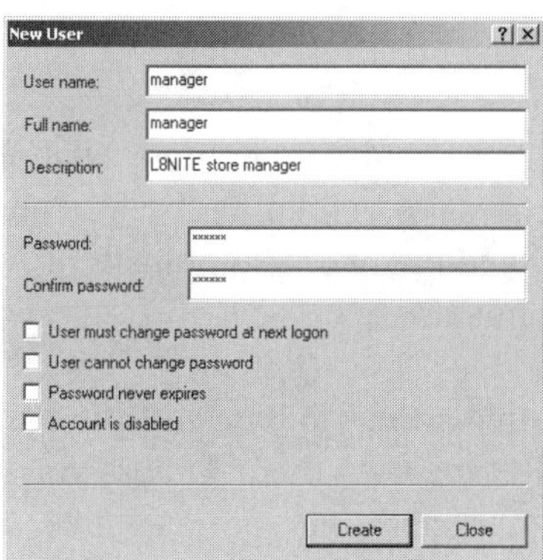

Repeat the foregoing steps to create a user called employee with the following information:

Field	Value
User name	employee
Full name	employee
Description	L8NITE store employee
Password	ibmdb2
User must change password at next logon	disabled

Creating Users on Linux

Users can be created on Linux using the useradd command. To create users, you must be logged in as root. In the following example, su is used to switch to the root user, followed by commands to add the employee and manager users (both of whom will use the password ibmdb2).

```
$ su -
# adduser manager -p ibmdb2
# adduser employee -p ibmdb2
```

11.5 Authentication and Authorization

When you connect to DB2 and access some data, at least two security operations take place: authentication and authorization. *Authentication* is the process of validating that you are whom you claim to be. This is usually done via a user ID and password combination. After authentication succeeds, a connection is established to the database.

A successful connection, however, does not imply unfettered access to data and database objects. You will have access to tables you created because you own them. Unless you created a database object, or you have SYSADM or DBADM authority, or you were otherwise granted access (discussed next), you will not have access to the object.

Whenever a user attempts to access a database object, DB2 will automatically check whether the user has sufficient privileges to perform the desired operation. Because all our application tables were created using the SYSADM user, manager and employee do not have any access to these tables. Let's now grant sufficient privileges for the manager and employee users to perform their roles.

Manager User

We assume that the manager user is nontechnical but has a business need to view and modify any data in any table. At the same time, we must protect the manager from accidentally damaging the database, and that is why we do not simply let managers use the SYSADM user ID. We should grant SELECT, INSERT, UPDATE, and DELETE privileges to manager for all tables and views. For the following instructions, be sure to be logged in to the operating system as the SYSADM user.

Step 1: Switch to the Control Center Advanced view.

If you are using the Control Center Basic view, select Customize Control Center from the Tools menu. Switch to Advanced view.

Step 2: View tables to grant privileges.

Expand the Control Center object tree to All Databases > L8NITE > Tables.

Step 3: Grant the required privileges to manager.

Expand the DB2 Control Center object tree, and right-click on the CUSTOMER table. Select the Privileges menu item to view the Table Privileges dialog box (Figure 11.13).

Figure 11.13 Opening the Table Privileges dialog box

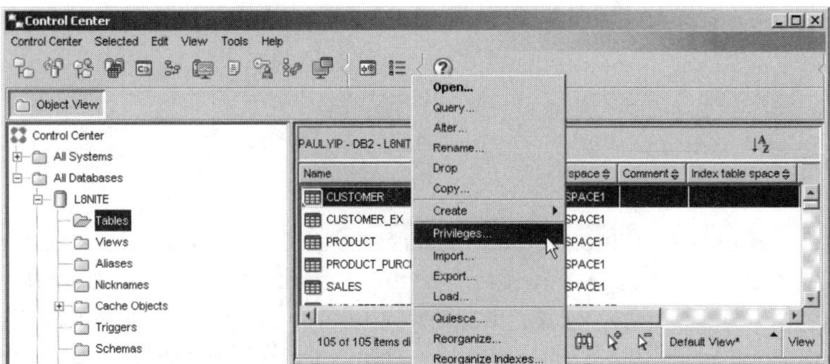

In the Table Privileges dialog box, you can see all the privileges granted (Figure 11.14). You can see that the db2admin user is listed, and double check marks are shown for the SELECT, INSERT, UPDATE, and DELETE privileges. The double check mark means that users have privileges because they originally created the tables.

Click on the Add User button, and select Manager. Select OK to close the Add User dialog box.

Figure 11.14 CUSTOMER table privileges

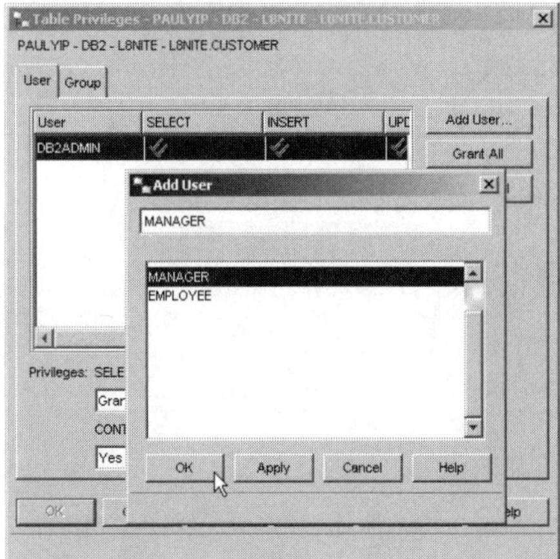

Initially, you will see that the manager has been added to the user list but has no privileges. To grant SELECT, INSERT, UPDATE, and DELETE privileges to manager, change the SELECT, INSERT, UPDATE, and DELETE privileges to Yes in the pull-down menus (Figure 11.15).

Click Show SQL to familiarize yourself with the SQL being issued under the covers.

Figure 11.15 Grant privileges to MANAGER

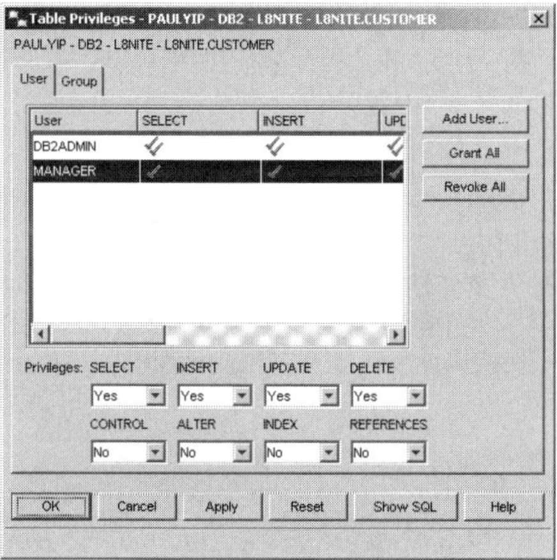

Click OK to save the changes.

Repeat step 3 for the PRODUCT, PRODUCT_PURCHASES, and SALES tables for the manager user. Also, be sure to grant the SELECT privilege to the reporting views PRODUCT_SALES_RANKING and NO_VISIT_30_DAYS created in Chapter 9, Working with Data. (Hint: Navigate to the Views folder in the Control Center object tree.)

Employee User

The employee should have access to data only on a need-to-know basis.

In the CUSTOMER table, the application allows new customers to be added at any time. Therefore, employees should be able to insert into the CUSTOMER table. Also, it is conceivable that an existing customer entering the store may want to update information in our system. Therefore, UPDATE on the CUSTOMER table also should be allowed. Employees have no need to delete customer data, so we should not grant the DELETE privilege on the CUSTOMER table to employees.

The employee at the L8NITE store operates only the point-of-sale terminal. He or she does not purchase new products to be sold at the store; this is done by the manager. However, the application needs to be able to display products for employees operating the application. Therefore, employees need the SELECT privilege on this table.

The PRODUCT_PURCHASES table is used whenever a new purchase is made. The employee may insert new rows into this table as purchases are made. The employee should not be allowed to delete purchases made in the past. If a correction needs to be made, it should be performed by the manager.

The SALES table is used to map product purchases to a customer. As with the PRODUCT_PURCHASES table, the employee may insert new rows into this table as purchases are made. An update operation on SALES is part of the sales transaction, and the employee will therefore require the UPDATE privilege on SALES. The employee should not be allowed to delete sales made in the past.

As part of a transaction, the PRODUCT table contains the retail price, which must be retrieved during a transaction, and the inventory must be updated as products are purchased. Therefore, the employee should have SELECT and UPDATE privileges on PRODUCT.

Table 11.2 summarizes the privileges to be granted given the requirements we've outlined. You should now repeat step 3 from the preceeding section, but for the employee user.

Table 11.2 Privileges to Be Granted to employee User

Table Name	SELECT	INSERT	UPDATE	DELETE
CUSTOMER	Yes	Yes	Yes	No
PRODUCTS	Yes	No	Yes	No
PRODUCT_PURCHASES	Yes	Yes	No	No
SALES	Yes	Yes	Yes	No

Inquiring Minds: What Are the Other Privileges?

Database Privileges:

- CONNECT allows users to connect to the database.
- BINDADD allows users to create new packages in the database.
- CREATETAB allows users to create new tables in the database.
- CREATE_NOT_FENCED allows users to create nonfenced user-defined functions or stored procedures.
- IMPLICIT_SCHEMA allows users to create objects in a schema that does not already exist.
- QUIESCE_CONNECT allows users to access the database while it is quiesced.
- CREATE_EXTERNAL_ROUTINE allows users to create stored procedures written in C, Java, OLE, and COBOL.

Schema privileges:

- CREATEIN allows users to create objects within the schema.
- ALTERIN allows users to alter objects within the schema.
- DROPIN allows users to drop objects within the schema.

Table space privileges:

- USE allows users to create tables within the specified table space. This privilege cannot be used on the SYSCATSPACE or any system temporary table spaces.

Table and view privileges:

- CONTROL provides the user with all privileges for a table or view as well as the ability to grant those privileges (except CONTROL) to others.
- ALTER allows users to alter a table or view.
- DELETE allows users to delete rows from a table or view.
- INDEX allows users to create indexes on a table.
- INSERT allows users to insert rows into a table or view.
- REFERENCES allows users to create and drop a foreign key, specifying the table as the parent in a relationship.
- SELECT allows users to retrieve rows from a table or view.
- UPDATE allows users to update data in a table or view. This privilege can also limit users to updating specific columns only.
- ALL PRIVILEGES grants all the foregoing privileges except CONTROL on a table or view.

Package privileges:

- CONTROL provides users the ability to rebind, drop, or execute a package as well as the ability to grant these privileges (except CONTROL) to others.
- BINDADD allows users to bind new packages to a database.
- BIND allows users to rebind (reoptimize) an existing package.
- EXECUTE allows users to execute a package.

Index privileges:

- CONTROL allows users to drop an index.

Routine privileges:

- EXECUTE allows users to execute user-defined functions.

Sequence privileges

- USAGE allows users to use NEXTVAL and PREVVAL expressions on a sequence object.

11.6 Group Privileges

In the preceding section, we defined user privileges explicitly and granted access on a user-by-user basis. You should be aware, however, that DB2 can also manage privileges by operating system group. Although we discuss group privileges here, we are not using it for our application.

Suppose the store has many managers and employees:

- Managers: Mary and Michael
- Employees: Eugene, Eric, and Eva

Rather than grant explicit privileges for each of the five users, you could create two operating system groups called managers and employees. You would then add Mary and Michael to the managers group. Similarily, Eugene, Eric, and Eva would be added to the employees group.

Instead of granting privileges to specific users as we did earlier, you would grant privileges to the groups. Mary and Michael, being members of the managers group, would then have the necessary privileges. Similarly, Eugene, Eric, and Eva would have privileges granted to the employee group.

Managing security at the group level can simplify the life of a database administrator. For example, should Eva be promoted to become a manager, the administrator need only remove her from the employees operating system group and add her to the managers operating system group.

Group Privilege Considerations

When you implement a security scheme using group membership, it is important to understand the difference between group and user privileges recognized by DB2.

When you grant privileges to a user directly, the user is said to have been granted explicit privileges. In the database system catalog tables, the user is directly recognized as having been granted the privilege. When a group is granted privileges, members of that group are said to have implicit privileges inherited through group membership, and DB2 associates the privilege only with the group name in the system catalog tables at runtime, and not with the users of the group.

Consider the following scenario:

- USER1 is granted explicit SELECT privilege to T1.
- GROUP1 is also granted SELECT privilege to table T1.
- USER1 becomes a member of GROUP1.
- USER1 is removed from GROUP1.

In this example, USER1 still retains the SELECT privilege granted to USER1. In other words, to revoke a privilege granted to a user, you must revoke the privilege directly from the user.

11.7 The PUBLIC Group

In addition to defining and leveraging operating system groups, DB2 internally defines a group called PUBLIC. Any user who successfully connects to DB2 is implicitly a member of the PUBLIC group.

When a database is created, the following privileges are granted to PUBLIC:

- CREATETAB: Any users who can connect can create their own tables as long as the fully qualified table name does not conflict with the name of an existing table and an appropriate table space exists.
- BINDADD: Any user can bind new packages. (For example, SQL procedures, when compiled, become packages bound to the database.)
- CONNECT: Any user can connect to a database provided that he or she supplies a valid user ID and password combination recognized by the authentication service.
- IMPLICIT_SCHEMA: Schemas, when they do not exist, will automatically be created.
- USE privilege on the USERSPACE1 table space: All users can create tables in the default table space userspace1.
- SELECT privilege on the system catalog views: All users can view data in the system catalog views grouped in the SYSCAT schema.

You can also use the PUBLIC group for your own database objects. In the following example, we show you how to grant the SELECT privilege to the PUBLIC group.

Step 1: Select the table on which to change privileges.

Right-click on the PRODUCT table, and select Privileges from the pop-up menu.

Step 2: Add the PUBLIC group to permissions.

Figure 11.16 Granting privileges to the PUBLIC group

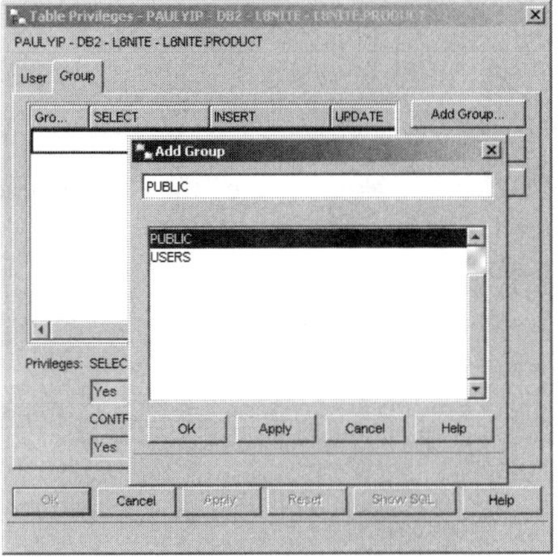

Select the PUBLIC group from the list of available groups (Figure 11.6).

Select the Group tab in the Table Privileges dialog box, and click the Add Group button.

Step 3: Grant the SELECT privilege to PUBLIC.

Select the PUBLIC group. Select Yes from the pull-down list for the SELECT privilege.

Click OK to save the changes.

All users who can connect can now view data in the PRODUCTS table.

11.8 Authentication Modes

When connecting to a database, by default DB2 authenticates users by comparing the supplied credentials with those defined at the server. This behavior is controlled in the database manager configuration (DBM CFG) file. Table 11.3 summarizes other options available.

Table 11.3 Authentication Options

Authentication Type	Description
SERVER (default)	Authentication takes place on the server containing the database.
CLIENT	Authentication takes place on the client where the application is invoked.
SERVER_ENCRYPT	Authentication takes place on the server containing the database. Passwords are encrypted at the client and decrypted at the server.
KERBEROS	Authentication takes place using the Kerberos security mechanism.
SQL_AUTHENTICATION_DATAENC	Authentication takes place on the server containing the target database, and connections must use data encryption.
SQL_AUTHENTICATION_DATAENC_CMP	Authentication takes place on the node containing the target database, and connections must use data encryption when available.
GSSPLUGIN	Authentication takes place using an external GSS API-based plug-in security mechanism.

If the database server and client are on the same machine, the default value of SERVER will suffice. If the client and server are separate, however, it would be wise to use the SERVER_ENCRYPT setting, which encrypts passwords before they flow over the network.

CLIENT authentication allows users to authenticate at the clients. Therefore, DB2 may provide services with minimal information about users at the server. If the user is able to log in to the client operating system, DB2 will trust that the client has authenticated the user and allow him or her to connect to DB2 without sending credentials across the network. This authentication mode is generally not recommended unless you have carefully considered its security implications.

KERBEROS is a third-party network authentication protocol that employs a system of shared secret keys to securely authenticate a user in an insecure network environment without exposing a text user ID or password. Using Kerberos provides the advantages of single sign-on access to resources, such as a DB2 UDB server, and the centralization of user (principal) administration. Before DB2 v8.2, Kerberos was supported only on Windows operating systems that support Active Directory. Authentication support is now extended to DB2 UDB for UNIX environments using a security plug-in.

The configuration parameter values SQL_AUTHENTICATION_DATAENC and SQL_AUTHENTICATION_DATAENC_CMP are discussed in section 11.10.

GSSPLUGIN allows DB2 to use customized security modules. The ability to create custom security plug-ins presents you with alternatives to the authentication methods currently provided by DB2. This is a new feature in DB2 v8.2, and eventually, you may even be able to buy a package of plug-ins from third-party providers rather than write your own. To help you write your own security plug-ins, the sqllib/samples/security/plugins directory (installed by default) contains sample source files for various types of plug-ins.

We now look at how you can change the authentication mode using the Control Center.

Step 1: Open the instance configuration file (DBM CFG).

DB2 instance parameters cannot be changed from the Basic view. If you are not already using the Control Center Advanced view, switch to it now by selecting Customize Control Center from the Tools menu.

In the Control Center object tree, navigate to All Systems > (hostname) > Instances > DB2 (or db2inst1 on Linux).

Right-click on the instance object (DB2), and select the Configure Parameters menu item (Figure 11.17).

Figure 11.17 Viewing DBM (instance) parameters

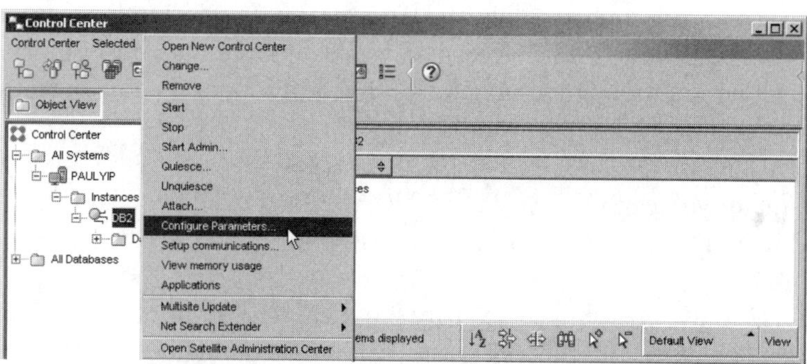

Step 2: Change the AUTHENTICATION parameter.

Modify the AUTHENTICATION parameter as desired (Figure 11.8).

Figure 11.18 Modifying the AUTHENTICATION mode

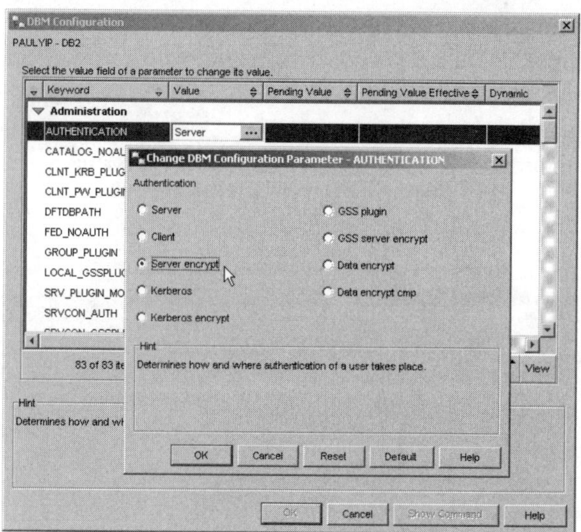

Step 3: Restart the instance.

Stop the instance by right-clicking on the instance object (DB2) and selecting the Stop menu item. Check the Disconnect Applications option to ensure that the stop is successful.

Wait for a confirmation that the instance has been stopped. Start the instance by right-clicking on the instance object (DB2), and select the Start menu item.

11.9 Data Encryption

DB2 v8.2 has the capability to perform both column-level encryption and encrypted network communication between client and server. Each encryption facility serves a different purpose, and both can be employed together to increase security in the database.

Column Value Encryption

To encrypt column data, three built-in scalar functions are used (Table 11.4).

Table 11.4 DB2 Column Encryption Functions

Function Name	Description
ENCRYPT	Encrypts data using a password. An optional hint can be provided.
DECRYPT_BIN DECRYPT_CHAR	Decrypts data using a password. There is no difference between DECRYPT_BIN and DECRYPT_CHAR.
GETHINT	Retrieves the hint stored with an encrypted value.

Another related SQL statement is

```
SET ENCRYPTION PASSWORD '<password>'
```

When you use encryption functions, a password is required for the encryption (the password is used to help scramble the value). You can either set the password for an entire session (so that all ENCRYPT function calls in the same transaction use the same password by default) or explicitly provide the password. The ability to use passwords for encryption aligns nicely with the way data should be protected: Only users who have the correct password for a given encrypted value can view that information. Even SYSADM users will not be able to access encrypted data without the right password. To reduce the chance that passwords may be completely lost, DB2 encryption functions incorporate user-supplied password hints, which are stored with the encrypted value.

Note: Values to be encrypted cannot exceed 32,663 bytes if hints are not used. If hints are used, the limit is reduced to 32,631 bytes.

Note: Passwords must be at least 6 bytes long, up to a maximum of 127 bytes. Hints are optional and can be up to 32 bytes long.

Let's start with some examples. In the first scenario, sensitive data, such as a credit card number, is stored. The users log in with their user ID and password. For this example, we'll use the sample data in Table 11.5.

Table 11.5 Column Encryption Sample Data

Parameter	Value	Notes
User ID	SAM	
Password	funnybone	min size = 6 bytes max size = 127 bytes
Hint	elbow	max size = 32 bytes
Credit Card Number	1111222233334444	

To support the following two examples, a simple credit card table is defined as follows:

```
CREATE TABLE creditcard (
       userid VARCHAR(100) NOT NULL,
       data VARCHAR (100) FOR BIT DATA)
```

Note: The return type of the ENCRYPT function is VARCHAR FOR BIT DATA. Therefore, the column type for encrypted data must be declared as such.

Although credit card numbers usually do not exceed 20 digits, we defined the data column to be significantly larger because the value is expanded when encrypted using this calculation:

```
encrypted data length =
  + bytes of nonencrypted data
  + 8 bytes
  + the number of bytes to the next 8-byte boundary
  + 32 bytes (if hint is used)
```

Example 1: Encryption with SET ENCRYPTION PASSWORD

SET ENCRYPTION PASSWORD is useful for defining an encryption password to be used for an entire transaction. Note that when you use default passwords, hints are not supported. If you wish to use hints for encryption, see the next example, which calls ENCRYPT with explicit password and hint values.

Before you call ENCRYPT, set the default password:

```
SET ENCRYPTION PASSWORD 'funnybone'
```

Note: To use SET ENCRYPTION PASSWORD, you must turn off auto-commit. A COMMIT will clear the default password.

The application can use the ENCRYPT function as follows:

```
INSERT INTO creditcard (userid, data)
   VALUES ('SAM', encrypt('1111222233334444'))
```

The application can then use DECRYPT_BIN or DECRYPT_CHAR to retrieve the encrypted value:

```
SELECT DECRYPT_CHAR(data,'funnybone')
  FROM creditcard WHERE userid='SAM'

===> 1111222233334444
```

Example 2: Encrypting Data with Password and Hint

If you want to employ hints, you must specify password and hint values with each call to the ENCRYPT function. There is no need to use SET ENCRYPTION PASSWORD.

The application can call the ENCRYPT function as follows:

```
INSERT INTO creditcard (userid, data)
VALUES (   'SAM',
           encrypt('1111222233334444','funnybone', 'elbow'))
```

If SAM forgets his password, use the GETHINT function to retrieve the hint:

```
SELECT gethint(data) FROM creditcard WHERE userid='SAM'

===> elbow
```

The application can then use DECRYPT_BIN or DECRYPT_CHAR to retrieve the encrypted value:

```
SELECT DECRYPT_CHAR(data,'funnybone')
  FROM creditcard WHERE use rid='SAM'

===> 1111222233334444
```

11.10 Data Communications Encryption

SQL_AUTHENTICATION_DATAENC means that connections must use data encryption. If the client does not support encryption, the connection will not be allowed.

The other encryption mode, SQL_AUTHENTICATION_DATAENC_CMP, allows for a compatibility mode with downlevel products that do not support the new authentication type. For such products, the use of this authentication type allows a connection using SERVER_ENCRYPT, and the encryption of data is not required. Any product that supports SQL_AUTHENTICATION_DATAENC will use full data encryption.

Use the following steps to configure a DB2 server for data encryption.

Step 1: Configure the server for data encryption.

If you are not already using the Control Center's Advanced view, switch to it now by selecting Customize Control Center from the Tools menu.

To enable data encryption, change the authentication method at the server instance from the default of SERVER to SQL_AUTHENTICATION_DATA_ENC.

In the Control Center object tree, navigate to All Systems > (hostname) > Instances > DB2 (or db2inst1 on Linux).

Right-click on the instance object (DB2/db2inst1), and select Configure Parameters from the pop-up menu (Figure 11.19).

Figure 11.19 View instance configuration

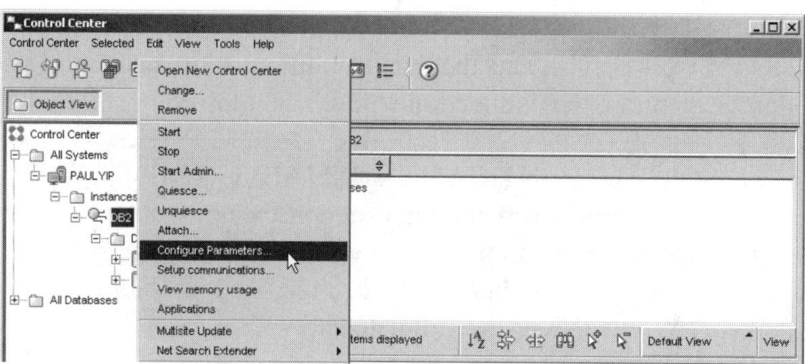

The default value of the AUTHENTICATION parameter is Server (Figure 11.20). Change the parameter to Data Encrypt, and click OK.

Figure 11.20 Changing the AUTHENTICATION parameter

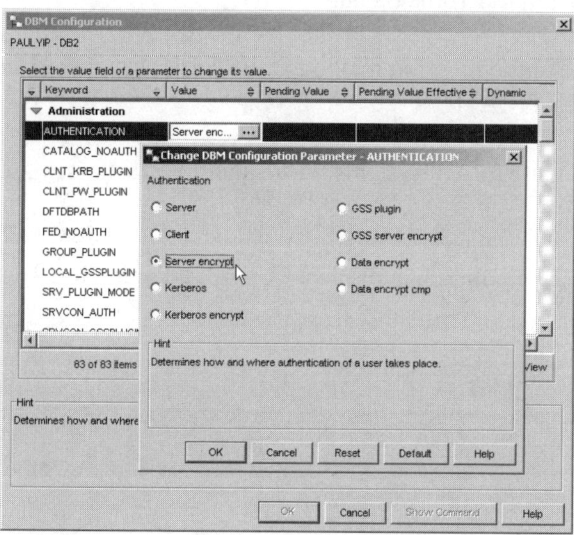

The change will take effect after an instance restart. Stop the instance by right-clicking on the instance object (DB2/db2inst1) and selecting the Stop menu item. Check the Disconnect Applications option to ensure that the stop is successful.

Wait for a confirmation that the instance has been stopped. Start the instance by right-clicking on the instance object again and selecting the Start menu item.

Step 2: Configure the client for encrypted communication.

After the server has been configured using data encryption, clients should catalog databases as usual. One minor observation: Ensure that you select an authentication type as one of

- Value in server's DBM configuration (assuming that the server has already been configured for data encryption)
- DATA_ENCRYPT to ensure that the client uses data encryption (Figure 11.21)

Figure 11.21 Configuring client to use encryption

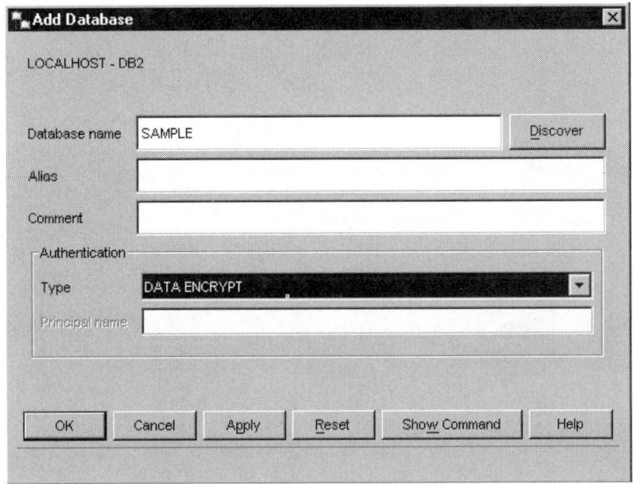

11.11 Summary

In this chapter, you learned about the basics of DB2's security model and security features. You learned how DB2 leverages the operating system (or other authentication mechanism) to identify and authenticate users and how this behavior can be changed through the

AUTHENTICATION parameter in the DBM CFG. You also learned about some security considerations regarding the default installation of DB2 on Windows and related best practices.

After the database server is secured at a system level, you can further secure DB2 at the object level so that users can access tables only in ways that they need to. Object privileges can be managed at the individual user level or at the group level. The special PUBLIC group was discussed, as were the default privileges granted to this group.

Finally, to further secure data access, you learned how to exploit DB2 facilities to encrypt not only data stored within tables but also network transmission of data.

CHAPTER 12

Deploying to Production

In this chapter, you will learn:

- How to generate scripts to re-create the L8NITE database using the Control Center
- How to export procedures and functions using the Development Center
- How to refine and package scripts to simplify deployment
- The capabilities of both SQL and operating system scripts
- How to leverage DB2's silent install feature

12.1 Introduction

Now that the L8NITE database application is completed, you need to consider how to deploy the database from your development environment to one or more production environments. Often, the people involved in developing an application do not actually implement the software at the customer location. Therefore, deployment should be made as simple as possible. Typically, scripts are used to automate creation of database objects once the database software has been installed.

First, we'll look at how to extract and customize DDL for objects. Then we'll demonstrate how to combine them with operating system scripts for increased deployment flexibility. This, combined with DB2's silent install capability, can make application deployment repeatable, consistent, and serviceable.

12.2 Extracting DDL from the Database

Deploying a database requires careful consideration of what must be deployed and how best to deploy it. Our goal is to make re-creation of the L8NITE database as straightforward and repeatable as possible. Often, this is done by using SQL scripts, which can be immediately executed after DB2 has been installed.

Database objects should be grouped by their types in separate files. Table 12.1 provides an example of how the L8NITE database objects can be grouped.

Table 12.1 SQL Scripts for the L8NITE Objects Grouped by File

Script Name	Objects
schema.ddl	Tables and related objects (views, indexes, constraints, etc.)
triggers.ddl	Triggers
app_objects.ddl	Functions and stored procedures

In the following subsections, you will learn how to generate SQL scripts for each type of object.

Tables and Related Objects

SQL scripts (DDL) for tables, views, indexes, constraints, and related objects are easily extracted using the Control Center.

Step 1: Generate the table DDL.

In the Control Center, right-click the L8NITE database object and select Generate DDL from the pop-up menu, as shown in Figure 12.1. This will launch the Generate DDL dialog box.

Note: You can also extract DDL for individual tables by right-clicking a table object and selecting Generate DDL from the pop-up menu.

Figure 12.1 Generate DDL for an entire database

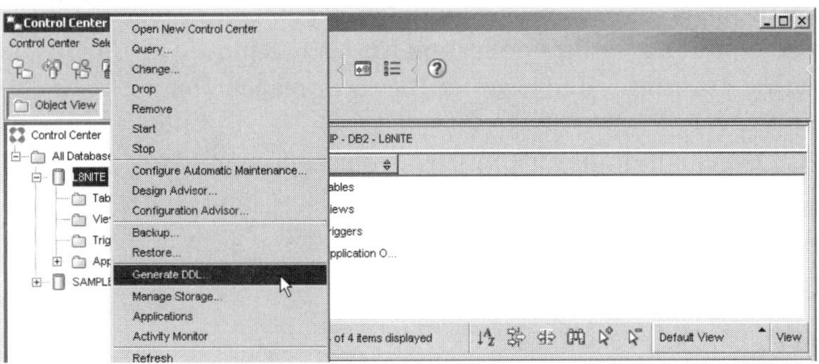

Step 2: Specify options for DDL generation.

In the Generate DDL dialog box, you can specify additional options for the generated DDL. In general, you will want to specify the options shown in Figure 12.2.

Figure 12.2 Generate DDL dialog box

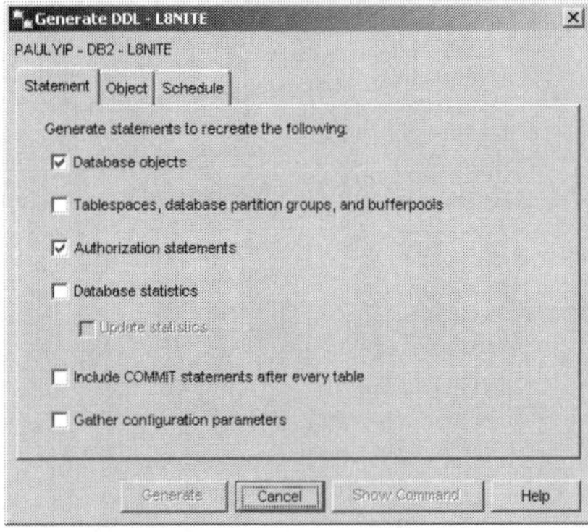

In your own applications, if you created additional table spaces, also select Table Spaces, Database Partition Groups, and Buffer Pools.

The Database Statistics option has not been selected because the statistics that are relevant to your development environment are probably incorrect for the production environment. Similarily, the database manager and database configuration parameters that affect performance can be redetermined after the application has been deployed. To do this, you use the Configuration Advisor, as discussed in Chapter 10, Performance Tuning.

Next, take a look at the Object tab (Figure 12.3). Here you specify precisely the objects you wish to generate DDL for.

Figure 12.3 Select objects for DDL generation

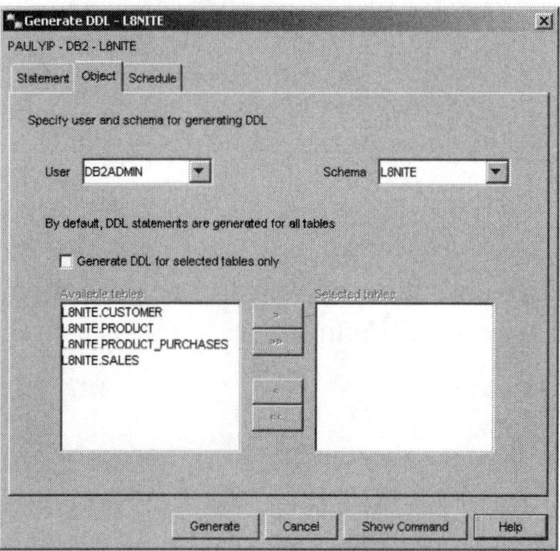

The User pull-down menu is used to specify objects by creator, and the Schema pull-down menu is used to filter the objects by schema. In this case, we wish to generate only the DDL for tables created by DB2ADMIN in the L8NITE schema.

Click the Generate button to start DDL generation.

Step 3: Review the generated DDL.

The result of this operation is a single script with all the SQL statements for all the related objects specified, as illustrated in Figure 12.4.

Figure 12.4 Generated DDL output

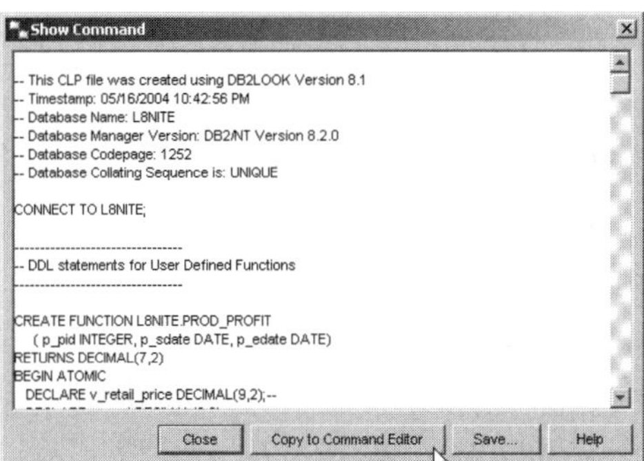

Create a directory called L8NITE, and save the file as schema.ddl in the new directory.

To review this script, click the Copy to Command Editor button or copy it to your preferred text editor.

Note that the script requires some manual tweaking. For example, you'll notice that DDL for functions and triggers is included in the script even though we requested DDL for tables only.

Move the CREATE TRIGGER statements to a separate file called triggers.ddl, and save this file in the L8NITE directory created earlier. Although we have only a single trigger in the L8NITE application, it is considered a best practice to separate objects by their types, as illustrated in Table 12.1.

For now, we recommend removing the following types of statements from all scripts:

- CONNECT TO database statements
- DISCONNECT statements
- CREATE FUNCTION and CREATE PROCEDURE statements (DDL for functions will be regenerated using the Development Center)
- Unnecessary comments

At this point, you should have two scripts:

- l8nite\schema.ddl: DDL for tables, views, indexes, constraints
- l8nite\triggers.ddl: DDL for triggers

For your reference, these files have been provided on the book's Web site.

Database Application Objects

The DB2 Development Center can be used to export DDL for user-defined functions and SQL stored procedures.

Step 1: Initiate export from the Development Center project.

Launch the Development Center, and open the project used to create the functions and procedures described in Chapter 8, Working with Functions, Stored Procedures, and Triggers.

Note: You can also create a new project and import existing procedures and functions into it. See Appendix A, Development Center, for more information.

Then right-click on the project object (as illustrated in Figure 12.5), and select the Export menu item.

Figure 12.5 Export from database

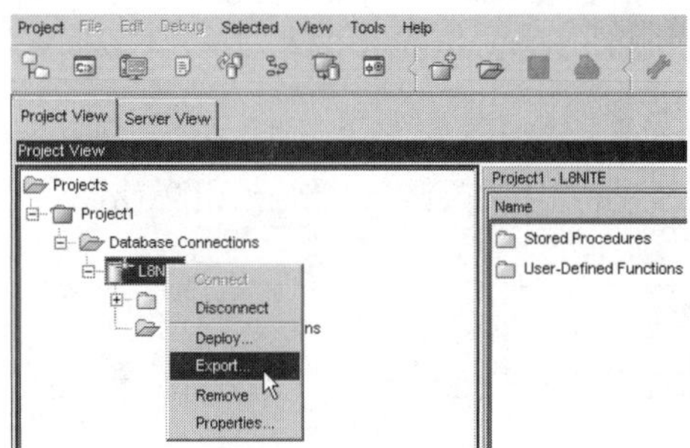

This will invoke the Export wizard.

Step 2: Select objects to export.

In the first step of the Export wizard, indicate the objects you wish to export. In the case of the L8NITE database, you will want to export everything, as illustrated in Figure 12.6.

Figure 12.6 Select objects to export

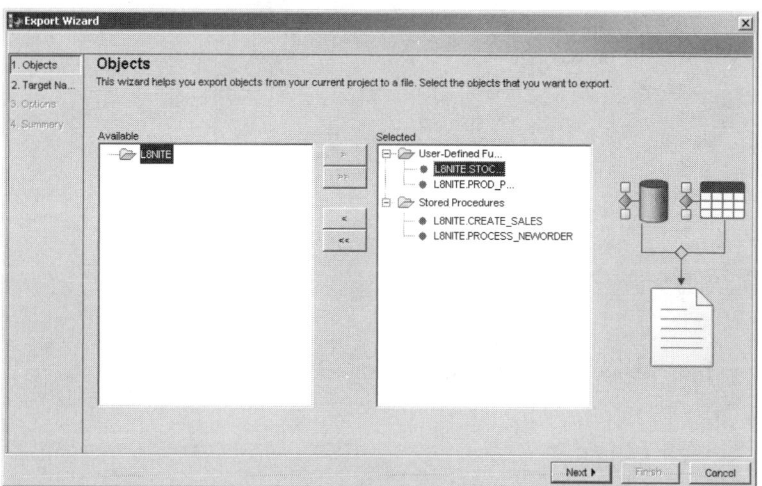

Click Next to continue.

Step 3: Specify the export target.

In the second step of the wizard, specify the path and file name where you would like the objects to be exported.

Figure 12.7 Select target file

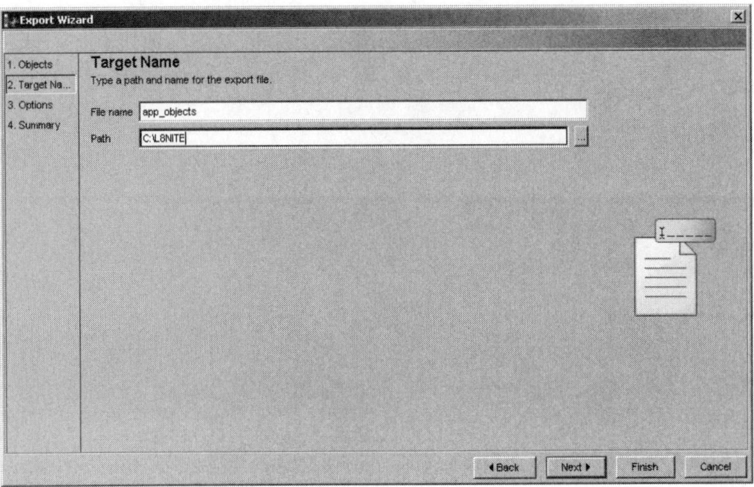

Specify the following values for the target name (Figure 12.7):

- File name: app_objects
- Path for Windows: c:\L8NITE
- Path for Linux: /home/db2inst1/L8NITE

Click Next to continue.

Step 4: Specify export options.

In the Options step, you can specify the export type. For the greatest deployment flexibility, we recommend exporting the objects as SQL scripts that can be tweaked and packaged with the schema and trigger scripts created earlier.

Select the Create an Export Script option, as illustrated in Figure 12.8.

Figure 12.8 Select export type

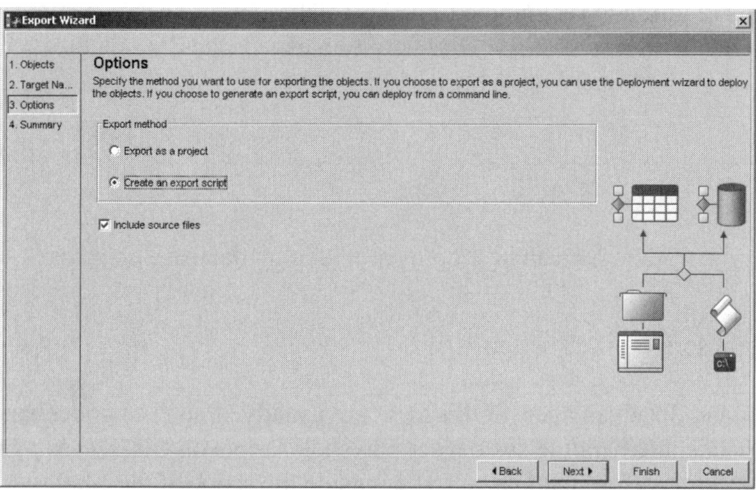

Click the Next button to view a summary, or Finish to generate the SQL script. When exported, the file will be compressed using the file name and path specified in step 3.

Step 5: Uncompress and cleanse the export file.

If you uncompress the exported file, you will see a single script that contains all functions and procedures. You'll also notice that, unlike schema.ddl and triggers.ddl, the @ character is used for the end-of-statement delimiter. The use of this delimiter is discussed in the next section.

For now, perform the following tasks to cleanse the script for deployment:

- Remove unnecessary comments. For example, the following lines are not required:
  -- connect to L8NITE user DB2ADMIN using Password
  ...
  -- CONNECT RESET (at the bottom of the script)
- Rename the exported file to app_objects.ddl for file naming consistency with the schema.ddl and triggers.ddl files.

- Relocate the app_objects.ddl file to the L8NITE directory if necessary.

Now that all the scripts required to rebuild the L8NITE database have been generated and cleansed, we will show you how to leverage DB2 scripting capabilities.

12.3 Scripting

There are two forms of scripting that can be employed to deploy database objects:

- SQL scripts
- Operating system scripts (shell scripts)

Both have advantages and disadvantages. SQL scripts are usually simpler to understand and can be platform independent. Operating system scripts (shell scripts on UNIX) have greater flexibility because they can perform actions or logic outside the scope of the database. A disadvantage of operating system scripts is that they are usually specific to a platform or command shell.

Entire books are available on scripting. The primary focus here will be SQL scripting, with only light treatment of operating system scripts. As you will soon see, SQL and operating system scripts can be combined to provide greater deployment flexibility.

The Scripting Environment

To run scripts that interact with DB2, you must have a DB2 command-line environment.

On Windows, the DB2 command-line environment is launched using the db2cmd.exe command. You can launch it from: Start > Programs > IBM DB2 > Command Line Tools > Command Window.

Or you can use the run window: Start > Run > db2cmd (Figure 12.9).

Figure 12.9 Opening the DB2 command window

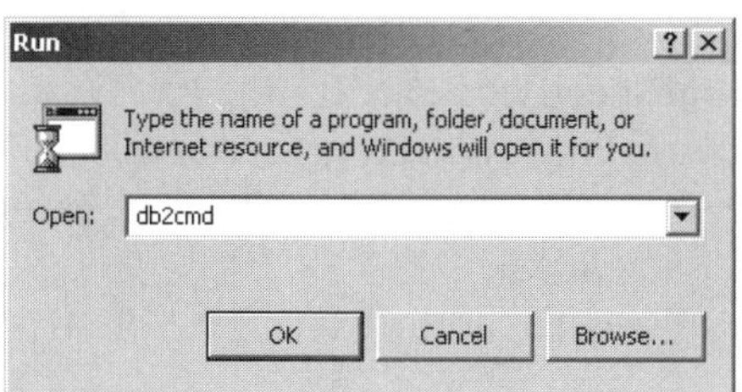

On Linux, the DB2 command-line environment is automatically initialized when you log in to the system as the instance user (for example, db2inst1). The environment can also be configured manually using the script /home/db2inst1/sqllib/db2profile. Any user can inherit the scripting environment for the instance by sourcing this script. For example:

```
$ source /home/db2inst1/sqllib/db2profile
```

SQL Scripts

Consider the sequence of SQL listed in Figure 12.10.

Figure 12.10 A basic SQL script

```
CONNECT TO L8NITE;

SET SCHEMA L8NITE;

CREATE TABLE L8NITE.PRODUCT
     ( product_id INT NOT NULL,
       description VARCHAR(40) NOT NULL,
       cost DECIMAL(7,2) NOT NULL,
       retail_price DECIMAL(7,2) NOT NULL,
       inventory int NOT NULL,
       minimum_inventory INT NOT NULL WITH DEFAULT 0,
       PRIMARY KEY (product_id));

SELECT * FROM PRODUCT FETCH FIRST 10 ROWS ONLY;
```

The primary characteristics demonstrated by this script are as follows:

- A statement or query can span multiple lines.
- Each statement is terminated by a semicolon. DB2 scripts use the semicolon as the default delimiter.
- The script uses a CONNECT statement without specifying user ID and password. Therefore, when this script is executed, the current operating system user ID will be used to connect to the database. Alternatively, you can connect to a database before running the script and remove the CONNECT statement.
- A SET SCHEMA statement is used to change the value of the CURRENT SCHEMA register variable.
- Any SQL or Command Line Processor (CLP) command can be used.

This script can be executed from the DB2 Command Editor or from the operating system command line. Assume that this script is called script1.db2 (the script name or extension is not important, but .ddl, .db2, and .sql are commonly used). To run the script from the command line, you can use the following:

```
db2 -t -v -f script1.db2 -z script1.log
```

Note: If you get the error "DB21061E Command line environment not initialized," then you are not running the script within the DB2 command-line environment. Review the earlier subsection on the DB2 scripting environment.

The foregoing statement has several parts:

- The -t flag indicates that statements use the (default) semicolon statement terminator.
- The -v flag means "verbose" and causes DB2 to output the command being executed. If you do not specify this flag, only a success or failure message is displayed as the script executes.
- The -f flag and the subsequent file name indicate that the input is contained in a file.
- The -z flag and the subsequent file name specify an output file for appending the screen output for later analysis (if required).

When running scripts for triggers, functions, and stored procedures, you often must use an alternative delimiter because the default delimiter (the semicolon) is already used within the body of these objects. Consider the example in Figure 12.11.

Figure 12.11 A script using a nondefault delimiter

```
CONNECT TO L8NITE@
SET SCHEMA L8NITE@

CREATE FUNCTION L8NITE.PROD_PROFIT
     ( p_pid INTEGER, p_sdate DATE, p_edate DATE)
RETURNS DECIMAL(7,2)
BEGIN ATOMIC
   DECLARE v_retail_price DECIMAL(9,2);
   DECLARE v_cost DECIMAL(9,2);
   DECLARE v_err VARCHAR(70);

   SET (v_retail_price, v_cost) = (
         SELECT SUM(retail_price), SUM(cost)
            FROM product p, product_purchases pp, sales s
          WHERE p.product_id = pp.product_id
               AND pp.sales_transaction_id = s.sales_transaction_id
               AND p.product_id = p_pid
               AND DATE(s.transaction_timestamp) BETWEEN
                       p_sdate AND p_edate);

   SET v_err = 'Error: product ID' || CHAR(p_pid) || ' was not found.';
   IF (v_retail_price IS NULL OR v_cost IS NULL) THEN
       SIGNAL SQLSTATE '80000' SET MESSAGE_TEXT = v_err;
   END IF;

   RETURN (v_retail_price - v_cost) / v_cost * 100;
END@
```

You can see that the semicolon is used within the function L8NITE.PROD_PROFIT(). The CREATE FUNCTION statement contains other statements and actually ends with the keyword END. Therefore, for this script to execute properly, a different end-of-statement terminator (the @ symbol in this case) must be specified. To run this script (script2.db2), use the following statement:

```
db2 -td@ -v -f script2.db2 -z script2.log
```

This statement is very similar to the preceeding example, with one key difference: The -td@ flag indicates that statements are terminated with the @ delimiter.

For the L8NITE database, schema.ddl uses the default delimiter, whereas triggers.ddl and app_objects.ddl use the @ delimiter. Therefore, the SQL scripts created in the preceding section could be executed as follows:

```
db2 -t -v -f schema.ddl -z schema.log
db2 -td@ -v -f triggers.ddl -z triggers.log
db2 -td@ -v -f app_objects.ddl -z app_objects.log
```

Note: The -z flag causes output to be appended to the specified file. Therefore, it is a good idea to delete log files before execution of DB2 scripts so that output from a previous script execution is not mixed with output from the current script execution.

Deployment of the L8NITE objects, however, can be simplified and made more robust by combining these commands with operating system scripts.

Operating System Scripts

Another way to automate creation of database objects is to use operating system scripts. The topic is vast, however, and a full discussion is beyond the scope of this book. We provide some basic examples because SQL scripts and operating systems scripts are often employed together to simplify deployment.

The biggest benefit of using an operating system script is that you can pass parameters into it, making it more flexible. Consider the Windows script create_database.bat in Figure 12.12 and the equivalent LINUX *bash* shell script in Figure 12.13.

Note: If you get the error "DB21061E Command line environment not initialized," then you are not running the script within the DB2 command-line environment. Review the earlier subsection on the DB2 scripting environment.

For the L8NITE application, an operating system script will be used to

- Establish a connection to the database
- Remove old log files, if any
- Execute SQL scripts: tables.ddl, triggers.ddl, app_objects.ddl

Figure 12.12 Windows script, create_database.bat

```
set DBPATH=c:

rem -- the database name must be 8 characters or fewer
set DBNAME=L8NITE
set MEMORY=20

db2 create database %DBNAME% on %DBPATH% AUTOCONFIGURE USING MEM_PERCENT %MEM-
ORY% APPLY DB AND DBM

db2 connect to %DBNAME% user %1 using %2

del schema.log triggers.log app_objects.log

db2 set schema l8nite
db2 -t -v -f schema.ddl -z schema.log
db2 -td@ -v -f triggers.ddl -z triggers.log
db2 -td@ -v -f app_objects.ddl -z app_objects.log
```

To execute this script, you can use

```
create_database.bat db2admin ibmdb2
```

Some observations:

- This script is a batch file (as indicated by the .bat extension) that is directly executed on the Windows command line.
- Parameters can be passed into the script. In this example, the first parameter is %1, which is assigned the value "db2admin." The second parameter, %2, is assigned the value "ibmdb2."
- Script variables can also be used. In this example, the database name and its creation location are represented by %DBNAME% and %DBPATH%, respectively. For additional flexibility, these values can be changed before actual deployment.
- Operating system scripts can be combined with SQL scripts. In the last few lines, schema.ddl, triggers.ddl, and app_objects.ddl scripts are executed. These scripts do not contain any CONNECT statements because they inherit the connection from the parent script.

Figure 12.13 is the Linux equivalent of the Windows script in Figure 12.12

Figure 12.13 Linux bash shell script, create_database.sh

```
DBPATH=/home/db2inst1

# The database name must be 8 characters or fewer
DBNAME=L8NITE
MEMORY=20

. /home/db2inst1/sqllib/db2profile

#clean up log files
rm schema.log triggers.log app_objects.log

db2 create database $DBNAME on $DBPATH AUTOCONFIGURE USING MEM_PERCENT $MEMORY
APPLY DB AND DBM

db2 connect to $DBNAME user $1 using $2
db2 set schema L8NITE

db2 -t -f schema.ddl -z schema.log
db2 -td@ -v -f triggers.ddl -z triggers.log
db2 -td@ -v -f app_objects.ddl -z app_objects.log
```

To execute this script, use

```
chmod +x create_database.sh
create_database.sh db2inst1 ibmdb2
```

Some observations:

- Before you can execute a bash script, its execution bit must be set using chmod +x.
- Parameters can be passed into the script. In this example, the first parameter is $1, which is assigned the value "db2inst1." The second parameter, $2, is assigned the value "ibmdb2."
- Script variables can also be used. In this example, the database name and its creation location are represented by $DBNAME and $DBPATH, respectively. For additional flexibility, these values can be changed before actual deployment.

- Operating system scripts can be combined with SQL scripts. In the last line, the SQL scripts are called after a connection has been established. The SQL scripts therefore do not require their own database CONNECT statement.

To bring it all together, the final packaging of database scripts will appear as follows:

```
l8nite\create_database.bat
l8nite\create_database.sh
l8nite\schema.ddl
l8nite\triggers.ddl
l8nite\app_objects.ddl
```

As you can see, the scripts are clean and well organized. All configurable options for deployment (such as database name, drive location, and connection information) are parameterized and are centrally located in the operating system script. The .ddl scripts do not contain any database connection statements and inherit their connection from the parent OS script.

At deployment time, the deployer can simply execute

```
Windows: create_database.bat <SYSADM user ID> <password>
Linux: create_database.sh <SYSADM user ID> <password>
```

12.4 Important Deployment Considerations

The Production System

Every application should specify a minimum hardware requirement.

For example, the L8NITE application requires an average desktop PC, which can be purchased at a modest price point. At the time of this writing, a retail desktop PC with the following features can be purchased for less than $1000:

- Intel Pentium 4 3.0GHz with hyperthreading
- Windows XP Professional (XP Home Edition is not supported for DB2 servers)
- Two 40G hard drives
- 512MB RAM

- Network card
- CD-ROM drive

Note that two 40G disks are specified as a requirement so that they can be mirrored (the operating system will use one disk to maintain an exact copy of the other at all times). If one drive fails, the system can continue to function, providing a window of opportunity to replace the defective drive with little or no interruption.

Although not absolutely required, some form of disk redundancy is recommended to ensure that a single disk failure will not cause the system to crash. This is important because the transaction logs and backup files for the database will be stored on the same file system. Both Microsoft Windows and Linux support disk mirroring. Refer to the product documentation for each of these platforms for information on how to configure this.

DB2 Express Installation

DB2 Express should be installed on the production machine as you did in Chapter 2, Getting Started. A typical installation will install the product and create a default instance, configuring it to use TCP/IP communications on port 50000 by default.

Customizing a Database

As mentioned earlier, every application should specify a minimum hardware requirement. Deployment environments vary, however, and it is therefore important to tune the database specifically for each environment. We recommend running the DB2 Configuration Advisor discussed in Chapter 10, Performance Tuning, to establish a customized performance configuration for each deployment target.

Application Seed Data

Application seed data is the minimum amount of data that must exist in the database before it can function. In the L8NITE application, the only required data is product information. For each product sold by the store, a row of data for its inventory count, wholesale cost, retail price, and minimum inventory must be entered.

The L8NITE application does not have an interface to allow the store owner to quickly enter this product information. However, the following options are available:

- As the developer, you can enter the product information in the development environment (for example, from the Control Center), export the data to an IXF file, and load it into the production database.
- The owner can enter the data into a spreadsheet, save it as an ASCII delimited file, and load it into the database.

All other data—customer, sales, and product purchases—are created as real transactions are processed in the store.

For your own applications, you may have significantly more seed data. You can export this data from the development database using the Export utility, likely in DEL format. This data can be included with the DDL scripts and loaded as a secondary step using the LOAD or IMPORT utility. EXPORT, LOAD, and IMPORT are all discussed in Chapter 9, Working with Data.

Security

After the application has been deployed, don't forget to implement and test security policies. Security was discussed in Chapter 11, Implementing Security. For Windows environments, we recommend using Local System Accounts for DB2 services. This minimizes the chances of DB2 not being able to start because of changed passwords.

12.5 Supplemental: Implementing Silent DB2 Installation

In the deployment scenario discussed earlier, DB2 software is installed manually by the deployer using a typical install with default options. Some may want to go further and make DB2 completely invisible to their customers by embedding the DB2 installation process with the application installation.

To implement silent DB2 installation, the steps and configuration information you would normally provide through the setup screens are provided in a script called a DB2 installation *response file*. Here, we provide you with an example of such a response file, which installs DB2 silently using a typical installation, and show you how to use it.

Figure 12.14 Sample response file

```
## To perform a silent install of DB2 Express using this file:
## setup.exe /u l8nite.rsp

# General Options
PROD                            = UDB_EXPRESS_EDITION
LIC_AGREEMENT                   = ACCEPT
FILE                            = C:\Program Files\IBM\SQLLIB
INSTALL_TYPE                    = TYPICAL
AUTOSTART_FIRST_STEPS           = NO


# General information for instance to be created
INSTANCE                         = DB2
DEFAULT_INSTANCE                 = DB2
DB2.NAME                         = DB2

# Default Instance Logon Settings
DB2.USERNAME                    = db2admin
DB2.PASSWORD                    = ibmdb2
```

As you can see in Figure 12.14, comments are prefixed with a # symbol. You can also use an * to prefix comments. This response file tells DB2 to install using these options:

- Accept the license agreement.
- Use the default instance name DB2 (on Linux, you can use db2inst1 instead).
- The instance (and other services) will be configured to use user ID db2admin and password ibmdb2.

To install DB2 using a response file, run setup.exe on the command line with a response file parameter. For example:

<CD-ROM>:`setup.exe /u l8nite.rsp`

For more information on performing a response file installation, please see Chapter 6 of the DB2 product manual, "DB2 Installation and Configuration Supplement."

12.6 Summary

In this chapter, you learned how to extract the DDL for objects created in your development environment into scripts so that they can be packaged for simplified and repeatable deployment. You learned how to work with both database and operating system scripts and studied their advantages and disadvantages. Other important deployment considerations were also discussed.

After the application has been deployed, you can set up automated maintenance to keep the system healthy and protect it from data loss. Automation of production maintenance is covered in Chapter 13.

CHAPTER 13

Automating Maintenance in Production

In this chapter, you will learn:

- How to create a maintenance plan for database activities
- How to monitor DB2 to ensure the health of the system
- How to manage the storage space needed for your database
- About High Availability Disaster Recovery (HADR)

13.1 Introduction

Now that the L8NITE database application has been deployed, you need to consider how to properly maintain the database in your production environment.

A database may start out small and have very few users, but it can quickly grow in size and number of users. It is crucial to monitor the health of the database as this occurs. Fortunately, by leveraging DB2 Express' autonomic features, you can automate many of these maintenance tasks.

13.2 Database Operational View

The Control Center has an operational view that is essential to the ongoing maintenance and health of your database. The operational view, invoked by selecting any database object in the object tree, will give you a concise snapshot of various activities occurring on the database (Figure 13.1).

Figure 13.1 Database Operational View

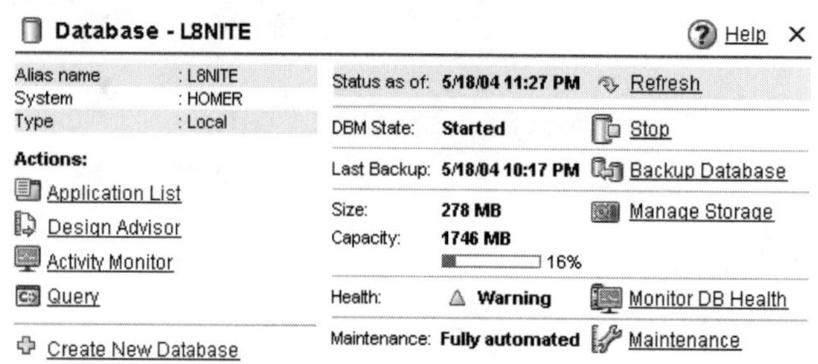

Through this operational view, you can see at a glance

- Whether the database is up and running
- When the database was last backed up
- How much storage is remaining
- The overall health of the database
- Whether it has been configured for automated maintenance

The operational view also includes quick links to related tasks. For example, if a database backup is overdue, the Backup Database link will launch the Backup wizard.

Conducting routine maintenance on your database will ensure its performance and efficiency. There are three main maintenance activities that should be performed periodically on all databases:

- Backup
- Reorganization
- Statistics

13.3 Backups

Backups are a cornerstone of all maintenance plans. Regular backups must be taken to ensure the lifelong integrity of the database. With a regular backup strategy, you can minimize the risk of losing important information if the database is damaged because of hardware failure or human error.

There are two main types of backups: online and offline. Each type has its own advantages and disadvantages, which we will discuss. Database log files are intimately intertwined with backups. We will explain each of these concepts.

Offline backups are the easiest and most traditional type. Offline backups require the database to be shut down so that a full copy of the database can be made. The backup is a complete, consistent copy of the database. It can be used in and of itself to completely restore a database to the state it was in at the time the backup was created.

Online backups have the distinct advantage that they can be done while the database is online. No interruption or window is needed. However, because the backup is done while the database is online, data within the database can change from the time the backup is started until it is finished. These changes are logged in the database logs and require that archival logging be used. The logs used during an online backup must also accompany the backup image to ensure that a point of consistency is reached if and when you want to restore the backup image. DB2 makes this easier with an option to include the database logs used during the course of an online backup inside the backup image itself.

Database logs are used to log all data changes within a database. These logs are used for crash recovery so that in the event of a failure, the database can be automatically restored to a point of consistency. Unfinished transactions can be rolled back, and committed transactions can be finished. Database logs can also be used during database recovery. After a backup image is restored, the logs can be used to roll the database forward to a specific point in time. This ensures that all the transactions performed between backups can be recovered. To roll a database forward, the logs must be kept and archived. By default a new database does not keep its logs around and therefore must be configured to do so.

Inquiring Minds: Incremental Backups

Incremental backups are extremely valuable for large databases. Incremental backups back up only the data that has changed since the last backup. This creates a consistency point so that the database logs do not have to roll forward through all the data changes, but it does not require the space needed for a full database backup. Incremental backups are delta changes from previous backups, and therefore all the previous backup images are required. A chain of incremental backups also may be required, as well as the last full database backup. DB2 automatically uses all the images to restore the database to its last backup state so that the administrator does not have to keep track of which backup images are needed.

13.4 Disaster Recovery

In Chapter 12, you set up your system to mirror the entire database, including logs, on two hard drives of your system. This is an excellent setup to maintain high availability of the system. However, it does not provide you with sufficient disaster recovery capabilities in case of catastrophic failure, such as a fire, where you could potentially lose your entire system.

To recover your entire database back to the point where you lost it, you will need two items. The first is your latest backup. The second is all the logs that were created after your last backup was performed. It is best to keep your backup and logs on a completely different system from your database, a system that hopefully is also in a completely different location. You can achieve this in several ways.

- CD: Copy all logs and backups to removable media, and take it home every night.
- Remote file system: Connect your database server to a remote file server, and copy your logs and backups to that remote server.
- Archival storage: Copy your backups and logs to an archival storage facility, such as Tivoli Storage Manager, Net.Backup, or Legato.

13.5 Database Log Management

Database logs are critical to the recoverability of your database in case of a failure. Because the logs are so important, you need to ensure that you have a method to retrieve them in case of failure. Depending on the current configuration of your database, you may be in either log retention (archive) or circular logging mode.

With *circular logging* (the default), transactions are recorded in files in a circular fashion. By default, there are three preallocated log files. DB2 writes transaction information to these log files in sequence, starting with the first file. As each file is filled, DB2 moves to the next. When the third log file is filled, the first log file is reused, and so on. Circular logging requires almost no maintenance because the transaction log files are continuously reused and do not grow.

With *log retention logging*, the log files are not overwritten. Rather, as they become filled with transaction information, they are copied to another location for safe storage. There is slightly more maintenance required to monitor the archive logs because they continuously consume disk space until older log files are removed. The good news is that DB2 can handle much of this ongoing maintenance for you, as shown later in this section.

In the event that the database is damaged, the first step in recovering the data is to restore it from the most recent backup image. The type of logging used has implications for data recovery.

- If circular logging was used, then any transactions that have occurred since the backup was taken are lost. If the business retains a record of transactions on paper, however, those transactions can be reentered manually to minimize data loss.

- If log retention logging was used, transactions that have occurred since the backup was taken can be recovered by using the retained log files. You can replay transactions that would normally be lost if circular logging were used.

Management of log retention logging systems is critical. Not only do the logs need to be in separate physical storage from the database, but also space management of the logs is essential. Common implementations will move their inactive logs to an archival system such as Tivoli Storage Manager or another large storage server. DB2 can do this automatically for you. Let's modify the L8NITE database to adopt a log retention approach and move the inactive logs to a different location.

From the Control Center object tree, go to Control Center > All Databases > L8NITE > (right-click) Configure Database Logging… (Figure 13.2).

Figure 13.2 Configure Database Logging wizard

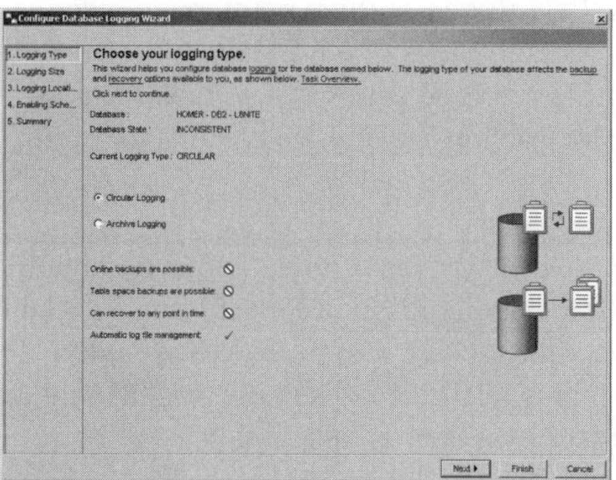

Step 1: Introduction page.

Select Archive Logging, and then click Next.

Figure 13.3 Configure Database Logging wizard: Archive logging

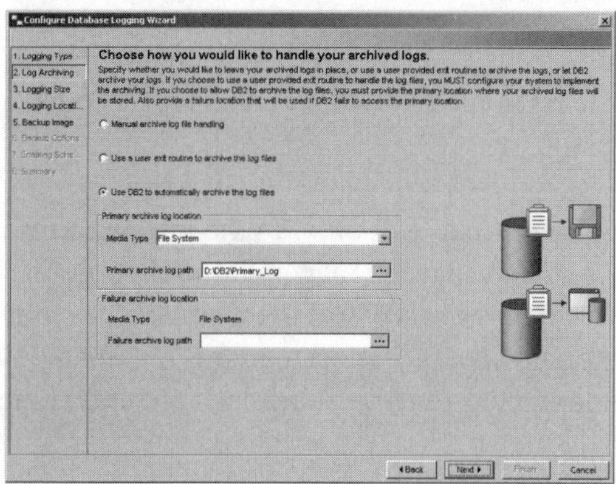

Step 2: Log Archiving page.

Select Use DB2 Log Manager to handle the archive log files, and specify a location where they will be copied to (Figure 13.3). Then click Next.

Step 3: Explore the options.

Explore the options, such as log size and the location for logging to occur.

Step 4: Backup Image page.

Choose to back up your database. To switch to log retention logging, a backup must be performed.

Click Finish to implement your changes. The wizard will change all configuration parameters to match your criteria. If your database was originally in circular logging and you changed it to log retention logging, a full offline backup will be done at this time.

13.6 Table Reorganization

Reorganizing tables and indexes (or *reorgs,* as they are commonly known), is essential to database maintenance. As data gets inserted and deleted from tables, they can become fragmented; there may exist holes of wasted space, and rows of data may span more than one block of data. Reorganizing a table is similiar to defragmenting a Windows file system. Wasted space is reclaimed, and data is reorganized to make data retrieval more efficient. Tables that are frequently modified will benefit most from regular reorganization. There is less need to reorganize tables that are static or do not change much at all.

Like backups, reorg has an offline and an online option. Offline reorg is faster and more efficient and is generally preferred by most administrators if the database usage allows it. Online reorg works well for small tables.

Fortunately DB2 can automate all your reorg needs. Later in this chapter you will learn how to automate table reorganization.

13.7 Statistics

Gathering statistics, or *runstats* as it is commonly known, is essential for maintaining optimal performance of your database. Runstats gathers statistics on the tables, such as the number of rows, indexes, data group sets, and so on. These statistics are used by DB2 whenever queries are executed.

When a query is executed there are many different ways that it can be performed within the database. DB2 relies heavily on database statistics to determine the best way to resolve a query. Therefore, when database statistics are up-to-date, DB2 will make more informed decisions on how to choose the right execution plan. As with table reorganizations, how often you should gather statistics depends highly on how often the data within the table changes.

13.8 Notification and Contact List

In the following sections, we'll show you how to automate database maintenance. When you automate activities, a form of notification should be set up so that e-mail can be sent to you whenever a maintenance operation fails. You can also have an e-mail sent if an operation is successful so that you can be reassured things are running smoothly.

DB2 administration tools maintain a contact list that is shared by the Task Center, Health Center, and databases using automated maintenance.

In the following sections you will learn more about these tools. But first, let's set up and configure the contact list to be used for the remainder of this chapter. The contact list is managed from the DB2 Health Center.

Step 1: Launch the Health Center from the Control Center.

From the Control Center, launch the Health Center from the Tools menu (Figure 13.4).

Figure 13.4 Launch the DB2 Health Center

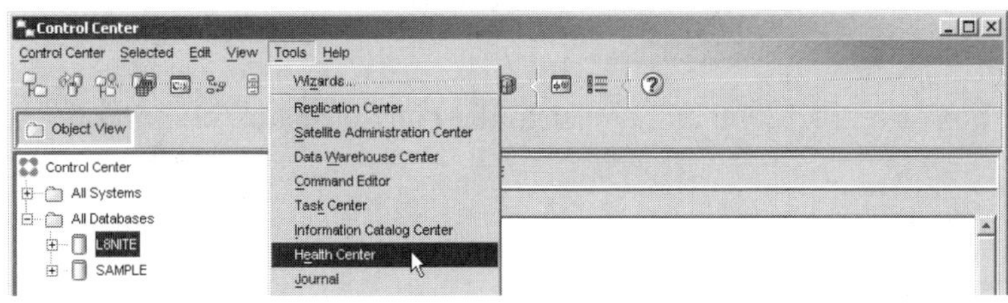

Step 2: Open the contact list.

From the Health Center menu, select Configure > Alert Notification (Figure 13.5).

Figure 13.5 Configure alert notifications

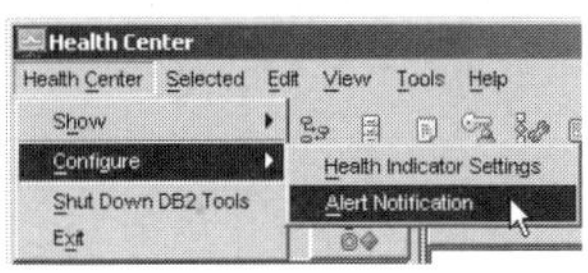

Step 3: Add notification contacts.

At the top of the Configure Health Alert Notification window, you should see a pull-down menu with the prompt Select an Instance (Figure 13.6). Select DB2 (or db2inst1 if you are using Linux).

Figure 13.6 Configure Health Alert Notification

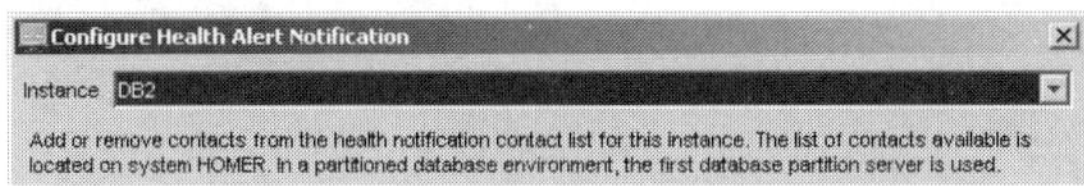

Click the Manage Contacts button at the lower-left corner of the window to add new contacts.

> **TIP:** You can also create groups of contacts if more than a single person needs to know about certain activities.

In the Contacts dialog box (Figure 13.7), add a user to the contact list by clicking the Add Contact... button.

Figure 13.7 Add contacts

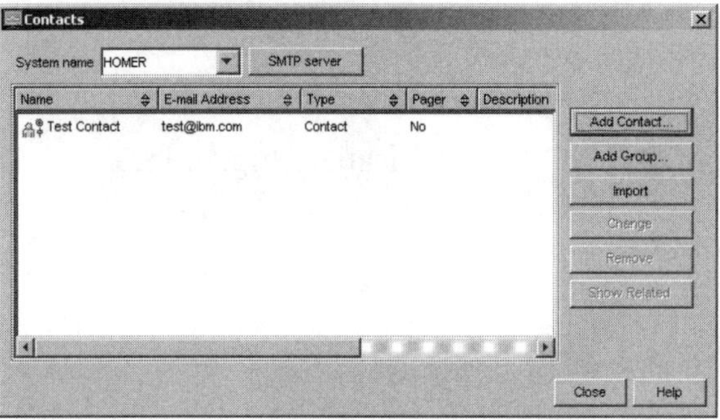

Enter the name, e-mail address, and a description for the new contact (Figure 13.8). Test the contact you just added. A success message should be returned.

Figure 13.8 Add new contact and test notification

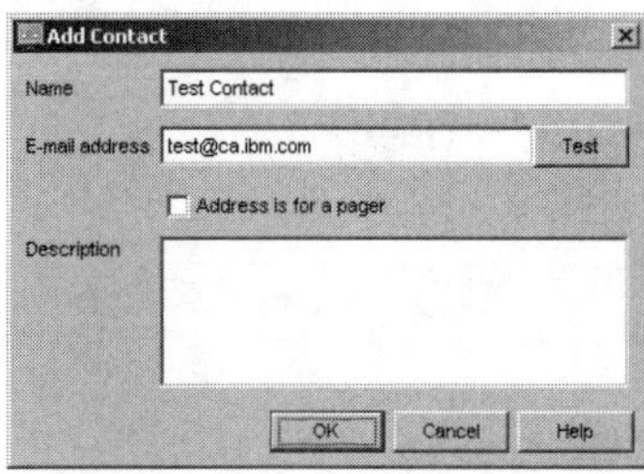

If sending a test e-mail is not successful, then do the following:

- Click OK to create the contact.
- Click the SMTP server button in the Contacts dialog box.

The most common cause of e-mail notification failure is the SMTP (e-mail) server setting. It either has not been set or was not set up properly. Most e-mail servers can act as your SMTP server.

In the dialog box, enter an SMTP server and click OK (Figure 13.9).

Figure 13.9 SMTP server dialog box

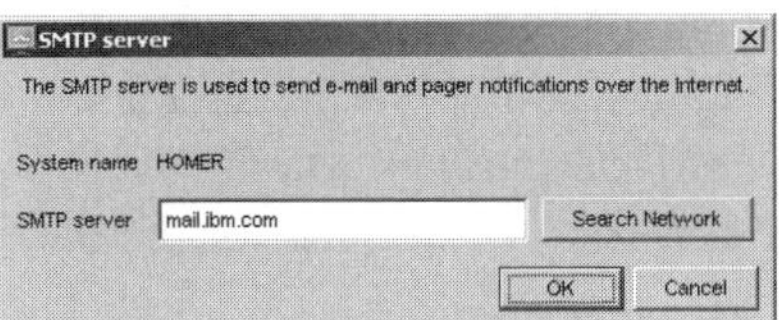

Return to the Contacts dialog box to test e-mail notification.

13.9 Automating and Scheduling Maintenance

In previous sections, we discussed three key maintenance activities: backup, reorganization, and statistics. You can perform these maintenance tasks manually or take advantage of DB2 automation capabilities.

There are two ways to automate maintenance. You can

- Let DB2 automatically perform maintenance operations for you
- Create scripts to perform maintenance and schedule regular execution of your scripts

Automated Maintenance

Fully automated maintenance puts the regular maintenance activities such as backup, reorg, and runstats into the hands of the database itself. Based on configuration parameters that you specify, the database will automatically back itself up, reorg, and perform runstats on tables. You provide the database guidelines to govern when the database can run maintenance activities (called a *maintenance window*). The database, in turn, will determine if and when maintenance is needed and whether it should be run during the maintenance window.

Before we configure the L8NITE database to use automated maintenance, let's explore it a little more. Let's discuss the nature of maintenance windows and explore how evaluations are performed.

A maintenance window defines a period of time when a database is allowed to perform maintenance activities such as database backup, table reorganization, and statistics update. Remember, this does not mean that DB2 will always perform maintenance during a given window; rather, it will perform maintenance only if it is required. Maintenance windows traditionally fall during times when a database is less busy or even inactive (for example, in the middle of the night). A maintenance window is a way for you to tell the database when it is OK to perform maintenance activities. The database still determines whether a maintenance activity is needed. Two maintenance windows can be defined for the database:

- Offline maintenance window
- Online maintenance window

Offline maintenance windows are used for offline maintenance activities such as table reorganization and offline backups. During an offline window, the database may become inaccessible and any connected applications may be affected. Choosing an acceptable offline window is an important consideration.

Online maintenance windows are used for online maintenance activities such as runstats or online backup. Online maintenance windows can be defined for any time, because a database remains fully accessible by all applications. The maintenance activities, however, will consume resources, so care must still be taken.

Inquiring Minds: Throttling Utilities

Utilities, such as online backup, can be *throttled* to limit their impact on a running workload. UTIL_IMPACT_LIM, a configuration parameter part of the database manager configuration parameters, limits the amount of impact a utility will have on the workload. A value of 10 limits a utility to impact a given workload by no more than 10 percent. This capability is very useful for systems that must be available 24x7 with very few low periods. Throttling enables you to perform maintenance without impacting availability.

The database will keep track of operations performed on itself to determine how often maintenance is required. For example, the database will track how much data has changed in the database to determine whether a backup, reorg, or runstats is needed. If the database determines that a maintenance activity is needed, it will be performed during the next appropriate maintenance window.

Configuring Automatic Maintenance

You can influence how the database determines whether a maintenance activity is needed as well as how it is performed. This is set up using the Configure Automatic Maintenance wizard. If you created your database using the Create Database with Automated Maintenance option, then much of this configuration may already be done. However, the wizard provides you more control and lets you change the existing configuration. Now that you have learned about automated maintenance, let's configure the L8NITE database to use it.

Step 1: Launch the Configure Automatic Maintenance wizard.

From the Control Center object tree, right-click the L8NITE database object and select Configure Automatic Maintenance… (Figure 13.10).

Figure 13.10 Configure Automatic Maintenance

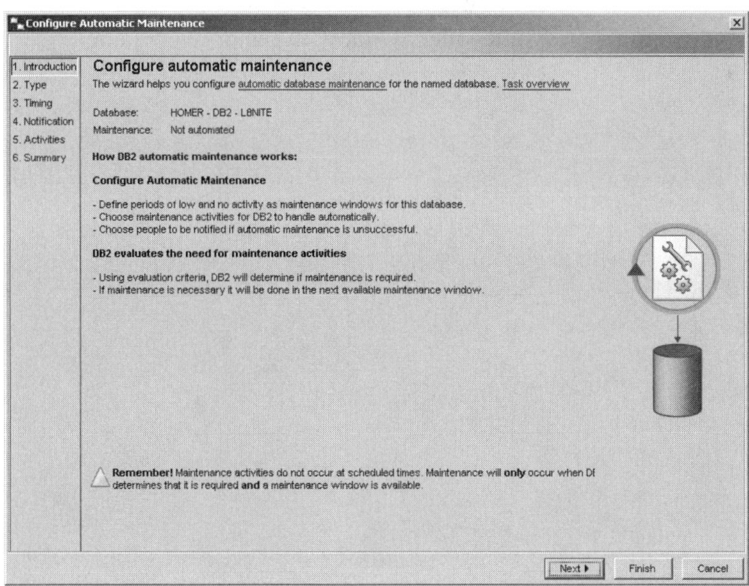

Explore the current settings of automated maintenance on the introduction page. If you created your database using the Create Database with Automated Maintenance option, then you may already have your maintenance automated. You can see from the introduction page the three types of automatic maintenance activities: backup, reorg, and runstats. You can also see that there are two types of maintenance windows: online and offline.

Step 2: Type page.

From the Type page, you can choose to disable all automated maintenance, or you can change your automated maintenance settings. We want to change the current automated maintenance activities.

Step 3: Timing page.

On the Timing page, configure the two maintenance windows to be used for all your maintenance (Figure 13.11). Let's configure the offline window to be every Saturday and Sunday night from midnight to 6 AM.

- Start time, 00:00 (midnight)
- Duration: 6 hours
- Only on selected days: Saturday and Sunday

You can verify your offline automatic maintenance window in the preview pane.

Figure 13.11 Change maintenance window specification

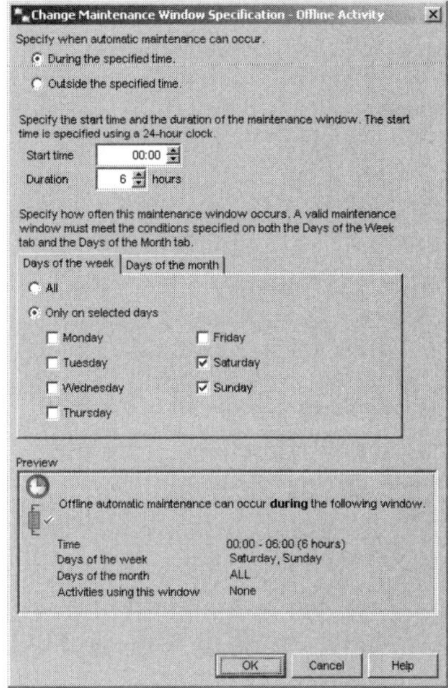

Repeat, making the online window every night from 8 PM to 6 AM.

Step 4: Notification page.

Choose the notification contact in case an automated maintenance activity fails for some reason. You have already configured your notification, so this should be complete, but it is another way to manage your contacts and troubleshoot your notification. Automated maintenance is tied into the Health Monitor, so the same notification is shared between the two.

Step 5: Activities.

Explore each configuration activity (Figure 13.12). You can choose to individually automate or not automate specific activities as well as choose whether you want to be notified of particular activities. You can also change the configuration of how the activities will be run.

Figure 13.12 Configure maintenance activities

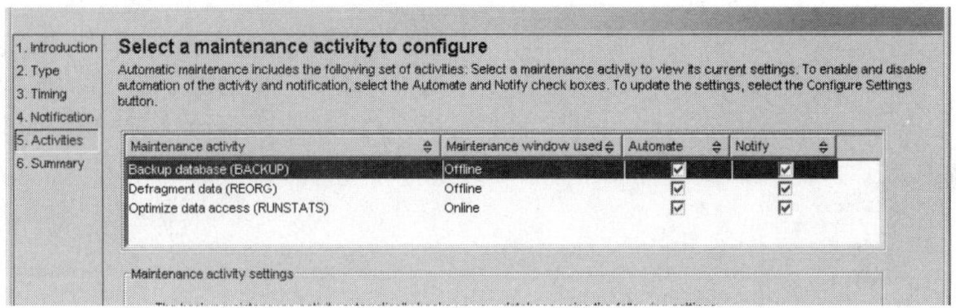

Step 6: Configure backup.

By default, you should not have to configure specific automatic maintenance activities. However, it is probably a good idea to configure at least the backup location for your automated backups. Ideally, just as with logs, you would like to store these on a different physical drive than the database itself, so that in the case of disk failure, you can still restore your database using the backup. From here you can also choose the minimum frequency of backups and the type of backup to perform. If you choose to have offline backups performed, they will be done during the offline automatic maintenance window. If you choose to have online backups performed, they will be done during the online maintenance window.

Whether you choose to use automated maintenance or scheduled maintenance, it is an important decision for the overall health of your database. Not performing maintenance should not be an option, and automated maintenance may not be the right choice for all. The full control you get using a scheduled maintenance approach may be needed to keep your database healthy within your system.

Scheduled Maintenance Using the Task Center

Scheduling the maintenance activities yourself is more time-consuming than using automatic maintenance, but it puts you in full control. Each table may need a unique maintenance schedule depending on how much the data within it changes. The need for backups may change from week to week, depending on the amount of data changed within the database. Scheduling your maintenance enables you to pick the exact time you would like an activity to be performed. To do this, you create scheduled tasks in the Task Center.

The Task Center is the central location for all scheduled activities within the DB2 administration tools (Figure 13.13). It is the main interface where all tasks for all systems can be created, edited, and scheduled. You can get to the Task Center through the toolbar or launch it from the Tools menu.

Launch the Task Center from the Control Center menu: Tools > Task Center.

The Task Center stores the tasks in a tools catalog database that is read by a scheduler. The scheduler then executes tasks on the system by using the DB2 Administration Server (DAS). The DAS is an important aspect of all Control Center remote administration. The DAS is used to perform server-side commands and activities that either cannot be or should not be performed by the client. The real benefit of remote scheduling is that the client does not have to be on for scheduled tasks to be run. In the simplest case (and recommended for most configurations), the scheduler system and run system should run on the same physical machine and use the same database.

Figure 13.13 Scheduling architecture overview

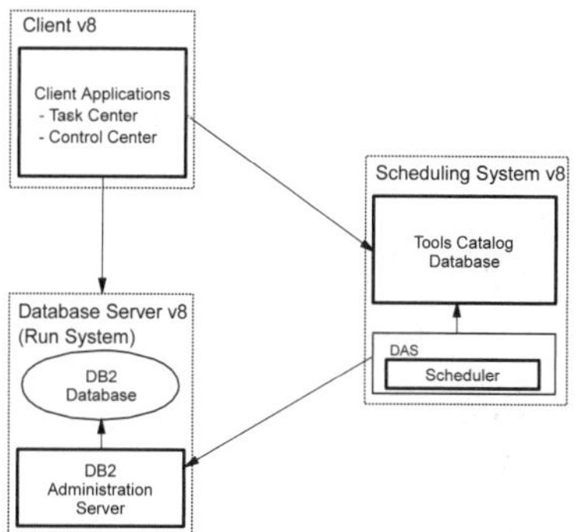

Using the Control Center, let's create a scheduled offline backup to run once a week.

From the Control Center object tree, navigate to Control Center > All Databases > L8NITE > (right-click) Backup… (Figure 13.14).

Figure 13.14 Backup wizard

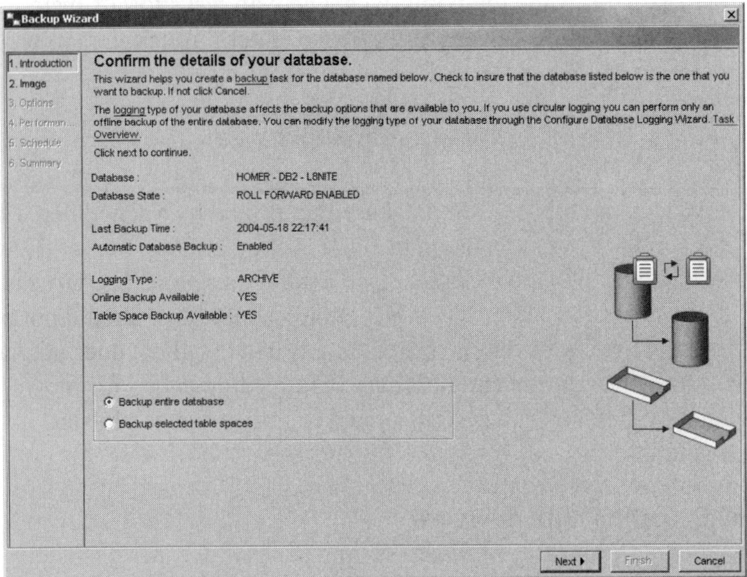

Step 1: Introduction page.

Choose to perform a full offline database backup.

Step 2: Image page.

Select the destination of the backup image. Just as with automatic maintenance and database log management, you want to have your backup image in a location where you can guarantee that it can be retrieved. You can explore the Options page and Performance page, but the defaults are most likely sufficient because DB2 will automatically perform the database backup in the most optimal way.

Step 3: Schedule page: enable the scheduler.

If the scheduler has not yet been enabled, choose to enable it now.

Figure 13.15 Create tools catalog

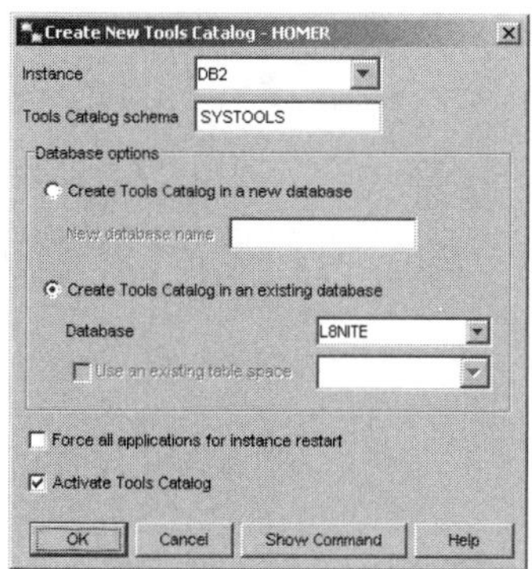

- Select the system to create the tools catalog on, and create a new tools catalog (Figure 13.15).
- Specify a schema for the tools catalog, and choose to create it in the existing L8NITE database.
- Select OK.

Step 4: Schedule page: schedule the backup.

Now that the tools catalog has been created and configured, choose to create a schedule for task execution (Figure 13.16).

Specify a schedule to be run once a week, every Sunday at 1:00 AM.

Figure 13.16 Schedule dialog box

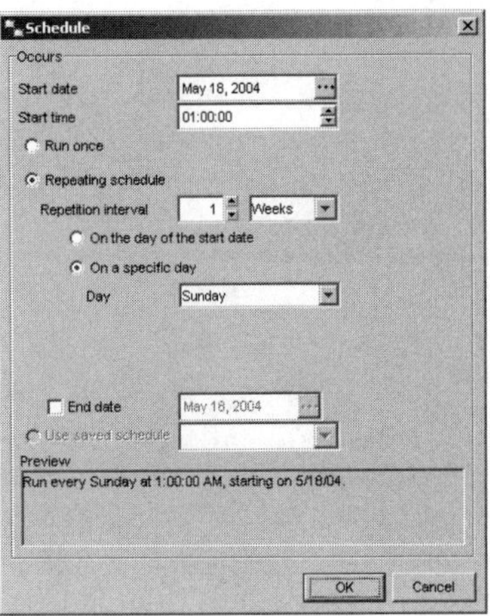

Specify a user ID and password for the backup execution to run under. The user ID and password must be valid for the database server (run system)—not the client and not the scheduler system.

Step 5: Summary page.

On the Summary page, choose Launch Task Center (Figure 13.17). Review the tasks that are going to be created. When you are satisfied with the scheduled task you are about to create, choose Finish. The Task Center should open automatically, with the backup task now created.

Figure 13.17 Task Center

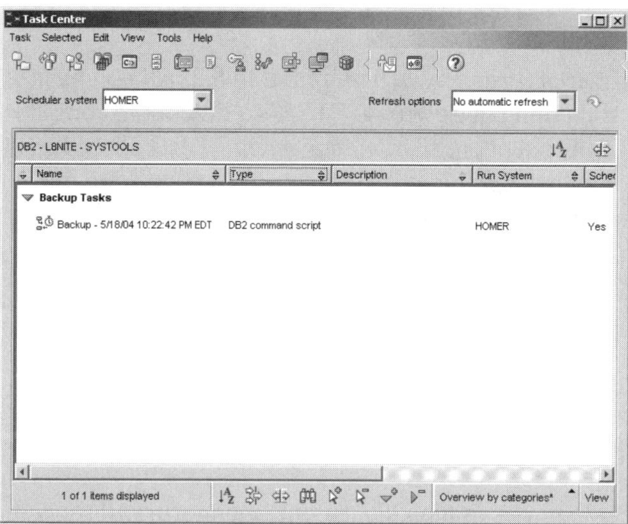

The Task Center can be used to schedule any type of script, whether or not it is created through the Control Center. The advantage of creating tasks through thc Control Center rather than manually is that they can then be edited in the original dialog box where they were created. The tasks will be run at their scheduled time from the system where you choose to create the tools catalog, but they will be run on the system where the database exists. This server-side execution is essential so that there are no dependencies on the client where the task was created.

You can see previous executions of your tasks in the Journal. Explore the task we just created, and see that dependent activities can be performed and notifications can be sent in case of task success, failure, or both.

13.10 Health of the Database

Beyond basic maintenance activities that can be proactively and routinely performed, there are many other aspects of a database that can affect its performance, stability, and longevity. We call all these aspects of a database its *health*. The health of a database needs to be monitored and analyzed proactively to ensure that as workloads change the overall health of the database remains optimal. This seems like a lot of work, and it can be if you do it yourself. Fortunately DB2 has a Health Monitor that does this for you.

The DB2 Health Monitor is preconfigured and on by default in DB2 v8.2. All you have to do is supply an e-mail address in case something goes wrong. OK, it's a little more complicated than that, but essentially, that's it. The concept is called *management by exception*. In other words, you have to act or manage only those problems that are the exception from the norm, and only these exceptions will be brought to your attention. There are two main components for monitoring DB2's health:

- Health Monitor
- Health Center

Health Monitor

The DB2 Health Monitor is an agent that runs in the DB2 engine, monitoring all aspects of the database health, from memory allocations, space management, and file system free space to even monitoring the automated maintenance activities you set up earlier. There are more than 30 health indicators with DB2. The power of the Health Monitor is that you don't need to know about any of them. You only need to begin to understand them when a health indicator alert is raised. A health indicator can be in its normal state or in one of the three alert states shown in Table 13.1.

Table 13.1. Health Indicator Alert States

Attention	Informational alert indicating a nonnormal state
Warning	A noncritical state that does not require immediate attention but may indicate a nonoptimal system
Alarm	A critical condition requiring immediate action

Each health alert has a set of recommended actions that can be performed to correct the root cause of the exception. The Health Monitor contains a sophisticated recommendation advisor that guides you through the needed corrective actions.

Health Center

The Health Center is a graphical tool for interacting with the Health Monitor. The Health Center breaks down the health alerts on a system by instance, database, and table space. For each health alert, a recommendation advisor within the Health Center will guide you through corrective actions.

If you haven't configured the notification and contact list, please return to section 13.8 and do so now. Choose a contact to be informed of health alerts, and then close the dialog box. Then follow these steps.

Step 1: Simulate a health alert.

To test that the Health Monitor is properly configured, let's artificially create a warning.

We will reduce the sort warning threshold from a default of 90 percent to 0 percent. When the alert condition is resampled, an alert will be raised and the recommendation engine will be demonstrated.

From the Health Center menu, select Configure > Health Indicator Settings. This will invoke the Health Indicator Configuration launchpad. Click the Instance Settings button to launch the Instance Health Indicator Configuration dialog box (Figure 13.18).

Figure 13.18 Instance Health Indicator Configuration

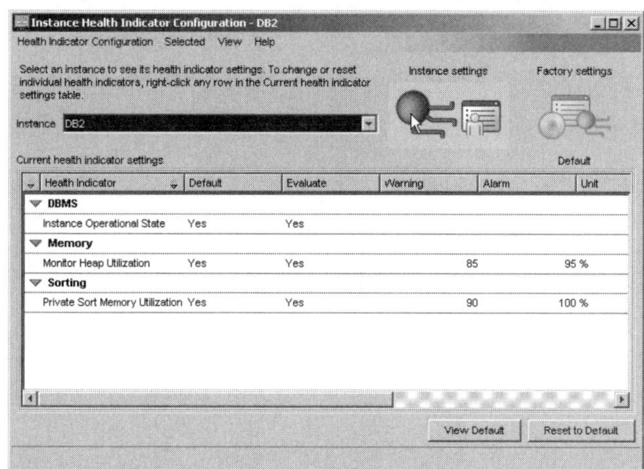

In the Instance Health Indicator Configuration dialog box, do the following:

- Select the DB2 or db2inst1 instance in the pull-down menu.
- Right-click Private Sort Memory Utilization (in the Sorting category), and click Edit from the pop-up menu.
- Change the Warning threshold to 0.
- Click OK .
- Close the Health Indicator Configuration dialog box and launchpad to return to the Health Center.

Step 2: Wait for the health alert.

The health indicator for sort utilization is evaluated approximately every five minutes. When it is next evaluated you should receive a warning alert for exceeding the sort threshold. You should also receive a notification in your e-mail.

Note that this change is not causing a problem in DB2 itself. We are simply making the Health Monitor overly sensitive about sorts to create a health alert.

When the health alert is generated, you will see that the icon for DB2 is now yellow (Figure 13.19).

Figure 13.19 Health Center with sort warning

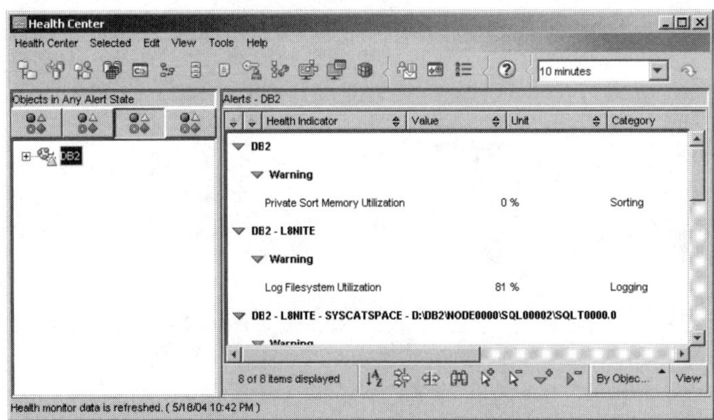

A health alert implies an unhealthy condition. However, the DB2 Health Center can step you through fixing the problem with the built-in Recommendation Advisor.

Step 3: Invoke the Recommendation Advisor.

Right-click the "Private Sort Memory Utilization" alert, and select Recommendation Advisor... from the pop-up menu. This will start the recommendation process (Figure 13.20).

Figure 13.20 Recommendation Advisor

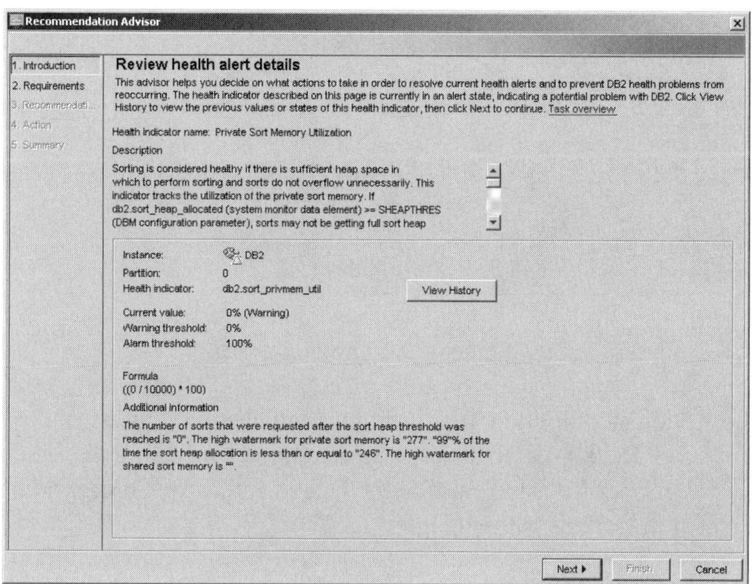

Review the information provided. The Recommendation Advisor will ask on the Requirements page whether you have run the Design Advisor, because sorting can sometimes be eliminated by creating a new index. For the purposes of this artificial alert, specify Yes. Navigate to the Recommendations page (Figure 13.21).

Figure 13.21 Recommendation Advisor: Recommendations

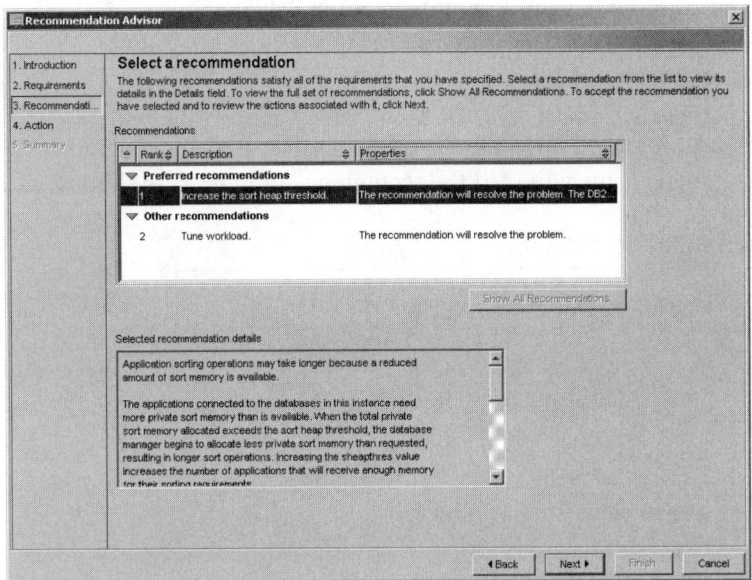

Click Next to review the recommendations. Select a recommendation.

Click Next to move to the Action step. Review the recommended changes, but do not implement the recommendation. Recall that this alert was generated by making the Health Monitor overly sensitive. The proper fix is to return to the Health Indicator Configuration dialog box and click the Reset to Default button (Figure 13.22).

Figure 13.22 Reset default health indicator thresholds

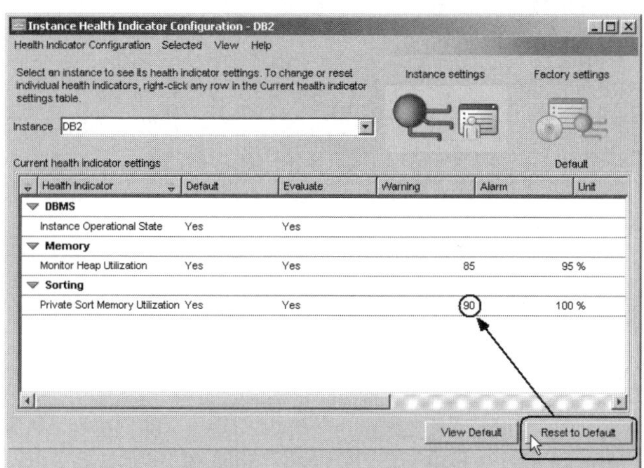

13.11 Storage Management

The management and monitoring of storage consistently rank among the most common tasks for all database administrators. In the case of the L8NITE database, the database grows only as transactions are processed. If the database runs out of disk space, the application will not function properly until more disk space is added.

In the Control Center's operational view (Figure 13.23), you can see at a glance how much storage is being used and how much is left.

Figure 13.23 Control Center Operational View

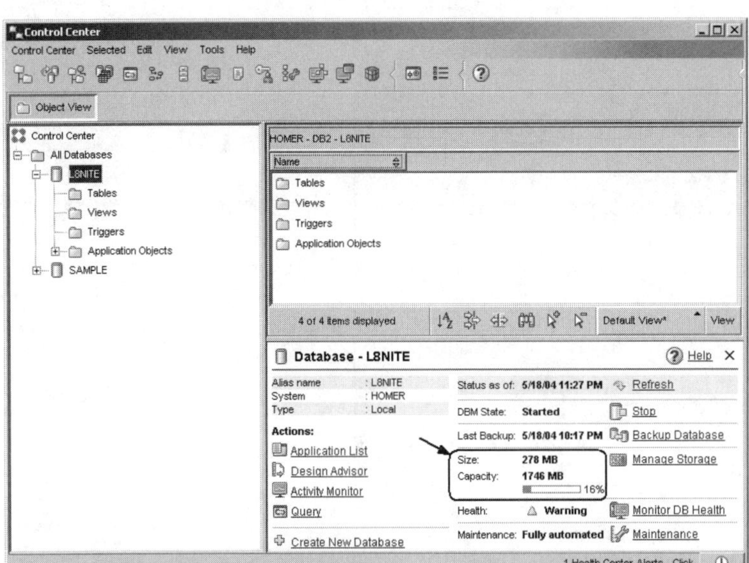

However, this storage indicator provides only the current state of storage. Knowing how quickly the database is growing over time would be useful for planning storage upgrades or other alternatives (such as deleting or archiving older, unneeded data).

DB2's Storage Management tool can gather storage information, called a *storage snapshot*, on a regular basis for further and future analysis. These snapshots, when taken regularly over a period of time, can be used to predict the future storage needs of the database. The tool uses a stored procedure that can be run at any time or can be scheduled as part of a weekly or monthly maintenance cycle. This stored procedure populates a set of storage management tables within your database that the Control Center can use to help you analyze the growth of the database, table spaces, and containers.

The storage information is also highly dependent upon up-to-date statistics. Therefore, be sure to keep statistics up-to-date so that the information is accurate. If you use automatic database maintenance or scheduled statistics collection (runstats), this should not be a problem.

For the L8NITE database, we'll set up the Storage Management tool to take a storage snapshot once a week.

From the Control Center, select the L8NITE database and click the Manage Storage link in the operational view.

Figure 13.24 Control Center Operational View: Launch Storage Management

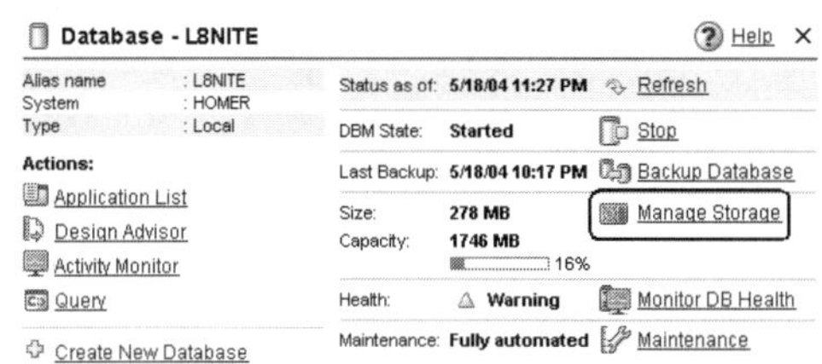

If this is the first time you are using the Storage Management tool, a launchpad will guide you through the process of creating your storage snapshot maintenance (Figure 13.25).

Figure 13.25 Storage Management Setup launchpad

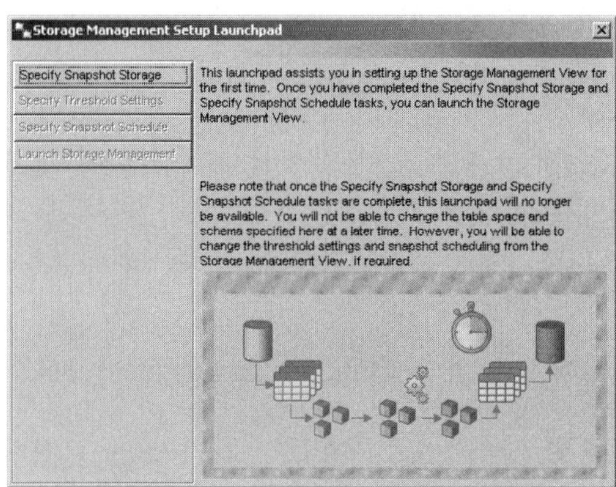

Click the Specify Snapshot Storage button. You are prompted to select a table space in which to create the storage snapshot tables. Select the default table space, USERSPACE1.

Click the Specify Snapshot Schedule button. Your scheduling capabilities should be configured to create tasks from the preceding section. If it is not, create the tools catalog by following the onscreen instructions.

Figure 13.26 Schedule periodic storage snapshots

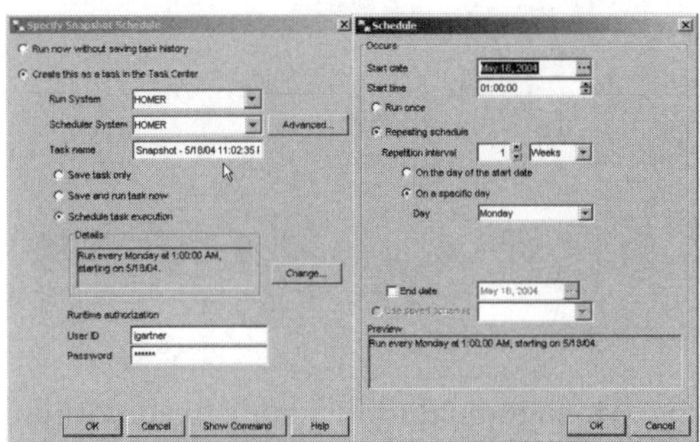

- Specify the task name L8NITE storage.
- Select Schedule Task Execution.
- Configure the task to run every Monday at 1:15 AM.
- Specify the user ID db2admin (or db2inst1) and the appropriate password.

Your storage snapshot schedule should now be set up (Figure 13.26). However, you will be unable to see the storage allocations of your database until at least one snapshot has been taken.

Launch the Specify Snapshot Schedule dialog box again, and choose Run Now to capture a snapshot immediately. You should now be able to launch the Storage Management tool.

The Storage Management tool is organized in a tree structure similiar to that of the Control Center, with the exception that it is organized according to the physical layout of the database as opposed to the conceptual one.

Figure 13.27 Storage snapshot

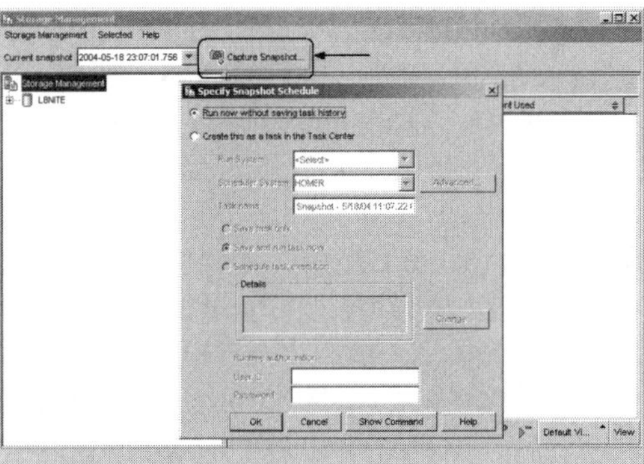

- Click Capture Snapshot, and choose Run Now. This will be the second time you've captured storage snapshot information (Figure 13.27).
- Right-click the L8NITE database, and select Show Historical Snapshots... from the pop-up menu (Figure 13.28).

Figure 13.28 Historical analysis of database size

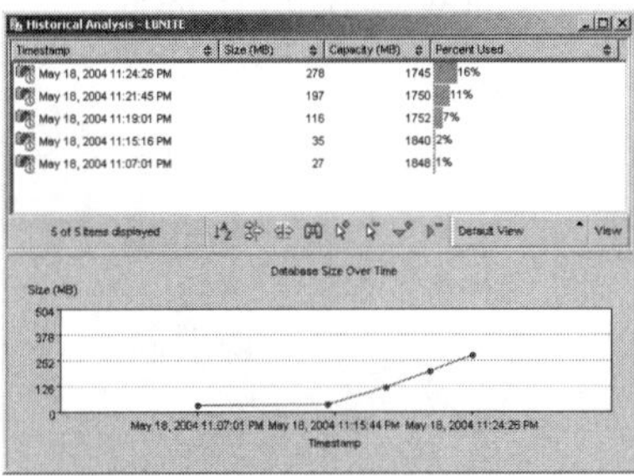

From here you can compare the database size over time. The more frequent the snapshot, the more accurate the graphing will be. However, each snapshot takes up storage in the database.

13.12 Supplemental: High Availability and Disaster Recovery

"Hope for the best, but prepare for the worst" is an old English proverb. The quote could not be more true today with our total dependence on computers. Availability 24x7 is no longer a want, but a need. With real-time purchasing systems available 24 hours a day on the Internet, downtime is not an option, so a highly available system infrastructure is needed.

The Enterprise Server Edition of DB2 v8.2 has a feature called High Availability Disaster Recovery (HADR). HADR (Figure 13.29) creates a hot standby database to be used in case the main database becomes unavailable for some reason. A copy of the database is maintained at all times as a secondary database, and committed database logs are shipped from the primary database to the secondary database and played on the secondary database. In this way, if the primary database ever becomes unavailable, an up-to-date secondary database is available to be used. Database takeover can be forced in times when downtime of the primary database is required for whatever reason, such as hardware maintenance. During a takeover, the primary database becomes the secondary and the secondary the primary, the roles of the databases being swapped.

Another feature of DB2 v8.2 that plays an important role in highly available systems is the concept of *client rerouting*. If all clients are pointing to a single database and it becomes unavailable, and if a different database takes over the responsibilities of the primary database, the clients need to be automatically rerouted to the new primary database.

Figure 13.29 High Availability Disaster Recovery (HADR)

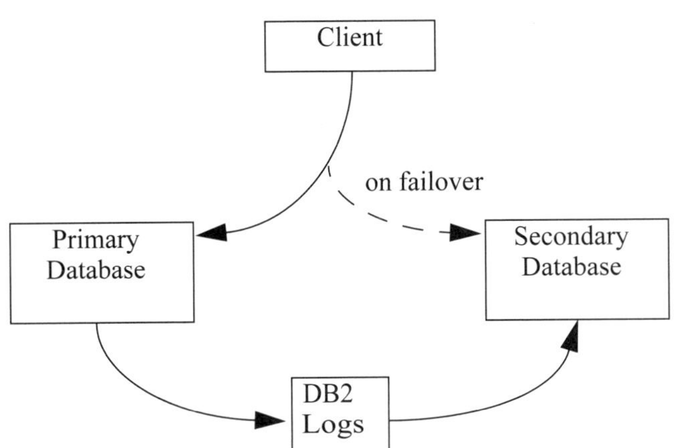

To set up HADR, a copy of your database must be made and configuration parameters set that will point the databases toward one another as partners. HADR must then be started. Client reroute is a set of configuration parameters that also points a client to both systems as available database servers.

A wizard is available to completely set up and help monitor your HADR configuration. You can get to it from the Control Center object tree: Control Center > All Databases > L8NITE > (right-click) High Availability Disaster Recovery… > Setup...

We will not step you through setting up an HADR configuration but will leave it as an exercise. A good way to test whether HADR is applicable to you and to evaluate it is to create a copy of the L8NITE database on the same machine and instance and test a takeover from one to the other. The setup wizard will guide you completely through this process. To test the takeover from one database to the other, you can use the Manage HADR operational dialog box.

13.13 Summary

When you go into production, the ongoing health and maintenance of your database are important aspects of maintaining a viable application for your clients to use. From regularly backing up the database to routinely ensuring that the data is properly represented and defragmented, all aspects of database administration are needed. Fortunately technologies such as automated maintenance and health monitoring can all but eliminate many routine tasks.

However, a certain level of involvement will be needed. Every database is different, and every environment it runs in is different, so use the tools given to you to their fullest potential. You may realize that certain capabilities or tools may not be needed or may not serve your needs in your environment; this is part of evaluating and settling on a maintenance plan.

Doing nothing about maintenance is not an option. Regular database backups are the absolute minimum that should be performed so that in the case of catastrophic failure, you and your data are protected. Even if your database is small, insignificant, embedded, or even hidden, the automated maintenance and health monitoring can save you time later in the life of your database. With more advanced databases, you should look even further into storage allocations, scheduled maintenance, or even high availability. HADR can be an easy, low-cost alternative to machine failover scenarios, where everything must have a redundant backup in case of failure.

Going into production can be a very anxious time for many database administrators. If you've done your homework and have set up the system fully and completely, maintenance is one less thing to worry about.

13.14 Exercises

1. Configure the L8NITE database to use automated maintenance with a backup directory of D:\Backups.

2. Configure a common contact list to be used for alert notification. Create five user contacts and create a group which includes the the first two users. Then create a second group which includes the first group and the remaining three users.

3. Artificially force a sorting health alert.

4. Schedule a storage snapshot to be taken once a week, every Sunday at 9 PM.

5. Configure the L8NITE database as an HADR configuration. Keep it simple by putting the standby database on the same machine and instance as the primary L8NITE database.

6. Configure the clients to automatically failover to the secondary database if the primary database becomes unavailable.

CHAPTER 14

Troubleshooting Tools

In this chapter, you will learn:

- How to find information about explicit errors returned by DB2
- How to use the Activity Monitor to troubleshoot ongoing database activity
- How to use an event monitor to gather information on hard-to-catch problems
- Where to get additional help

14.1 Introduction

When problems with DB2 arise, it can be difficult to know where to start troubleshooting. First, you must know what an error is trying to tell you, and then you must gather more information to understand how the problem occurred.

DB2 comes with a set of graphical tools to simplify problem determination and resolution. Finding out more information about an error can be as simple as typing the error code in the Command Editor, as you will soon see.

Not all problems have error codes, however, and these are more difficult to resolve. For example, if your application performance starts to degrade or resources start to get locked up, error codes are not necessarily returned, and you may need to take proactive action to understand what activities are occurring at that moment. The Activity Monitor can be very useful in these situations.

Yet another class of problems are those that are difficult to catch or reproduce. Without a repeatable test case, it's difficult to gather relevant information (if you can gather any at all) to fix the problem. DB2 event monitors can be employed to automatically gather information for you whenever problems happen, without user intervention.

In addition to IBM technical support, there is a large community of DB2 users who actively participate in discussion groups and publish articles. Therefore, we also include a set of important resources that may help you find solutions to problems.

There is no single methodology for fixing all kinds of problems. Troubleshooting is an art form. By reading this chapter, however, you will understand how to use the core tools available.

14.2 Interpreting Error Codes

When you encounter a database error, you first need to understand what the error is saying. Every interaction with DB2—whether through SQL or other means (such as the various programming interfaces)—is classified as either successful, successful with warnings, or unsuccessful (error encountered).

For every error returned by DB2, there is always an associated SQLCODE and SQLSTATE. SQLCODEs are usually more informative for troubleshooting problems, whereas SQLSTATE is more standards-based. SQLSTATEs are based on the ISO/ANSI SQL standard.

SQLCODE is an integer status code specific to DB2 and is consistent across DB2 for Linux, UNIX, and Windows. There are some SQLCODEs that are common across all database vendors, such as +100 (which means "not found"), but the vast majority of codes do not overlap across various database products. In general (there are few exceptions), the rules for SQLCODEs are as follows:

- SQLCODE = 0: The command was successful.
- SQLCODE > 0: The command was successful, but returned a warning.
- SQLCODE < 0: The command was unsuccessful and returned an error.

SQLSTATE is a five-character string that conforms to the ISO/ANSI SQL92 standard. Messages associated with SQLSTATEs are more general in nature. Rules for SQLSTATE also exist. The first two characters of SQLSTATE are known as the SQLSTATE class code.

- A class code of 00 means that the command was successful.
- A class code of 01 implies a warning.
- A class code of 02 implies a not found condition.
- All other class codes are considered errors.

The following are examples of error messages.

```
SQL0911N The current transaction has been rolled back because of a deadlock or
timeout.  Reason code 2. SQLSTATE=40001

SQL0100W  No row was found for FETCH, UPDATE or DELETE; or the result of a
query is an empty table.  SQLSTATE=02000

SQLCODE SQL0911N means -911 (error, with N implying negative) and SQL0100W
means +100 (warning, with W implying warning). The SQLSTATEs associated with
these errors are 40001 and 02000, respectively.
```

When you encounter an error, you can always find more information about the error by using a question mark to prefix the SQLCODE in the Command Editor. For example, if your application received SQLCODE -811, it translates to SQL0811N, and you can find more information about the error as illustrated in Figure 14.1.

Figure 14.1 Finding more information about SQLCODEs

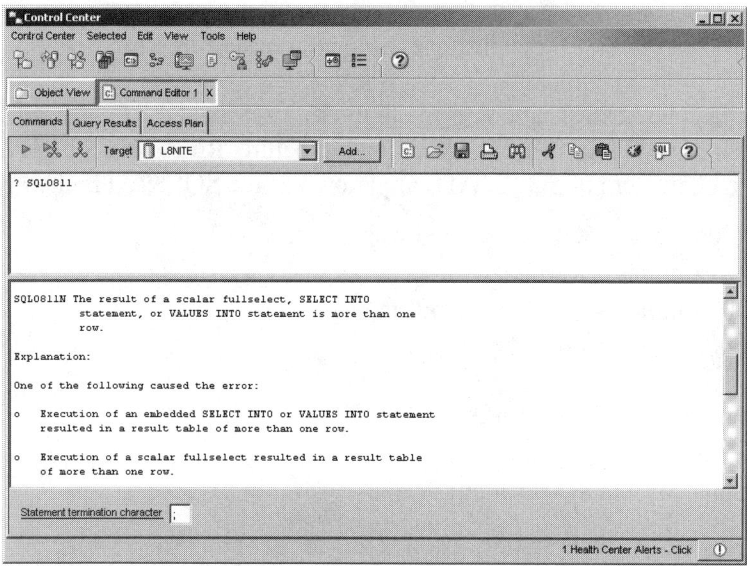

The output returned will repeat the error text associated with the code and will list the conditions in which the error is returned. If you scroll down to see the tail portion of the output messages, the User Response section (Figure 14.2) can be very helpful.

Figure 14.2 User response output for SQL0811N

User Response:

Ensure that the statement contains the proper condition specifications. If it does, there may be a data problem that is causing more than one row to be returned when only one is expected.

Federated system users: isolate the problem to the data source failing the request (refer to the problem determination guide to determine which data source is failing to process the SQL statement) and examine the selection criteria and data for that object.

sqlcode : -811

sqlstate : 21000

You can also find more information for an error using SQLSTATE, as illustrated in Figure 14.3.

Figure 14.3 Finding more information about SQLSTATEs

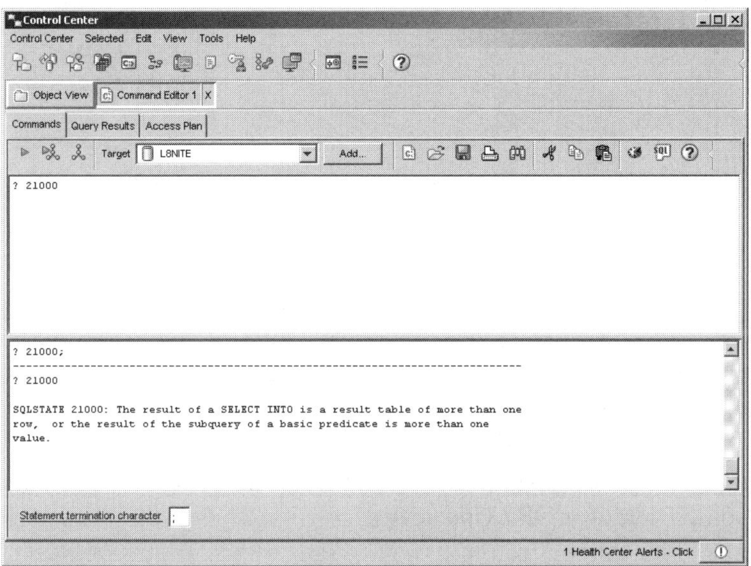

14.3 DB2 Defects and Applying FixPaks

Sometimes, a problem you encounter is caused by a defect in the DB2 product itself. IBM regularly releases fixes for problems through software patches called FixPaks. New features are also included in FixPaks.

Installation of FixPaks also changes the version number of the installed product. When DB2 version 8 was first released, the version number was 8.1.0. Applying a FixPak changes the minor number of the version: DB2 v8.1.1, DB2 v8.1.2, DB2 v8.1.3, and so on.

Between DB2 versions 8.1 and 8.2, six FixPaks were released. In FixPak 7, because there were many new features, the product was released as DB2 v8.2. Customers who were using any version of DB2 version 8.1 could get to version 8.2 by applying FixPak 7.

To see the FixPak level of DB2, select About from the Control Center Help menu (Figure 14.4). As you can see, the product level indicated is DB2 version 8.1.7.x, implying DB2 version 8.2.

Figure 14.4 Viewing the current DB2 product level

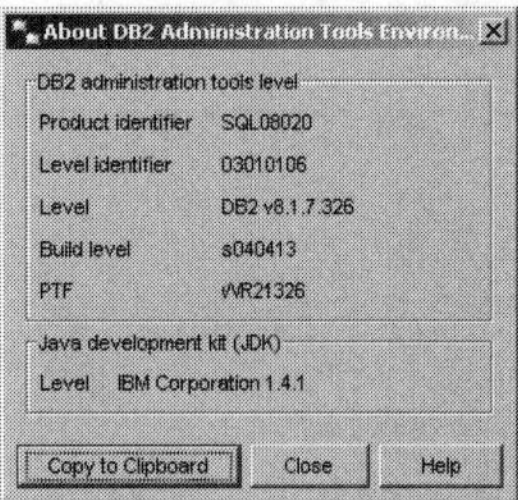

You can download FixPaks from http://www.ibm.com/software/data/db2/udb/support.html

Click on the link Download FixPaks and Clients.

On Windows, you can also check for updates at any time by clicking Start > Programs > IBM DB2 > Information > Check for DB2 Updates.

When you are developing new applications, we generally recommend using the latest available FixPak to benefit from the latest fixes and features. Included with each FixPak is a text document with instructions on how to apply it (the instructions differ between Windows and Linux). Be sure to read the instructions carefully.

In the remaining sections, you will learn about additional graphical tools that can help you troubleshoot other classes of problems. These tools have a strong dependency on the DB2 Administration Server (DAS). The DAS has been mentioned before, but because the tools will not function without it, we elaborate on its purpose and setup in the next section.

14.4 The DB2 Administration Server

The DB2 Administration Server (DAS) is a special background process that runs on DB2 servers to support DB2 tools. Many of the troubleshooting tools we will discuss rely on the

DAS to gather information about the system and perform certain tasks. Therefore, it is important to ensure that the DAS is running on the server, or else you may enounter communications errors.

The DB2 Administration Server is registered as DB2DAS in the Windows Services dialog box (Figure 14.5). Ensure that it is running.

Figure 14.5 The DB2 Admin Service (DB2DAS)

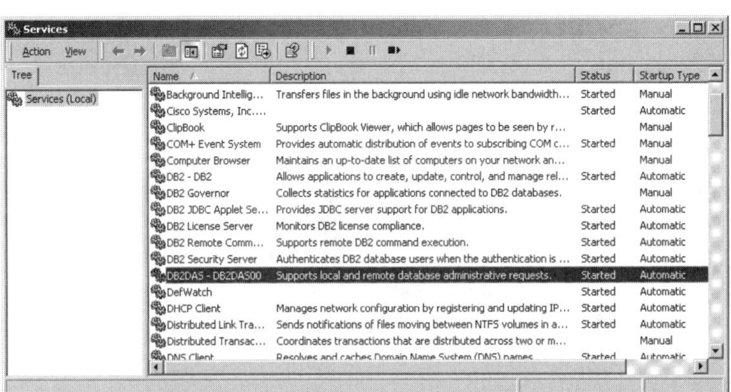

On Linux, the DAS process is called dasusr1 and runs as the user dasusr1 by default. If the process is not running, change to the dasusr1 user and run the command db2admin start.

```
su - dasusr1
db2admin start
```

14.5 DB2 Journal

The Journal is a good place to start looking for information on system-level problems. The Journal is simply a DB2 DBA's activity journal in an online form. The Journal can be opened from the Tools menu of any graphical DB2 utility. The Journal has four tabs:

- Task History: This is a record of all attempted scheduled tasks and their success status (configured through the DB2 Task Center).

- Database History: This gives you a record of database activities performed (such as backups, restores, loads, reorgs, etc.).
- Messages: This contains a history of messages returned by DB2 tools such as the Control Center and the Command Editor. This is useful if you wish to recall and compare old error messages, or if you close a dialog box too quickly by accident.
- Notification Log: This log contains DB2 system-level messages. Critical errors are recorded here.

Figure 14.6 shows the DB2 Journal.

Figure 14.6 The DB2 Journal

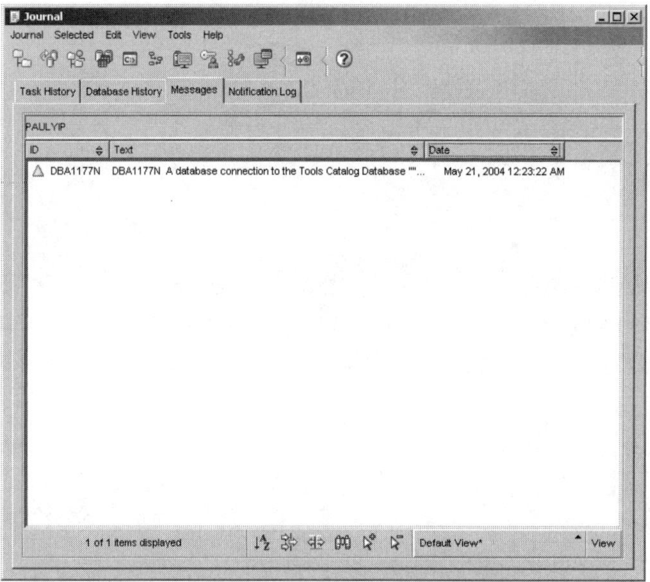

14.6 Activity Monitor

Before DB2 Express v8.2, troubleshooting complex performance and resource consumption problems required you to gather performance statistics using the command line or SQL (snapshot functions). This process, called *snapshot monitoring*, requires extracting data from DB2's built-in performance monitors. For a given type of monitor, dozens or even hundreds of performance metrics could be returned for analysis. Although snapshot monitoring provides a wealth of information, it can be overwhelming for many inexperienced DB2 users. With all the information returned, it is challenging to identify what should be monitored given a problem. It is also a time-consuming task to manually obtain and sort out all the monitor data needed.

Troubleshooting DB2 is significantly easier with the introduction of a new graphical tool called the Activity Monitor. The Activity Monitor helps you concentrate on a small set of prearranged monitor data to quickly locate relevant information related to a symptom. You can then perform some action to resolve the problem (or invoke another tool for further investigation).

Out of the box, DB2 provides many predefined monitoring tasks to address the most common problems. The Activity Monitor focuses on monitoring application performance, application concurrency, resource consumption, and SQL usage. Reports generated by the Activity Monitor provide recommendations. These recommendations can help you diagnose the cause of database performance problems.

To resolve a problem through the Activity Monitor, you must first set up a monitoring task. A *monitoring task* is the set of reports and filter settings that you define in order to collect specific snapshot data. DB2 ships with predefined monitoring tasks for gathering relevent monitor data and generating reports for common problems. You can also create your own monitoring tasks. To demonstrate use of the Activity Monitor, we can create a monitoring task on the L8NITE database.

Step 1: Start the Activity Monitor.

To launch the Activity Monitor, select the L8NITE database object in the Control Center object tree, and click the Activity Monitor link in the object details panel (Figure 14.7).

Figure 14.7 Launching the Activity Monitor

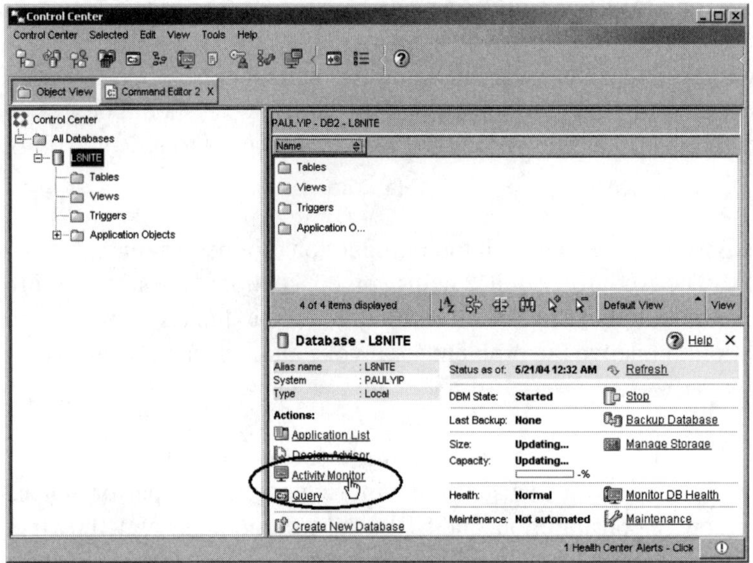

This will invoke the Set Up Activity Monitor wizard.

Step 2: Select a monitoring task.

In the second step of the wizard, you are prompted to select a monitoring task. Listed by default are the system-defined monitoring tasks, a collection of predefined reports for troubleshooting common problems.

Figure 14.8 Selecting a monitoring task

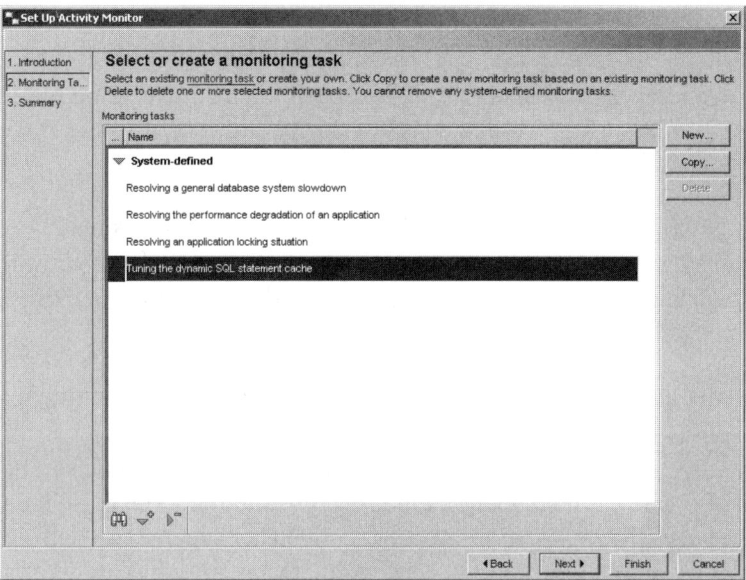

For our example, select the monitoring task called Tuning Dynamic SQL Cache, and click Next (Figure 14.8).

Step 3: Review Activity Monitor setup summary.

In the final step, a summary of the reports to be created by the Activity Monitor is shown. Click Finish to launch the Activity Monitor interface.

Step 4: Select a report.

Initially, no information appears in the Activity Monitor until you select a report from the pull-down menu. Select a report, and you will see that information is returned about queries that have been executed recently.

Now that you have these reports collected, what can you do with them? Troubleshooting query execution problems is really an art form, but here are some ideas on what to look for in each of the reports:

- Dynamic SQL statements in the cache with the longest average execution time: Among these statements, try to determine the source of the long execution times. For example, is the SQL reading or writing an unnecessarily large set of rows? Is the statement performing a lot of sorts?

- Dynamic SQL statements in the cache with the largest number of rows read: Among these statements, is it possible to create an index so that the number of rows read is reduced? Consider submitting this query to the Design Advisor to explore indexing opportunities.

- Dynamic SQL statements in the cache with the largest number of rows written: Of primary concern is whether there are rows written for SELECT statements. This means that a data sort operation was required but overflowed the available sort heap. It may be possible to create an index to avoid the sort operation or to increase the value of maximum sort heap (SORTHEAP in DB CFG). For other statements (INSERT, UPDATE, DELETE), assess whether it is appropriate that many rows are written.

- Dynamic SQL statements in the cache with the largest number of internal rows written: Internal rows written is the number of rows inserted, updated, or deleted from the database as a result of triggers or referential constraints defined as ON DELETE SET NULL or ON DELETE CASCADE. In such cases, you may have to analyze the access plans of SQL within triggers, or look for indexing opportunites on the table where foreign keys exist (to make the foreign key access more efficient).

Change the refresh pull-down option from No Automatic Refresh to 5 Seconds. This means that the Activity Monitor will collect information about database activity that relates to rows read by dynamic SQL statements every five seconds. Assuming that no activity is occurring on your database at the moment, the report should remain stable.

Other monitoring tasks are available, and we leave it as an exercise to explore how each one may be useful in solving your runtime problem.

14.7 Diagnosing Locks

Diagnosing locking problems can be very difficult. By "locking problems," we generally mean lock contention. In Chapter 7, Maximizing Concurrency, we discussed the basics of DB2 isolation levels, locking behavior, and other aspects of concurrency. When you do run into a problem with locking, you should first be clear on whether the problem is a deadlock or a lock-wait.

Deadlock

This occurs when application A is waiting on application B to release locks, while application B is waiting for application A to release locks. Neither transaction is able to complete until DB2 forces one application to roll back (thereby releasing its locks and allowing the other transaction to complete). In this subsection, we discuss troubleshooting lock-waits, using the application list in Control Center and the Activity Monitor.

Deadlocks are hard to catch at the moment they occur because DB2 automatically detects cyclical dependencies and forces one application to roll back its transaction. Therefore, another tool is usually used for deadlocks. Troubleshooting deadlocks using event monitors will be discussed later in this chapter.

Lock-Wait

A lock-wait occurs when one application is waiting for resources that another application is holding. The following are the two most common symptoms of lock-wait:

- Symptom 1: The following error has been returned:
  "SQL0911N The current transaction has been rolled back because of a deadlock or timeout. Reason code 68. SQLSTATE=40001".

Identifying the message as reason code 68 is critical because it means that the error occurred because of lock-wait. If it were reason code 2, the error would be due to a deadlock. To troubleshoot deadlocks, see the later discussion on event monitors.

- Symptom 2: The application or database appears to hang.
  The Java program, LockingApp.java, simulates a lock-wait situation (Figure 14.9).

Figure 14.9 LockingApp.java

```
import java.lang.*;
import java.sql.*;

class LockingApp
{
  public static void main(String argv[])
  {
    try
    {
      String url = "jdbc:db2:l8nite";
      Class.forName("com.ibm.db2.jcc.DB2Driver");

      Connection conA = DriverManager.getConnection(url);
      System.out.println ("Connection A established...");

      Connection conB = DriverManager.getConnection(url);
      System.out.println ("Connection B established...");

      Statement stmtA = conA.createStatement();
      Statement stmtB = conB.createStatement();

      System.out.println ("conA: autocommit OFF");
      conA.setAutoCommit(false);

      //Connection A inserts a row without committing
      stmtA.executeUpdate(
         "insert into l8nite.product values (0,'product x',10,14,10,1)");
      System.out.println ("conA: insert successful");

      //Connection B tries to read uncommitted row (Lock-Wait)
      System.out.println ("conB: attempting SELECT...");
      ResultSet rsB = stmtB.executeQuery("select * from l8nite.product");
      rsB.next();

      System.out.println ("conB: SELECT successful...");
    }
    catch (Exception e)
    {
       System.out.println(e);
    }
  }
}
```

The application establishes two connections—conA and conB—and purposely creates a lock-wait problem. conA inserts a row into the PRODUCT table without committing, while conB tries to select all rows from the table, including the row just inserted.

The sample code, LockingApp.java, is also available for download from the book website.

Run this application locally on your machine as follows:

```
javac LockingApp.java
java LockingApp
```

The application should hang after indicating that the connections have been established. You can easily validate whether a lock-wait has occurred by selecting the database in the Control Center, and clicking the Application List button in the object details panel, as illustrated in Figure 14.10.

Figure 14.10 Launching the application list

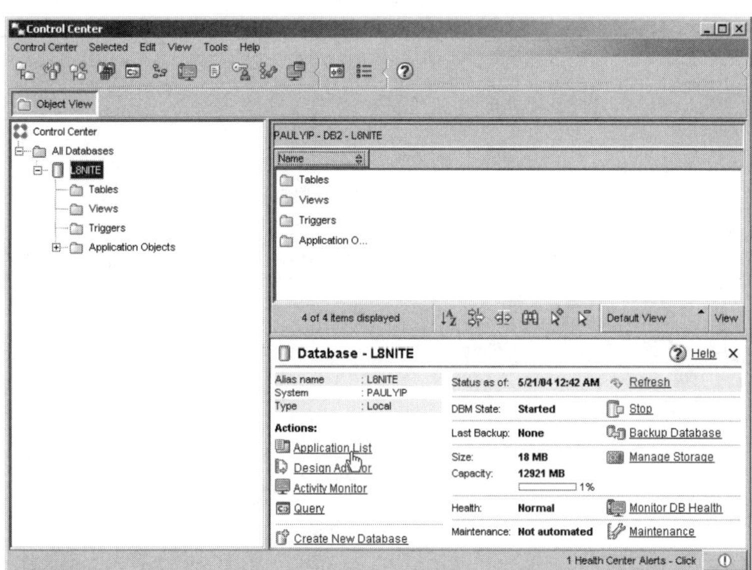

As illustrated in Figure 14.11, you can readily see whether an application is in "lock-waiting" state in the application list. Very likely, it is waiting on resources held by one of the two applications in "UOW Waiting in the Application." *OUW-waiting* means that the connection is idle and waiting on the application to issue the next database operation.

Figure 14.11 Identifying applications in lock-wait in the application list

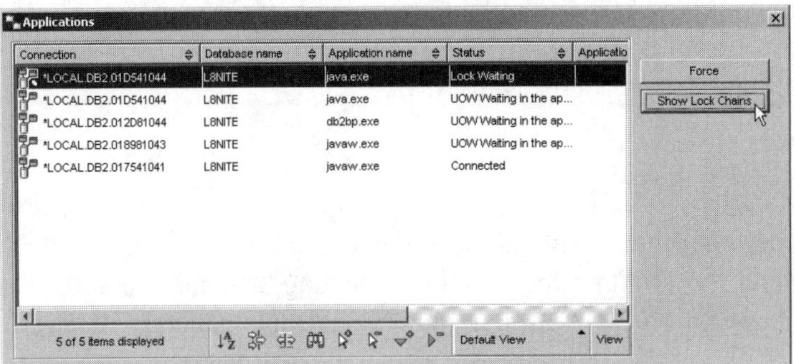

To find out where the lock contention is occurring, you can select the application in lock-wait state and click the Show Lock Chains button (Figure 14.12).

Figure 14.12 View lock chains for a lock-waiting application

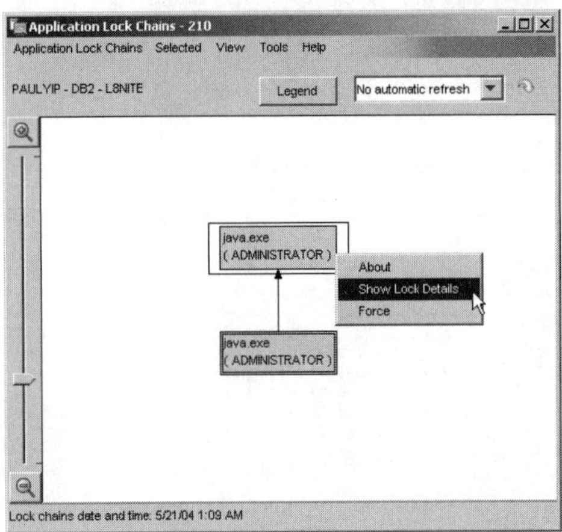

As you can see in Figure 14.12, the contention is occurring between two applications. The application identified by the double-lined box is the application you selected to open the lock chains window (the application in lock-wait). The direction of the arrow indicates the order in which applications are waiting on one another.

Right-click on the object causing the lock-wait, and select Show Lock Details from the pop-up menu to reveal more information about that application.

Figure 14.13 Application Lock Details

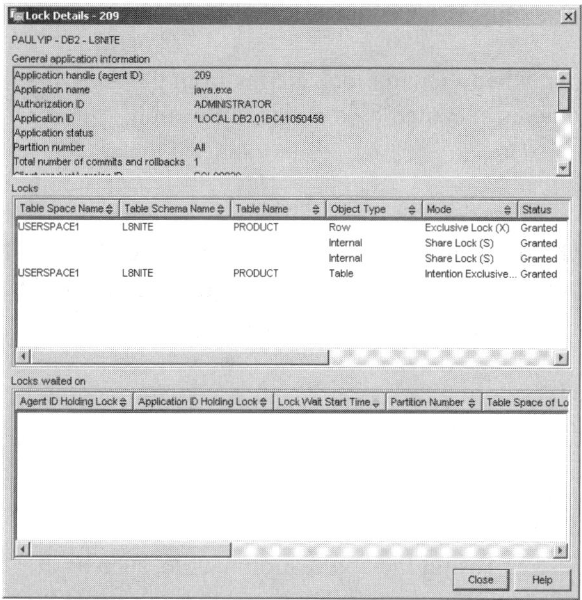

Figure 14.13 shows the details of the application causing the lock contention. In the first window, you see information about the application name, user authentication used, and other important information such as the number of locks it is currently holding and whether any lock escalations have occurred (something that could also be causing other applications to lock-wait). If lock escalations are occurring, redesign your transaction or increase the database configuration parameters LOCKLIST or MAXLOCKS (or both). For more information on these parameters, see Chapter 7, Maximizing Concurrency.

In the middle section, you see the list of locks that have been acquired so far. Looking carefully at this lock list, you can see that two object locks have been acquired, and one internal lock has been acquired. New users often jump to the incorrect conclusion that the *intent exclusive* lock (IX) on the table is the same as a full exclusive lock. An IX lock is usually acquired in conjunction with a row lock. In this case, the IX lock has been acquired in conjunction with a *row exclusive* lock (X). The row exclusive lock would have been acquired because the row was just inserted, updated, or deleted but not yet committed.

To resolve this locking problem, you must investigate why the application has inserted, updated, or deleted the row but has not committed the transaction. For example, is it waiting on something unnecessarily or something unrelated to the database before it can commit? Refer to Chapter 7, Maximizing Concurrency, for best practices in transaction design.

You can find out even more information when viewing lock chains from the Activity Monitor, such as the most recent statements executed by a given application.

Step 1: Launch the Activity Monitor.

Take note of the application handle, which is visible in the title bar of the Lock Details dialog box. Looking back at Figure 14.13, for example, the Lock Details dialog box shows that the application handle is 209.

Launch the Activity Monitor with the monitoring task Resolve an Application Being Locked Up by Some Other Application. Select any report.

Step 2: Open the Show Latest Statements window.

Select the application causing the lock-wait (using the application handle, such as 209), and select Show Latest Statements from the pop-up menu, as illustrated in Figure 14.14. (You may have to increase the limit for the number of applications displayed.)

Figure 14.14 View statement history for application causing lock

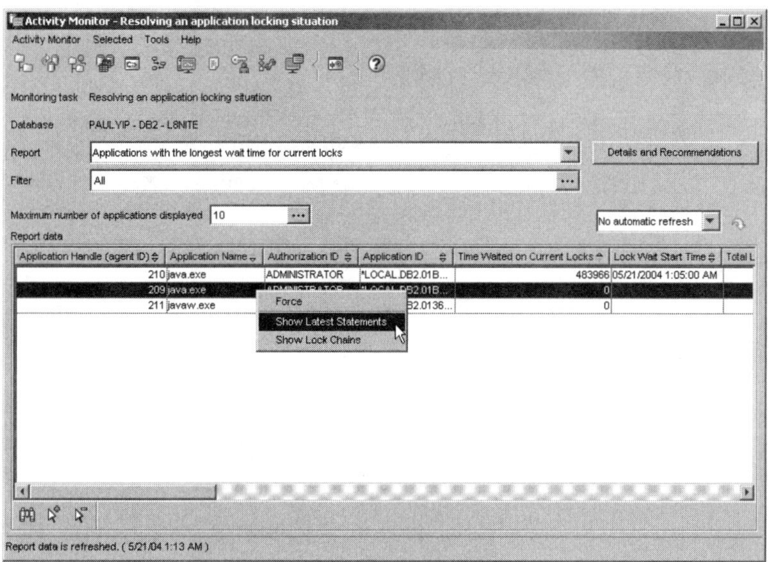

Step 3: View the latest statements.

Select any report in the Application Statements window, as illustrated Figure 14.15, to see the most recent SQL issued by the application. As you can see, the INSERT statement into the PRODUCT table (without committing) is the cause of the lock-wait.

Figure 14.15 View application statements

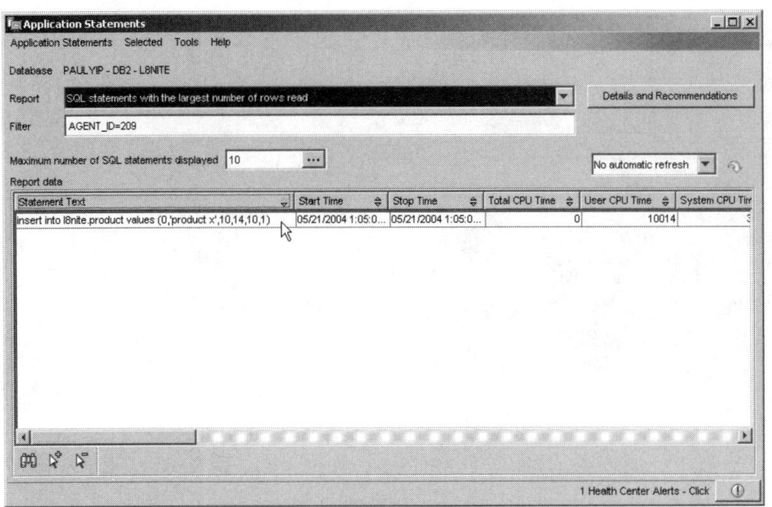

14.8 Event Monitors

The preceding section showed how the Activity Monitor can be used to capture information on activities that were occurring as they were occurring. There are some types of problems, however, that happen rarely or randomly when no one is watching, and this makes it difficult to gather information related to those problems. For example, the occurrence of a deadlock may be difficult to predict. DB2's deadlock detector process scans for deadlocks every 10 seconds (by default) and resolves deadlocks by forcing an application to roll back. Therefore, even when a deadlock does occur, you have a limited time to identify and gather information on the problem.

An event monitor is a tool that gathers information based on events. Events represent transitions in database activity, such as connections, deadlocks, statements, and transactions. For the scenario described earlier, an event monitor for deadlocks will help you automatically capture troubleshooting information when they happen.

Creating event monitors, regardless of type, is simple. Here we will describe how to create an event monitor for deadlocks, but the same steps are used to create any type of monitor.

Step 1: Switch to the DB2 Control Center Advanced view.

Event monitors cannot be created from the Control Center's Basic view. Switch to the Advanced view by selecting Tools > Customize Control Center > Advanced.

Step 2: Create an event monitor.

Expand the object tree for the SAMPLE database, and right-click on the Event Monitors folder. Select Create from the pop-up menu (Figure 14.16).

Figure 14.16 Creating an event monitor from the Control Center

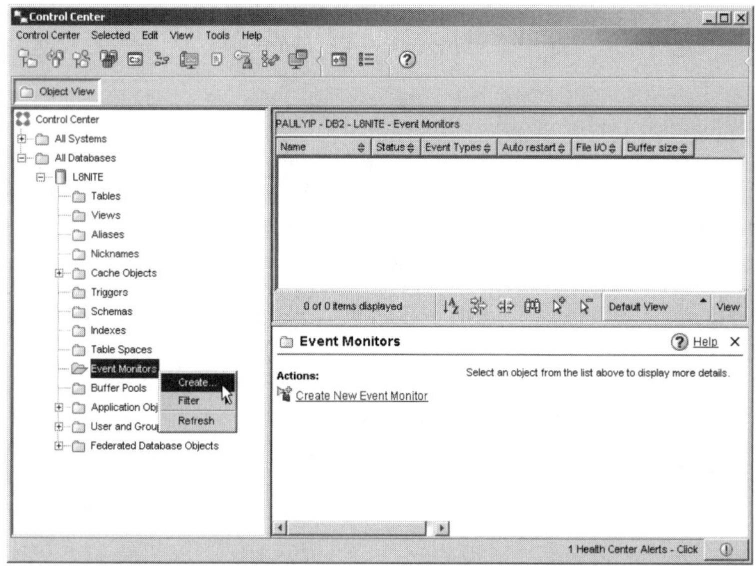

Step 3: Specify event monitor details.

In the Create Event Monitor window, specify a name for the monitor you are about to create. Note that the event monitor name cannot contain spaces. Select Deadlocks and With Details, and click OK (Figure 14.17).

Figure 14.17 Defining event monitor details

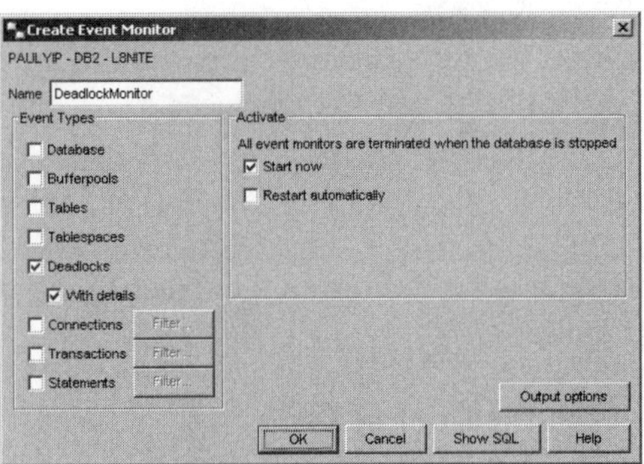

Step 4: Simulate a deadlock scenario.

A windows batch program has been created to simulate a deadlock scenario in deadlock.bat. The files described here are available from the book website. The batch program launches two scripts to simulate two applications that will deadlock:

- deadlock_app1.sql
- deadlock_app2.sql

Application1 (deadlock_app1.sql) performs the following:

- Creates a table called deadlock.t1
- Inserts a value into deadlock.t1 without committing
- Waits for 20 seconds

While application1 is waiting, Application2 (deadlock_app2.sql) performs the following:

- Inserts a value into deadlock.t1 without committing
- Selects all rows from deadlock.t1, which results in a lock-wait (on Application1)

Application1, after the 20 seconds expire,

- Selects all rows from deadlock.t1, which also results in a lock-wait (on Application2)

A deadlock occurs because Application1 and Application2 are lock-waiting on each other, and one application must be forced to roll back to break the lock contention. The DB2 deadlock monitor process will force one of the applications to roll back within 10 seconds (by default).

To run this scenario, run the deadlock.bat batch file.

Step 5: Analyze the event monitor information.

For improved performance, event information is buffered and not immediately written to disk. This means that even after a monitor has captured data, it may not be available for analysis. Stopping the monitor, however, will cause the monitor to flush its buffer to disk.

Right-click on the event monitor object, and select Stop Event Monitoring from the pop-up menu (Figure 14.18).

Figure 14.18 Stopping the event monitor

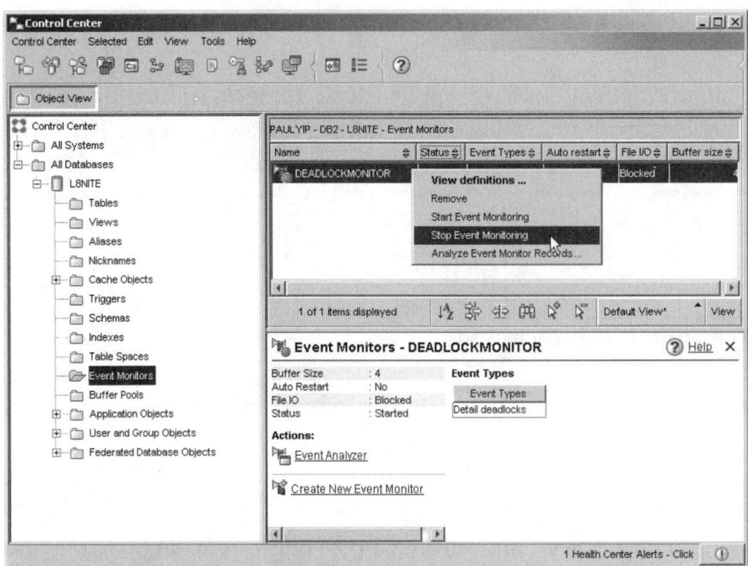

Right-click on the event monitor again, and select Analyze Event Monitor Records to launch the Event Analyzer tool (Figure 14.19).

In the first screen, you see a list of events that have occurred. Right now, there is only the one deadlock event we simulated. To find out more, use the analyzer tool to perform a series of drill-downs into the collected data. The current depth of analysis is Monitored Periods.

Because we are looking for deadlock information, we'll start by drilling down to Monitored Periods > Deadlocked Connection.

Figure 14.19 Deadlock events

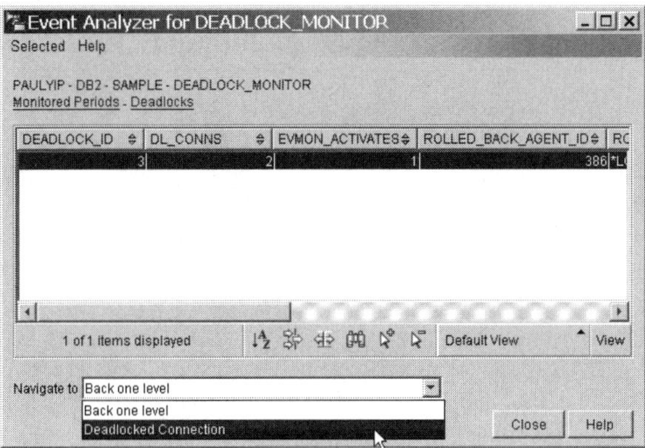

You can see in Figure 14.19 that information for one deadlock occurrence has been collected. To see which application connections were involved in the event, drill-down further to Monitored Periods > Deadlocks > Deadlocked Connection.

Figure 14.20 Connections involved in deadlock event

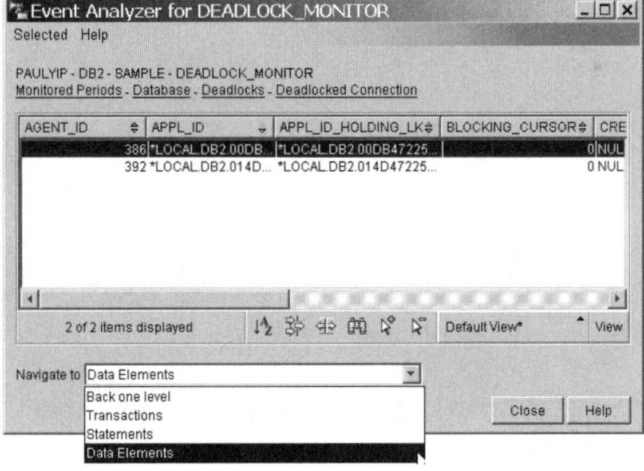

You can see in Figure 14.20 that two connections were involved, as expected. Scrolling across the information can reveal additional information about the applications. To see the intricate details of each connection, such as what SQL statement was executed when the deadlock occurred, drill down further to Monitored Periods > Deadlocks > Deadlocked Connection > Data Elements.

Figure 14.21 Data Elements of deadlock event, including SQL involved

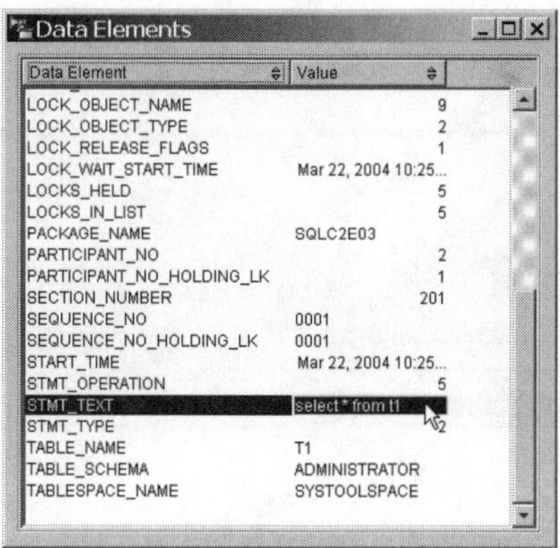

The SQL involved in the deadlock can be seen in Figure 14.21

14.9 Other Sources of Help

A wealth of other information sources is available to help resolve problems. Here is a description of the more well-known resources.

IBM DB2 Support Home Page

www.software.ibm.com/data/db2/udb/support.html

Access the IBM DB2 Support knowledge base. Especially useful are the DB2 Technotes, which document problems experienced by other users and their solutions.

IBM Virtual Innovation Center

http://www.developer.ibm.com/welcome/vic.html

Register your company with the virtual innovation center for technical support.

DB2 Newsgroup

comp.databases.ibm-db2

This newsgroup is monitored by professional DB2 users and DB2 developers. The problem you have may have been identified and resolved by others in the newsgroup.

DeveloperWorks DB2

http://www.ibm.com/developerworks/db2

This Web site has many useful technical articles about tips, tricks, and experiences with DB2 that may be able to help with a particular problem you have.

14.10 Summary

This chapter guided you through the primary tools used to troubleshoot DB2 problems. First, we described how you can quickly find more detailed information for a given DB2 error using either the SQLCODE or the SQLSTATE code and get information on recommended user actions for each error.

Not all problems return error codes, however, and these are more difficult to resolve. In such cases, the Activity Monitor and event monitors can be very useful.

The Activity Monitor is used when you are trying to diagnose a problem that relates to an ongoing operation or activity. The Activity Monitor, with its built-in snapshot and reporting capability, can help you answer questions such as, What is the source of lock contention being observed? Why is the database slowing down? Which SQL is taking the longest to execute? Which SQL is reading the most rows?

An event monitor is another tool you can use to troubleshoot a different class of problems—those that are difficult to catch because they disappear quickly. Event monitors collect information automatically and are triggered by events rather than requiring a user to actively wait for the problem to repeat.

We also provided some important resources for troubleshooting problems. There is no single methodology for fixing all kinds of problems. By reading this chapter, however, you have armed yourself with an extensive set of tools to fix problems more quickly.

APPENDIX A Development Center

The material in this appendix was adapted with permission from the book, *DB2 SQL PL Essential Guide for DB2 on Linux, UNIX, and Windows, i5/OS, and zOS* by Janmohamed, Liu, et al. (Pearson Education, 2004).

A.1 Introduction

The DB2 Development Center (DC) is an easy-to-use, integrated development environment (IDE) for building and debugging DB2 application objects (Figure A.1).

Figure A.1 The DB2 Development Center

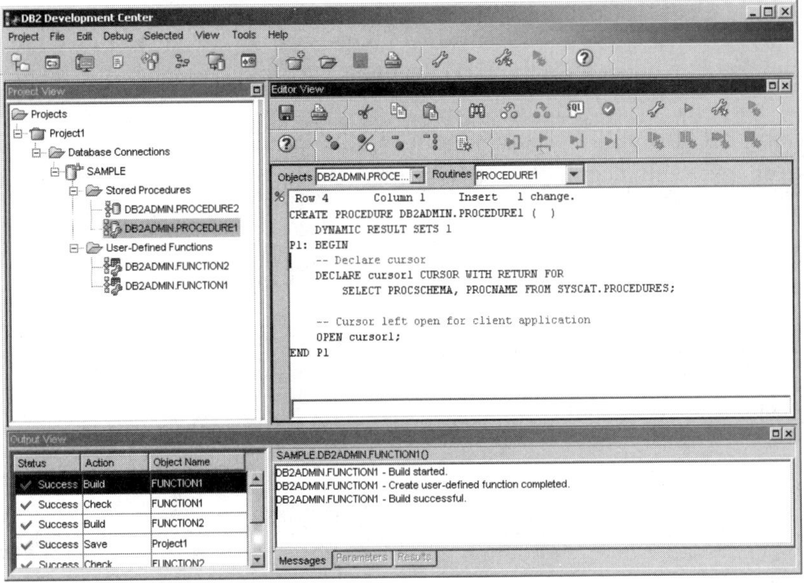

With the Development Center, you can

- Create, build, and deploy Java and SQL stored procedures
- Debug SQL stored procedures using the integrated debugger
- Create, build, and deploy user-defined functions (UDFs)

NOTE: A Microsoft .NET Visual Studio add-in is also available for DB2 that allows you to easily develop DB2 applications using a unified development environment. For more information, see

http://www.ibm.com/developerworks/db2/library/techarticle/0311alazzawe/0311alazzawe.html

A.2 Installing the DB2 Development Center

The Development Center is packaged with all DB2 UDB for Linux, UNIX, and Windows Server installation CDs as well as with the DB2 Application Development Client CD.

For all new development efforts, we recommend using the latest available FixPak to take advantage of performance enhancements and bug fixes. Be sure to apply the same FixPak level at servers as well as clients (if separate).

DB2 FixPaks and client software are available for free download at

http://www.software.ibm.com/data/db2/udb/support.html

Follow the link for DB2 FixPaks and Clients.

NOTE: DB2 version 8.2 is the same as DB2 version 8.1 with FixPak 7 applied.

DB2 for Windows

Before you do anything else, check to ensure that the Development Center has not already been installed. The Development Center can be launched from the DB2 Development Tools menu (Figure A.2).

Figure A.2 Development Center menu location in Windows

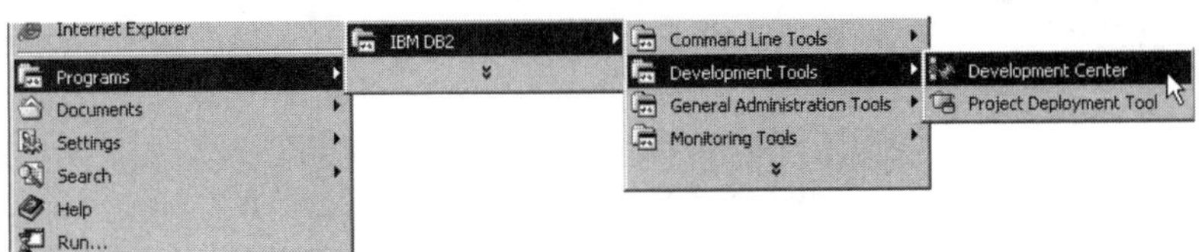

On Windows, there are three types of installation: typical, minimal, and custom. When you use a typical installation, Application Development Tools is included by default, and hence so is the DB2 Development Center.

If you perform a custom installation of DB2, ensure that the Development Center (under Application Development Tools) option is selected, as illustrated in Figure A.3.

Figure A.3 Selecting Development Center during custom installation

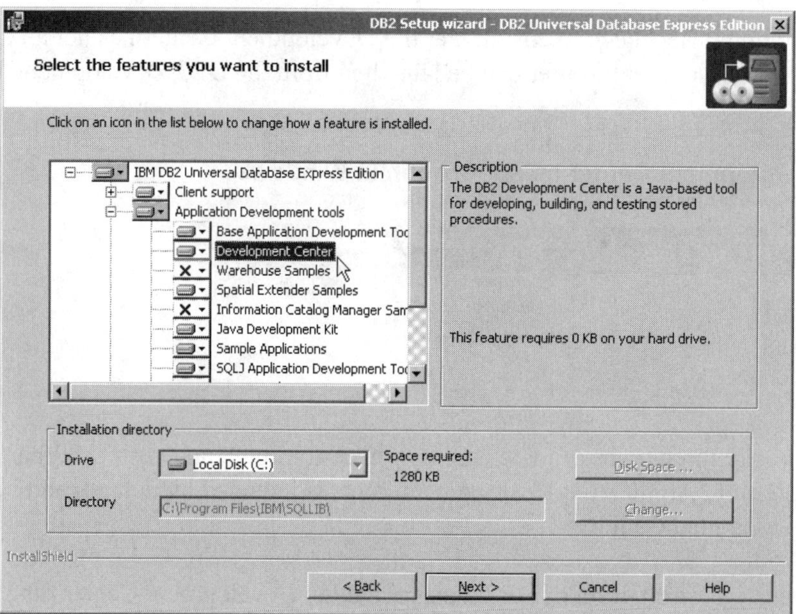

If you have already installed DB2 but did not select Application Development Tools, you can change your existing installation in the Windows Control Panel (Add/Remove Programs), as shown in Figure A.4.

Figure A.4 Using Control Panel to modify an existing installation

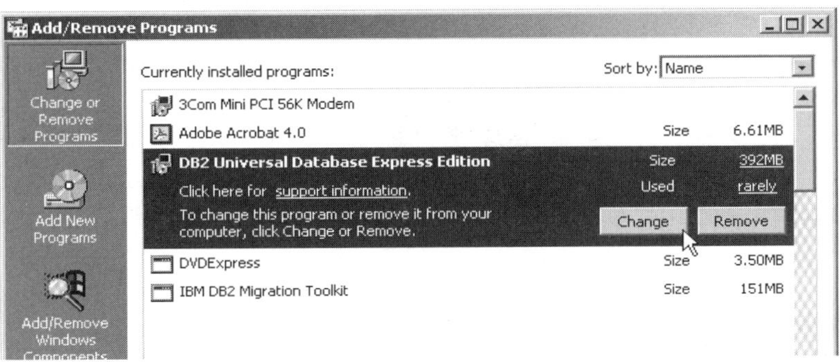

The DB2 installer will look for the required files from previously known install locations. If the required files are not found, you will be prompted to provide the location of a DB2 installation image.

DB2 for Linux and UNIX

Before you do anything else, check to ensure that the Development Center has not already been installed. To launch the Development Center, log in to the system as an instance user (such as db2inst1) and type db2dc.

NOTE: The Development Center (db2dc) can also be run by a noninstance user who has sourced the DB2 instance environment script db2profile.

```
Example:
$ source /home/db2inst1/sqllib/db2profile
$ db2dc
```

When you install DB2 for Linux and UNIX, the Development Center is not installed by default. Be sure to select a custom install if you intend to use the Linux or UNIX system to run the Development Center.

In the custom installation, ensure that the Development Center option (under Application Development Tools) option is selected.

Figure A.5 Selecting the installation of the DC

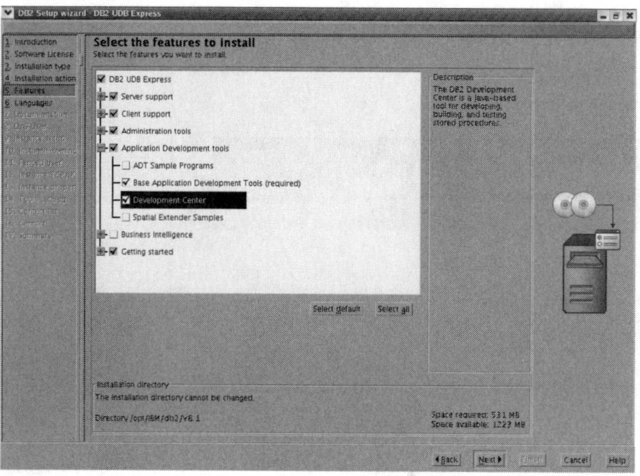

If you have already installed DB2 but did not select Development Center, simply run the install program again. You do not have to uninstall. If you have applied a FixPak since the original installation, you will have to re-apply it before attempting to start DB2 again.

A.3 Using the Development Center for the First Time

The first time you launch the Development Center, you will be greeted with the Development Center launchpad (Figure A.6). Click the Create Project button at the upper-left corner of the window to begin.

Figure A.6 The Development Center launchpad: Creating a project

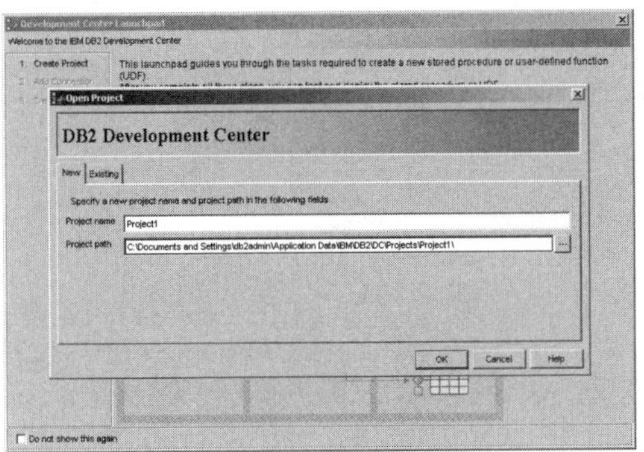

To start developing database application objects, you must first create a new project. A *project* is a logical grouping of related database application objects. The set of all objects in a project, however, may be only a subset of all database application objects already existing on a system.

For example, a single database may be shared by two applications called application A and B. Each application has its own unique set of stored procedures and functions stored in the same database. You might then define a project that contains only objects for application A, and a separate project that contains only objects for Application B. In this way, you can limit your workspace to include only those objects related to the immediate task at hand. It is also possible to open and work with multiple projects at the same time. Projects will be discussed in more detail later.

The second step of the launchpad helps you define a connection for the project (Figure A.7). Click Add Connection.

Figure A.7 Adding a connection to a project

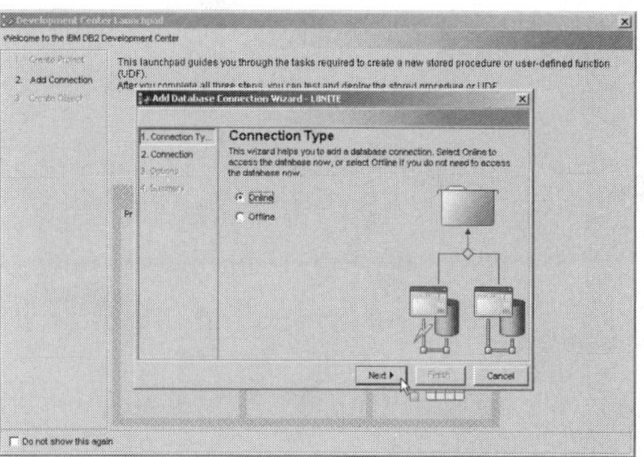

An online connection means that the database is accessible immediately. Generally, this is what you want to do. You would create an offline connection if the database is not currently available for connection. Click Next to continue.

Figure A.8 Select a database and provide connection information

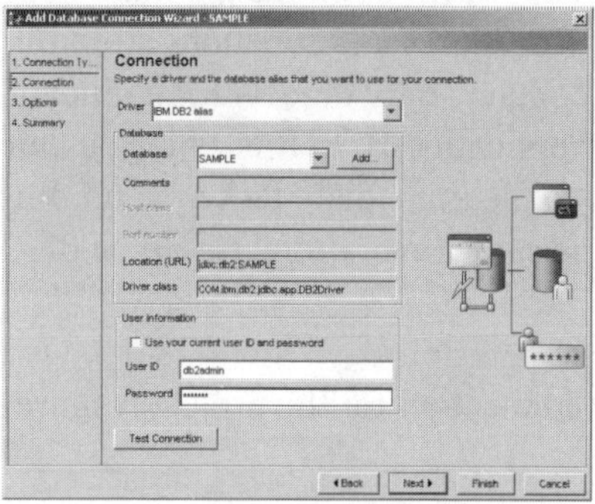

DB2 then prompts you to select the database connection from the pull-down menu (Figure A.8). The SAMPLE database is selected in this case. If there is a remote database that you wish to access but is not configured on your client, you can click the Add button.

Before you can move to the next step, you must provide a user ID and password for connecting to the selected database. You may provide a user ID and password explicitly or use your current network user ID and password. Remember that DB2 uses operating system authentication services. If you do not have a solid understanding of how DB2 implements security, we recommend that you use the IDs in Table A.1.

Table A.1 Default user IDs for DB2 UDB Linux, UNIX, and Windows

Platform	Platform Default SYSADM
Windows	db2admin
UNIX/Linux	db2inst1

Before continuing, click the Test Connection button to verify that the connection works.

After the first two steps, you can accept the remaining defaults and click Finish. Feel free to view the remaining steps of the wizard, but the default values usually suffice. The remaining steps are for specifying additional options such as overriding the default schema.

The final step displays a summary of the connection (Figure A.9). Click Finish to create the connection. This will return you to the Development Center launchpad.

Figure A.9 Connection summary

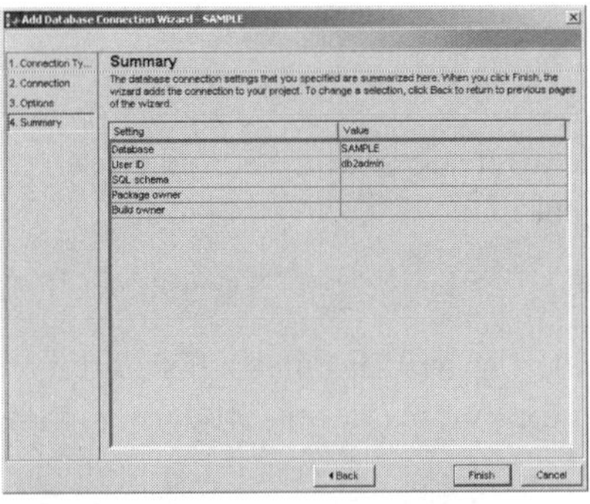

Now that you have a project (Project1) and a database connection object (to SAMPLE), the launchpad can help you create your first stored procedure. Click Create Object, and you will see the New Object dialog box. Click OK to invoke the Create SQL Procedure wizard (Figure A.10).

For the purposes of this tutorial, you can directly click the Finish button to accept all defaults and create your first object using the Development Center (but feel free to step all the way through the wizard if you wish). This will create a small sample procedure.

Figure A.10 Creating a sample stored procedure

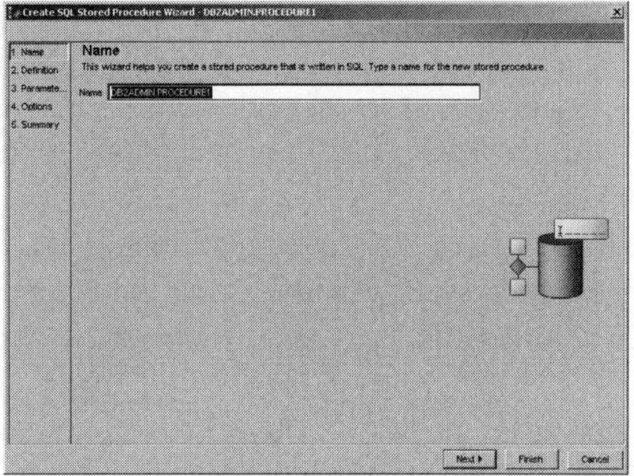

You can now close the launchpad to view the fruits of your labor in the Development Center interface.

NOTE: You can open the Launchpad after the DC has started by selecting the Launchpad option from the Project menu.

The procedure created appears as PROCEDURE1 in the SAMPLE database's stored procedure folder (Figure A.11). You can see in the Output view (lower-left corner) that the build was successful.

Figure A.11 First look at the DB2 Development Center IDE

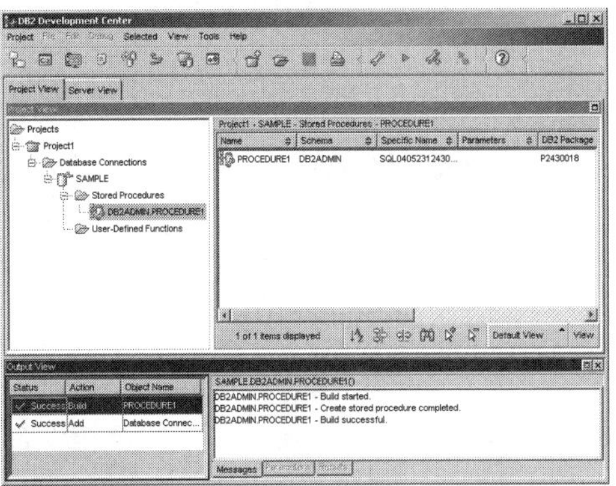

You can retrieve the source code for an object by double-clicking its icon, pressing Ctrl+E while highlighting the object, or by right-clicking it and selecting the Edit menu item. This will open the Editor view (Figure A.12).

Figure A.12 The Editor view

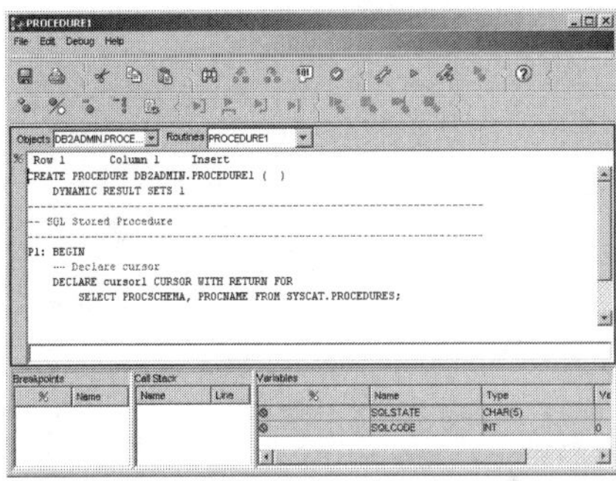

A.4 Development Center Views

The Development Center has four main views, as illustrated in Figure A.13.

The Server view allows you to look at objects that exist at the server and may or may not be part of your current project. From the Server view, you can import objects into your current project so that they also appear in your Project view.

The Project view allows you to navigate between projects. Currently, only one project is open (Project1). It is also possible to open multiple projects at the same time.

The Output view keeps a history of actions taken and the resulting messages for each action.

The Editor view is not opened by default, but you have already seen it (Figure A.12). It is opened automatically if you edit or view the source code for an object. When you launch the Editor view, you may notice that the Editor window is its own stand-alone window (by default). For some, it can be awkward to have to switch between the main Development Center window and the Editor view. Therefore, in the next section, we show you how to customize the Development Center to help you be more productive.

Figure A.13 The views of the Development Center

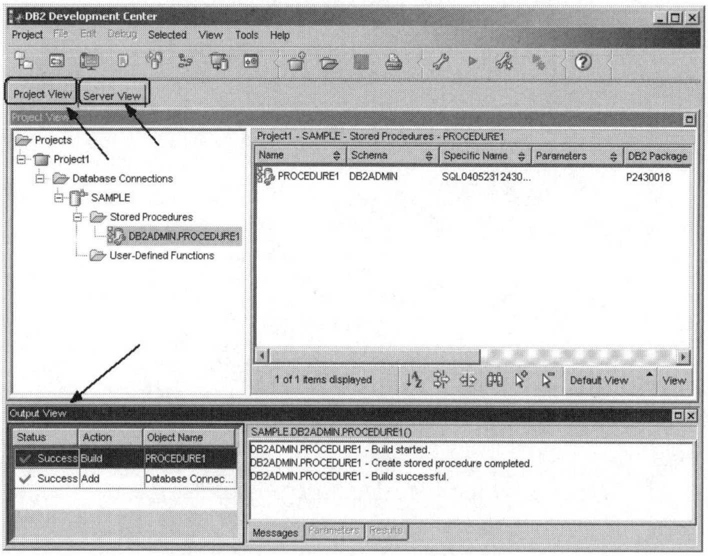

A.5 Customizing the Development Center

All the Development Center views are dockable and can be rearranged according to your preferences. To rearrange a dockable component, simply use a mouse to grab the view's header and drag it to the desired location.

NOTE: To identify dockable components in the Development Center, move the mouse icon around the screen until you see the hand icon .

When you click and hold the mouse on the component, the hand icon will change to a closed hand. While pressing the mouse button, drag the icon to various parts of the screen to rearrange the component. When you drag the mouse to various parts of the Development Center interface, a separate indicator will appear, indicating how the component will be docked if the mouse button is released.

Dozens of docking orientations are possible. A few examples are listed in Table A.2. The indicator that appears depends on where you drag a component.

Table A.2 Examples of Docking Orientations Available

Guide	Position
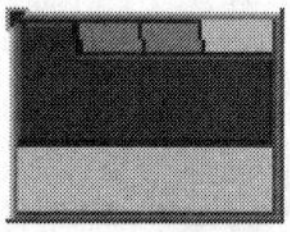	Dock the current component to the top half of the Development Center as the first tab.
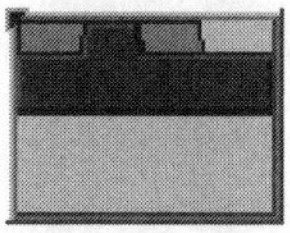	Dock the current component to the top half of the Development Center as the second tab.
	Dock the current component to the lower-left corner of the Development Center as a panel.
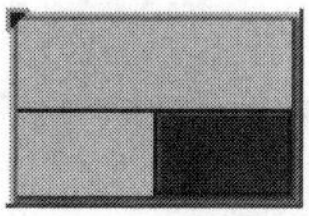	Dock the current component to the lower-right corner of the Development Center as a panel.
	Dock the current component to the right window of the Development Center as a panel.

To illustrate, let's walk through the process of rearranging components as illustrated in Figure A.14. The following customizations will be made:

- The Editor view will be docked to the main Development Center window.
- The debugging views will be hidden.
- The Server view will be closed.
- The Project view will be simplified.

Figure A.14 A customized Development Center

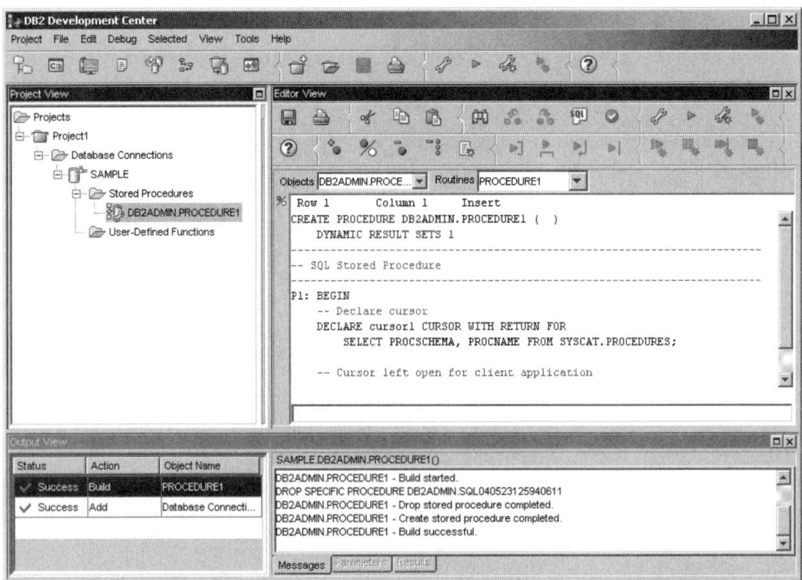

Open the Editor view on the procedure PROCEDURE1 (Figure A.15)

Figure A.15 Opening the Editor view on the source code for procedure1

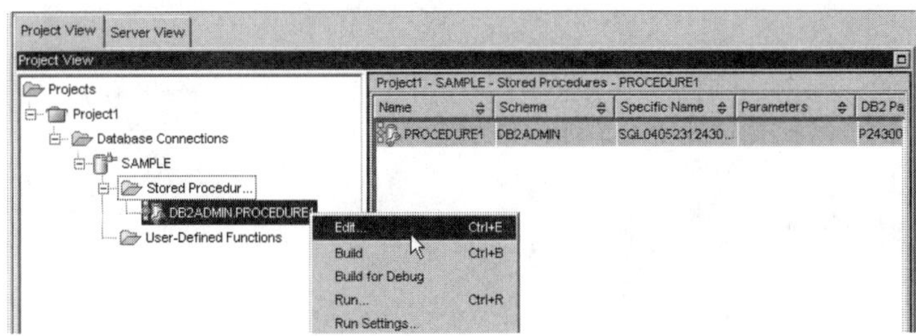

The Editor view will be opened in its own window by default. Wave the mouse around the Editor window (near the top) until you see the white hand icon (Figure A.16).

Figure A.16 Grabbing the Editor view as a docking component

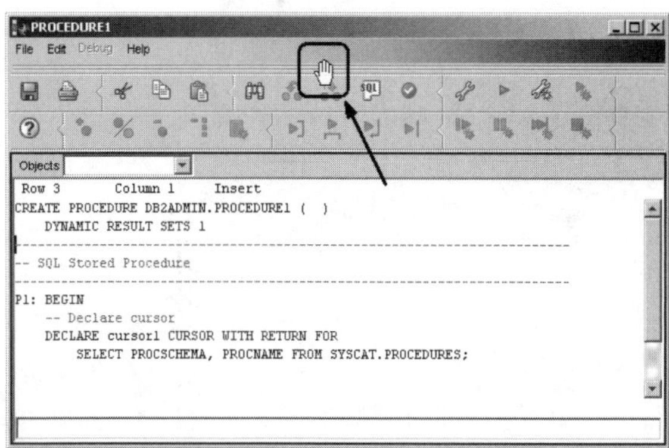

Click, hold, and drag the window to the upper-right corner of the Development Center. Look for a pop-up image like the one you see in Figure A.17, which indicates how the window will be docked.

The Editor view then becomes docked within the main interface of the Development Center. After a docking operation, you may have to resize the Editor window so that the Editor view is of usable size.

Figure A.17 Docking the Editor view to the main interface

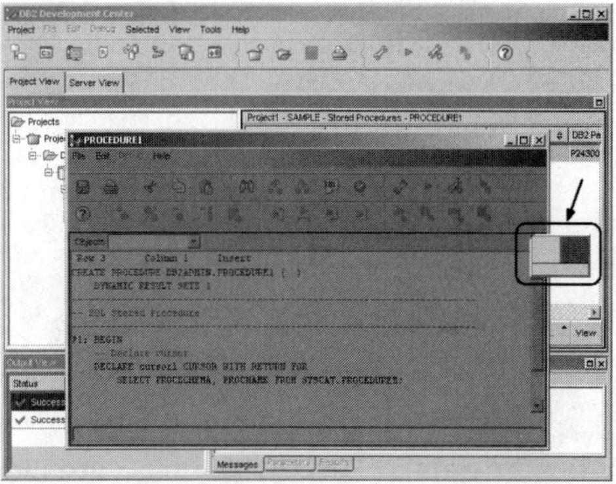

You can also hide the debugging views in the Editor to free up space. Toggle the Show Debug Views button, as seen in Figure A.18.

Figure A.18 Toggling show/hide debug views

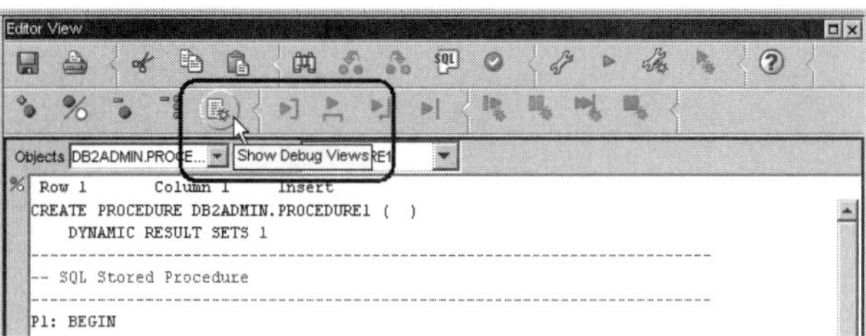

You can also remove windows that you don't immediately need. Select the Server View tab, and close the window by clicking the close window button as illustrated in Figure A.19.

Figure A.19 Closing the Server view

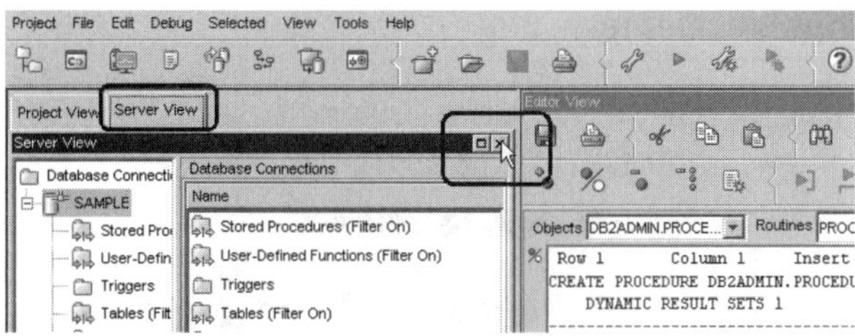

To bring back the Server view, you can always reopen it from the View menu.

The only remaining view in the upper-left corner is the Project view. However, the Project view window is divided awkwardly. You can refine this layout by sliding the divider out of the way to the right (Figure A.20).

Figure A.20 Resizing the Project View panel

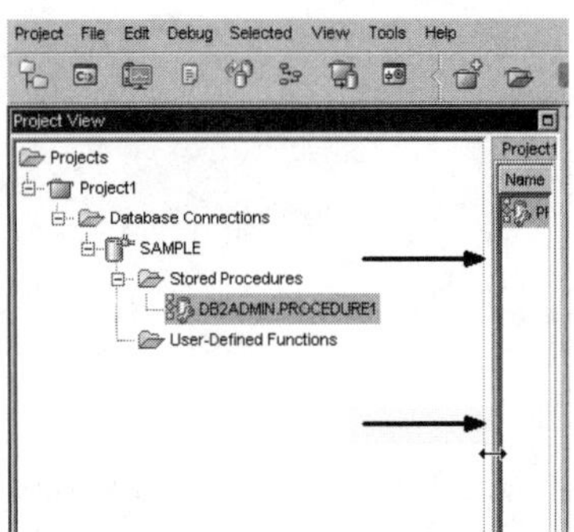

The final layout should now look like Figure A.21.

Figure A.21 Customized Development Center

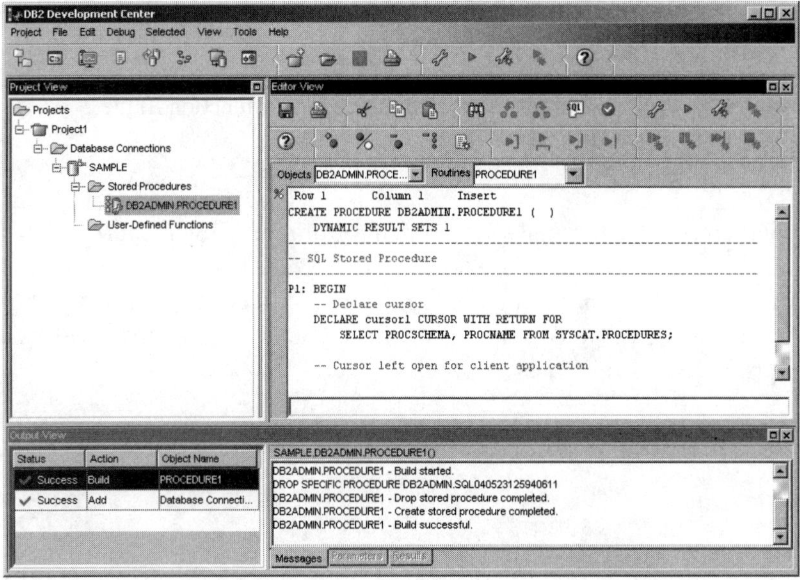

Of course, this is only an example of what you can do. You should experiment with docking windows in different places to see which orientations make you the most productive. If the windows ever become severely disoriented, you can always start over by selecting Reset Views from the View menu.

A.6 Running Procedures

Continuing our example, you can run procedure PROCEDURE1. Before a procedure can run, it must first successfully build in the database. Table A.3 describes the icons related to building and running procedures.

Table A.3 Icons for Building and Running Procedures and Functions

Icon	Action	Description
	Build Object	Builds the current object.
	Run Object	Runs the current procedure or function. If the object has not been built or has been updated since the last build, the Development Center can automatically (re)build it before running it.

PROCEDURE1 is fairly simple. It executes the following SQL query:

```
SELECT PROCSCHEMA, PROCNAME FROM SYSCAT.PROCEDURES;
```

The resulting rows are returned to the application (the Development Center, in this case) for fetching by leaving the cursor open.

Select PROCEDURE1 and click the Run button. The Development Center detects that a cursor has been returned and automatically fetches rows back from it.

You will be able to see the rows fetched back in the Results tab of the Output view, as seen in Figure A.22.

Figure A.22 Viewing data returned by cursors

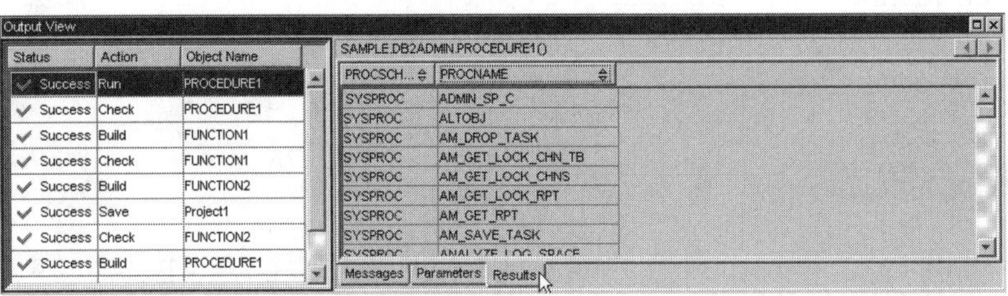

If you are running a function or a procedure with OUT parameters, the results will appear in the Parameters tab of the Output view. PROCEDURE1 does not have any parameters. Therefore, no values are listed here (Figure A.23).

Figure A.23 Viewing input and output parameter values

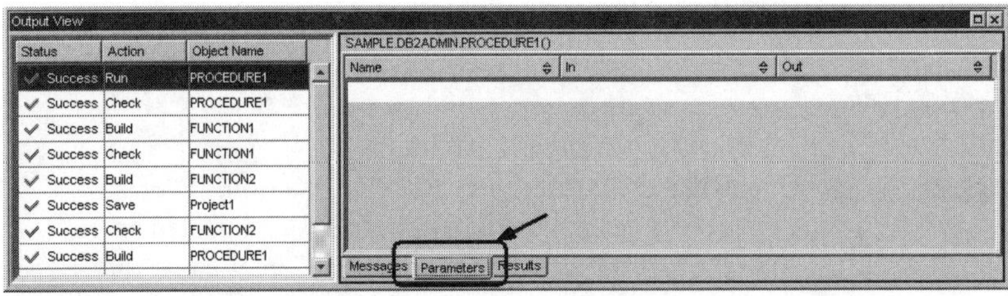

Stored Procedure Run Settings

Additional Run options are available in the Development Center.

Figure A.24 Setting stored procedure settings

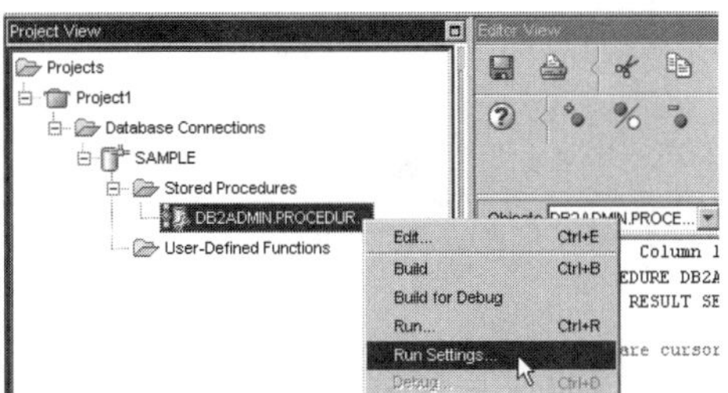

By changing the Run settings of a procedure, as shown in Figures A.24 and A.25, you have the option of not having any changes committed. With this option, after a procedure has finished executing, all changes will be automatically rolled back.This is useful for keeping the state of the database consistent while you debug your code. Scripts can also be set to run before or after the procedure executes. This gives you greater control over the testing environment of stored procedures.

Figure A.25 Setting stored procedure run options

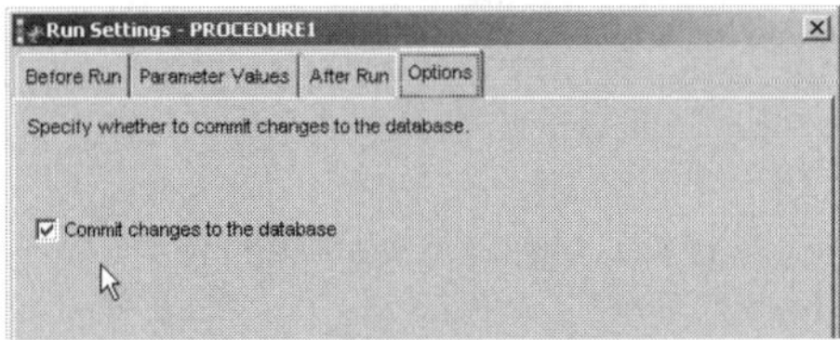

A.7 Debugging Stored Procedures

The Development Center offers a complete range of debugging tools for stepping through a procedure. The debugger is integrated into the Editor view. When a debug session is started, the Development Center will either open a window for the current procedure or use an existing window if the procedure is already being edited.

Debugging Basics

Table A.4 describes the icons used to initiate and terminate a debug session.

Table A.4 Debugger-Related Icons

Icon	Action	Description
	Build for Debug	Builds a stored procedure in debug mode.
	Run in Debug Mode	Runs a stored procedure in debug mode. This button is enabled only if the procedure was built for debug.
	Pause Debug	Temporarily stops debugging.
	Resume Debug	Resumes a paused debug.
	Terminate	Stops run in debug mode. Uncommitted changes will be rolled back.

A procedure must be built in debug mode in order for the debugging capabilities to be used. If a procedure is built in regular mode, attempts to run it in debug mode will result in the procedure simply being run normally.

After a procedure is run in debug mode, you can use the stepping buttons to walk through the lines of code one by one. Table A.5 describes the icons used for stepping through source code.

Table A.5 Icons for Controlling Debugger Stepping

Icon	Action	Description
▶]	Step Into	Traces through code one line at a time.
▶|	Step to Cursor	Runs the procedure to the line of code where the cursor is currently placed or the next breakpoint.
	Step Over	Executes a block of code or a call to a nested procedure without stepping through their substeps. This allows you to avoid tracing entire blocks of code that you are not interested in.
	Run to Completion	Runs the procedure to the end, ignoring all breakpoints.
	Step Return	Exits the procedure immediately from the current point in the code.

As you step through code in debug mode, you can view the state of all variables in the variables section of the debug view, as illustrated in Figure A.26.

Figure A.26 View or change variable values in a debug session

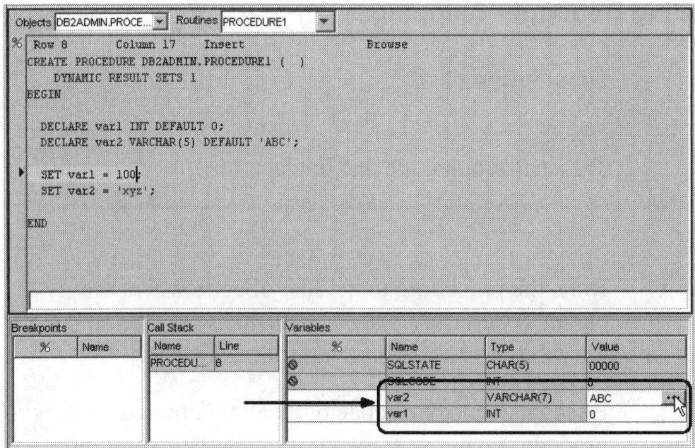

NOTE: When execution has paused in debug mode, variable values can be manually changed midflight if required (with the exception of SQLCODE and SQLSTATE).

Breakpoints

A procedure can often be quite long, and having to step through many lines of code to reach the section of interest can be tedious. To alleviate this, you can add a breakpoint to the code that will halt the execution of a procedure when that point is reached by the debugger. Multiple breakpoints can be added to a procedure, and each breakpoint will be indicated by a red dot. A breakpoint is useful if you want to check the current values of a variable at a particular point in the code to ensure that the procedure is performing as expected.

Table A.6 describes the icons used to manipulate breakpoints.

Table A.6 Icons for setting and manipulating breakpoints

Icon	Action	Description
	Add Breakpoint	Adds a breakpoint at the current cursor position.
	Remove Breakpoint	Removes the breakpoint at the current cursor position.
	Toggle Breakpoint	Enables or disables an existing breakpoint. If no breakpoint exists, it will be added.
	Remove All Breakpoints	Removes all defined breakpoints.

You can also add, remove, or toggle a breakpoint by clicking in the leftmost column of the Editor view while the arrow is on the line of code where the break should occur (Figure A.27).

Figure A.27 Adding a breakpoint

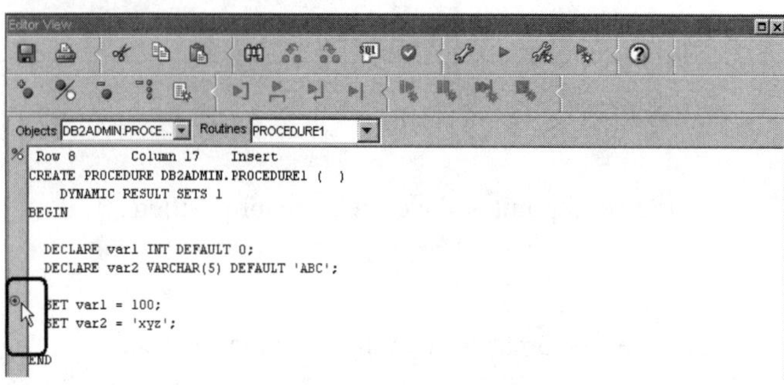

You can reach a breakpoint in a procedure by clicking the Step to Cursor icon. The code will execute until the current cursor position or the first breakpoint is reached.

Debugging Nested Stored Procedures

A stored procedure may call additional procedures, and this can make debugging complicated. The Development Center debugger has been designed to simplify this task. The parent stored procedure from which the debugger is initially started must be built in debug mode. When another procedure is called, at each nested level it is checked to see whether it is also in debug mode. If the nested procedure has not been built in debug mode, it will be executed normally until it completes. If the nested procedure is also in debug mode, an edit window will be opened for it and the debugger will begin to step through it. Consider the example shown in Table A.7.

Table A.7 Example of Debugging Nested Stored Procedures

Procedure	Build Mode	Procedure Called
Proc1	Debug	Proc2
Proc2	Debug	Proc3
Proc3	Normal	Proc4
Proc4	Debug	

Table A.7 represents a series of stored procedure calls: Proc1 calls Proc2, which calls Proc3, which calls Proc4. All are built in debug mode except for Proc3. A developer initially debugs

Proc1 by stepping through it. The debugger will execute the procedure one line at a time until the call to Proc2 is reached. An edit window for Proc2 will then be opened, and it will be stepped through because it was built in debug mode. The debugger will stop when the call to Proc3 is reached and will run the procedure normally. The debugger will renew stepping through the code when the call by Proc3 to Proc4 is reached. Upon the completion of Proc4, the debugger will return to running Proc3 normally, without any debugging options. At the completion of Proc3 the debugger will resume stepping through the procedure in Proc2's edit window. Upon completion of Proc2, the debugger will return to the original calling Proc1. Debugging will finish when Proc1 completes.

You can perform more complex debugging tasks by adding breakpoints in nested procedures, as shown in Table A.8. The initial procedure will run normally until the breakpoint is reached in a nested procedure. The nested procedure with the breakpoint must be built in debug mode to allow the procedure to be stepped through after the breakpoint is reached. The nested breakpoints can be reached by using the Step to Cursor icon. If multiple breakpoints are embedded in the procedures, then clicking on the icon again will cause the program to execute until the next breakpoint is reached.

Table A.8 Example of Debugging a Nested Procedure Using Breakpoints

Procedure	Build Mode	Procedure Called
ProcA	Debug	ProcB
ProcB	Normal	ProcC
ProcC	Debug (with breakpoint)	

In Table A.8, ProcA is run in debug mode. The Step to Cursor icon is then clicked. ProcA makes a call to ProcB, which will be executed normally and the code will not be debugged. The execution will continue until ProcB calls ProcC and the breakpoint in ProcC is reached. You can then step through ProcC starting from the breakpoint. Upon completion of ProcC, the debugger will return to executing ProcB normally until its completion. Finally, ProcA will be stepped through until it is completed.

Combining the mixture of debugged and non-debugged procedures with breakpoints allows you to easily find and test problems that may be buried many levels down in a nested procedure. You can test procedures for correctness by ensuring that the top-level procedure is performing correctly until the first nested procedure call. A breakpoint can then be added just after the call so that earlier tested code does not have to be stepped through. As each layer of the procedure is fully tested, you can move the breakpoint, or you can prevent the procedure from being debugged by building it in normal mode. Stored procedures that call dozens of other procedures or are thousands of lines long can then be tested on a component or sectional basis.

A.8 Working with Projects

The Development Center uses projects to logically group a set of related application objects for the developer. A project can even reference application objects from multiple databases. Also, multiple and varying copies of the same procedure can be open in different projects. Each project will have its own local copy of all its procedures. This code can be saved, and it will not overwrite copies from other projects. The procedure code will be saved into the database when it is built. If a different copy of the procedure from another project is built, the new code from the second project will overwrite the code from the first project at the database server. The following example illustrates:

- There are two projects—projectA and projectB—and both contain a copy of procedure procTest from the same database.
- User1 opens projectA and edits its copy of procTest to have a return code of 4.
- User2 opens projectB and edits its copy of procTest to have a return code of 3. There are now two versions of the procedure open.
- User1 then builds procTest. If the procedure is now run, the return code will be 4. The code for procTest that User2 has open is not affected by User1's actions.
- User2 then builds her copy of procTest. User2 will be asked whether she wants to drop the old copy of the procedure (built by User1) and build a new one. If she chooses to build the procedure, then the return code of the procedure will be 3.

You can create new projects by selecting New Project from the Project pull-down menu. Multiple projects can be open in the Development Center at the same time. You can open projects from the Project pull-down menu by selecting the Open option. The Remove Project option will delete the project from memory but will not delete the application objects that were successfully built on the database. Be sure to save all your projects to ensure that all your changes to the project are kept. If you do not save the project and have not built the stored procedure, then your changes will be lost. Procedure changes will not take effect in the database until they are built, despite the project having been saved.

Importing Stored Procedures

Often, an SQL procedure that you wish to work with has already been written by someone else or exists in another project. The Development Center allows you to quickly create a new procedure from code that is saved elsewhere.

After you have opened a project, you can import a procedure by right-clicking on the stored procedure folder icon and selecting Import, as illustrated in Figure A.28.

Figure A.28 Importing a stored procedure

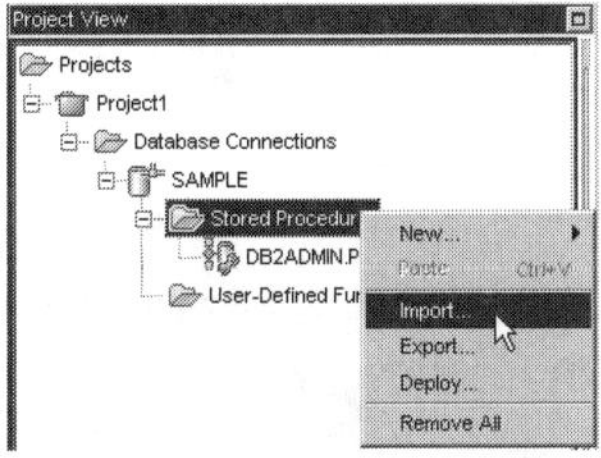

There are two sources from which a procedure can be imported. The procedure can be directly extracted from a database, or it can be read from a file. The database import option allows you to use filters to limit the search for procedures that may exist in a database. The file system option will allow you to import a procedure either from a file or from another project. These two options are shown in Figure A.29.

Figure A.29 Import from a file or another database

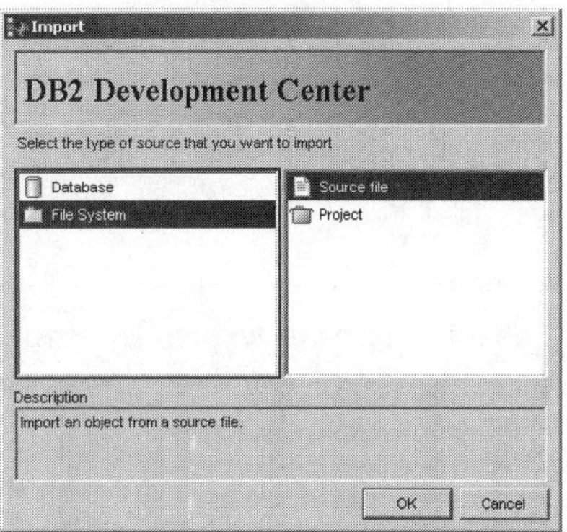

Another convenient way to import database application objects directly from a database is through the Server view in the Development Center. If your Server view is not open, open it from the View menu. In the Server view, you will see the procedures that currently exist in the database. Right-click on any object, and select Add to Project (Figure A.30).

NOTE: If you wish to add multiple objects to your project, use the Import feature from the Project view. If you wish to quickly add only one or a few objects, using Add to Project from the Server view is faster.

Figure A.30 Adding objects to the current project from the Server view

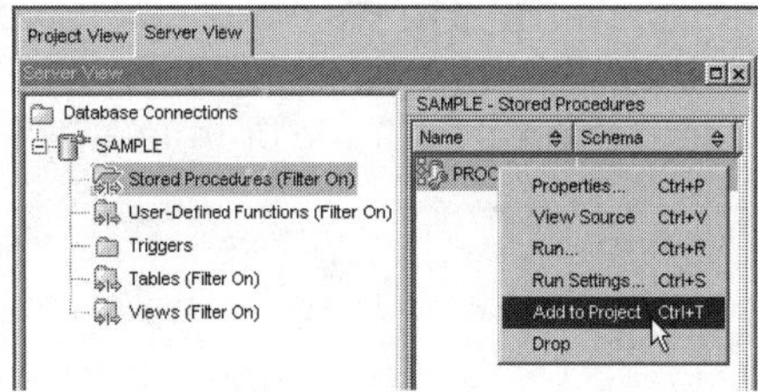

A.9 Summary

The DB2 Development Center is a powerful IDE for developing stored procedures in all DB2 platforms. By defining multiple projects (which can share the same database), you can manage related database application objects with ease. The integrated debugger allows you to debug complex SQL procedures, even if they make nested procedure calls. Debugging concepts and strategies were highlighted in this appendix.

Index

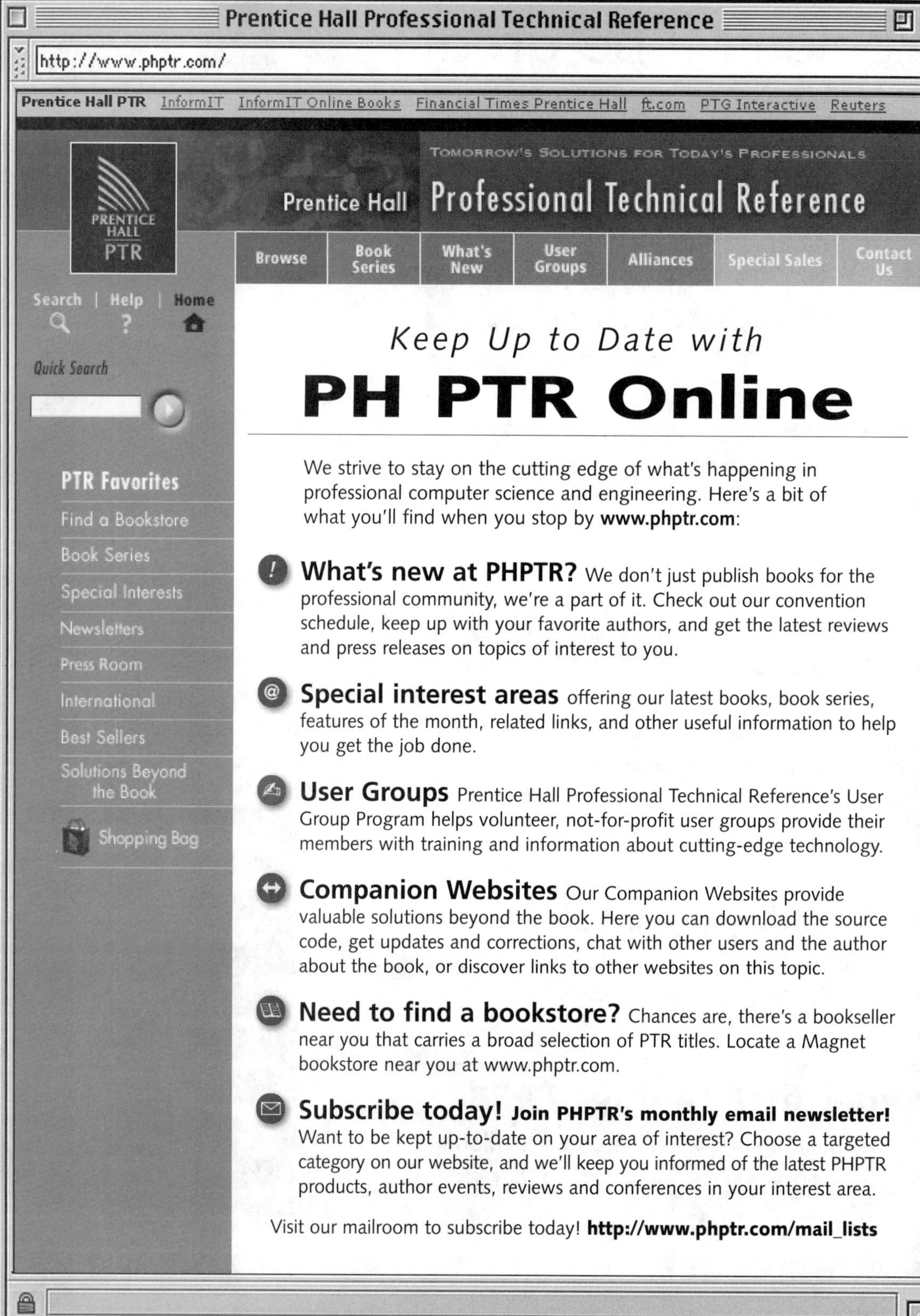
Prentice Hall Professional Technical Reference
http://www.phptr.com/
Prentice Hall PTR InformIT InformIT Online Books Financial Times Prentice Hall ft.com PTG Interactive Reuters
Tomorrow's Solutions for Today's Professionals
Prentice Hall Professional Technical Reference
PRENTICE HALL PTR
Browse
Book Series
What's New
User Groups
Alliances
Special Sales
Contact Us
Search | Help | Home
Quick Search
PTR Favorites
Find a Bookstore
Book Series
Special Interests
Newsletters
Press Room
International
Best Sellers
Solutions Beyond the Book
Shopping Bag
Keep Up to Date with
PH PTR Online
We strive to stay on the cutting edge of what's happening in professional computer science and engineering. Here's a bit of what you'll find when you stop by www.phptr.com:
What's new at PHPTR? We don't just publish books for the professional community, we're a part of it. Check out our convention schedule, keep up with your favorite authors, and get the latest reviews and press releases on topics of interest to you.
Special interest areas offering our latest books, book series, features of the month, related links, and other useful information to help you get the job done.
User Groups Prentice Hall Professional Technical Reference's User Group Program helps volunteer, not-for-profit user groups provide their members with training and information about cutting-edge technology.
Companion Websites Our Companion Websites provide valuable solutions beyond the book. Here you can download the source code, get updates and corrections, chat with other users and the author about the book, or discover links to other websites on this topic.
Need to find a bookstore? Chances are, there's a bookseller near you that carries a broad selection of PTR titles. Locate a Magnet bookstore near you at www.phptr.com.
Subscribe today! Join PHPTR's monthly email newsletter!
Want to be kept up-to-date on your area of interest? Choose a targeted category on our website, and we'll keep you informed of the latest PHPTR products, author events, reviews and conferences in your interest area.
Visit our mailroom to subscribe today! http://www.phptr.com/mail_lists